Skill Set

Strategies for Reading and Writing
in the Canadian Classroom

SECOND EDITION

Skill Set

Strategies for Reading and Writing
in the Canadian Classroom

SECOND EDITION

Lucia Engkent

OXFORD

UNIVERSITY PRESS

OXFORD
UNIVERSITY PRESS

8 Sampson Mews, Suite 204, Don Mills, Ontario M3C 0H5
www.oupcanada.com

Oxford University Press is a department of the University of Oxford.
It furthers the University's objective of excellence in research, scholarship,
and education by publishing worldwide in

Oxford   New York

Auckland   Cape Town   Dar es Salaam   Hong Kong   Karachi
Kuala Lumpur   Madrid   Melbourne   Mexico City   Nairobi
New Delhi   Shanghai   Taipei   Toronto

With offices in

Argentina   Austria   Brazil   Chile   Czech Republic   France   Greece
Guatemala   Hungary   Italy   Japan   Poland   Portugal   Singapore
South Korea   Switzerland   Thailand   Turkey   Ukraine   Vietnam

Oxford is a trade mark of Oxford University Press
in the UK and in certain other countries

Published in Canada
by Oxford University Press

Copyright © Oxford University Press Canada 2011

Library and Archives Canada Cataloguing in Publication

Engkent, Lucia Pietrusiak
Skill set : strategies for reading and writing / Lucia Engkent. — 2nd ed.
ISBN 978-0-19-544169-7
1. English language—Composition and exercises.
2. College readers. 3. English language—Grammar—Textbooks.
4. English language—Rhetoric. I. Title.

PE1408.E486 2011   428   C2010-906557-3

Cover image: Getty Images/Erik Isakson

Oxford University Press is committed to our environment. This book is printed on
Forest Stewardship Council certified paper,
harvested from a responsibly managed forest.

Printed and bound in Canada.

4 5 6 — 16 15 14

Contents

Part 2   Reading Selections

Introduction

Introduction for the Instructor

This text is intended for students who need to hone their English writing and reading skills in order to meet future academic demands. It was developed in a non-credit college course for students who had not achieved the required reading and writing skills for the credit English course. The students in this course were of different backgrounds and mixed abilities: some were native speakers of English who were reluctant readers, some were newly arrived international students who had university degrees from their native countries, and some were immigrants who had spent many years in the Canadian school system and spoke English fluently. These students were taking regular college courses in their own discipline at the same time that they were studying English. In addition, some of the material was tested in English as a Second Language (ESL) academic preparation classes.

Although some institutions have separate streams for ESL students and native speakers, at this level the two groups have enough in common that they can be taught together. Even some of the grammatical errors are similar. Instructors see incorrect verb forms, article and preposition errors, difficulty with complex sentence structures, and misuse of vocabulary. Reluctant readers struggle with the more complex vocabulary and structures of academic English.

Skill Set is very much a product of the classroom. It focuses on the problems generally seen in the writing of students in the developmental English course. The exercises address problems these students have, such as distinguishing general and specific points in order to write supporting statements in paragraphs. Some of the sample paragraphs and essays were generated from student writing assignments. In addition, many of the sentences used for error correction in Unit 7 were taken from student writing samples.

Organization of the Text

This book is designed to let instructors move around from section to section as needed. It is organized so that smaller units (vocabulary and sentences) are discussed before larger units (paragraphs and essays), but that does not mean units have to be tackled in that order. The material is organized by skill areas, such as constructing complex sentences and writing topic sentences, so you can focus on the weaknesses your students have.

It is important to remember that students do not come to a course like this with a blank slate. They have been introduced to the writing process and essay structure. They do not have to master sentence structure before they move on to paragraphs, and they may even chafe at working on paragraph structure when they want to write essays.

You may wish to move on to the unit on paragraphs (Unit 4) after a brief introduction to writing (Unit 1) and then work on grammar (Units 3 and 7) and vocabulary (Unit 2) in bits as students practise writing paragraphs and then essays. You can draw from Unit 6, Rhetorical Skills, as you assign different types of writing tasks. You can do a different reading each week, in any order you wish, according to your curriculum, your students' needs, and your own tastes.

Paragraphs and Essays

Students are given an opportunity to work on independent paragraphs before they move to the essay. This allows them to practise their skills in shorter writing assignments before they progress to the essay. The focus is on the basic academic skills of making points and supporting them.

Some educators argue against teaching the five-paragraph essay since it is so formulaic and not "real world" writing. However, it is a useful pedagogical structure that teaches the skills students need for all kinds of writing—the ability to organize thoughts, present ideas, and support them. Whether they have to write a cover letter for a job application or a business report, they still have to introduce a topic, divide their arguments into well-structured body paragraphs, and write a conclusion—just as they do in an essay. Students who are struggling with writing benefit from having a well-defined structure to follow.

Readings

Reading and writing go hand in hand. It is not enough to add some readings to a writing text as an afterthought. Students who have weak writing skills often have weak reading skills, and this must be addressed. Good reading comprehension is paramount—no instructor would deny that as skills are ranked, understanding the main idea of a newspaper article is surely more important than being able to fix a comma splice. Furthermore, to become good writers, students need to read more in order to learn about the written language—its structures and vocabulary.

It is essential to test students' reading ability with comprehension questions, paraphrasing, and summarizing. Otherwise, it is easy to miss students' reading problems.

The readings in this text serve several functions. First, they give students an opportunity to improve their reading skills and their vocabulary. Second, students are asked to look at sentence, paragraph, and essay structures in the readings so that they can carry over what they learned about grammar and writing into their reading. They can see different writing styles at work. Third, the readings provide the students with interesting subjects to discuss and write about.

The non-fiction readings are presented in seven thematic units (Units 9–15). Each unit has two readings, which may differ in style as well as in content. Moreover, because of the thematic organization, each unit presents a wide range of possible writing topics. Different writing styles are explained and discussed. Sometimes students are asked to distinguish between journalistic and academic styles so that they can more easily use the latter style in their essays.

In addition, the book contains four fiction readings—three short stories and one excerpt from a novel. It is important to include fiction in students' reading diet because they sometimes have difficulty understanding the difference between fiction and non-fiction. Moreover, fiction captures and exercises the imagination.

Besides the typical comprehension questions, discussion topics, and assignment suggestions, the readings are accompanied by vocabulary study and notes on structure and technique. These elements are intended to make students more conscious of the language as they read. They can then apply what they learned about vocabulary and sentence structure to actual words and sentences in the reading.

Vocabulary Study

In developmental English courses, building vocabulary is crucial. Spoken English uses a fairly small range of words, so reluctant readers have limited exposure to less common words and need more guidance to learn the patterns that can help them make connections between words. For that reason, this text has work on collocations, parts of speech, and common roots and affixes.

Each of the readings is accompanied by a variety of vocabulary exercises. Students can use the context to find the meaning of the less common, more difficult words in a matching exercise. A parts-of-speech chart allows students to figure out the derivatives of some more common words, including words from the Academic Word List. In addition, lists draw students' attention to idioms, common expressions, and collocations. The exercises are designed to make students more conscious of the words and expressions they come across; they are not just supplied with the definition and asked to read on.

Grammar

Grammar can be a contentious issue. Instructors all agree that grammar instruction is necessary, but there is so much to learn and practise that the areas to focus on must be carefully chosen. Moreover, exercises may have little carry-over to actual writing assignments; some students excel at grammar exercises but make errors on the same points in their writing. Error correction and the construction of complex sentences are two areas that are more like real writing work. In this text, the sentences used for error correction are taken from actual student writing.

Assignments

Assignments are left open-ended so that you can tailor them to your class needs. For example, if your class is still working on paragraph structure when you do a particular reading, your assignments will focus on paragraphs. If you are working on reports or research essays, you can choose a topic for students to explore in such an assignment. You may want to specify length and format.

Answer Key

Answers to many of the exercises can be found in the Answer Key at the end of the book; these exercises are marked with a key icon.

Exercises with answers readily available in the dictionary and more open-ended exercises do not have answers in the book, but many are available in the online Teacher's Resource.

Teacher's Resource

The online Teacher's Resource offers help for beginning instructors as well as supplemental material. It includes sample course outlines and lesson plans, answers to exercises not in the Answer Key, and sample quizzes.

Introduction for Students: Developing Study Skills

Skill Set is a book that will help you improve your reading and writing skills, but it cannot do so if you do not do your part. It is important to develop good study habits in order to be successful in college or university.

Using the Textbook

A good way to start any course is to become familiar with the course textbook. Look over the table of contents to learn what the book covers. Read the introduction. Check out what the appendices have to offer—sometimes there is a good reference list. Look at the index, and be prepared to use it to find specific information.

If the textbook is borrowed or if you are planning to resell it, you probably want to keep it fairly clean. However, a textbook makes a much better study tool if you mark it up as you read it. Use highlighting judiciously—to mark only important sentences, not big chunks of text. Highlighting is used to draw your attention, so you do not need it for tip boxes or lists that already summarize information for you. Write brief explanatory notes or definitions in the margins or on sticky notes.

Preparing for Class

Students are often assigned reading to do before class. It could be an article, a story, or a chapter of the textbook. The instructor then organizes the class on the presumption that students have done the required reading. Students who come unprepared find themselves sitting in class not understanding what is being said. It is a waste of their time and money because they are not getting the value out of class that they have paid for in their tuition. The class discussion also suffers when students have not read the material to be discussed. Instead of having a lively discussion of the issues raised in the reading, students must endure listening to the instructor lecture for a long stretch.

If you have been asked to read an article or story from this text, you should spend time going over it as often as necessary for you to understand it. Some exercises may be assigned as homework, but even if they are not, you should read the notes, do the vocabulary exercises, and be prepared to answer comprehension questions and discuss the reading.

As you read, you may come across words and concepts that you are not familiar with. With the wealth of online information available at your fingertips, there is no excuse for not looking up these references. Many dictionaries have online versions. Proper names of people and places and historical references can easily be found with a search engine such as Google. A good student is a curious student.

Time Management

One of the biggest changes students face when they make the leap from high school to post-secondary school is the need for time management skills. In high school, your time is often managed for you. Much of your work is done in class, and your assignments may be divided into smaller chunks. In college and university, however, you may have several weeks to complete an assignment, but how and when you do it is your responsibility. For every hour spent in class, you are expected to do two or three hours working on your own.

It is important to use some sort of calendar to organize your semester. Schools often provide specially printed handbooks or agendas for this purpose. Alternatively, you could use an electronic format, whether it be on your laptop or phone. Make sure your class schedule is in there, as well as the important dates in the school year, such as holidays and exam week. Enter test and assignment due dates as you get them. Make daily and weekly "to do" lists, and use them.

Start assignments as soon as you get them while the instructions are fresh in your mind. Work on them in manageable chunks. Finish early so that you can review everything before you hand it in. Getting an assignment done early clears the way for other work. It also helps you avoid last-minute problems such as a malfunctioning computer. (Remember to back up all your work on other media.)

Review and study your material as the course goes on. Last-minute cramming is never as productive as keeping up with the flow.

Your schedule should allow for some flexibility and downtime. Take breaks, get some fresh air and exercise, and try to get enough sleep. Your mind will function much better if your body is healthy.

Multi-tasking

The use of technology today encourages multi-tasking. Students have multiple windows open on their computer screen. They send text messages while they walk, talk, and study. However, the human brain has not evolved to handle more than one task at a time. It can switch rapidly between tasks, but it cannot do two at once. Studies show that you lose time and efficiency when you try to multi-task. You will work more efficiently if you commit to the task at hand and avoid distractions. While background music can be beneficial, anything that draws your attention away from your work is a problem.

Active versus Passive Learning

People learn something much better when they are active rather than passive learners. Active learning requires doing something—taking notes, summarizing material, asking questions, making comments, and talking about the topic. Passive learning is just reading or listening. Even telling your roommates or family about what you studied in class will help you remember it.

Taking Notes

College and university instructors expect you to take notes in class. This does not mean just copying down what the instructor writes on the board or shows on a screen. You need to process the information that is being presented to you and write down the main ideas. Pay attention to what the instructor stresses as important.

A good strategy is to flesh out the notes after class while the information is still fresh in your mind. For example, you can write down the meanings of the new vocabulary items you jotted down during class.

Reading notes are also useful. You can summarize a chapter in a few notes after you have read it to aid your comprehension and memory. Moreover, the notes are useful when you study for tests and exams.

Keeping a separate vocabulary notebook allows you to create a useful learning tool, much like your own dictionary. Write down new words and expressions. Put in grammatical information, such as the part of speech. Write down the phrase or sentence that the word appeared in. Jot down the meaning and related words.

Following Instructions

While some people think that following instructions is only for mindless automatons, it is vital in the workplace where failure to do so can result in lost work hours and added expense or even lead to life-threatening situations. In school, following instructions is the key to getting good grades. One of the common complaints of all instructors in any institution is that students often do not do what they have been asked to do.

Read written instructions carefully, more than once. For example, you can read them when you first get an assignment, while you are working on the task, and again as a final check before you hand the work in. Highlight important instructions you do not want to overlook. Listen to oral instructions carefully, taking notes. Instructors repeat directions because they are so important and because students often do not pay enough attention to them.

Developing Language Skills

Students who are learning English as a second language (ESL) should recognize that it takes years to develop language skills to reach a high enough level to function in an English-speaking academic environment. If their goal is a diploma or a degree from a Canadian institution, they must work at their language skills all the time—not just for the duration of English class. They need lots of exposure to both written and spoken English, so they should read, watch educational television, and surf the Internet in English.

Students whose native language is English have mastered the spoken language, but if they do not read much, they may still be considered language learners for written English. They also need to build their vocabulary and learn about the structures of academic English.

Learning from Mistakes

Making a mistake creates an opportunity to learn. Indeed, learning would not take place without mistakes. Of course, errors also mean lower marks, so you should try to avoid making them. However, for those mistakes you do make, make sure you learn from them and avoid them in the future.

Writing instructors spend a lot of time marking essays. They write in corrections and comments. Students who take the time to go over their marked essays can see where they had problems and where they need to improve for the next assignment.

Practice

In his 2008 book *Outliers*, Malcolm Gladwell explains what leads to success and shows that talent and skill are not enough. One important factor is that it takes 10,000 hours of practice to become a world-class expert at something. Wayne Gretzky undoubtedly had a lot of natural talent, but he would not have become "The Great One" without the hours he spent practising his hockey skills every winter on his backyard rink.

While you do not have to put in 10,000 hours and become an expert essay writer, it is necessary to realize that you cannot hope to become a competent writer without lots of practice. Take advantage of any practice opportunity you are offered. Some instructors will mark practice essays and will allow you to rewrite essays.

Some students find journal-writing a low-pressure way to practise expressing ideas in writing. A journal is a notebook that you write in every day. You can record your thoughts about almost anything—a movie you saw, a class you attended, what you think about a political issue, or your observations of your classmates. Keep in mind who may read your writing. If you are keeping a journal as part of your class work, your audience is your instructor. If the journal is just for you, you do not have to be as careful about what you say.

Reading comprehension and speed also improve with practice. At the end of Unit 8 are some tips for building reading skills.

Furthermore, writing in a journal and reading a chapter in a novel are good ways to wind down at the end of the day. Studies show that looking at television and computer screens immediately before bedtime can interfere with sleep rhythms.

Seek Help

Colleges and universities offer many services to help students succeed. They may offer a study skills course, for example. The library may have tutors and seminars. Conversation groups may be arranged for ESL students. Remember that you have paid for these services in your tuition fees, so take advantage of them.

It is also a good idea to ask questions in class when you do not understand something. Do not be shy about it—chances are other students are wondering the same thing. Moreover, the instructor would prefer that such general questions be asked during the class instead of several students asking the same question immediately after class.

If you have concerns about the course or your progress in it, be sure to talk to your instructor before taking a drastic measure such as dropping the course. Sometimes students give up prematurely, thinking they have no chance of passing the course when in fact they are making good progress.

Abbreviations and Conventions Used in the Text

n:	noun
v:	verb
adj:	adjective
adv:	adverb
tr:	transitive (verb)
U:	uncountable (noun)
C:	countable (noun)

For the readings, numbers in square brackets refer to the number of the paragraph where a vocabulary item can be found.

Acknowledgements

This material was class-tested at Seneca College in Toronto and at Renison College at the University of Waterloo. Thank you to my students, whose work provided the base for many of the examples and exercises. I would also like to acknowledge the suggestions and support of my colleagues, especially Adriana Neil, Dina Chipouline, Jeannine Maxfield, Dara Lane, Christine Morgan, Carolyn Samuel, and Susan Bates.

And as always, a big thank you to my family—my husband, Garry, and my children, David, Susan, and Emily. They contributed their literary criticism, editing, and writing skills to the cause.

Lucia Engkent

Part 1

Skill Development

Unit 1

Writing Skills

One of the first steps to becoming a good writer is recognizing the difference between speaking and writing. Even though the written system is fundamentally based on spoken language, the differences can be quite marked. Most important, you can learn the written language only by reading. If you read little, chances are that your writing will be at the wrong register (level of language)—it will be just a written-down version of speech.

In English, the differences between versions lie in both vocabulary and sentence structure, with the everyday spoken language being more limited than the written. This is just a generalization, however, since there is a wide variety of spoken and written forms. A casual conversation differs from a formal speech, while a text message sent on your cellphone is written language but is more like the spoken form.

In spoken English, you use tone of voice, gestures, and context to get your meaning across. You can get away with calling something a "thing-amajig," for example, if you can point to the item in question. You can get immediate feedback if your communication is unsuccessful—ranging from the bewildered look on the listener's face to direct questions such as "What do you mean?"

In written English, you have no such back-up system. Your meaning must be clear from the outset. You must anticipate what your readers need to know. You have to use precise vocabulary. (Imagine reading instructions for a new digital camera that tell you to "hook that dangly piece to the thingy over there.") Consequently, written English calls upon the huge vocabulary of English more than the conversational language does.

You speak mainly in simple sentences, but in writing you use longer, more complex sentences. You can layer meaning with clauses. Your attention span is greater when you read than when you listen, and you can go back and check meaning, so you can handle complexity better in written form. Academic English, the language of essay writing, is even more sophisticated. For your English course, you need to be able to produce this level of language. It will be useful to you in the work world in both business and technical writing.

Addressing Audience and Purpose

Your first job as a writer is to consider why you are writing (your purpose) and who your readers are (your audience). You may write to inform, persuade, or entertain your readers. The purpose of a technical manual is to give information. A novel or short story entertains and perhaps along the way informs and enlightens its readers. Academic essays are arguments—presenting ideas to explain them and persuade the readers of their soundness.

What you write has to be tailored to your audience, so you need to know who will be reading your document. Imagine telling someone how to use a new portable music player—instructions to your technophobic grandparents would be very different from instructions to your techno-savvy classmate. Recipe directions for an experienced cook would be different from those for a novice. You might write an essay about traditions in your native country, but you need to say enough to make your essay clear to readers who may never have visited that country or are not familiar with the traditions.

The information you give and the words you use will vary depending on your audience and purpose:

> **That patient is suffering from separation anxiety disorder, but I think it is developing into full-fledged agoraphobia. I'd like to try cognitive behavioural therapy.** (audience: another psychologist; purpose: to give information for a treatment program)

> **It's okay, sweetie. Don't cry. Your mama will be back soon.** (audience: small child; purpose: to reassure and calm the child)

Knowing what your audience knows and needs to know is not easy. It can be especially difficult if your audience is diverse, but keep in mind that you cannot follow your document around to explain it, so it is better to give too much information than too little.

The writing you do in school is artificial in that it is not communication of new information. You are writing to a teacher or professor who is an expert on the subject. Your essay on sibling rivalry is not going to tell your psychology professor much that he or she does not know; however, it will tell the professor how well you have learned the required material, researched the topic, and expressed your ideas. Sometimes you may be tempted to leave out information that you know the professors have, but it may be required for the logical links in your argument.

In an English composition class, your primary audience is your instructor, and you must satisfy his or her requirements in order to earn a good grade. Some instructors are sticklers for grammar, going as far as failing a paper for a single run-on sentence. Other instructors are more laid-back, looking for clarity more than perfection. Some instructors prefer students to take writing assignments seriously and do not appreciate humour or satire.

Some assign personal, creative writing tasks. Others make students practise a more formal and objective academic style to pave the way for business and technical writing. Some accept a conversational style; others prefer a more formal one. However, no matter what style they prefer, all good writing instructors should make their expectations clear.

You may be tempted to throw up your hands in frustration if your English instructor prefers a style very different from the one your last instructor did, but remember that the same thing applies in the work world. Supervisors often vary in their expectations, and you may have to relearn how to do a job for a different boss.

> For the writing in your English course, your audience is your instructor, and your purpose is to show the instructor what you have learned, how you can connect ideas, and how well you express those ideas.

The Principles of Good Writing

Whatever the type of writing, whatever the audience and purpose, the qualities of good writing remain the same. Documents should be legible, clear, and concise. They should engage and inform the reader.

Clarity

Above all, written communication must be clear to the reader. Otherwise, it does not succeed as communication and is essentially worthless. When you speak, you have immediate feedback for your words because of your inter-action with your audience. As a writer, you cannot follow your document around to every reader to make sure that it is understood. Clear, simple language is always preferable to overly ornate, complicated language. Just remember that simple does not mean overly simplistic.

To achieve clarity, you must choose your words carefully. You cannot just point to something if you forget the name of it. You cannot get away with imprecise words like "stuff" and "whatever." The vocabulary of the written language is much larger than that of everyday spoken language, and these words are needed to ensure precision and clarity. You can get by with fewer words in your everyday speech, but for good writing you need an arsenal of words. You also need to use the vocabulary correctly. For example, a student wrote, "Men do not carry purses because purses are too big for men to carry without a handbag. Therefore, men have to put their purses in their clothes bag." This is confusing because the student mixed up the words *purse* and *wallet* and did not know the word *pocket*.

It is difficult for writers to evaluate the clarity of their own writing. They may not know they are using words incorrectly. They may be relying on references that may not be clear to their audience. One way to improve clarity is to let a document sit for a while and come back to it with fresh eyes. Getting a second opinion is also vital. That is why published works go through several readers and editors.

A piece of writing can follow basic grammar rules and be technically "correct" yet not be clear:

> Cars come in many forms as perceived by a viewer. In the past century, cars have contributed to many criteria of human development. To view cars as an advantage is a benchmark, but to view them as a disadvantage is a learning curve. Owning a luxury car can be an advantage and disadvantage.

In academic writing, clarity depends on support. Essay writing hinges on making points and supporting them with examples and explanations. This support is crucial to the clarity of the points. For example, an essay that claims "high school does not adequately prepare students for college" needs to include specific statements such as "high school students do not have to take notes while the teacher is talking" and "assignments are broken down into steps so that students do not have to manage their time by themselves."

Content

Writing is judged by what it has to say. In English class, your writing is evaluated by the strength of your argument—the logic of your conclusions, the support for the points, the suitability of the examples. Instructors may disagree with your point of view, but as long as the argument is sound and well expressed, they will not give you a low mark.

One important aspect of content is how well the paragraph or essay addresses the topic question. It is important that you understand exactly what the instructor is asking you to do. Be sure to ask your instructor if you do not understand the assignment. Stay focused on your topic question as you write so that you do not wander off topic.

Writers build on what other writers say. The more you read, the easier you will find it to come up with ideas for your essays. For example, as you read newspaper stories of accounts of gang violence and the editorials and comments of people discussing the issue, you will get a better understanding of the complexity of the problem. When you write an essay suggesting ways to tackle the problem, your ideas will be founded on this strong understanding.

Conciseness

Unless you are writing a novel, conciseness is valued in writing. Business and technical communication must be short and to the point. No one likes to read more than they have to, unless they are reading for pleasure. Wordiness frustrates readers; it not only causes readers to lose interest but also confuses them.

You can make your writing economical by eliminating unnecessary repetition, using complex sentences instead of many short sentences, choosing precise vocabulary instead of descriptive phrases (for instance, saying "widow" instead of "woman whose husband died"), and eliminating unnecessary phrases.

Students faced with a required length for an essay assignment may pad their writing because they don't know what to say. This is always a mistake. Writing instructors know when you are padding and will not consider such an essay to be high-quality writing.

You can see examples of wordy writing and practise editing for conciseness in the exercises on page 234.

Coherence

Because written communication lacks the visual cues that speakers rely on to let listeners follow the flow of ideas, it needs to be more structured. Logical order and transition signals are essential for coherence. Coherence is explained in Unit 4 on paragraph skills.

Correctness

Writing should be correct—that is, free of grammatical, spelling, and punctuation errors. Sometimes these errors are serious—they impede comprehension. Some are minor; readers can understand what is meant, but they may get annoyed, and their impression of the writer's ability and even credibility will be negatively affected.

While perfection is impossible to attain and even professional writers make spelling and grammatical errors, it is important to strive for some degree of standard English. If you have trouble with spelling, first memorize words that are used frequently. Use all the tools available to you, such as dictionaries and spell checkers. Above all, recognize that your poor spelling is a problem, and strive to improve.

As for grammar, again, you cannot achieve perfection, especially since rules change over time and even experts can disagree over correctness. For instance, the caution against not ending an English sentence with a preposition is actually based on a mistaken reference to Latin grammar. Winston Churchill supposedly said, "That is a rule up with which I will not put" to show the absurdity of that "rule."

Concentrate on the most important aspects of grammar. For example, students with English as their second language always have trouble with articles and prepositions because much of the usage is idiomatic. However, verb forms are fairly straightforward and vital to the comprehension of sentences, so students should be sure to learn the rules and use them. They should also pay attention to common slips—such as the –*s* ending on third person singular verbs (e.g., "he walks").

Also coming into play is your instructor's take on errors. Sometimes essays are marked with deductions for each error. In that case, you have to play it safe and keep your writing as clean as possible. However, you can go too far if you use only basic words in simple sentences. Most instructors would rather read a more sophisticated essay with more mistakes than a simplistic error-free paper.

Expression

Good writing is a pleasure to read. The vocabulary is interesting, and the sentence length and structure is varied. English offers a treasure trove of words and expressions; the most successful writers are those who can use that vocabulary effectively. That does not mean that you should load up your sentences with the most multi-syllabic words you can find but rather that you should choose the appropriate word to express whatever you want to say. Good prose is simple and straightforward but not simplistic.

Understanding the Writing Process

Essentially, there are three stages to the writing process: planning, writing, and editing. These stages can be broken down into smaller steps. For instance, planning includes choosing a topic, brainstorming, and outlining. Several drafts may be written in the second stage. Editing includes making both major revisions and minor corrections.

Writers do not always progress from one stage to the next in an organized fashion. Working on a computer allows writers to go back and forth in their writing, changing their plans and editing as they write, until they are satisfied with the final product. However, students often benefit from following a more orderly process. They may skimp on the planning stage, not thinking enough about what they want to say and how they want to say it. They also tend to give the editing stage short shrift. They look for obvious mistakes they have made but are reluctant to toss out or rework full sentences, especially sentences they have sweated over. Of course, students sometimes do not have the luxury of time for their assignments. When they have to write an essay in class, they have to get words on paper fast.

Planning

Choosing a topic is generally the first step in the planning process. How much choice you have depends on your instructor and the nature of the assignment. Although students sometimes grumble about the choice of topics and say that they want to choose their own, students given complete freedom to choose a subject often produce a less satisfactory essay. Instructors generally tailor essay questions to the needs and interests of their students and relate them to the readings and discussions in the course.

You often have to narrow your subject down from the question asked. Most cover a broad range of ideas. For example, an essay topic might be "Discuss one of the problems that second-generation immigrants face." You may choose to narrow this further by writing about one specific ethnic group. Often, you are given a choice whether to disagree or agree with a statement or to write about advantages or disadvantages.

If you cannot decide among a selection of topics, do some brainstorming on two or more of them. If you jot down some ideas in point form, you will be able to see which issue you have more to say on. Pick the subject you are most comfortable with.

Sometimes students are asked to show the process in the work they submit. They may be asked to include the brainstorming, essay outline, and/or drafts with the final product. You can read more about brainstorming and outlining in Unit 5.

Writing

As you write your first draft, follow your outline, and make any necessary changes. At this point, you do not have to worry about perfection. You can correct spelling and grammatical errors in the editing stage. Essentially, you want to get your ideas down in the proper place. Remember to support your ideas with explanations and examples. Academic writing is all about making points and supporting them. You can see how this is done in Units 4, 5, and 6.

Editing

Editing involves making both major changes and minor corrections to your draft. You may want to revise what you have said, changing parts of the essay around and taking out sections. Do not hesitate to delete what does not work in your essay—even if you feel you worked hard to get the sentences written. One difference between professional writers and student writers is that professionals tinker with the wording until they are satisfied with it.

Remember that you have to proofread carefully. It is better if you do this after the essay sits for a day so that you can view it with fresh eyes. This is impossible to do with an in-class writing assignment, but if you do not leave take-home writing assignments until the last minute, you will see what a difference it makes to let your writing rest a bit.

Unit 7 gives you a chance to practise your editing skills.

Writing Personally and Impersonally

A personal voice in writing is important and indeed unavoidable, but many documents in business and technical writing have to be less personal and more objective. Because of long years of practice with compositions in English class, you may be able to handle personal writing more easily. You are probably used to personal assignments like "What I did on my summer vacation" but may have more difficulty with topics like "Why vacations are necessary for a healthy workforce." Therefore, as a college student, you should practise writing impersonally so that you can be prepared for the work world. For instance, you might have to produce a business letter that represents the company viewpoint instead of your own.

One way of looking at impersonal writing is that it means writing in the third person (*he, she, they*) instead of the first person (*I*). It also means being objective, looking at something academically. For example, instead of arguing that an increase in tuition fees is wrong because you cannot afford it, you can argue that the government should pay more because public spending on post-secondary education is an investment in society. You use more passive voice in impersonal writing, but keep in mind that too much passive bogs down the passage and makes it difficult to follow.

Student writers often overuse *I* in their essays, coming up with such phrases as "In my opinion, I personally think that . . . ." If you say, "SUVs are a waste of money," that is clearly your point of view, and you don't need to say, "I think SUVs are a waste of money." Moreover, from a grammatical point of view, a sentence such as "I think that the college should lower its parking rates" has the emphasis on the main clause "I think." You can use "I think" and "in my opinion" in your essay when you need to emphasize that this is your point of view, but use such expressions sparingly—only when you really need the emphasis.

Unless you say otherwise, your writing is your opinion. If you say, "Many people think smoking is a personal, free choice," you are distancing yourself from that idea; the reader expects the next sentence to express a "but" idea that shows your viewpoint: "However, teenagers start to smoke without a true, rational decision, and they get hooked quickly and cannot stop."

You need to develop a sense of when personal writing is appropriate. Instructors will indicate whether an essay should be personal or impersonal by the assignment question. For example, "Would you want to be married?" is a personal question, but "Discuss the benefits of marriage" indicates that a less personal response would be appropriate.

Even in an impersonal essay, you are giving your opinion and speaking from your experience. You can give personal examples, but make sure that they are appropriate and need to be expressed personally. Sometimes they are general examples that could apply to anyone. For example, if you are arguing that students cannot afford an increase in tuition fees, a personal example would be "I was so poor that I lived on macaroni and cheese. I had a friend who lived on his version of 'tomato soup,' which was boiled water flavoured with ketchup." In an academic essay, you might say, "Students can't even afford food. They are forced to go to food banks or live on macaroni and cheese or boiled water flavoured with ketchup."

Remember that personal writing is not wrong. You need to be able to write both personally and impersonally, but usually you need more practice in the latter. Notice also that it is a matter of degree; you can make something more or less personal. Moreover, it is possible to take impersonal writing too far. Governments and businesses use this style when they want to obscure who actually performed an action.

You will read examples of both personal and impersonal writing in this text, in both sample paragraphs and essays and the readings. Check the sample essays beginning on page 169 for an example of two treatments of the same topic.

To make writing less personal and more objective:
- use the third person (*he, she, they*);
- use the passive voice (but judiciously—do not overuse the passive);
- make general statements that apply to many people.

Exercise 1.1

Rewrite the following personal statements to make them impersonal. You will have to generalize:

Example: Now that my children have left home and I am approaching retirement, I would prefer to move to a bungalow. It would be easier to keep a smaller house, and I would not have to subject my arthritic knees to stair-climbing.

For empty-nesters approaching retirement, a bungalow is a good choice of house. The smaller size makes it easier to keep clean, and the lack of stairs makes it kinder to arthritic knees.

1. I like driving on the highway. I don't have to worry about so many distractions. The traffic is all travelling in the same direction, so I only have to worry about lane-changers and the occasional traffic jam.

2. My friend wants a tattoo, but I think it's a mistake. She'll regret it when she gets older. She may no longer have the same interests, and the tattoo may not look as good later when the ink fades and her skin changes with age.

3. To cut down on my food preparation time, I often cook big batches of food on the weekend and freeze it. My family particularly enjoys the chilli, stews, and spaghetti sauce. I find that some soups also freeze well.

4. I don't think children should have TVs and computers in their bedrooms. In my opinion, they are too distracting. I wouldn't do my homework if I could play electronic games instead. I would just stay in my room and never talk to my parents and siblings.

Exercise 1.2

High school graduates have to make many decisions—which school to go to, which program to study. As college students, they must decide whether to live at their parents' home, on campus, or in accommodations shared with other students. How to travel to school is another decision.

Take one of the decisions you made recently, and give three reasons for your choice. Then rewrite the paragraph from an impersonal point of view.

Example: When I went to college, I decided to give up my car and rely on public transit. First, I would have good bus service from my apartment to the campus. By not having to pay for gas, insurance, parking, and maintenance, I could also save money from my meagre student budget. Finally, I could go partying without worrying about driving home.

College students often find it more practical to give up driving their own vehicles. Campuses are generally well served by public transit. Moreover, the costs of gas, insurance, parking, and maintenance take a huge bite out of a meagre student budget. Students can even enjoy the student lifestyle with less worry about driving home safely.

Using Appropriate Style

Every language has different styles and varieties. In spoken language, dialects and accents vary considerably. For example, in everyday conversation, Australians use a kind of English very different from the one Canadians use. Their accents are different, and the slang expressions can vary significantly from those of Canadians. However, since written English is more standardized than spoken English, essays written by Australians would not differ greatly from those written by Canadians.

Written language has forms different from those of spoken language even though writing is based on spoken language. It is not just a written-down version of speech. The spelling system is not phonetic, and writing has a larger range of vocabulary and more complex sentence structure. Yet some forms of writing, such as informal notes and text messaging, are closer to spoken language in form than to most types of writing.

Just as spoken language varies depending on the audience and situation (for example, people speak less formally to friends than to co-workers), written language can be conversational, as in a letter to a friend, or more formal, as in a business report. The term "academic writing" is generally used to refer to the style expected in essays and reports in college and university. While compositions in high school and ESL classes may be informal and personal, you need to graduate to the more formal and impersonal academic style because it is similar to the one used in business and technical writing.

It is also possible to write too formally. However, this is not a common problem among college and undergraduate students. It is more often seen in the writing of professionals and academics who use jargon and complex expressions, often obscuring what they mean. For instance, a business executive may write "at this point in time" instead of using a simpler word such as "now." As a demonstration of inflated language, common proverbs have been rewritten. For instance, "It is fruitless to become lachrymose over cascading lacteal fluid" is "There's no use crying over spilt milk."

North American society has moved toward greater informality. Casual work dress has replaced business suits in many occupations. People rarely use a title and surname, preferring to address business associates by their first name. Written communication has also seen a lessening in formality. For example, newspaper articles are more casual today. You can see this difference by comparing "The Strange Forces behind the Richard Hockey Riot" (page 338), which was written 50 years ago, to any of the other articles in this text or articles in current newspapers and magazines. In addition, business letters written decades ago show many outdated formal expressions, such as "I am in receipt of your letter dated the 24th of June."

Here is an example of different styles of language used to describe the same incident:

Conversational English

Well, the thing is, the guys did a real good job on that project. They busted their butts getting all the info together. And they figured out all the stuff that could come up. Like, let's say, the power went out, they'd have this back-up plan all set to go. And they made this list of people to call, you know, if you had some sorta problem. [67 words]

Academic English

The team did a commendable job on that project. They all worked diligently to assemble the required information. They planned for contingencies such as power blackouts and prepared an emergency contact list. [32 words]

Notice that conversational language uses more words but the words are shorter.

The writing style used in this textbook varies. Explanations are written in a semi-formal style to make them more accessible to you, the reader.

The use of *you* is necessary because directions are being given. The sample paragraphs and essays are in a slightly more formal style—in the style you might be required to produce in your English class. Many of the readings in the text are in a less formal, journalistic style. You can learn from reading all kinds of styles. Moreover, your instructor should give you direction as to which type of writing style you are expected to use for assignments.

Conversational English	*Academic English*
• regional (different dialects, accents)	• standardized
• mostly spoken but also written to friends (letters, email, chat messages) and in dialogue in novels and short stories	• mostly written but also in formal speeches
• immediate feedback so speaker knows what listener needs to understand	• writer must anticipate what reader knows and what questions reader will have
• meaning from gestures, tone of voice	• meaning from punctuation, use of space
• use of visuals from situation, scene	• some use of visuals from pictures, graphics
• personal (use of *I* and *you*)	• less personal, more detached and objective
• *you* for people in general	• focus on third person (*he, she, they*)
• imprecise words (*stuff, thing*)	• more use of passive voice to depersonalize
• very limited vocabulary (~2000 words)	• precise vocabulary for clarity
• basic English has only 800 words	• huge vocabulary in use (~20,000 words)
• conversational markers (*let's see, well now, you know*)	• use of transition markers to show relationship of ideas (*moreover, however*)
• short, simple sentences	• longer, more complicated sentences
• use of slang, colloquialisms	• little idiomatic language
• contractions to show speech forms (*don't, gonna, would've*)	• contractions not used
• sentences starting with co-ordinate conjunctions (*and, or, but, yet, so*)	• use of conjunctive adverbs (*however, nevertheless, furthermore*)
• conversations can meander, digress; ideas may not be fully explained or completed	• in long, structured paragraphs; with logical sequence; ideas supported and explained; with introductions and conclusions
• repetition, interruptions	• more development, less repetition
• shorthand among friends, relatives referring to common experiences	• reference to other works of literature, film, history, current events

Understanding the Use of *You*

In modern English, *you* is used for both the person being addressed directly (in writing, this would be the reader) and for people in general:

> You should check your assignment over carefully before you hand it in.

> In that neighbourhood, you can hear the sound of airplanes flying into the airport.

The use of *you* has become common in many forms of writing, such as newspaper and magazine articles, but you should avoid it in your essay writing. Since academic writing is impersonal, you should not address your reader directly. As for the other use of *you* to mean *people*, this usage is conversational style and, again, not suitable for essays. For instance, instead of saying, "You should look both ways before you cross the street," you could say, "It is important to look both ways before crossing the street" or "People should look both ways before they cross the street." Sometimes students run into problems with the *you* form because they switch references:

> When those children grow up, they will be very surprised to see that life is hard and you have to do things for yourself. If you don't baby your child, they will grow up to be adults who can think for themselves.

These sentences are confusing because the *you* in the first sentence refers to the children but the *you* in the second sentence refers to the parents. Moreover, the writer switches between *you* and *they* for the same people.

Remember that command sentences, also known as imperatives, are also considered to be *you* sentences. A statement like "Consider the differences between these two types of students" actually has an implied subject *you*, the person doing the action.

In textbooks like this one, *you* is used to address the readers—the students—directly. In journalistic writing, *you* is often used to give a more casual, friendlier tone. Because writing today is generally less formal, *you* is used frequently, and many students find it almost impossible to avoid. It is worth practising, however. While some instructors may accept a conversational tone in your essays, most do not accept the use of *you* in academic writing.

To eliminate *you*, choose a noun that represents the group being discussed, and use third person plural (the plural also helps you avoid the messy he/she problem). For instance, instead of saying, "When you are looking for a job, you should network and exploit your contacts," you can say, "Job hunters should network and exploit their contacts."

Exercise 1.3

Rewrite the following sentences to eliminate *you*:

Example: You need to see the student advisor to change your timetable.

Possible rewrites: Timetable changes must be approved by the student advisor.

Students should see their advisor to change their timetable.

1. The smallest problem with a luxury car will cost you a lot of money because the parts are harder to find and you have to pay the person for his or her time.

2. In order the pass the test, you must memorize the rules and road signs in the driver's handbook.

3. You can be successful at college if you attend class, pay attention to the instructor, and do your homework.

4. You could spend hours watching TV and YouTube videos and waste your whole day.

5. You can see teenagers hanging around the mall with nothing to do.

Exercise 1.4

Generally, a piece of writing stays in one style of language. Academic pieces that use hip hop slang would be disconcerting to readers, and a newspaper column in an overly formal tone would sound unfriendly and cold. The following article breaks this rule to create a humorous effect. The author switches from formal language to conversational English throughout the piece.

1. What are the features of conversational English that this article contains? (Use the chart on page 13 as a reference.) Consider the verb forms, the beginnings of sentences, and the use of questions. Are these features suitable for use in an essay?

2. Find examples of conversational expressions (such as "let's see") that would be inappropriate in an essay.

3. Find three idioms in the article.

4. Find examples of slang.

5. Find examples of "legalese"—overly formal language that a lawyer (or politician) would be likely to use.

6. What one word could be used instead of "children's children" and "children's children's children"?

7. What are some slang words you would use to describe "scientists, with their oversized glasses and little slide rules and pocket protectors"?

8. How does the author create humour in the article? What do you find particularly funny?

9. How do you know that the author is not serious about his opposition to environmental initiatives, that he is in fact kidding?

A Global Warming Deal to Do Nothing Still Possible
by Linwood Barclay

1   If, as it appears, the Kyoto Protocol to reduce global warming is going straight into the toilet, it's time to consider drafting a new deal that all of the world's nations can get behind.

2   Let's face it. The United States isn't signing on to Kyoto. Australia's not on board. Russia isn't going to ratify the agreement. And our soon-to-be Prime Minister is kind of waffling about it, too. So it's finished. It's done. It's over. The deal to cut greenhouse-gas emissions has gone up in smoke. But that doesn't mean an agreement regarding global warming is impossible. It just needs to be worded a bit differently.

3   Chances are, world leaders like US President George W. Bush and Russian President Vladimir Putin and even our own Paul Martin would be more likely to consider an agreement with the following provisions:

4   "Be it resolved that, given that the worst effects of global warming—continents disappearing under oceans, skin frying the moment you step outside, that kind of thing—aren't likely to happen for another hundred years or so, there's no sense getting your shorts in a knot about it today. Why not take in a ball game instead, so long as it's not outside."

5   "We are united in the belief that it's not our own children, and maybe not even our children's children, who will be devastated by global warming. In all likelihood, it will be our children's children's children. And ask yourself this, 'What have they done for you lately?' Have you seen so much as a thank-you card from any of them?"

6   "It is acknowledged, without prejudice, that while massive Hummer-style SUVs may contribute to the problem of global warming, they're also part of the solution. Those suckers sit high enough that when the oceans start rising, you'll be drier longer than that guy in the Neon."

7   "The people of the nations of the world are in agreement that, well, you've got to die from something, right? You could spend billions trying to curb emissions, then cross the street and get hit by a bus."

8   "We must accept, unreservedly, that it is within the realm of possibility that maybe we're just plain wrong about how dangerous these greenhouse gases really are. Isn't it possible the scientists, with their oversized glasses and little slide rules and pocket protectors, are not only the people we beat up in grade school but a bunch of naysayers who've got it all wrong? Consider this: Who could have imagined that not just one but both Matrix movie sequels would suck? If something like that can happen, anything's possible."

9   "As responsible nations we are committed to the financial well-being of our citizens. Strict environmental protection rules stifle economic growth. We believe strongly in the principle of being able to make as much money as we can and acquiring really neat things, right up until the moment that we collapse onto the sidewalk, hacking and wheezing and gagging."

10   "You have to admit, sometimes, when the sun is setting, and the rays hit the smog clouds just the right way, it can be quite beautiful."

11   "It is hereby affirmed that we, the leaders of the world, must get re-elected every few years, and that's not going to happen without substantial campaign donations from the leaders of the business community, and given that it is the aforementioned business community that has to pay the costs of greater environmental controls, well, do we have to connect the dots for you here or what?"

12   "Just for fun, let's go to David Suzuki's place and let the air out of the tires of his hybrid car."

13   Now there. Isn't that something our world leaders, visionaries every one, could sign on to?

[from the *Toronto Star*, 5 Dec. 2003, p. G1]

Good Writing
- is clear and concise;
- fits the audience and purpose;
- has something interesting to say;
- has correct grammar, spelling, and punctuation;
- uses a variety of words and sentence structures.

Academic-Style English

- is used for school essays and carries over to business and technical reports;
- is impersonal and objective (no *I* or *you*);
- is structured with developed paragraphs;
- has points made and, above all, supported;
- uses precise vocabulary and longer, more complex sentences;
- does not use contractions, slang, or conversational expressions.

Vocabulary Skills

Words and expressions are the building blocks of language. Grammar tells you how the words fit together, but without words there is no meaning. Having a large vocabulary at your command makes you a better reader and writer. You can increase your vocabulary through wide and attentive reading, but an understanding of how words work will also help you. You need to be able to identify the basic parts of speech and differentiate between nouns, verbs, adjectives, and adverbs. When you learn new words, you should learn about their usage—grammatical and stylistic. Words fit into patterns—how they relate to words with similar meanings, words with similar roots, and words that tend to appear together. Moreover, many grammar mistakes in writing are actually vocabulary errors. For example, you might use the wrong preposition with a verb ("gambles in" instead of "gambles on," for instance), but there is no grammar rule that explains this; it is simply part of the usage pattern of that particular verb.

The English language offers its users the largest vocabulary of any language. English is like a huge stew into which many ingredients have been added. The base is a Germanic language brought to England by the Anglo-Saxon tribes 1500 years ago. Added to that are Norse words and structures brought by Viking raiders who settled on the west coast of England. The most significant addition was Norman French because it practically doubled the vocabulary of Anglo-Saxon English. The 1066 invasion by William the Conqueror meant that for many years the nobility spoke French while the common people spoke English. The French words gradually blended into the Anglo-Saxon base so that we have many synonyms such as *help*, which has an English base, and *aid* from French. Later on, English, like other European languages, acquired technical and scientific words with roots in Greek and Latin, words like *television*, *microscope*, and *psychology*. This mongrel background of English also makes the spelling system seem chaotic, since words from different languages may follow different spelling conventions.

Written language uses a richer vocabulary than spoken language. It is difficult to estimate vocabulary size. One reason is that we can argue over what counts as a word. For example, the word *jerk* can refer to the act of pulling, a type of chicken dish, and a rude person, so should it be counted as three different words or three different meanings of one word? Usually, the decision is made by lexicographers who can count the number of entries in their dictionaries. Another difficulty is the number of technical terms and the words from different varieties of English. Even the most educated of speakers know relatively few of the possible words of English—which is over a million. Moreover, our active vocabulary (the words we use) is smaller than our passive vocabulary (the words we understand).

It is important that writers take advantage of this richness of vocabulary. First of all, it is necessary for accuracy. People speaking English can get away with imprecise words like *stuff* and *thingamajig* because they can point to the object in question and determine whether the listener understands. However, writing requires precision of vocabulary to achieve clarity.

In addition, you can keep your readers' interest by varying the words you use. A passage that repeats the same word again and again can become tedious. You can use a thesaurus (a dictionary of synonyms and antonyms) to remind yourself of other words you can use for a concept, but you must keep in mind that synonyms may have similar meanings in one context but they are not always interchangeable. For example, you can tell someone to either *concentrate* or *focus* on an assignment, but *concentrate* is also used in chemistry to talk about concentrations in solutions and *focus* is used for cameras.

In order to increase the size of your vocabulary, you must understand the basics of how words are used and formed, be able to use reference tools, and find patterns and connections so that you can learn words in groups and not individually. Your brain stores words with connections to other words. Reading a variety of texts will expose you to a wide range of words and their uses.

Recognizing Parts of Speech

Words are labelled according to their class or part of speech, which denotes the function that they have in a sentence. The traditional divisions of parts of speech are nouns, pronouns, verbs, adjectives, adverbs, conjunctions, prepositions, and interjections. Nouns, verbs, adjectives, and adverbs are content words; they are in an open class to which words are constantly being added. In contrast, words like conjunctions and prepositions are in a closed class; they are function words with grammatical meaning in the sentence but little lexical meaning. Increasing your vocabulary means increasing the number of content words you know.

The part of speech label figures prominently in dictionary entries because it is so important. As you work on expanding your vocabulary, you need a sense of the different parts of speech so that you can learn new words in various forms. For example, if you study the word *reciprocate*, which is a verb, you can also learn the corresponding noun *reciprocity* and adjective *reciprocal*.

It is important to be able to distinguish nouns, verbs, adjectives, and adverbs in a sentence:

> He will <u>succeed</u> this time. [verb]
> His <u>success</u> depends on the amount of effort he puts in. [noun]

> He was considered a <u>successful</u> man. [adjective]
> He <u>successfully</u> turned that company around. [adverb]

Sometimes the form of the word is the same, but the function differs:

> I need a <u>light</u>. [noun]
> Could you please <u>light</u> the fire? [verb]
> It's so warm outside that all we need is a <u>light</u> jacket. [adjective]

> Time <u>flies</u> like an arrow.
> Fruit <u>flies</u> like a banana.

Understanding parts of speech can help you build your vocabulary and avoid grammar mistakes such as the following:

> He is a violence man. [He is a <u>violent</u> man—adjective, not noun, required]

> He lacks of the skills necessary for the job. [He lacks the skills necessary . . . —the preposition only goes with the noun *lack* (as in "the lack of skills") and not with the verb (as in "he lacks the skills").]

An intensive and extensive knowledge of grammatical terminology is not necessary for writing grammatical English, but you should have a basic sense of the different parts of speech to guide you in sentence construction and in vocabulary building.

Nouns

Nouns and verbs are fundamental to a sentence. Nouns are essentially the names of persons, places, things, animals, and ideas. Examples of nouns are *girl, house, desk, cow,* and *beauty.*

Concrete nouns refer to things you can touch, such as *stone, chair,* and *eggs,* while **abstract nouns** name emotions and qualities, such as *love, truth,* and *success.*

Proper nouns are specific names and are capitalized (*Tom, Vancouver, the Bible, Saskatchewan, Mr. Smith*).

Collective nouns refer to a group of people and things but are singular, such as *staff, team,* and *herd.*

Compound nouns are two words that are used together as a unit. Different parts of speech can be combined. For example: *girlfriend, bookcase, boom box, lunch break, slip-knot, mini-bar.* The unit can be two separate words, hyphenated words, or one word. It is often difficult to tell how a compound should be written; dictionaries might disagree, more than one form might be acceptable, and the compound may evolve from a two-word combination to a single word. For example, *web page* is gradually becoming *webpage.* Consult a recent Canadian dictionary if you need an authoritative source of information.

Uncountable nouns are not generally pluralized or used with indefinite articles (*a, an*). They include liquids (*milk, water*), gases (*air, helium*), things that are in grains (*sand, salt*), and abstract qualities (*beauty, truth*). Some tricky uncountable nouns are *advice, clothing, equipment, furniture, information, mail, paper, news, research, software, time,* and *work.*

Sometimes a noun can have both an uncountable and countable usage:

> She had a lot of <u>work</u> to do for her assignment. She still had to go to the museum to view the <u>works</u> of arts.

> We don't have much <u>time</u> to do this project. We have to check everything three <u>times</u>.

> I need more <u>paper</u>. I have to write a <u>paper</u> on *Othello.*

Some uncountable nouns have an expression that can be used when you want a countable item. For example, you can ask for "a piece of advice" or "a slice (or a loaf) of bread." Luggage cannot be counted, but bags and suitcases can. You cannot count furniture, but you can count individual pieces like chairs and tables. You cannot count paper, but you can count individual pieces or sheets. You cannot say that you have "many works" to do, but you can have many tasks, chores, or jobs.

Pronouns take the place of nouns and refer to them:

> I, me, my, mine, myself
> you, your, yours, yourself
> he, she, it, him, her, his, hers, its, himself, herself, itself
> we, us, our, ours, ourselves
> they, them, their, theirs, themselves

Position

Nouns are crucial to a sentence. They tell what is being talked about. Nouns can be the subject of the sentence, the object of the verb, or the object in a prepositional phrase:

> The **secretary** [subject] hid the **key** [direct object] behind the **mirror** [object in a prepositional phrase].

Nouns appear after determiners (*a, an, the, this, that, these, those, my, your, his, her, its, our, their*):

> the house, a boy, his book, their names, this boat, that restaurant

Adjectives may come in between the determiner and the noun:

> the old house, the red-haired boy, his only book, their former names, this expensive boat

Note, however, that nouns can often function as adjectives, sometimes forming compound forms:

> grocery store, biology book, garage door opener, bus stop

Plural forms

Nouns can be singular (meaning *one*) or plural (*more than one*). For most nouns, an −*s* is added to make the plural form:

> book/books, holiday/holidays, computer/computers, year/years

Nouns that end in *–s*, *–sh*, *–ch*, or *–x* have an *–es* plural ending:

> box/boxes, bus/buses, church/churches, kiss/kisses, wish/ wishes, watch/watches

Nouns that end in *–y* not preceded by a vowel have an *–ies* plural ending:

> story/stories (but storey/storeys), spy/spies

Nouns that end in *–f* or *–fe* end in *–ves* in the plural:

> knife/knives, half/halves, wife/wives

Some nouns that end in *–o* take an *–es* ending:

> hero/heroes, potato/potatoes (but studio/studios)

Irregular plurals

Words that have the same form for singular and plural:

> deer, fish, moose, sheep, shrimp

Plural forms ending in *–en*:

> child/children, man/men, woman/women, ox/oxen

Words from Latin and Greek that use Latin and Greek plurals (these are gradually being replaced by the *–s* plural of English):

> criterion/criteria
> datum/data (the singular form is rarely used now)
> medium/media
> phenomenon/phenomena
> appendix/appendices
> thesis/theses, analysis/analyses

Plural nouns with no singular form:

> clothes, scissors, pants, trousers

If you are not sure of the plural form of a noun, look it up in the dictionary.

Some common noun suffixes

–age	breakage, marriage, mileage
–ance, –ence	alliance, difference, reference, silence
–er, –or	actor, escalator, instructor, inventor, teacher
–dom	freedom, kingdom, wisdom
–hood	knighthood, neighbourhood
–ism	feminism, heroism, plagiarism, realism
–ist	artist, cyclist, finalist, racist, typist
–ity	capability, fatality, inability
–ment	document, enjoyment, entertainment
–ness	goodness, happiness, sadness
–ship	friendship, kinship
–sion, –tion	celebration, fusion, nation, permission

Exercise 2.1

Identify the nouns in the following list:

song	forest	likelihood
popular	darken	folder
good	shadow	national
Paris	understand	prettiness
future	wilderness	Tanya
dreamer	take	beauty
careful	mortality	hardship
upon	naysayer	repetitive

Exercise 2.2

Give the noun form of the following words (e.g., decide – decision).
Note that some nouns have the same spelling as the verb or
adjective form:

1. competent (adj.)

2. enrich (v.)

6. real (adj.)

7. invite (v.)

Exercise 2.2 – *continued*

3. speak (v.)
4. wealthy (adj.)
5. clear (adj.)

8. stable (adj.)
9. deny (v.)
10. contribute (v.)

Verbs

Verbs are words that describe actions (*jump, swim, wave*) or states (*be, seem, signify*). Like nouns, they are crucial to a sentence. Verb tenses are discussed in Unit 3 as part of sentence structure.

Verb forms

English verb structures are less complicated and have fewer forms than those of most other European languages. English verbs have only three regular verb endings: *–s, –ing, –ed*. The base form of the verb is the infinitive without *to* (e.g., *make, seem, wear*), and it is used to make the simple present tense.

To make the different forms of the verb, you need to know three main parts:

Base	Past tense	Past participle
walk	walked	walked
study	studied	studied
run	ran	run
swim	swam	swum

While regular verbs use the *–ed* ending for the past forms, irregular verbs vary. Check your dictionary for the past tense and past participle of irregular verbs.

Auxiliary verbs

The verb in a sentence may be more than one word. For example, the auxiliary (helping) verbs *be* and *have* form part of the verb in the perfect and continuous tenses. Modal verbs (e.g., *could, should, may, would*) can also be part of the verb:

The group is <u>travelling</u> to the exhibition by bus.

I <u>have been</u> to Paris many times.

She <u>could have gotten</u> more work done.

The verbs *be*, *do*, *have*, and *will* can be verbs on their own or can function as auxiliary verbs:

> Even though he <u>is</u> late, he <u>is going</u> to the competition.

> I <u>do</u> enough work around here. I <u>do not wish</u> to take on more.

> She <u>has</u> no money. She <u>hasn't received</u> her student loan yet.

> The king <u>wills</u> that the ceremony proceed. It <u>will be</u> spectacular. (Note that the use of *will* as a main verb is rare.)

Active and passive

The auxiliary verb *be* is used with the past participle to make the passive voice:

> The ball <u>was hit</u> hard to left field, but it <u>was caught</u>.

In the active voice, the subject of the sentence is the one doing the action, while in the passive voice the subject of the sentence is the receiver of the action:

> I <u>signed</u> the receipt, but she <u>did not give</u> me a copy. [active]
> The receipt <u>was signed</u>, but I <u>was not given</u> a copy. [passive]

The use of passive voice is explained on page 68.

Phrasal verbs

Some verbs are completed by one or two adverbial particles, commonly known as prepositions:

> She <u>slept in</u> and missed class, so then she <u>fell behind</u> and had trouble <u>catching up</u>.

> I <u>got up</u> at noon, but I was still tired.

Verbals

Words that are based on verbs but do not function as main verbs are called verbals. They include participles, infinitives, and gerunds.

Verb forms that act as adjectives are called **participles**. **Active participles** end in *–ing* and show that the person or thing is doing something, while **passive participles** end in *–ed* and show that something is being done to someone or something:

The group <u>performing</u> next is the favourite to win the competition.

The <u>elected</u> officials were sworn in on Tuesday.

An **infinitive** is the simple, base form of the verb, with or without *to*:

He seemed <u>to shrink</u> before my eyes.

I need another computer program <u>to do</u> the editing.

She helped them <u>reorganize</u> the whole department.

Gerunds end in –*ing* and act as nouns:

<u>Waiting around</u> is more difficult than doing something.

<u>Dancing</u> is great exercise.

I recommend <u>taking</u> the bus instead.

One of the trickier aspects of English is figuring out whether a verb takes the infinitive or the gerund to complete the idea. Note these examples:

I <u>intend to leave</u> next Thursday. I <u>suggest taking</u> the train.

I <u>enjoy playing</u> the piano. I <u>want to take</u> more lessons.

Sometimes a verb takes both forms, but a different meaning is expressed:

He stopped <u>talking</u> and listened to the odd noise.

He ran into some old friends downtown, so he stopped <u>to talk</u>.

There is no definitive grammar rule that explains why some verbs require the gerund and some the infinitive. Sometimes hypothetical, unfulfilled ideas tend to be expressed with the infinitive, while real happenings tend to be found with the gerund:

I <u>hope to complete</u> a marathon this year. (hypothetical, a wish)

I <u>enjoyed running</u> the marathon. (actually happened)

This problem of infinitive versus gerund causes particular difficulty for ESL students. Lists of the different verbs for these structures are given in Unit 7. As you develop your vocabulary, note which forms are required with each verb—whether a verb takes a direct object (this type of verb is called *transitive*), whether a certain preposition follows the verb (as in *rely on*), as well as whether it takes the gerund or the infinitive. These aspects of language should be considered part of vocabulary since there are few grammar rules to guide such usage.

Affixes that make verbs

be–	bejewel, belittle, bewitch
en–	enable, endanger, enjoy, enlarge, envision
–en	blacken, lighten, soften, toughen
–ate	activate, discriminate, motivate
im-, in-	impassion, imperil, inflame
–fy	identify, notify, signify, solidify, unify, verify
–ize	idealize, maximize, realize, recognize, sympathize

Exercise 2.3

Give the verb form of the following words (e.g., sign – signify):

1. description (n.)

2. evasive (adj.)

3. inspirational (adj.)

4. facilitator (n.)

5. white (adj.)

6. threat (n.)

7. authority (n.)

8. defiant (adj.)

9. pursuit (n.)

10. expansion (n.)

Adjectives

Essentially, adjectives describe nouns. They usually appear before the noun in English, as in these examples:

> <u>brown</u> dress, <u>tall</u> man, <u>close</u> escape, <u>unparalleled</u> beauty, <u>questionable</u> actions

They also appear after the verb *to be* and other verbs that describe the state of something:

> Working in this classroom is <u>difficult</u>. The air feels <u>stuffy</u>. The noise is <u>annoying</u>.

Several adjectives can be used together. A comma is used between them if they are describing a similar attribute (in other words, if an *and* sounds right):

> the <u>big brown</u> hen

> the <u>typical French-Canadian</u> house

> an <u>itsy-bitsy</u>, <u>teeny-weeny</u>, <u>yellow polka-dot</u> bikini

Sometimes nouns work as adjectives, as do verbals like active (*–ing* verbals) or passive (*–ed* verbals) participles:

> library book, welcoming committee, chosen participants

Phrases can be used as a unit to describe a noun; they are usually hyphenated:

> His <u>stick-in-the-mud</u> attitude annoys me.

> It's a <u>10-year-old car</u>, so it often requires repairs.

Note that these adjective phrases are used in the singular:

> I wouldn't touch him with a <u>10-foot pole</u>. [not "10-feet"]

Determiners, which include qualifiers and articles, are a subclass of adjectives that are considered function words:

> a, an, the, this, that, these, those

Comparative and superlative forms

Different forms of the adjective are used to make comparisons. For comparing one thing to another, the comparative form is used. It is formed by adding an *–er* ending to words of one or two syllables. For longer words, *more* appears before the adjective:

> She is <u>taller</u> than I am, but I have <u>longer</u> legs because I have a <u>shorter</u> torso.

> That is the <u>more expensive</u> of the two options.

The superlative form is used when the comparison is between one thing and two or more. It is formed with the *–est* ending or the addition of *most* before the adjective:

> He was the <u>brightest</u> child in the class.

> Of the three options, that is the <u>most cost-effective</u>.

> That is the <u>most ridiculous</u> idea I have ever heard.

Less and *least* are used as the opposite of *more* and *most*:

> She is <u>less experienced</u> than I am.

> They were <u>the least prepared</u> team in the competition.

Adjective suffixes

–able, –ible	able to, suitable for	acceptable, capable, flexible
–en	made of	golden, wooden
–ful	full of	awful, beautiful, grateful, powerful
–ic, –ical	relating to	classical, comic, musical, public
–ive	tending to	descriptive, pensive, sensitive
–less	without	careless, worthless
–ous, –ose	quality, state	grandiose, mountainous, poisonous, verbose
–y	having, being like	funny, sunny, hairy

Exercise 2.4

Give the adjective form of the following words (e.g., wonder – wonderful). There may be more than one form, and the adjective may have the same form as the word given:

1. mist (n.)
2. comedy (n.)
3. operate (v.)
4. force (n.)
5. experiment (v.)

6. accept (v.)
7. stress (n.)
8. disaster (n.)
9. science (n.)
10. publicity (n.)

Exercise 2.5

Match the adjectives in the list to a noun below, using each one once: brute, extensive, frantic, heartfelt, jagged, limited, masked, secret, tempting, tough:

1. _____ ballot   6. _____ offer

2. _____ force   7. _____ opponent

3. _____ haste   8. _____ sympathy

4. _____ hole   9. _____ visibility

5. _____ intruder   10. _____ vocabulary

Exercise 2.6

Fill in the blanks with suitable adjectives:

1. The _____ house was _____ and _____.

2. Several _____ children played around the _____ park.

3. The _____ robots completed the _____ work.

4. A _____ hat lay on the _____, _____ ground.

5. A _____ _____ toy was the last item at the _____ auction.

Adverbs

Adverbs explain how, when, or where something is done:

He closed the door <u>quickly</u>.

<u>Yesterday</u> we met in the boardroom.

We like to eat lunch <u>nearby</u>.

Some adverbs are formed from adjectives, with the addition of the suffix –*ly*:

carefully, quickly, realistically, slowly

Adjectives that end in –*ly* (such as *friendly*, *lonely*, *miserly*) do not have an adverb form:

The dog was friendly. The dog wagged his tail in a friendly way.

Adverbs that are not formed from an adjective are mostly function words and include many different kinds of adverbs:

time: now, then, yesterday, never

place: there, here, nearby

Some adverbs are intensifiers:

very, quite, highly, rarely

Exercise 2.7

Give the adverb form of the following words (e.g., careful – carefully):

1. simple (adj.)
2. real (adj.)
3. true (adj.)
4. signify (v.)
5. uneasy (adj.)

6. brutality (n.)
7. haze (n.)
8. absurd (adj.)
9. frequent (adj.)
10. evidence (n.)

Exercise 2.8

Add adjectives and adverbs to the following sentences:

1. The man walked down the block.
2. The deer ran away.
3. The mother took her children to the park.
4. The car sped down the street.
5. The machine emitted smoke.

Reviewing parts of speech

Exercise 2.9

Decide which type of word goes in each blank—a noun, verb, adjective, or adverb. After you have labelled each blank, fill in appropriate words to fit the sentence:

1. A _____ book lay on the _____, next to the black _____.

2. The student _____ his homework. He went back to his _____ to get it.

3. The _____ couple _____ in the park _____ watching the _____ at play.

4. Jack _____ placed the _____ top back on the _____.

5. She prefers _____ music when she feels _____.

Exercise 2.10

Fill in the blanks in the following chart:

Noun	Verb	Adjective	Adverb
agreement			
	anger		
			beautifully
		developmental	
excess			
		high	
			legally
	manage		
politics			
		soft	

Mastering Spelling

English spelling is not only difficult, it can be downright maddening because it is not consistent with the pronunciation of words. For instance, the *–ough* combination can have many different pronunciations, as seen in the words *cough*, *through*, and *although*. This does not mean you should just give up. English spelling does have patterns that can be learned, and there are tools to help you. Some words you will just have to memorize.

Because English has absorbed so many words from different languages, it has also acquired spelling features of the words. Moreover, the Latin alphabet it uses is ill-suited to the sounds of a Germanic language like English. Some scientific and technical terms are based on Greek words, which has another alphabet. To make things more complicated, pronunciation has altered over the years, while spelling has not changed as much. For example, the silent letters in words like *knight* used to be pronounced.

English spelling is an obvious target for reformers. They argue that it is chaotic and unnecessarily difficult to learn. Counter-arguments include the fact that a phonetically based spelling system (one based on sounds) would hide some semantic relationships (those based on meaning). For example, the words *sign* and *signify* are related (both come from the Latin *signus* for *sign*), but their kinship would not be as evident if *sign* were spelled *sine*.

Whether you are for or against English spelling reform, the fact remains that your responsibility as a writer is to spell the words as they are currently accepted. In the world outside the classroom, spelling is also important. A misspelled document reflects badly on its author. For example, a resumé with misspellings is likely to go straight into the reject pile. Some people are poor spellers, and they have to work at it much harder than other people. Even avid readers can be bad at spelling.

Tips for Improving Your Spelling
- Be careful. Many spelling mistakes are the result of carelessness such as miscopying from a source document.
- Learn basic spelling rules and patterns (some are given on the following pages).
- Recognize common letter combinations (e.g., *–ought*).
- Learn standard prefixes and suffixes.
- Learn common Greek and Latin root words.
- Use mnemonic devices to help you remember spelling (e.g., "The principal is your pal.").
- Use a dictionary. (If you have trouble locating the word, concentrate on getting the first few letters right. Try possible alternate spelling combinations. For example, if the word starts with an *s* sound, try looking under *s*, *c*, *sc*, and *ps*.)

- Use a computer spell checker, but do not rely on it to catch all your errors.
- Proofread your work carefully, looking especially for words you have trouble with.
- Make a list of words you often misspell, and practise them by writing them out several times.
- Go over any spelling mistakes when you get writing assignments back.
- Have someone give you a spelling quiz to see whether you have learned the words on your list.

The silent *e*

Many words end in a silent −*e*, which generally serves as a sign to show how the previous vowel is pronounced. This pronunciation is sometimes called the "long" vowel, pronounced the same as the vowel's name. Compare these examples:

> mat/mate
> bid/bide
> bit/bite
> bad/bade
> hop/hope
> rip/ripe

This silent *e* is dropped when endings with a vowel are added to the base word but kept if the ending begins with a consonant. In contrast, words that end in a single consonant coming after a single vowel have that consonant doubled if the final syllable is stressed. This helps distinguish between such words as *dining* (eating) and *dinning* (loud noise). Note that verbs that end in −*e* may go to a double letter form in the past participle if the pronunciation changes, such as in *bite/bitten* and *write/written*.

Base word	+s	+ed	+ing	with affixes
hope	hopes	hoped	hoping	hopeful
hop	hops	hopped	hopping	hopper
file	files	filed	filing	
fill	fills	filled	filling	filler

Exercise 2.11

Add the ending to the following base words:

1. smile + ing
2. tile + ed
3. require + ment
4. fade + s
5. wade + ing

6. complete + ed
7. comprise + ing
8. shade + s
9. settle + ed
10. erode + ing

Doubling consonants

If a word ends in a single vowel and single consonant and this last syllable is stressed, the final consonant is doubled before the endings:

fit + ed = fitted
begin + ing = beginning
develop + ment = development (last syllable not stressed)

Sometimes the American spelling of a word has a single consonant whereas Canadian spelling has a double consonant, as in *traveled* versus *travelled*.

Exercise 2.12

Add the ending to the following base words:

1. wed + ing
2. wait + ed
3. dream + less
4. dip + ed
5. control + ed

6. chug + ing
7. occur + ence
8. keep + ing
9. grunt + ed
10. drip + ing

Words with −*y*

The −*y* ending often creates problems for spelling. Look at the word forms below. How are they grouped? Which words give you trouble? Think of ways to help you remember the spelling.

study, studies, studying, studied
muddy, muddies, muddying, muddied
ready, readies, readying, readied
die, dies, dying, died
dye, dyes, dyeing, dyed
notify, notifies, notifying, notified
try, tries, trying, tried
lay, lays, laying, laid
play, plays, playing, played
portray, portrays, portraying, portrayed
stay, stays, staying, stayed
day, daily
enjoy, enjoys, enjoying, enjoyed
boy, boys

Words with *ei* or *ie*

In elementary school we learned the rule "Write *i* before *e* except after *c* or when sounded as *a*, as in *neighbour* and *weigh*." This rule helps, but it does not cover all the cases. If the sound is a short *e* or a long *i*, the *ei* is often the correct spelling (as in *their* or *height*). The *ie* spelling is generally more common than *ei*. Exceptions include *caffeine* and *protein*.

Exercise 2.13

Decide which words in the list follow the spelling rules described here. Can you think of ways to help you remember the words that do not?

beige	caffeine	chief
believe	ceiling	conceive
counterfeit	piece	shield
either	receive	veil
freight	reign	weight
friend	retrieve	weird
heir	seize	yield
leisure	sheik	

Greek letters

Some of the trickiest words to spell come from Greek, which uses a different alphabet, some letters of which are familiar from their use in mathematics (such as *pi* π). While some Greek letters have an obvious one-to-one corre-spondence with the Roman alphabet used for English (such as *alpha* α and *a*), other Greek letters are represented by two-letter combinations in English. For instance, the *ps* combination found in words like *psychology* is from the Greek letter *psi* ψ. The letter combination *ph* sounds like an *f* in English words, but its use shows us the word is from Greek, from the letter *phi* φ.

Etymology (the historical sources of a word) can help you figure out the pronunciation of *ch* in English. Greek words (which are often scientific or technical words) have the *ch* pronounced like a *k* sound because it comes from the Greek letter *chi* χ. This explains the common short form *Xmas* for *Christmas* because the letter *chi* looks like an *x*. If the word is a common, simple one and does not have typical Greek spelling combinations, it is probably a true English word in which the *ch* is pronounced as in *church* and *chicken*. French words (like *chef* and *champagne*) have the *ch* pronounced like *sh*, but these are less common.

If you know you are dealing with a scientific or technical term, expect that it might have the Greek spelling patterns. Here are some examples of words from Greek:

> chronology, chaos, psychology
> philosophy, photography, phonetics
> psychiatrist, psyche, psychic

Words often confused

Many spelling mistakes occur because different words sound alike. Here are some common ones that cause spelling problems:

> accept: receive
> except: not
> > She couldn't <u>accept</u> the fact that we wanted all the
> > T-shirts <u>except</u> for that one.
>
> advice: noun
> advise: verb
> > I <u>advise</u> you not to take his <u>advice</u>.
>
> affect: usually a verb
> effect: usually a noun
> > He studied the <u>effects</u> of pollution on the wetlands and
> > found that global warming <u>affects</u> the ecology.

cite: to reference
sight: ability to see, something you see
site: a place
> The students had to <u>cite</u> the web<u>sites</u> they used for their project in their bibliography.
> She lost her <u>sight</u> in an accident when she was four years old.

desert: arid land with little vegetation
dessert: something sweet at the end of a meal
> Chocolate makes a good <u>dessert</u>, but it would melt in the heat of the <u>desert</u>.

hear: to listen
here: not there
> Did you <u>hear</u> that funny noise over <u>here</u>?

it's: it is, it has
its: possessive, belonging to it
> <u>It's</u> funny when the dog chases <u>its</u> tail.

loose: not tight
lose: to be unable to find something
> That bathing suit is so <u>loose</u> that you are going to <u>lose</u> it in the water.

passed: to have gone by, to have succeeded in a test
past: previous time
> I <u>passed</u> my driving test and my lifeguard certificate in the <u>past</u> two weeks.

personal: belonging to a person
personnel: human resources
> She hired her <u>personal</u> secretary through the <u>personnel</u> department.

principal: most important, person in charge of a school
principle: a basic rule
> The <u>principal</u> of the high school said it was a matter of <u>principle</u>.

quiet: little or no noise
quite: rather
> Although it was <u>quiet</u> in the house, it was <u>quite</u> hot.

right: correct, not wrong
rite: ceremony
write: to put words on paper

> That's <u>right</u>. Joanne can <u>write</u> a description of the religious <u>rite</u> for her assignment.

stationary: in one spot
stationery: writing supplies

> I exercise on a <u>stationary</u> bicycle.
> We ran out of letterhead paper, so I had to call the <u>stationery</u> store.

than: comparative
then: adverb of time

> <u>Then</u> I learned that he was faster <u>than</u> I am.

their: belonging to them
there: adverb, like *here*
they're: they are

> <u>They're</u> waiting for <u>their</u> luggage to arrive over <u>there</u> in the lounge area.

to: preposition
too: also, and used with other words such as *much* and *few* to show excess
two: the number after *one*

> I'd like <u>two</u> cards <u>too</u>, please.
> I gave the report <u>to</u> the manager.
> The company showed <u>too</u> little growth to satisfy the stockholders.

wear: put on clothes
were: past tense of *to be*
where: in which place
we're: we are

> <u>Where</u> are you going? You <u>were</u> just out.
> <u>We're</u> going to the mall because we have nothing to <u>wear</u> for the dance.

weather: climate
whether: if

> <u>Whether</u> we go on the hike or not will depend on the <u>weather</u>.

which: question word

witch: a woman who is believed to have magical powers
> There were several women dressed as <u>witches</u> at the Halloween dance. <u>Which</u> one was Joan?

who's: who is, who has

whose: possessive, belonging to whom
> <u>Who's</u> been eating my porridge?
> <u>Whose</u> shoes are these?

woman: singular

women: plural
> The three <u>women</u> met with another <u>woman</u> for lunch.

you're: you are

your: belonging to you
> <u>You're</u> going to get <u>your</u> jacket wet.

Exercise 2.14

Choose the correct word to complete the sentence:

1. The _____ [woman, women] _____ [whose/who's] been appointed to the committee is a lawyer _____ [to, too, two].

2. You forgot to _____ [cite, site, sight] that reference in _____ [your, you're] bibliography. You'll _____ [loose, lose] marks.

3. The temperature _____ [affects, effects] the result _____ [weather, whether] or not you change that setting.

4. I need _____ [to, too, two] collect _____ [to, too, two] more gems to finish this level of the game.

5. He _____ [passed, past] my house an hour ago, so he should be _____ [their, there, they're] by now.

6. The students had to change _____ [their, there, they're] seats because they could not _____ [hear, here] very well. _____ [Than, Then] the fire alarm went off.

7. Because Hassan had worked at the company longer _____ [than, then] the others, he gave them some _____ [advice, advise] about getting along with the supervisor.

Exercise 2.15

In pairs, give each other a spelling test of words chosen from the list of common misspellings below. Make a study list of the words you have trouble with:

a lot	definitely	occur
accommodate	dependent	occurred
accomplish	descendant	opinion
accumulate	develop	parallel
achievement	development	pastime
acknowledge	dining	phenomenon
aggravate	embarrassed	precede
all right	emphasize	preference
almost	entrance	prejudice
analyze	environment	prevalent
answer	especially	proceed
apartment	exaggerate	professor
apology	exercise	pronunciation
appropriate	fascinate	receive
argument	February	recommend
athlete	foreign	relevant
beginning	forty	religion
believe	fourth	religious
business	government	repetition
calendar	grammar	restaurant
cemetery	height	rhythm
changeable	humorous	schedule
chosen	immediately	secretary
column	indispensable	seize
coming	interesting	separate
committee	knowledge	sincerely
competitive	license	speak
conscience	manoeuvre	speech
conscientious	marriage	studying
convenience	necessary	succeed
convenient	noticeable	surprise
criticism	occasion	technique

Exercise 2.15 – *continued*

temperature	truly	Wednesday
thorough	Tuesday	writing
tragedy	usually	written
tries	vacuum	

Recognizing Roots and Affixes

Words can be formed from root words from Greek and Latin. For example, the Greek word *phone* for sound is found in English words like *telephone* (sound from far away), *microphone* (small sound), and *phonetics* (the study of speech sounds). An affix is a group of letters attached to the front or end of a word to change its meaning. There are two kinds of affixes—prefixes and suffixes. Prefixes are attached at the front of the word. A prefix can make a word negative, such as in *clear* and *unclear*. Suffixes are found at the end of the word, changing its part of speech. The suffix *–ify* is a verb ending, as shown in the words *beautify* and *modify*. Common suffixes like these are listed in the first section of this unit, Recognizing Parts of Speech.

Knowing some common root words and prefixes and suffixes can help you figure out the meaning of unfamiliar words, especially those in science and technology. Learning these word forms can help you expand your vocabulary.

Prefixes may change their spelling slightly depending on the first letter of the root word. For example, the negative prefix *in–* becomes *im–* before *b*, *p*, or *m* (*impossible*, *impenetrable*) and *ir–* before *r* (*irrefutable*). *Sub–* (under) can also appear as *sub–*, *suc–*, *suf–*, *sug–*, *sup–*, and *sus–* (as in *sustainable*). These spelling changes depend on phonetic rules—the sound (and therefore spelling) is adjusted to make the word easier to pronounce. For example, *irreplaceable* is easier to say than *inreplaceable*.

Negative prefixes

Many different prefixes are used to change a word to a negative or opposite meaning. The most common of these prefixes are *in–* and *un–*, usually used with adjectives.

Note that the prefix *in–* can also mean *in*, as in the word *inhale*. This may cause confusion as in the word *inflammable*, which means that something is likely to go up "in flames"—not that it will not burn. Therefore, to avoid such confusion, warning signs are likely to say *flammable* and *nonflammable*. Other words for which the *in–* prefix is not negative include: *inbred*, *incorporate*, *indent*, *indrawn*, *inform*, *input*, and *inspire*.

It is also important not to confuse *anti–* (against) with *ante–* (before), which appears in words like *antebellum* (before the war) and *antenatal* (before birth).

a–	without, not	apolitical, atypical
an–	without (before vowels)	anarchy, anaemia, anonymous
ant–	against, opposed to (before vowels)	antacid, Antarctic, antonym
anti–	against, opposed to	antibiotic, antifreeze, antiperspirant
contra–	against	contraceptive, contradict, contravention
counter–	against, opposite	counter-clockwise, counterproductive
de–	away from	debug, decriminalize, de-ice, deplane
dis–	absence, apart	dishonest, dislike, disreputable
dys–	bad, difficult	dyslexic, dysfunctional
in–	not	inanimate, inconsiderate, insufficient
il–	not (before l)	illegitimate, illegal, illogical
im–	not (before b, p, m)	imbalance, immobile, impolite
ir–	not (before r)	irrefutable, irreplaceable
mal–	bad, badly	malformed, malnourished
mis–	wrong, badly	misspell, mistake, misunderstand, mistreat
non–	not	nonconformist, nondescript, non-fiction
pseud(o)–	false	pseudonym, pseudo-science
un–	not	undesirable, unimpressed, unthinkable

In addition, some English words, such as *bad*, *evil*, *ill*, and *wrong*, are attached to other words, usually with a hyphen, to create negatives and opposites: *bad-tempered*, *bad-mouth*, *evildoer*, *ill-treatment*, *ill-advised*, *wrong-headed*. The suffix *–less* can also make words negative (*careless*, *faithless*).

Exercise 2.16

By adding or deleting prefixes, give the opposite of the following words:

able	competent	grateful	quote
ability	continue	hero	readable
active	discolour	implausible	regular
addictive	divisible	informed	renewable
amoral	excusable	interesting	represent
argument	favourable	justified	successful
appetizing	finite	literate	toxic
audible	flexible	malnutrition	unworthy
believable	forgettable	manage	usable
behave	formal	patient	visible
classified	function	practice	wise

Prefixes of size and quantity

ambi–	both	ambiguous, ambivalent
bi–, bin–	two	bicycle, bilingual, binoculars
cent–	hundred	centigrade, centipede, century
dec–, deca–	ten	decathlon, decibel, decimate
di–	two	diode, dioxide
hyper–	over	hyperactive, hyperbole
macro–	large	macrocosm, macroeconomics
mega–	great	megabyte, mega-city, megalomania
micro–	small	microbe, microbiology, microfibre
mill–	thousand	millennium, millisecond
mono–	one	monogamy, monologue
multi–	many	multi-faceted, multiplex

omni–	all	omnipotent, omniscient
pan–	all	Pan-American, pandemic, pandemonium
poly–	many	polyglot, polygamous, polygon
quasi–	partly	quasi-intellectual, quasi-professional
semi–	half	semi-detached, semi-sweet
tri–	three	trio, triangle
ultra–	beyond	ultra-conservative, ultrasound
uni–	one	unicorn, unification

Other number prefixes include *duo–* (two), *quarto–* (four), *quint–* (five), *hept–* (six), *sept–* (seven), *octo–* (eight), and *nono–* (nine).

Exercise 2.17

Match the word on the right with the correct definition on the left:

1. ambidextrous _a_
2. bigamist _k_
3. centennial _g_
4. decade _h_
5. hypersensitive _____
6. mega-mall _d_
7. millipede _e_
8. monologue _f_
9. monotheism _b_
10. multilingual _l_
11. multimedia _____
12. panacea _____
13. triathlete _____
14. triplicate _____
15. unicycle _____

a) being able to use both the right and the left hand (usually for writing)
b) belief in one god
c) cure-all
d) huge shopping mall
e) insect with many legs (possibly a thousand)
f) long speech spoken by one actor in a play
g) 100-year anniversary
h) period of 10 years
i) single-wheeled cycle often used by acrobats
j) someone who competes in three events (running, swimming, biking)
k) someone who gets married when he or she still has a legal spouse
l) speaking many languages
m) three copies of something
n) too sensitive to something
o) using more than one medium of expression, such as audio and video

Prefixes of location and direction

ante–	before	antedate, antechamber, anterior
circum–	around	circumference, circumstance, circumvent
co– (com/n/l/r)	together	cooperate, connect, co-worker
ex–	out	exit, explode, exhale
in– (il–, im–, ir–)	in	incision, imprison
inter–	between	interfere, interrupt, interview
intra–, intro–	within	intravenous, introduce
peri–	around	perimeter, peripheral, periscope
pre–	before	predict, pre-emptive, preview
post–	after	postpartum, post-secondary
re–, retro–	again, back	recite, retrograde, return
sub–	under	subliminal, subtitle, subzero
super–, sur–	above	superior, supreme, surcharge
syn–, sym–	with	symphony, symposium, synchronize
trans–	across	transform, translate, transportation

Exercise 2.18

Match the word on the right with the correct definition on the left:

1. antenatal _____
2. circumpolar _____
3. collaborate _____
4. excise _____
5. inhale _____
6. intermingle _____
7. intramural _____
8. postdate _____
9. post-graduate _____
10. prehistoric _____
11. renovation _____
12. submarine _____
13. superman _____
14. symphony _____
15. transit _____

a) around or near one of the earth's poles
b) before recorded history
c) boat that goes under the sea
d) breathe in
e) cut out
f) make like new again
g) man who is superior to all others
h) mix together
i) musicians playing with others in a group
j) related to before a birth
k) studies undertaken after graduating with a university degree
l) system to move people across town
m) taking part within a school's walls, especially sports
n) give a later date
o) work together with someone

Greek and Latin roots and affixes

arch	first, chief	hierarchy, monarch
audi, audit	hear	audio tape, audition
auto	self	automobile, autobiography
ben, bene	good	beneficial, benign
bibl, biblio	book	bibliography, Bible
bio	life	biology, biometrics
chron	time	anachronism, chronology, synchronize
corp	body	corporal punishment, incorporate
dic, dict	speak	contradict, dictation, predict
doc, doct	teach	doctor, indoctrinate
eu	good	euphemism, euthanasia
fac, fact	make, do	faculty, manufacture
graph, gram	write	biography, graphology
liter	letter	literal, literate
log, logy	word	dialogue, meteorology
man, manu	hand	manager, manicure, manually
mis, mit	send	admit, commission, missive
phil	love	philosophy, Philadelphia
phon	sound	phonetics, symphony, telephone
scrib, script	write	describe, prescription, subscript
son	sound	sonogram, sonorous
spect	look	inspect, spectacles, spectator
spir	breathe	inspiration, expire
tele	far	telecommute, telegraph
ven	come	venue, convention
vid, vis	see	audiovisual, revise, videotape
voc, vok	call	evocative, vocal, vocation

Exercise 2.19

Determine the meaning of the underlined words by using the meanings of the roots and affixes, and make a list of related forms (such as an adjective form related to a noun) where possible:

1. Magellan led the first <u>circumnavigation</u> of the globe.
2. Jan is a marine <u>biologist</u> who specializes in the <u>vocalizations</u> of dolphins.
3. Don't worry. That was just a <u>sonic</u> boom from a jet.
4. He pronounced his <u>dictum</u>, and everyone obeyed.
5. He's a true <u>bibliophile</u>; he has crammed bookshelves into every room.
6. The <u>corpse</u> was discovered in the <u>factory</u>.
7. The <u>transmission</u> was unclear because of the static.
8. The <u>philanthropist</u> was a <u>benefactor</u> for many worthwhile charities.
9. The <u>eulogy</u> was so stirring that many of the mourners broke down in tears.
10. He asked the professor if he could <u>audit</u> the course.

Recognizing Collocation

Some words go together, and some do not. The word *collocation* (made from *co*, for "with," and *location*) refers to probable word combinations. For example, *say*, *speak*, *talk*, and *tell* have the same basic meaning but collocate with different words. We can "tell a secret" but not "speak a secret." We "speak a language" but "say a word." We "talk tough" but "tell the truth." We "say thank you" but "talk over a problem."

Collocation can include adjectives that go with nouns (*antique furniture* but not *ancient furniture*), verbs that go with nouns (*offer advice* but not *award advice*), prepositions or particles that complete verbs (*depend on* someone but not *depend for* someone), and noun combinations (*time management* but not *price management*).

Collocations are probable word combinations. Online tools, such as the Corpus of Contemporary American English, can pull out sentences using a specified word, thus showing which words generally occur with it. Even if they are unfamiliar with the concept of collocation, native speakers of a language are likely to feel that certain word combinations sound better than others. ESL students, however, often use unlikely word combinations, especially if they translate from their native language or use a bilingual dictionary that does not explain usage. Some ESL dictionaries list collocations in their word entries, and the *Oxford Collocations Dictionary for Students of English* specializes in this feature of English.

To learn collocations, pay attention to how words are used, and look for common word combinations. It is important to get a sense of which words sound right together. You can test your ability to spot collocations in the following exercises.

Exercise 2.20

In the following list of verb + noun combinations, cross out the unlikely ones, leaving the collocations:

Example: take a course, ~~study a course~~, ~~make a course~~, pass a course

1. take a test, work a test, follow a test, run a test
2. ask a request, make a request, want a request, grant a request
3. conduct research, make research, carry out research
4. drop a hint, take a hint, see a hint, have a hint, give a hint
5. lose experience, make experience, lack experience, acquire experience
6. run up a debt, make a debt, settle a debt, take a debt
7. do a method, adopt a method, work a method, follow a method
8. follow a reason, give a reason, take a reason, hold a reason
9. show a risk, follow a risk, run a risk, make a risk, take a risk
10. gain support, take support, run support, provide support

Exercise 2.21

Match the word in the left column with one in the right column to complete the collocation:

Adjective	Noun
border	attack
calculated	hesitation
daring	material
hazardous	matter
momentary	patrol

Exercise 2.21 – *continued*

Adjective	Noun
reasonable	rain
subtle	reminder
torrential	request
urgent	risk
weak	tea

Understanding Connotation

It is not enough to know the meaning of a word; you must know its connotation—the emotional impact it makes. For example, the word *murder* is much stronger than the word *kill*. A person is complimented when he is called *generous* but insulted when he is called a *spendthrift*. Words have a lot of power and should be used carefully. Make sure you understand the connotation of the words you use in your writing. As you expand your vocabulary, pay attention to the connotation of the new words and expressions.

Exercise 2.21

With a partner, consider the connotation of the following groups of words. Do they have the same meaning? Which are positive, and which are negative? Which are stronger? Think of three pairs of words that have different connotations.

1. house, home
2. cheap, inexpensive
3. thrifty, stingy, economical
4. arrogant, confident
5. mentally ill, crazy
6. old geezer, senior citizen
7. handyman's special, dump, fixer-upper
8. unemployed, between jobs
9. secretive, sneaky
10. slender, thin, slim, anorexic, skinny, scrawny, emaciated, svelte

Using Synonyms and Antonyms

Synonyms are words that have similar meanings, while antonyms are words that have opposite meanings. However, it is important to remember that even though two words may be synonyms, they may not be interchangeable. There may be slight differences of meaning, connotation, or collocation.

Using synonyms and antonyms allows you to make your writing more interesting. English offers such a rich vocabulary that it is a waste to repeat the same word again and again. For instance, instead of using the word *car* over and over again in a paragraph, you could use synonyms like *automobile* and *vehicle* to vary your vocabulary.

Thesauruses, books of synonyms and antonyms, are useful tools for reminding a writer of other possible word choices. However, you should not just blindly choose a synonym from a thesaurus. First make sure you know how the word is used.

Exercise 2.22

Replace the underlined words or expressions with other words or expressions that have similar meanings. Try coming up with a synonym yourself, but use a thesaurus if you get stuck. You might have to adjust the sentence by adding prepositions with verbs, for example.

1. The stranger's act of <u>kindness</u> <u>astonished</u> the beggar, who was <u>accustomed</u> to abuse.
2. Samson's <u>riddle</u> was <u>baffling</u> to everyone who tried to <u>solve</u> it.
3. Every day, newspapers <u>warn</u> their <u>readers</u> about some health <u>hazard</u> related to common foods. After a while, people become <u>sceptical</u>.
4. He made a <u>rookie</u> <u>error</u> by <u>expecting</u> his <u>staff</u> to <u>correct</u> the problem.

Understanding Idioms

An idiom is an expression in which the figurative meaning is different from the literal meaning. *Figurative* means that the whole expression gives a picture (think of a figure) that is different from the meaning of the individual words (the word *literal* is related to the word *letter*; think of it as letter by letter or word by word). For example, the idiom *let the cat out of the bag* does not literally refer to a cat and a bag; it means *reveal a secret*. To *kick the bucket* means to *die*; this idiom has led to the expression "bucket list" (a personal list of things someone wants to do before he or she dies).

Idioms are generally more conversational in style. For example, "Same-sex marriage is a political hot potato" is more informal than "Same-sex marriage is a controversial issue." You can use some idioms in formal, academic essays, but use them judiciously. If there is another, more standard way to express the same meaning, use that if you want to be more formal. The more idiomatic language you use, the more conversational your writing becomes.

Exercise 2.23

Here are some more examples of idioms. In groups, discuss the meaning of the idiom, and rewrite the sentence replacing the idiom with other words:

1. If we don't find the bug in this program soon, we are going to be up the creek without a paddle.
2. I didn't want to make the announcement yet, but as usual Mark jumped the gun.
3. Of course she copied his essay. She was caught red-handed.
4. I can't afford to go to restaurants every day for lunch, so I brown-bag it.
5. She was all set to bring up the problems from last year, but I told her it was best to let sleeping dogs lie.
6. Tomas was not expecting an inheritance because he's the black sheep of the family.
7. Whenever her mother starts lecturing her, it goes in one ear and out the other.
8. This assignment is going to be a piece of cake.
9. I'm not going to tell him. I don't want to be the one in hot water.
10. I can't eat anything right now. I have an oral presentation to make next class, and I've got butterflies in my stomach.

Exercise 2.24

In small groups, make a list of 10 idioms that you know. Compare it to the other groups' lists, looking for common ones. Which ones would be most useful for ESL students to learn?

Using Jargon

Jargon is technical language, such as medical terminology, legalese, and computer terms. The word often has a negative connotation because it is extended to mean wording that is not clear. Writers are often told to avoid jargon, but it actually depends on the audience. If the intended readers or listeners have the right background to understand the technical language, then jargon is not only appropriate, it is necessary. It allows the professionals within that group to communicate effectively and concisely. For example, a doctor can tell another doctor that a patient has a *subcutaneous haematoma* but would tell the patient that it is a lump. Avoid using jargon if your audience would not understand the words.

Some words start out as jargon and move into common usage. Computer terms like *input* and *output* are now used for non-computer purposes.

Exercise 2.25

Identify the fields these groups of words come from:

1. IV, contusion, ICU, carcinoma, septicemia
2. plaintiff, subpoena, writ, affidavit, pro bono
3. boot, blog, mouseover, CPU, data compression
4. escrow, tenancy in common, lien, title search
5. vehicle trespass, B&E, complaint, disorderly conduct

Recognizing Colloquialisms and Slang

Another aspect of vocabulary learning is recognizing that certain words do not belong in academic essays. The differences between conversational and academic style are explained in Unit 1. Native speakers will already be comfortable with the words and expressions of conversational English, but they might have to learn how to categorize them. ESL students, on the other hand, are probably still learning these words and expressions—probably from the street and not the classroom—and must learn about appropriate usage.

The word *colloquialism* is used to describe informal, conversational language. A word like *kid*, for example, may be marked "colloquial" or "informal" in the dictionary. This means that it is not suitable for more formal speaking or writing situations. In an academic essay, it would be more appropriate to use *children* instead of *kids*.

Slang goes one step further than colloquialism. Slang is a type of language common in casual speech. Because it is characteristic of a group (such as teenagers or rap musicians), it sounds odd when used by non-members.

For example, middle-aged parents are ridiculed when they try to sound like their teenaged children. In addition, slang changes over time. In the 1920s, young people would have called something really good *the cat's pyjamas* or *the bee's knees*. In the 1950s, they would have described it as *neato* or *swell*, then *groovy* in the sixties. At the end of the twentieth century, teens used *awesome* and words like *bad*, *sick*, and *wicked* to describe something that was in fact very good. Slang also varies regionally: A British teenager is more likely to say "Brilliant!" whereas a Canadian might say "Sweet!"

Obscenity is another kind of language that is more common in spoken language than in written. Again, attitudes have changed. In 1939, audiences were shocked when Rhett Butler said to Scarlett O'Hara, "Frankly, my dear, I don't give a damn" in the film *Gone with the Wind*. Today, movies are filled with profanity, and the "f-word" may appear in almost every line of dialogue. Newspapers are a good guide as to what is generally accepted in a society, but even though the word appears in print, it is not appropriate for academic writing. Overly formal, stuffy language is also not appropriate in most situations. A real estate agent talking about the *purveyance of a domicile* instead of the *sale of a house* would confuse and put off most clients. Remember that the primary purpose of writing is to give information clearly and concisely. Write to communicate, not to impress.

Exercise 2.26

Rewrite the sentences to replace the underlined slang words and expressions with more formal ones:

1. When his boss reassigned the project, Jamal freaked out.
2. When we wanted to add a casino night to the fundraising plans, he nixed the idea.
3. He's so worried about the project that he's a basket case.
4. They spent the day goofing off and fell behind schedule.
5. She's always mooching fries from everyone at lunch but will never buy her own.
6. He was all doom and gloom about the agency's chances of winning that contract.
7. Coming off the roller coaster, he stumbled, turned green, and tossed his cookies.
8. He did squat on this project, so he doesn't deserve credit.

Using Dictionaries

Dictionaries are extremely powerful tools for learning vocabulary. The information given extends beyond simply the meaning of the word; it includes the part of speech, pronunciation, different forms of the word, and even the etymology (the word's history—where it comes from). Dictionaries for language learners, such as the *Oxford Advanced Learner's*, guide students in how to use the words with example sentences and lists of collocations.

Students today are more likely to use electronic sources for dictionaries. These may be in the form of online dictionaries, phone apps, or dedicated devices. Students should check out the different resources available and not just rely on a basic dictionary. ESL students should not rely on translation dictionaries because they can be misleading and often give little information about the word's usage.

Print-form dictionaries are far from dead, however. Many schools allow students to use book dictionaries for tests and exams; electronic formats are prohibited because there is no way to limit them to just a dictionary function. Bibliophiles (look that word up if you don't know the meaning) love the look and feel of a beautiful dictionary. Moreover, they can benefit from serendipity (another word to look up) to find new words.

If you need to buy a print-form dictionary for class, shop carefully. The best way to choose a dictionary in a bookstore is to "test drive" a few. Look up the same words in several dictionaries and compare the entries. Look up common words that may have many definitions (such as *set* and *like*) and more academic words (*enumerate*, *repatriate*). Check for the clarity of the definition and how much information is given. Make sure the pronunciation guide is easy to use. Look for a clear, legible typeface and a format that is easy to handle. Check the date of the dictionary to make sure it is a recent edition, not just a reprint. Check for current slang (words like *bling*, *geek*, and *diss*) to see whether the dictionary is up-to-date.

One common question about dictionary use is how to find a word in a dictionary if you do not know how to spell it. One technique is to concentrate on the beginning of the word. Even electronic dictionaries that guess at your word work much better if the first few letters are correct. Get to know possible letter combinations for sounds. For instance an *s* sound could be spelled with an *s*, a *c*, an *sc*, or a *ps*.

Dictionaries can help speed up the vocabulary learning process. You can learn a new word without consulting a dictionary, but you need to read it or hear it many times to learn the meaning from the context. A dictionary will provide you with the information you need to understand the word and be confident in using it.

Studying Vocabulary

Although you will not have a chance to look up every unfamiliar word you come across in your reading, it is a good idea to make a vocabulary list for any reading you study in class. Look up unfamiliar words in the dictionary. Write them in your notebook, along with a definition and any other useful information (part of speech, irregular forms, usage label, synonyms, collocations). Even if you do not go back and memorize this information, the fact that you have gone to the effort of writing it down means that you will remember it better. If you just look up a word in the dictionary and continue with your reading, you will not retain it as well.

Expanding vocabulary:
- Read a lot to increase your exposure to words and how they are used.
- Read a variety of types of material (newspapers, books, websites), on different topics, to widen the fields of words you encounter.
- Pay attention to the language when you read. Look out for new words.
- Try to guess the meaning of words from the context, and notice how they are used and which words accompany them.
- Use a dictionary to find out more about unfamiliar words.
- Keep a notebook for vocabulary you encounter. Notes can include grammar and usage notes, such as the part of speech and the collocation. Write down the phrase or sentence the word appeared in.
- Learn words in groups. For example, if you use a dictionary to look up the meaning of an unfamiliar word, check out the derivatives, collocates, and any synonyms or antonyms given. Make sure you understand differences in usage.
- The more you read, the more you will encounter the words, and then you will understand them better.

Sentence Writing Skills

Words are combined to make sentences, and sentences are combined to make paragraphs. In turn, the paragraphs form parts of essays, reports, letters, and any other forms of writing. The sentence is the basic unit of grammar—writing is judged grammatical or not based on the formation of the sentences. Sentences are also the most important structure for meaning, so it is important to get sentences formed correctly.

Students who need to improve their writing can benefit from a review of grammar rules. It can be an eye-opening exercise for native speakers who are not accustomed to looking at English in that way. ESL students, on the other hand, may be quite comfortable talking about the use of verb tenses and uncountable nouns. They may excel at grammar tests but have trouble writing grammatical sentences in their essays. Even though they may have spent years studying grammar rules, sometimes it helps to look at the structure of English in different ways.

Questions about grammar are not simple, black-and-white questions. Grammar, like other aspects of language, evolves and changes over time. For instance, the relative pronoun *whom* is dying in English, as is the subjunctive structure in conditionals (e.g., "if I *were* a rich man"). Moreover, what is considered acceptable in casual speech may be considered incorrect in standard academic writing. For example, we may say, "Here's the books you ordered" or "Everyone should pick their courses now." Written English tends to be more "correct" than speech.

As for grammar terminology, you may already be familiar with it, or it may be unfamiliar jargon to you. Knowing these terms is not essential for you in order to construct a good sentence, but the proper vocabulary makes it easier to explain grammar rules. However, terminology can vary. For instance, "continuous" verb tenses are also called "progressive." Do not worry about memorizing the terms, but try to get a feel for the structures they describe.

This unit offers a quick review of the major parts of a sentence at a fairly basic level. It is not meant to be a comprehensive look at grammar. (If you need to know more, consult a grammar book such as *The Oxford Practice Grammar*.) The explanations focus on the fundamental structures of the language so that you can recognize what is behind common errors and fix them. The exercises give you more examples and allow you to practise and discuss the rules. More practice can be had in Unit 7, which deals with editing and correcting errors.

Understanding Basic Sentence Structure

Essentially, a sentence starts with a capital letter and ends with a period (or question mark or exclamation mark). It is important for the reader to be able to tell where each sentence begins and ends. Especially when writing by hand, you need to make the sentence boundaries clear. Capital letters should be easily distinguishable from small letters, even if you use block printing, and a period should be easily distinguishable from a comma. Thus, the primary consideration is that a sentence should look like a sentence.

A sentence needs a subject and a predicate to qualify as a sentence. The subject is what you are talking about, and the predicate is what you are saying about it. The subject is a noun or a pronoun along with any modifiers. The predicate is the verb along with objects and their modifiers.

Here are some basic sentence patterns:

John fled. [subject + intransitive verb]

They opened the package. [subject + transitive verb + direct object]

Ahmed gave her a ring. [subject + verb + indirect object + direct object]

Yuki is an architect. [subject + linking verb + predicate noun or adjective]

She painted the room blue. [subject + verb + direct object + objective complement]

The house is over there. [subject + verb + adverbial]

The subject is a noun, noun phrase, or noun clause. A subject cannot appear in a prepositional phrase. A subject can be a compound subject, containing two or more nouns joined with *and*:

The <u>house</u> on the corner is slated for demolition. [single word subject; the noun *corner* is in a prepositional phrase and cannot be the subject]

<u>Walking to school</u> is one of the ways I get my exercise. [noun phrase as subject]

<u>That he ruined the day for his family</u> did not seem to enter his mind. [noun clause as subject]

<u>Jack, Amir, and Tim</u> enjoyed the pumpkin pie. [compound subject]

Verbs can be more than one word—auxiliary verbs along with the main verb. In a sentence, the predicate can include more than one verb:

He <u>should have been</u> more careful. He <u>could have been electrocuted</u>.

The children <u>ran</u>, <u>skipped</u>, and <u>hopped</u> across the field.

It is useful to be able to identify the core sentence—the basic parts without any modifiers. These basic parts include the subject and verb. Then you can tell whether you have a grammatical sentence or not. Here are some example sentences with the core parts underlined:

Yesterday <u>I paid</u> all my <u>bills</u> online.

My <u>brother fixed</u> the door <u>handle</u> with a screwdriver.

Screaming in fright, <u>Lynn ran</u> down the street.

The *Bluenose*, a fishing schooner from Lunenburg, Nova Scotia, <u>is</u> the <u>ship</u> depicted on the Canadian dime.

Sentences that are in the imperative mood—in other words, commands—look like one-word sentences, but the implied subject is *you*:

Stop! [You] Stop!

Take a chair. [You] Take a chair.

The minimum for a sentence is a subject and a verb. The subject and verb are also the basis of any sentence.

Exercise 3.1

For the following sentences, identify the subject, verb, and objects to get the core sentence:

1. Strolling through the park, Peter whistled a cheerful tune.
2. Surprisingly, my brother's soccer team, which had an abysmal record, won the game.
3. On Saturday night we went to the theatre to see an amateur production of *The Importance of Being Earnest*.
4. With her promotion, she can afford that European vacation.
5. One of the band members has decided to leave the group to pursue a career as a rapper.
6. His friend Tony is throwing the bachelor party.
7. My neighbour signed for my package but forgot to tell me he had it.
8. His flight leaves at eight, but he hasn't even packed yet.

Understanding Verb Forms

Verb endings (*–ing* and *–ed*) and auxiliary verbs (*be*, *have*, *will*) are used to make the different tenses:

Simple present: She <u>walks</u> to work every day.

Simple past: She <u>walked</u> to work yesterday.

Future: She <u>will walk</u> to work tomorrow.

Present continuous: She <u>is walking</u> to work right now.

Past continuous: She <u>was walking</u> to work when I saw her.

Future continuous: She <u>will be walking</u> to work from now on.

Present perfect: She <u>has walked</u> to work many times, but usually she takes the bus.

Past perfect: She <u>had walked</u> to work before he called to offer her a ride.

Future perfect: She <u>will have walked</u> to work by the time I can pick her up.

Present perfect continuous: She <u>has been walking</u> to work since the bus strike started.

Past perfect continuous: She <u>had been walking</u> to work before she decided to buy a car.

Future perfect continuous: She <u>will have been walking</u> to work for two years by the time she gets a car.

Present events

To express general facts, you use the simple present tense (as in this sentence). To describe actions that are occurring now (as in this clause), use present continuous (also called present progressive). To express past ideas that are relevant to the present, use the present perfect tense or present perfect continuous.

The earth is round. The sky is blue. Astronomers study stars. I walk to work every day.

I am studying Japanese as a third language, and I am finding the classes interesting.

Ellen has lived in Edmonton for six years. [This means that she still lives in Edmonton, in contrast to "Ellen lived in Edmonton for six years."]

Past events

Actions that happened in the past and are complete are described with the simple past tense. Actions that took place over a period of time are expressed with the past continuous. Actions that occurred before another past action are in the past perfect:

They opened the store three years ago, but this was the first time they made a profit.

Naomi was cleaning up the mess when her supervisor walked in.

He had studied Arabic for several years before he went to Egypt.

The past perfect form is used less frequently today. People tend to use the simple past for past actions, even if one happened beforehand:

> After he washed the car, it rained.

Future events

The simple future (with *will*) can be used for most actions that will take place in the future. The present continuous and *going to* also express future actions. The difference in meaning is slight, but the *will* form tends to be used with decisions just made, whereas the other forms refer to already decided upon events. The simple present is sometimes used for future scheduled events, often regular events:

> The band will take the bus to Halifax.

> The band is travelling to Halifax by bus.

> The band is going to take the bus to Halifax.

> The bus leaves at nine.

The tenses you will use most in your writing are simple present, simple past, and present perfect.

It is important not to shift tenses unnecessarily:

> Doug Howat claimed that he is not a loser, that he was just stuck in neutral. However, such underachieving young men are common in our society. He has finished school but did not know what to do with his life, so he was living at home, and his parents give him hints to leave. [shifts between present and past tenses]

> Doug Howat claims that he is not a loser, that he is just stuck in neutral. However, such underachieving young men are common in our society. He has finished school but does not know what to do with his life, so he is living at home, and his parents give him hints to leave. [corrected version]

Exercise 3.2

Write the correct form of the verb for the blank. More than one tense might be appropriate:

1. Tanya _____ [bring] her son along on the trip to the museum, and he _____ [behave] very well.

Exercise 3.2 – *continued*

2. Thomas _____ [see] a skunk in the woods, but he _____ [avoid] it because his teacher _____ [warn] him about skunks.

3. We _____ [eat] eggs for breakfast every day last week.

4. Our flight _____ [leave] at 10, but we _____ [have] to get there early.

5. On Mondays and Wednesdays, the students _____ [play] soccer after class.

6. I _____ [meet] you at seven in the restaurant. Don't be late.

7. We _____ not _____ [sleep] well because it was too hot in the residence.

8. Janice _____ [decide] to take a trip to Parliament Hill because she wants to learn more about Canadian history.

9. How many T-shirts _____ you _____ [buy] on our visit to Chinatown? I only _____ [buy] three.

10. Jeannie _____ already _____ [see] the museum exhibit, so she _____ [go] shopping and she _____ [meet] us at 4 o'clock this afternoon.

Auxiliary verbs

An auxiliary (helping) verb must be followed by another verb. The auxiliaries *be*, *have*, and *will* are used to make several of the tenses. Other auxiliaries include *do* and the modal verbs (*may*, *might*, *can*, *could*, *should*, *would*).

The chart reviews auxiliary verbs and how they are used:

Auxiliary	Verb that follows	Used for	Example
have	past participle (*-ed* ending for regular verbs)	perfect tenses	I have lived here for six months.
be (am, is, are, was, were, been, being)	present participle (*-ing* form)	continuous tenses	He is working now.
be (am, is, are, was, were, been, being)	past participle (*-ed* ending for regular verbs)	passive voice	The time was well spent.

Auxiliary	*Verb that follows*	*Used for*	*Example*
will	base form (infinitive without to)	future tenses	He will speak after the dinner.
do, did	base form (infinitive without to)	emphasis; negatives; questions	I did call her. You did not fail. Did he see them?
modal verbs (can, could, may, might, should, would, etc.)	base form (infinitive without to)	to express possibility, probability, conditions, etc.	They can walk there. She might be late. I would ask first.

The auxiliary verb determines which form of the verb follows it. If the sentence has several auxiliary verbs in a row, the last verb is the main one (underlined in the examples below):

He should have been <u>paying</u> attention in class.

He should have been <u>elected</u> president.

The verbs *be*, *have*, *do*, and *will* can also be used as simple verbs without another verb:

Richard <u>is</u> a hard worker.

They <u>have</u> $50 to spend on the gift.

He <u>did</u> the dishes right after dinner.

She was exhausted, but she <u>willed</u> her eyes to stay open. [rarely used as a main verb]

Modal verbs, however, can never be used alone. They must be followed by a verb, and it must be in the bare infinitive form:

They should redo the whole project. They can get the funding.

Furthermore, the *–ing* form of the verb is not a complete verb, so it cannot be used without an auxiliary as the verb in a sentence.

It is important to remember these verb patterns to avoid errors such as "I have saw" or "he can going." If you make these types of mistakes, check your verb forms over before you hand in your work.

Exercise 3.3

Choose which form of the verb should be used in the sentence:

1. He could not have _____ [be, being, been] waiting in the store. I would _____ [have, having, had] seen him.

2. Jamal was _____ [wait, waiting, waited] a long time before the clerk finally served him.

3. She had _____ [wrote, writing, written] several versions of the essay before she was finally happy with one.

4. I might _____ [be, being, been] able to help you with that problem. I can _____ [contact, contacts, contacting] my brother-in-law. He is a paralegal.

5. The problem could have been _____ [solve, solving, solved] without violence.

6. Anne should _____ [has, have, having, had] complained earlier. It's _____ [be, been, being] so long now that it's harder to prove.

7. They will _____ [take, taking, took] the package along and pass it on to her sister.

8. She may _____ [be, been, being] promoted when Richard leaves.

9. Didn't you _____ [follow, followed, following] that explanation? It could have _____ [be, been, being] shorter, but it was fairly clear.

10. She could have _____ [reads, read, reading] those chapters before the class. She had enough time.

Transitive and intransitive verbs

A transitive verb requires a direct object to complete it. For example, the verbs *see*, *deny*, and *have* are incomplete without an object:

I saw five whales.

He denied the accusation.

I have change for a twenty.

Many verbs can be used both transitively and intransitively:

> Michael spread the fertilizer over the lawn. [transitive]

> The fire spread quickly. [intransitive]

> She likes to read. [intransitive]

> I read the newspaper with breakfast. [transitive]

In dictionaries, verbs are generally marked as "transitive" and "intransitive." Check to see which abbreviations your dictionary uses for these two words.

Only transitive verbs can be used in the passive voice (see page 70).

Exercise 3.4

Determine whether these verbs are transitive or intransitive by deciding whether the sentences are correct or not as they stand. If you need an object to complete the verb, then the verb is transitive. Fill in the blanks with an appropriate object, where necessary:

1. Heather saw _____ last week.
2. They ate _____ late yesterday.
3. He rejected _____.
4. She swam _____ quickly.
5. Melanie caught _____ last week.
6. Ivan told her _____.
7. His actions irritated _____.
8. Jon whistled _____ and the dog came.
9. The songs included _____.
10. She bought _____ at the mall.

Using Active and Passive Voice

In an active sentence, the grammatical subject does the action of the verb:

> James presented the proposal, but his supervisor rejected it.

In the passive voice, the subject is acted upon. You can make a sentence passive by moving the object before the verb to become the subject:

Anita painted the landscape. [active]

The landscape was painted by Anita. [passive]

For the passive voice, a form of the verb *to be* is used (*is, am, are*), and the main verb is in the past participle form, which ends in *–ed* for regular verbs. There may also be modal verbs in the structure (*will be, would be, may be*) or other verb forms (*have been, is being*):

The show will be cancelled if it rains.

The painting could have been forged.

The documents were shredded accidentally.

The exhibit was seen by thousands of people.

The active voice is preferred because it is easier for readers to understand, but the passive is useful when you want to de-emphasize who or what did the action. It is therefore common in technical writing. For example, lab reports are often written in the passive because it does not really matter who did the action.

The water was heated to the boiling point, and the solution was added.

The company was founded in 1845.

The parade was postponed because of the accident.

Some students have problems with the passive voice. They may form it incorrectly, not using the auxiliary *to be* or not using the past participle *–ed* verb form:

The document was wrote by hand. [incorrect]

The document was written by hand.

They may write a passive sentence when an active one would be more appropriate:

> The donations were recorded in the red notebook by John. [awkward]

> John recorded the donations in the red notebook. [better]

A general guideline is that if a "*by* phrase" to show the actor is necessary, the sentence should probably be in the active voice.

Another mistake is using verbs that are not normally found in the passive voice, such as intransitive verbs and verbs that express state. Verbs that are often incorrectly made passive include *become, belong, depend, exist, lack, occur, seem,* and *happen*:

> The mistake is happened because he was not paying attention. [incorrect]

> The mistake happened because he was not paying attention.

Only transitive verbs can be used in the passive voice because the direct object becomes the subject in the passive.

Exercise 3.5

Determine whether the following sentences are active or passive:

1. She bought all her textbooks online.
2. The manager corrected the mistakes and reprimanded the staff.
3. The car bomb exploded, killing five.
4. The interview was scheduled for 11:15.
5. His story was not believed by anyone.
6. The lawyer advised the client to stay quiet.
7. Finally, the winner was chosen.
8. I can't remember the last time we spoke.
9. Everyone enjoyed the concert.
10. The game was lost by a slim margin.

Go back over the sentences and decide whether the voice can easily be switched. If so, make active sentences passive and passive sentences active (you may have to add an agent doing the action).

Showing Singular and Plural

Both verb and noun forms are determined by the concept of singular (to show one thing or one person) and plural (more than one). Students need to make sure they understand the difference so they can put the *s*'s in the right place. Although the basic concept is simple, some cases can be confusing, and this is an area where many grammatical errors are made in sentences. For instance, ESL students may make errors such as "a teapots" or "John walk," and native speakers make agreement errors such as "one of the engineers were."

Unlike most European languages, which have many word endings, English has the *–s* ending doing triple duty: it is used to show plural nouns, possessive nouns, and third person singular verbs. For possessive forms, the *–s* is used with an apostrophe.

> The <u>computers</u> were down because of a virus. [plural noun— more than one computer]

> The <u>clown's</u> nose fell off. [possessive—the nose belonging to the clown]

> Jennifer <u>walks</u> to school every day. [third person singular verb form]

Most nouns in English have an *–s* added to them to show plural, with an *–es* ending if the original word ends in an *s*-like sound:

> bike/bikes, pie/pies, box/boxes, job/jobs, patient/patients, church/churches

Plural nouns, including irregular plurals, are discussed in Unit 2 (page 23). The determiners *a, an, another, each, every, this,* and *that* are singular:

> I want another folder. This one is all bent.

> Each of these rooms is too small.

The determiners *these* and *those* are plural:

> Have you checked over these results? This one looks off.

> I need some of those bigger envelopes. Where are they?

Words that end in *−one*, *−thing*, and *−body* (*everyone*, *anybody*) are singular:

> Is anybody home? Nobody is there. Everybody has gone.
> Something is missing.

The verb form has to agree in person and number with the subject. Many regular verb forms do not vary for singular and plural (e.g., *she waited*, *they waited*; *I sleep*, *we sleep*), but agreement is important for irregular verbs (which include the forms of the modal *be*, thus affecting passive and continuous verb forms) and in the simple present tense when the third person singular has an *−s* ending:

> He has a cottage on Lake Huron, while his parents have one
> further east.

> Laura bikes to work every day, but she wants to buy a car.

In order to get the proper verb form, you have to identify the subject. In the following examples, the subject is underlined once and the verb is underlined twice:

> One of the children is not coming.

> Kevin and Tom are cousins.

> The books in the hallway are donations for the charity book sale.

Showing singular and plural with subject/verb agreement and pronoun reference is a messy problem for writers in English. The main problem is that if the writer chooses an unspecified third person singular reference, he (or *he or she* or *he/she*) gets into a pronoun problem. Traditionally, *he* has been considered correct grammatically, but it is seen as sexist because it excludes females. In speech (and in some literature with authors as exalted as Charles Dickens), the *they* form is often used:

> A student should make sure they choose the right courses.

> A driver needs to check their rear-view mirror frequently.

This usage is so pervasive that even when the sex is obvious, the *they* turns up:

> The woman who wins the top model competition will get a
> contract with a prestigious agency, and they will get a chance
> to travel all over the world. [should be *she*]

You can get away with the *they* usage in casual speech, but remember that academic writing should be grammatically correct, so you need to find a solution to this problem. You can use *he or she* if you only need the reference once or twice, but a whole paragraph of *he or she* can be very tedious. Do not use *he/she*—it is not an actual word. Neither is *s/he*, which is an attempt at coining a new term. You can choose to alternate *he* and *she*, but you cannot do it in a single paragraph. In other words, do not give the person a sex change midway through a paragraph. One of the simplest things is to play it safe and avoid the problem by using a plural form:

Students should make sure they choose the right courses.

Drivers need to check their rear-view mirror regularly.
(Note that sometimes pronouns can be avoided: A driver needs to check the rear-view mirror regularly.)

The plural form does not always work out. For example, sometimes it is necessary to make one reference singular and one plural to avoid confusing pronouns:

Parents should raise their children so that they learn financial responsibility.

Parents should raise their child so that he or she learns financial responsibility.

It is important to stay consistent, however. Do not switch from singular to plural unnecessarily:

Finally, a spoiled child is often rude. Children who always receive all they want without thinking of anybody else rarely show appreciation and say "thank you."

Exercise 3.6

Choose the correct word form for the sentence (if both are possible grammatically, choose the more likely):

1. One of the car/cars broke down during the trip.
2. An apple/apples a day is/are recommended.
3. What I don't understand is/are why she has/have two of them.
4. The member/members of the school band is/are excused from the test.

Exercise 3.6 – *continued*

5. Every lamp/lamps packed in the plastic crates was/were broken.

6. A few of the poster/posters are left; we can sell them at the flea market/markets.

7. Emma take/takes dance/dances lesson/lessons every Tuesday/Tuesdays.

8. She corrected all the error/errors in the essay.

9. Several piece/pieces were missing. Each is/are hard to replace.

10. There were many mistake/mistakes, but they were not major one/ones.

Showing Possession

Possession means that something belongs to someone or something. This relationship is generally shown with possessive pronouns (*my, your, his, her, its, our, their, whose*) or an apostrophe and an *s* attached to a singular noun. After plural nouns that end in *s*, possession is shown by an apostrophe alone, without the *s*:

> My mother is coming to visit along with my sister and her husband.

> The accountants' report criticized Elizabeth's handling of the books.

> The Martins are staying at the Johnsons' condo in Florida.

> The children's toys were left all over the floor.

Sometimes you will see names that end in an *s* sound with just an apostrophe and no added *s*, just like plural nouns, as in *Moses' mother*, but it is acceptable to use one, as in *James's book*.

Other possessive pronouns are not used before nouns. These include *mine, hers, yours, theirs,* and *ours*. They do not have apostrophes:

> This is not my bike. That one over there is mine.

> They paid off the mortgage, so the house is now officially theirs.

> Whose shoes are these? I thought they were yours.

Possession is also shown with an *of* phrase. This is used for things and to indicate the source of something:

the mouth of the river

the model of the car

the author of the book

Sometimes this type of relationship (with objects, not persons) is expressed with an adjective. This adjective may be a noun functioning as an adjective:

the river mouth

the car model

Generally, English speakers prefer not to use the possessive form with *'s* with inanimate objects. For example, they would prefer to say "the car door" or "the door of the car" rather than "the car's door." However, there are no hard and fast rules for this usage.

Students who mistakenly add apostrophes to plurals may have trouble distinguishing possessive and plural forms. If there are two nouns in a row and the first one ends in an *s*, it is likely that the first noun is possessive. One way to check is to replace the word with a possessive pronoun (*his*, *her*, *its*, *their*); if the sentence makes sense with the substitution, the word in question is likely a possessive form:

Peter's [his] mother brought all the dishes [~~their~~] home.

The instructor lost the students' [their] exam papers.

Another mix-up is with the homophones *its/it's* and *whose/who's*. *It's* is a contracted form of *it is* or *it has*, while *who's* is a contraction of *who is* or *who has*. If the non-contracted form works in the sentence, there should be an apostrophe. *Its* and *whose* are the possessive pronouns:

It's [it is] time to figure out who's [who is] going to the conference.

Whose car is that? [who does the car belong to?—possessive]

It's [it is] funny to see the dog chasing its tail. [the tail belongs to the dog]

Since contractions are generally not used in academic writing, you can avoid using *it's* and *who's*.

Exercise 3.7

Identify the words showing possession, and add any necessary apostrophes:

1. It is Charles responsibility, but we should not ignore Peters involvement.
2. Her glasses broke when Tims brother stepped on them.
3. The childrens bedtime was moved up, and their nap time was shortened.
4. There were many videos, CDS, and DVDS at Megans garage sale.
5. Murphys Law says that if something can go wrong, it will.
6. The boys boat started sinking, but they made it to shore. They even rescued their belongings.
7. On Tuesdays we meet for lunch and discuss the students progress.
8. We need our own sleeping bags, but the tents are provided by the excursion company.
9. Ians car broke down, so we missed our rendezvous with the tour guides.

Using Determiners

Determiners are words that come before a noun to identify which person, place, or thing is being talked about. Determiners include articles (*a, an, the*), demonstratives (*this, that, these, those*), possessive forms (*my, your, his, her, its, our, their*), relative pronouns (*which, whose, what*), and indefinite determiners (*few, many, more, several, some*).

You do not have to learn the different terminology as long as you can use determiners correctly. One problem area (singular versus plural) is discussed on page 74. Relative pronouns are discussed as part of adjective clauses, on page 89. The use of articles can be troublesome, especially for ESL students. The usage is often idiomatic and different from the way articles are used in other languages.

The articles in English are *a, an,* and *the. A* and *an* are indefinite articles. They have the meaning of "one," so they are not used for plural forms. *The* is a definite article and is used with both singular and plurals.

Generally, the first time a noun is introduced, the indefinite article is used, but once the reader knows which thing is being referred to, a definite article is used to refer to something specifically:

I picked an apple off the tree. [one apple] The apple was red and juicy. [specifically, the apple I picked] I like apples. [apples in general] The apples in my uncle's orchard are especially good. [specific apples]

A is used before consonants, and *an* is used before vowel sounds. This usage depends on how the initial sound is pronounced, so both *a* and *an* appear before *h* and *u*:

a walk, a school, a book, a car, a dish, a fairy tale, a lovely scene

an article, an elephant, an island, an octopus, an ugly hat

an umbrella, a university, a hero, an hour

a/an herb [depending on individual pronunciation]

Remember that indefinite articles (*a, an*) cannot be used with uncountable nouns (introduced in Unit 2, page 22). Quantifiers such as *many* and *few* are used with countable nouns; uncountable nouns take *much*, *some*, and *little*:

I have little money left, but you can have a few dollars.

He didn't have much concrete information, but he had many contacts to recommend.

Few and *little* can be used with the indefinite article *a*, but the meaning changes slightly, changing from negative to positive. For example, if you asked your instructor if she could look at your essay draft and she said, "I have a little time right now," she is saying that she could look at it now because she has enough time to do it. However, if she answered, "I have little time right now," she is saying no and will probably suggest another time to meet. Compare the following examples:

Few students understood that complicated problem. [stressing the negative—perhaps the problem will have to be presented again]
A few students understood that complicated problem. [stressing the positive—perhaps more students than were expected to understand]

There is little water left, so we should get more.
There is a little water left; we probably have enough.

Proper names, such as the names of countries and institutions, may have articles in their name depending on the other words used in the name. For example, a country name has no article if it is plain (Canada, Russia, China), but an article is used when another noun like *republic*, *states*, or *union* is found in the name (the Dominion of Canada, the Soviet Union, the Republic of China). (See more examples of country names on page 308.) University names have an article if the word "university" appears first: the University of Toronto, but York University.

Exercise 3.8

Fill in the blanks with articles or other determiners where required:

1. I met several people on _____ trip. _____ student I met on the bus is going to _____ University of Ottawa. She wants to become bilingual, but _____ French is quite weak, so she's working with _____ tutor. She eventually wants to study _____ law, and she thinks _____ bilingualism is _____ asset for any profession.

2. They've decided to arrange _____ picnic for _____ park's anniversary. They are going to hire _____ clowns and _____ magicians. _____ neighbourhood high school band is going to perform in _____ band shell during _____ afternoon, and _____ local bands are going to play _____ more modern music in the evening. _____ food vendors will sell everything from _____ hot dogs to _____ ice cream.

3. We had _____ wonderful trip to Halifax. We visited _____ museum at _____ Pier 21. It told the story of European immigrants who disembarked at _____ pier. Many travelled by _____ train to _____ final destinations. I even found _____ name of _____ ship that _____ family came to Canada on. We also took _____ trip on _____ *Bluenose* replica ship. I love any kind of _____ sailboat, so _____ tall ship was _____ real thrill. We saw _____ display about _____ *Titanic* at _____ Maritime Museum of _____ Atlantic. Many of _____ *Titanic* victims are buried in _____ Halifax. _____ story of _____ 1917 Halifax

Exercise 3.8 – *continued*

explosion was really astonishing. _____ munitions ship blew up in _____ harbour, levelling _____ entire downtown area, killing 2000 and injuring 9000.

4. After _____ weeks of looking, I finally found _____ apartment. It's on _____ Baker Street, near _____ university. I'll be able to walk to _____ class, but I can take _____ bus when _____ weather is bad. It's _____ two-bedroom apartment. I'm going to share with _____ cousin. It's in _____ high-rise building, on _____ seventh floor. _____ living room is really nice because it has _____ picture window with _____ view of _____ river. We have some furniture from our parents, and we can get _____ few pieces from _____ garage sales or _____ thrift shop. I can't wait to have _____ own place.

Using Prepositional Phrases

Prepositional phrases are a frequent add-in to the basic sentence structure. Most specify time or place (when or where); some show the manner—how something was done. They are formed with a preposition followed by a noun phrase (a noun with articles and adjectives if required):

> in the house
>
> at school
>
> with the red hat
>
> in five minutes
>
> in a sloppy way

Prepositions:

> about, above, across, after, against, along, among, around, at, before, behind, below, beneath, beside, between, by, down, during, except, for, from, in, inside, into, near, next to, of, off, on, onto, out of, outside, over, past, through, to, under, until, up, upon, with, within, without

Notice how the prepositional phrases (underlined in the sentences below) add meaning to the sentence:

The girl threw the ball.
After her brother's taunt, the girl from next door threw the ball into the street.

Jack sat at the back of the bus to avoid the family with the crying baby.

Being able to identify prepositional phrases is important because by eliminating these phrases from the mix, you can isolate the core of the sentence (the subject and verb) and check to see whether the sentence is grammatical. A grammatical subject never appears in a prepositional phrase:

One of the soldiers was killed. [the subject is *one*, not *soldiers*]

The members of the choir were tired after the long rehearsals. [the subject is *members*, not *choir*]

Prepositions themselves pose problems for both people learning English as a second language and native speakers. The basic meanings are relatively straightforward, but they combine with verbs to make idiomatic combinations. Some verbs are completed by a specific preposition. For instance, we say *to rely on* and *to contend with* someone or something. Phrasal verbs are two and three-part verbs that are completed with prepositions (technically distinguished as particles, but they are essentially the same words). For example, we say someone is *getting by* on a reduced income and that someone is trying *to catch up*. Unfortunately, there are few rules that can help. One is that *up* usually adds the meaning of *completely* or *elaborately* (e.g., *dress* versus *dress up*). Most of these combinations, however, are idiomatic and must be learned individually. A good dictionary includes phrasal verbs and gives the prepositions that go with the verbs.

Exercise 3.9

Underline the prepositional phrases in the following sentences, and identify the main subject and verb:

1. Some of the best dinosaur fossils can be found at the Royal Tyrrell Museum in the Badlands area near Drumheller, Alberta.
2. In Quebec City, you can visit the Plains of Abraham, the site of the 1759 battle where the English forces defeated the French, putting Canada under the control of the British.

Exercise 3.9 – *continued*

3. The corner of Portage and Main is the downtown heart of
    Winnipeg and is considered the windiest intersection in the
    world.

4. Victoria, the capital of British Columbia, is located on
    Vancouver Island, whereas Vancouver is on the mainland and
    is a much larger city.

5. Niagara Falls is not the highest waterfall in the world, but the
    Horseshoe Falls, on the Canadian side of the border, is the
    world's largest by volume of water.

Exercise 3.10

Fill in the blanks with an appropriate preposition to complete the
prepositional phrase:

1. Chris plays road hockey _____ the summer to keep his skills
    sharp _____ his regular games _____ ice _____ the winter.

2. We went to see the Blue Jays play _____ Friday night. We had
    seats _____ the highest part _____ the stadium _____ the
    nosebleed section.

3. I found an apartment _____ my sister's house, and it's
    convenient _____ work, too. I'm looking forward to spending
    more time playing _____ my nephews. They like going _____
    the park and hanging _____ the monkey bars.

4. Marcus likes to laze _____ the couch _____ Sunday
    afternoons watching his favourite teams _____ television.

5. The shortstop hit the ball _____ _____ the park _____ his
    second home run _____ the game.

6. I love to swim _____ the early morning _____ the cottage. I
    can dive _____ the end _____ the dock. In a few strokes, I
    can swim _____ the bay _____ the small beach.

7. If you look _____ the bookshelf _____ the door, you'll find
    the slang dictionary _____ the top shelf _____ the other
    dictionaries.

8. The students play soccer _____ the park _____ class _____
    Wednesday afternoons. _____ the time they finish the game,
    it's getting dark.

Exercise 3.10 – *continued*

9. Ling and Albert are planning a destination wedding. It will take place _____ a resort _____ the island of St. Lucia.

10. I can't find the key. I looked _____ the hook, _____ my purse, _____ the desk, and even _____ the junk drawer. I checked _____ the desk to see if it had fallen.

Exercise 3.11

Add prepositional phrases to the following sentences:

1. The house was demolished.
2. The students are studying quietly.
3. The wall needs to be painted.
4. The band performed.
5. The rugby team won the game.
6. The movie is playing.
7. The children are running.
8. I fell.
9. The man drove.
10. Anna is studying Japanese.

Using Co-ordinate Conjunctions

The co-ordinate conjunctions are *and, or, but, for, so, nor,* and *yet.* They are used for joining sentences or parts of sentences:

Jesse <u>and</u> Kate were putting up new drywall.

We arrived tired <u>yet</u> happy.

They topped the pizza with pepperoni, mushrooms, <u>and</u> green pepper.

Marcus wanted to take fencing lessons, <u>but</u> he could not afford the gear.

You could see the Friday show <u>or</u> go to the matinee.

Punctuation of co-ordinate conjunctions can be tricky. For example, in the following sentences, a comma comes before the conjunction only when there is a full sentence afterwards:

> Martha installed a firewall and changed the passwords.
>
> Martha installed a firewall, and Sylvia changed the passwords.

When a list of items is given, a comma is optional before the *and*. British English favours using this "serial" comma, while American style tends to leave it out. Canadians, as usual, are in the middle. If you do opt to use a serial comma, use it consistently:

> Rob topped his hamburger with mustard, ketchup, and relish.
>
> OR: Rob topped his hamburger with mustard, ketchup and relish.

In conversational style, sentences often begin with a co-ordinate conjunction, but this should be avoided in academic writing. It is considered conversational style and, technically, not grammatical. This structure is very common in less formal writing, but do not use it in your academic writing:

> Students can be more comfortable taking online courses. They can work in a homey atmosphere, at ease in their favourite chair. <u>And</u> they don't have to get dressed up. <u>And</u> they can even work in their pyjamas. <u>So</u> they can enjoy the course more.
>
> Students can be more comfortable taking online courses. They can work in a homey atmosphere, at ease in their favourite chair. In addition, they don't have to get dressed up and can even work in their pyjamas. Therefore, they can enjoy the course more. [preferable for academic writing]

Exercise 3.12

Make the two sentences into one, using co-ordinate conjunctions and eliminating unnecessary words:

1. Peter had to get the transmission fixed. He had to get the brakes fixed.
2. Zach thought he passed his driver's test. He had to book another one.
3. Kate plays the piano. She plays the guitar.

4. My uncle was killed in a motorcycle accident. My mother won't allow me to get a motorcycle.

5. Erin's brother is an engineer. Erin's brother-in-law is an engineer.

6. Melissa could go to the University of Calgary. Melissa could go to the University of Alberta.

7. Ben thought he had a job on the oil rig. The job fell through.

8. We thought of holding my parents' anniversary party on a dinner cruise boat. We thought of holding my parents' anniversary party in the revolving restaurant.

9. Christine was supposed to pick Jim up at the train station. She forgot.

10. Suji couldn't understand the formula. She read the chapter again.

Parallel structure

When using co-ordinate conjunctions, you must ensure that each sentence part that you join has essentially the same grammatical structure. This is called parallel structure.

> Martha likes dancing and to sing. [not parallel]
> Martha likes dancing and singing. [parallel]
> Martha likes to dance and sing. [parallel]
> Martha likes to dance but hates to swim. [parallel]
> Martha likes to dance, but Dimitry prefers to sit on the side. [parallel]

The structures being joined can be single words, phrases, or full clauses. Sometimes the structures are in a series of elements. Again, the joined elements must have the same basic grammatical structure:

> On their vacation trip, they wanted to sit on a beach, eat great food, and they hoped to visit family. [not parallel]
> On their vacation trip, they wanted to sit on a beach, eat great food, and visit family. [parallel]

Ensuring parallelism can be difficult. You have to figure out what parts of the sentence are being linked. You can put them in a list to see if everything has the same structure and fits the sentence:

When Eli lost his keys, he looked	under the desk, beside the filing cabinet,
and	checked under the sofa cushions. [not parallel]

When you line up the elements and check them with the head of the phrase, you can see that "he looked under the desk" and "he looked beside the filing cabinet" are both grammatical, whereas "he looked checked under the sofa cushions" does not work.

When Eli lost his keys, he looked	under the desk, beside the filing cabinet,
and	under the sofa cushions. [parallel with three prepositional phrases]

Parallel structure is especially important in thesis statements where three elements are often linked to show the three ideas explored in the body paragraphs. You can practise parallel structure with thesis statements in Unit 5.

Exercise 3.13

For each list, choose which item is not parallel:

Example: washing dishes

setting the table

to pour the drinks [not parallel]

1. a good plot
    interesting characters
    kept the audience's attention
    exciting special effects

2. worried
    in a bad mood
    tired

Exercise 3.13 – *continued*

frustrated

hungry

3. strolling through the park

   running around the track

   rollerblading down the path

   walk around the block

4. made some appetizers

   put the beer in the fridge

   set the table

   tidy the living room

5. tour the Parliament buildings

   the bike paths around the city

   visit the National Gallery

   shop in the Byward Market

Exercise 3.14

Fill in the blank with a phrase that will fit the sentence and have parallel structure:

1. Marie topped the pizza with tomatoes, sausage, _____, and onions.

2. I was born in Edmonton, raised in Vancouver, and later _____.

3. College students can be high school graduates, mature students, and _____.

4. Her presentation was clear, concise, and _____.

5. To be successful, college students should attend class, manage their time, and _____.

Exercise 3.15

Correct errors in parallel structure:

1. Before the snow falls, we have to rake the leaves, plant some bulbs, and the mulch has to be spread.

2. At the cottage, Martin spends time on the lake canoeing, in his sailboat, and waterskiing.

3. An ideal job would have good financial compensation, a good work environment, and the co-workers have to be friendly.

4. For the make-over, her hair was coloured, cut, and a straightener was used.

5. The movie was R-rated because of excessive violence, the characters swore a lot, and nudity.

Writing Noun Clauses

Clauses are parts of complex sentences and have both a noun and a verb. Noun clauses can function as both subjects and objects:

> His behaviour was inexcusable. [noun subject]
> What he did was inexcusable. [noun clause subject]

> I understood his apology. [noun object]
> I understood that he was sorry. [noun clause object]

Words that may begin noun clauses:

> that, if, whether, when, where, what, why, how, who, whom, which, whose

Here are some examples of noun clauses:

> She asked whether I could come.

> They wondered if it would rain.

> The school accepts whoever wants to attend.

> I don't understand how they fixed it.

> Who will win the race is a mystery.

Many noun clauses begin with *that* (never *which*), but if the clause comes after the verb, the *that* can be eliminated if the sentence is clear without it:

> She realized [that] he was late.

Noun clauses that function as subjects should be relatively short. English doesn't like top-heavy sentences requiring the reader to wait for a long time to come to the verb because these sentences are more difficult to understand. They can be revised by using an *it* phrase:

> That we could still negotiate a fair deal after so many false starts is amazing. [awkward but grammatical]
> It is amazing that we could still negotiate a fair deal after so many false starts. [better]

Be careful with the word order in noun clauses that deal with questions. The question structure (using the verb *do* and inverted word order) is not used:

> They asked what time did she finish. [incorrect]
> They asked what time she finished.

> They wanted to know did she have time for another project. [incorrect]
> They wanted to know if she had time for another project.

Exercise 3.16

Construct a sentence with a noun clause to express the two ideas in one sentence, changing the wording where necessary:

Example: He was late. It was surprising.

> It was surprising that he was late. OR That he was late was surprising.

1. I was upset. The trip to Europe was cancelled just when my parents agreed to fund the trip.
2. Juan made so much progress in his English skills. His tutor was pleased.
3. The students were relieved. The assignment due date was extended.
4. She broke the world record in high jump. It was astonishing.
5. He came second in the class. It was a big surprise to her.

Exercise 3.17

Complete the noun clause to fit the blank:

1. She asked whether _____.

2. That _____ was disappointing.

3. How _____ was Jane's main concern.

4. He didn't understand why _____.

5. Whoever _____ is fine with me.

Writing Adjective Clauses

A clause is, in effect, another sentence added into a sentence, since it has both a subject and a verb. Adjective clauses, also called relative clauses, describe a noun and are introduced by relative pronouns (*who, whom, whose, what, which, why, that, when, where*):

> The woman <u>who led that protest march</u> is Jamie's cousin.

> The reason <u>that I am so tired</u> is that I stayed up all night finishing that essay.

> The cottage road, <u>which is not paved</u>, is impassable in the winter.

> The DVD <u>that he ordered</u> is not available anymore.

> The tourist <u>whose luggage was stolen</u> spent hours filling out a report.

Adding clauses to sentences is a good way to give extra information to a sentence without changing its main idea or focus. For example, if you want to identify someone but you do not want that identification to be the main idea of the sentence, you can use an adjective clause:

> My friend Liz, who went to Europe with me, is travelling to New Zealand this summer.

As in noun clauses, the *that* is sometimes eliminated if the meaning is clear:

> The reason [that] <u>I am so tired</u> is that I stayed up all night finishing that essay.

> The DVD [that] <u>he ordered</u> is not available anymore.

The relative pronoun *whom* is the correct form when the pronoun refers to the object of the verb or of the preposition. However, it is dying out in English usage. In conversation and informal writing it is almost never used, but it is more common in academic writing:

> The woman whom I met last week is a set designer.
> The woman who I met last week is a set designer. [commonly heard but not acceptable in academic English]

Punctuation is important in sentences that contain adjective clauses. Commas around the clause signal that the information is extra, that taking out the clause will not affect the meaning of the sentence. If there are no commas, the clause is essential to the meaning because it restricts who or what is being spoken about. In grammar terms, the first case is called a non-restrictive or non-defining adjective clause, while the latter case is a restrictive or defining adjective clause:

> The Class 2B students, who failed the test, have to attend a tutorial. [non-restrictive clause showing that all the students in Class 2B failed]
> The Class 2B students who failed the test have to attend a tutorial. [restrictive clause—only some of the students in Class 2B failed]

The relative pronoun *that* is used in restrictive relative clauses, while *which* is used for non-restrictive clauses:

> The course that she wanted to take is already full.

> The first year biology course, which is required in many programs, has several sections.

Exercise 3.18

Identify the relative clauses in the following sentences. Add commas where necessary (i.e., for the restrictive relative clauses):

1. Nunavut which was created from the Northwest Territories in 1999 has an Aboriginal government and Inuktitut as an official language.
2. The spot where the cottage will be built has a nice view of the lake.
3. Janice whom I taught last year is planning to be a teacher herself.
4. The company where she worked part-time in high school offered her a scholarship.

Exercise 3.18 – *continued*

5. The president of the college who uses a wheelchair has done much to improve the accessibility of campus facilities.

6. The apartment which I saw last week is still available.

Exercise 3.19

Combine the following sentences using relative clauses. Change the word order as necessary:

Example: We got married in the church. The church is being torn down.

The church where we got married is being torn down.

OR The church that is being torn down is the place where we were married.

1. I worked at the company part-time as a student. The company offered me a full-time position when I graduated.

2. The students forgot to do their assignment. Those students had to stay after class.

3. The singers were trained in Europe. The singers were most familiar with classical tradition.

4. We are meeting at a restaurant. The restaurant is on campus, next to the biology building.

5. Children come to the community pool to learn to swim. Their ages range from seven to twelve.

6. Some people keep exotic pets such as tarantulas, rattlesnakes, and piranhas. These people want to be different and prefer to live dangerously.

Writing Adverb Clauses

Adverb clauses (often called subordinate clauses) modify whole sentences and, like adverbs, tell when, where, why, or how something was done. They are introduced by subordinate conjunctions:

He studied hard for the test. He didn't get a passing grade.
Although he studied for the test, he didn't get a passing grade.

> Marie was late for the interview. The car broke down.
> Marie was late for the interview <u>because</u> the car broke down.

The adverb clause that begins with the conjunction is also called a subordinate or dependent clause, and the other half of the sentence is the main or independent clause. The clause is dependent because it cannot stand on its own; it depends on the main clause to make a complete sentence:

> Although he studied for the test. [incomplete sentence]
> He didn't get a passing grade. [complete]

> Because the car broke down. [incomplete sentence]
> Marie was late for the interview. [complete]

Here are the main subordinate conjunctions:

> after, although, as, because, before, even though, if, since, unless, until, when, where, whereas, whether, while

For most sentences, the subordinate clause can come either before or after the main clause:

> <u>If</u> you remove the cover first, it is easier to access the parts.
> It is easier to access the parts <u>if</u> you remove the cover first.

Note the punctuation. In the two sentences above, a comma separates the two clauses in the first one. The reader needs to know when one clause ends and the other begins. If the subordinate clause is second, the subordinate conjunction tells the reader that a new clause is starting, so the comma is unnecessary. Note also that there is no comma after the conjunction:

> Although, he was tired of hearing her complaints, he finished the job. [incorrect]

Often you have a choice whether to use a co-ordinate or subordinate conjunction. Some express the same meanings:

> <u>Although</u> Takeshi hates playing golf, he never misses the company golf day.
> Takeshi hates playing golf, <u>but</u> he never misses the company golf day.

(Note, however, that English does not allow both these conjunctions at the same time. "<u>Although</u> Takeshi hates playing golf, <u>but</u> he never misses the company golf day" is incorrect.)

A sentence with a co-ordinate conjunction is considered a compound sentence; both clauses have the same weight. A sentence constructed with a subordinate conjunction is considered a complex sentence. It allows you to express different levels of meaning. What is expressed in the subordinate clause is the less important (subordinate) idea; the main idea is in the main clause. For example, in an essay supporting school uniforms, you could say:

> Although school uniforms are often hideous, it is comforting to know that everyone is dressed the same and your style can't be found wanting.

The writer is acknowledging the lack of fashion in uniforms but is stressing the positive side (the idea that is in the main clause). If the sentence was flipped, it could be used in an essay discussing the disadvantages of uniforms:

> Although it can be comforting to know that everyone is dressed the same, it must be acknowledged that school uniforms are truly hideous.

This technique is discussed in "Conceding a Point," page 203.

You can write a sentence with more than one subordinate clause as long as you have a main clause to make it a grammatical sentence. But do not overload your sentence:

> While he was waiting for the train, wondering if it would ever come, he looked through a magazine because he was very bored, but even though the articles were interesting, he could not concentrate on the information given, as his thoughts kept coming back to the mistakes he had made in the job interview.

Note the differences between *although* and *even though*. They have the same basic meaning, but *even though* is stronger, showing a contrast that is surprising:

> Although he had done his training, he could not complete the marathon.
> Even though he had trained hard for months, he could not complete the marathon.

Remember that *even though* is always two words. The word *though* by itself is conversational style and not suited to essay writing.

Conjunctive adverbs (also called adverbial connectives) such as *however*, *therefore*, and *nevertheless* are often confused for subordinate conjunctions:

> He couldn't figure out how to install the sink, therefore he finally read the instructions. [incorrect]
> He couldn't figure out how to install the sink, so he finally read the instructions.

> Because he couldn't figure out how to install the sink, he finally read the instructions.
> He couldn't figure out how to install the sink; therefore, he finally read the instructions.

A conjunction can join two sentences together, while a conjunctive adverb is primarily an adverb. To join two sentences with a conjunctive adverb, you need to add something that will make the connection grammatical, such as a semicolon.

Conjunctive adverbs generally function as transition signals (listed on page 134). It is relatively easy to distinguish adverbs from conjunctions—an adverb can appear in different places in the sentence; a conjunction cannot:

> Gillian wanted to buy a modern house in the suburbs; <u>however</u>, Roy preferred an old fixer-upper downtown.

> Gillian wanted to buy a modern house in the suburbs; Roy, <u>however</u>, preferred an old fixer-upper downtown.

> Gillian wanted to buy a modern house in the suburbs; Roy preferred an old fixer-upper downtown, <u>however</u>.

> <u>While</u> Gillian wanted to buy a modern house in the suburbs, Roy preferred an old fixer-upper downtown.

> Gillian wanted to buy a modern house in the suburbs <u>while</u> Roy preferred an old fixer-upper downtown.

Notice that the subordinate conjunction *while* can only appear at the beginning of a subordinate clause, but the adverbial *however* can appear at the beginning, in the middle, or at the end of a sentence.

Exercise 3.20

Join the following pairs of sentences with a subordinate conjunction:

Example: I tried to install the wireless router. My system crashed.

> When I tried to install the wireless router, my system crashed.

1. Tim Horton had a hand in starting the business that bears his name. Laura Secord had nothing to do with the candy-making business.
2. The candy store was named after Laura Secord. The founder wanted a Canadian heroine as a trademark.
3. The Canadian flag is such a recognized symbol today. It did not have an easy road to design and official acceptance in 1965.
4. The first explorers came to Canada seeking a route to the Orient. They came back for the valuable fish and furs.
5. British Columbia agreed to join Canada. A railroad would be built to connect it with the eastern provinces.
6. The Canadian Pacific Railway took many years to complete. It was so difficult to build through the rock of the Canadian Shield in central Canada and the mountain ranges in British Columbia.
7. The United Empire Loyalists came north to Canada after the American Revolution. They wanted to remain British subjects.
8. Lacrosse is one of Canada's national sports. It is not very popular, especially when compared to hockey.
9. Tommy Douglas became a member of Parliament. He wanted to introduce the same reforms to Canada that he brought to Saskatchewan.
10. The Acadians were expelled from Nova Scotia. They settled in Louisiana.

Using Participles and Gerunds

A verb that ends in –*ing* can be many things. It may be part of a verb in one of the continuous tenses:

> Jamie was skating with David when she fell.

> Amanda is learning to skate.

It may be a gerund, a verbal that functions as a noun. In a sentence, a gerund can be both a subject and an object:

Wishing is not enough.

He hates waiting.

These gerunds can be completed by objects and modifiers:

<u>Seeing the whales up close</u> was an amazing experience.

<u>Running up the stairs</u> is good exercise.

She enjoys <u>walking alone</u>.

Verbals that end in *–ing* can also be participles, which function as adjectives:

<u>Running</u> water does not freeze readily.

The boys <u>running around the room</u> are my nephews.

The *–ing* form is in the active voice, while the *–ed* participles are used to express the passive:

Some politicians would like to see an <u>elected</u> Senate.

I love <u>freshly baked</u> bread.

Gerund phrases should not be confused with participial phrases. Both gerunds and participles end in *–ing*, but gerunds act as nouns while participles act as adjectives:

The woman <u>watching the dancers</u> is a talent scout. [participle describing the woman]

<u>Watching the dancers</u> is a good way to learn the choreography. [gerund phrase as grammatical subject]

Another tricky part of understanding and using gerunds is distinguishing the verbs that take gerunds and those that take infinitives (the *to* form of the verb):

I enjoy <u>walking</u> in the park.

I want <u>to walk</u> in the park.

See page 225 for a list of such verbs and exercises.

A common mistake that students make when they try to use a gerund phrase as a subject is that they add a preposition:

> By working all night is a bad way to write an essay. [incorrect]
>
> Working all night is a bad way to write an essay. [correct]
>
> By working all night, she finished the essay. [correct—the *by* phrase is not the grammatical subject]

Exercise 3.21

Here are some *–ing* phrases that could be used as gerund phrases or participle phrases. Write two sentences for each—one using the phrase as a gerund and one as a participle:

Example: running around the track

> I love running around the track. [gerund]
>
> Running around the track, I am often joined by a friendly dog. [participle]

1. sleeping in the corner
2. driving down the street
3. dancing every day
4. reading novels
5. confronting a burglar
6. talking on a cellphone
7. shopping for shoes
8. cheating at poker

Reducing Clauses to Phrases

When two clauses have the same subject, one clause can sometimes be reduced to make a phrase:

> Gillian, who is the former president of the club, stayed on to help her successor deal with the firings.
>
> Gillian, the former president of the club, stayed on to help her successor deal with the firings.

While they were going over the lesson, the students discovered a new problem.
While going over the lesson, the students discovered a new problem.
Going over the lesson, the students discovered a new problem.

If the clauses have different subjects, this type of reduction cannot be made:

While the students were listening to the lecture, the lights went out.
While listening to the lecture, the lights went out. [incorrect]

In these examples, note the changes:

We ordered the meal for the group before <u>we went</u> to the restaurant.
We ordered the meal for the group before <u>going</u> to the restaurant.

The movie was sold out <u>although it got</u> bad reviews.
The movie was sold out <u>despite having got</u> bad reviews.

Exercise 3.22

In the following sentences, reduce the underlined clauses to phrases where possible:

1. <u>When he was touring the house</u>, Marc noticed that it needed a lot of work.

2. The house, <u>which was located in a prime downtown area</u>, had large rooms and original wood panelling that needed to be stripped.

3. The powder room, <u>which was tucked under the stairway</u>, had pink tiles and 1970s fixtures.

4. <u>Because he had worked for his father's construction company</u>, he had the skills to do most of the work himself.

5. He particularly liked the stained glass, <u>which was almost 100 years old</u>.

6. Elena, <u>who was Marc's wife</u>, was reluctant to take on the project <u>because she didn't want to live in a construction zone for years</u>.

Exercise 3.22 – *continued*

7. Although she was handy with power tools and a paint brush, she preferred a place that required less work.

8. Because they both had demanding jobs, she wanted to have relaxing weekends, not more work.

9. If they did the work themselves, they could afford to live downtown.

10. After they weighed all the pros and cons, they put in an offer on the house.

Combining Sentences

When you use a co-ordinate conjunction, you create a compound sentence. When you use other clauses, you create a complex sentence. Sentences without clauses are called simple sentences. Simple sentences are more common in spoken English. In your writing, it is important to have a variety of sentence structures. It makes your writing more interesting to read and improves the flow of ideas. It lets you add information to a sentence without losing the focus of the main clause. It also makes your writing more sophisticated—at the higher level more suited to college and university work. A paragraph that contains only simple sentences sounds simplistic.

A clause is, in effect, another sentence added to a sentence. Clauses are different from phrases because they have the structure of a full grammatical sentence with a noun and a verb:

> Because he wanted to revise the whole paper, he threw out his drafts. [clause]
>
> The student who foolishly threw out his drafts wanted to revise the whole paper. [clause]
>
> Wanting to revise the whole paper, he foolishly threw out his drafts. [phrase]

Noun clauses work as subjects and objects, adjective clauses describe nouns, and adverb clauses use subordinate clauses such as *although* and *because*.

Exercise 3.23

Use phrases and clauses to write one to three concise sentences incorporating the ideas in the groups of sentences below:

Example: The five-dollar bill celebrates children at play.

There are different pictures of winter sport on the reverse side.

Children are shown playing hockey.

A child learning to skate is also depicted.

There is a picture of a toboggan.

There is a quotation from "The Hockey Sweater."

"The Hockey Sweater" is a famous short story.

"The Hockey Sweater" was written by Roch Carrier.

The five-dollar bill celebrates winter sport, with pictures of hockey, skating, and tobogganing and a quotation from "The Hockey Sweater," a famous short story by Roch Carrier.

1. Queen Victoria chose Ottawa to be the capital of Canada.
    She made the decision in 1857.
    In 1857 Ottawa was known as Bytown.
    Bytown was a small lumber town.
    Bytown's location was advantageous.
    It was farther from the American border.
    The other towns considered were all close to the border.
    It was on the border between French and English Canada.

2. The Hudson's Bay Company is Canada's oldest corporation.
    It started in 1670.
    It started with a land grant from King Charles II.
    The king's cousin was Prince Rupert.
    Prince Rupert and his associates started the corporation.
    The corporation controlled the fur trade in the area around Hudson Bay.
    The area of the land grant was the drainage area of rivers flowing into Hudson Bay
    This land grant gave the corporation control of 40 per cent of the current area of Canada.

Exercise 3.23 – *continued*

3. In the 1930s, the most famous Canadian was Grey Owl.
    He is considered Canada's first conservationist.
    He wrote books and lectured about saving the wilderness and the beaver.
    He died in 1938.
    After his death, newspapers told his real story.
    He said he was an Indian.
    He was actually an Englishman named Archie Belaney.
    Belaney came to Canada as a teenager.
    He was in love with the idea of living in the wilderness.
    He dyed his hair.
    He darkened his skin.
    He made up stories about his past.

4. The Confederation Bridge was opened in May 1997.
    It stretches from New Brunswick to Prince Edward Island.
    It is often referred to as the "fixed link."
    It is 12.9 kilometres long.
    It is the longest bridge over ice-covered salt water.
    It carries two lanes of traffic.
    Travellers pay a toll on leaving Prince Edward Island.
    They can go by the bridge or by ferry.

5. The building of the transcontinental railway led to the creation of Canada.
    British Columbia would only join the confederation if a railway were built.
    The railway was promised in the 1860s.
    The railway was completed in 1885.
    It was difficult to build.
    There were many political battles.
    It was very expensive.
    The areas in the Canadian Shield and the Rocky Mountains were particularly difficult.

6. Marilyn Bell was the first person to swim across Lake Ontario.
    She was 16 years old.
    An American woman was offered $10,000 to swim across Lake Ontario.
    Bell was asked to compete against her by a rival newspaper.
    Bell was not offered any prize beforehand.
    It took her 21 hours.
    She had to fight high waves, eels, and oil spills.

Recognizing Fragments and Run-on Sentences

Remember that a sentence must have a subject and a verb. A sentence fragment is an incomplete sentence:

> Going whale-watching off Vancouver Island.
>
> When I dug for dinosaur fossils in Drumheller.
>
> The actor who was chosen for the lead role.
>
> The small red brick house down the street.

To fix a sentence fragment, you need to find out what is missing and supply it:

> Going whale-watching off Vancouver Island was an incredible experience.
>
> When I dug for dinosaur fossils in Drumheller, I relived my childhood dream of being an paleontologist.
>
> The actor who was chosen for the lead role had to leave the production.
>
> The small red brick house down the street is for sale.

A run-on sentence, on the other hand, is essentially too much sentence:

> Graduates take entry-level jobs to get their foot in the door they do not want to be stuck there for years.

One kind of run-on sentence is a comma splice, in which a comma incorrectly divides the sentences:

> Polar bears live in the Arctic, they need the ice to live on.

Sometimes sentences can be considered run-on if they contain too many clauses—even though they are grammatical:

> When the waitress took the orders, which was difficult to do because of the noise of the hockey game, which was the final game of the season, so the hockey fans were out in full force and full voice, she misunderstood the customers' orders, and the kitchen prepared the wrong food, so the customers were angry and complained to the manager, who blamed the kitchen staff, but the waitress admitted she could not hear the order very well, so new meals were prepared on the house.

There are essentially three ways to fix run-on sentences: make two sentences, use a semicolon, or add a conjunction:

> The play had sold out its run was extended. [incorrect]
>
> The play had sold out, its run was extended. [incorrect, comma splice]
>
> The play had sold out. Its run was extended. [correct, two separate sentences]
>
> The play had sold out; its run was extended. [correct, semicolon]
>
> The play had sold out, <u>so</u> its run was extended. [correct, co-ordinate conjunction]
>
> <u>Because</u> the play had sold out, its run was extended. [correct, subordinate conjunction]
>
> The play had sold out; <u>therefore</u>, its run was extended. [correct, semicolon and conjunctive adverb]

Exercise 3.24

Decide whether the following sentences are fragments, run-ons, or correct sentences. Fix the fragments and run-ons:

1. Watching a soccer game on Sunday afternoon.

2. The goalkeeper came out to handle the ball the attacker managed to get a kick in to score a goal.

3. They managed another goal on a penalty kick, however the game was already lost.

4. Although they had been division champions. They could not get past the powerhouse teams.

5. I like to watch the children play soccer. Because they all travel in a bunch following the ball.

6. She has become addicted to reality shows on television, she especially likes the ones where she can vote on who is the most talented.

7. Eating snacks in front of the television set and not exercising.

Exercise 3.24 – *continued*

8. My children love to watch nature documentaries, which are a lot better than a steady diet of cartoons and music videos.

9. Infomercials, usually shown in the middle of the night, advertising a useless array of products.

10. Those infomercials, however, attract a large number of customers who cannot resist the sales pitch.

Using Punctuation and Capitalization

Punctuation is an important part of sentence structure. Readers rely on capital letters and end punctuation to tell them where sentences begin and end. Commas show the different parts of a sentence. Because sentences in academic English are more complex, the punctuation is crucial to the reader's ability to follow the sentence.

End punctuation

The end of a sentence is marked by a period, question mark, or exclamation mark. In essay writing, almost all of your sentences will end with a period; you should have very few questions and no exclamations at all.

Sentences should not end with three dots (an ellipsis mark). It gives the impression that the writer is not committed to the sentence and is just trailing off. (Ellipsis marks are properly used in academic writing in quotations to show that some words have been left out.)

Periods are also used with some abbreviations, such as shortened words (Prof. for Professor) and university degrees (M.B.A.). Initialisms (abbreviations formed from the first letter of words, such as ESL for English as a second language) and acronyms (like initialisms but pronounced as words, such as AIDS for acquired immune deficiency syndrome) rarely have periods between the letters. Check your dictionary or style guide if you are unsure of the usage.

Space

Space is an element of punctuation because it shows readers where paragraphs begin and end as well as showing word boundaries. Space also contributes to the readability of the document. A text that is too jammed with words is harder to read. Your résumé, for example, should have enough white space to make it attractive and readable.

There should be no space between the end of the word and the punctuation. A comma, for example, should never appear at the beginning of the next line, no matter how squished your words are at the end of the line.

In the old days of typewriters, typists were taught to leave two spaces at the end of a sentence. This is no longer the convention now that people use computers and proportional fonts; one space is sufficient.

Space is also important to show the beginning and end of paragraphs. Generally, paragraphs are indented with five spaces, or a half-inch tab space. Block-style paragraphing uses no indent but rather a blank line between paragraphs. Readers should be able to easily see where a new paragraph starts. Avoid sloppy, misleading spacing, such as indenting at the beginning of a page where there is no new paragraph.

Proper margins are important for all your documents—leave an inch on each side. Use left justification with a ragged right margin so that you will not have gaps in your lines of text or have to deal with hyphenation. Double-space assignments so that your instructor has room for corrections and comments.

Commas

Commas are placed in sentences, mainly to separate different parts of the sentence. Commas generally appear:

- after initial adverbs: Thankfully, we hailed the rescue team.

- between items in a list: We ate roast beef, mashed potatoes, green peas, and corn. OR We ate roast beef, mashed potatoes, green peas and corn.

- after adverb clauses: Because it was raining, we cancelled the picnic.

- before clauses introduced by co-ordinate conjunctions: I took a nap, and then we left.

- before and after modifying phrases or clauses: John, who is this year's president, gave a welcome speech.

The second example in the list above shows the optional use of a serial comma, a comma before the *and* in a list of several items (discussed on page 83).

Commas appear in lists of adjectives where the two adjectives have a similar function and could be replaced with an *and*:

> She told a strange, sad story about a beautiful Mexican dancer.

A missing comma can change the whole sentence:

Students come to class to learn not to have fun.
Students come to class to learn, not to have fun.

Commas are often inappropriately placed at breath stops in a sentence, such as between a subject and a verb, especially if the subject is long and complex. Other common comma errors include putting commas after *although* and *such as*.

Exercise 3.25

Insert periods, commas, and capital letters where needed in the following paragraph:

cleaning out my grandmother's cluttered musty old house after she died was a monumental task like many old people who had lived through unspeakable war and famine she was an incurable hoarder she kept old newspapers plastic bags and cardboard boxes she didn't trash out-of-date calendars she just tacked up a new one in a different spot on the wall we found new clothes that had been saved for a special occasion and never used her husband's clothes still hung in the closet even though he had passed away a dozen years earlier in the cold cellar were jars of pickled food that must have been 20 years old two full-size freezers were crammed with food some of the packages were many years old she felt safe with all her possessions and never wanted to let anything go

Apostrophes

There seems to be an epidemic of apostrophe overuse and misuse today, not only in students' writing but also on printed signs and even in some published works. Some people incorrectly bestow apostrophes on words ending in *s* and between *nt* letter combinations. As a result, we see miswritten words such as "chair's" and even "he wan't's."

Misplaced or missing apostrophes can result in misleading sentences:

The drill sergeant called the recruits names. [he called them names, mocking them]

The drill sergeant called the recruits' names. [he called their names out]

Were in trouble now. [should be "We're in trouble now."]

Essentially, apostrophes are used for contractions and possessive forms.

A contraction is a shortened form of words, such as *he isn't* for *he is not.* An apostrophe takes the place of dropped letters in a contraction. For example, in verbs contracted with *not*, the apostrophe replaces the *o* (*isn't, doesn't, can't*). The auxiliary verbs *be, have,* and *will* are sometimes contracted: *I'm going, they've noticed, she'll see, I could've done it.* Apostrophes can also show dropped numbers, as in "The radio station played hits from the '70s." They are **not** used in non-contracted verbs (*she tries, he listens*). Do not confuse the verb form *lets* ("he lets me take the car") with the contracted form *let's* (*let us,* as in "let's go").

Possessives are words that show that something belongs to something else (e.g., *Jim's car, the students' pet rabbit*). The possession can be a loose relationship, as in such phrases as *a day's work* or *a summer's day.* If you have trouble distinguishing possessive forms, see the section "Showing Possession" in this unit (page 74).

Apostrophes are **not** used before most plurals (*many ways, two different techniques*). The few exceptions are plurals when an *−s* alone would be confusing:

He got all A's and B's on his report card.

She dots her i's with circles.

Sometimes you might see apostrophes used in plurals of shortened words (e.g., *reno's* for *renovations*) and of number and letter combinations, but these are unnecessary:

He ordered CDs of hits from the 1960s and 1970s.

They booked two limos for transportation to the prom.

Exercise 3.26

Insert apostrophes where needed in the following sentences:

1. Susans brother has been living in his grandfathers house to help take care of him. Hes missed some classes but hes planning to make them up with night classes. The universitys online program lets him follow many different options.

2. Lets go to the Johnsons cottage this weekend. Weve had an open invitation for ages. Ill just give them a call to see if its okay. Itll be good to get away, and if we dont go now, who knows when well be able to get away?

Exercise 3.26 – *continued*

3 James always listens to his teachers instructions because he knows how important following instructions is to getting good marks.

4. Unlike his siblings, hes willing to take over his fathers business selling antiques.

5. The students work needed to be completely redone. I dont know why there were so many mistakes.

Colons

Colons (:) are used to show illustration of an idea. They can be used to introduce a sentence or a list. They should not be used after *are* or *such as*.

> The pizza dough requires few ingredients: flour, water, sugar, salt, oil, and yeast.

> My favourite sports are: soccer, swimming, and squash. [incorrect—colon is unnecessary]

> There was only one thing left to do: He had to contact his friend's parents to let them know what happened. [correct; the capital on *he* is optional]

Semicolons

Semicolons (;) are used between two related sentences and to distinguish items in a complex list where commas are needed:

> The soccer game was exciting to watch; the teams had each been previous champions.

> Dave was the strongest member of the team; however, he was let go because he could not get along with anyone.

> Canadian coins show a number of national symbols: the maple leaves on the penny; the beaver, the animal that brought many Europeans to Canada, on the nickel; the dime's *Bluenose*, a famous racing schooner from Nova Scotia; the caribou on the quarter; the loon on the dollar coin; and the polar bear on the two-dollar coin.

Quotation marks

Quotation marks ("...") or '...') are used to show that you are using some-one's exact words:

> Doug Howat claims, "I'm not exactly a slacker, but I am nonetheless stuck in neutral." (page 266)

For a quote appearing within a quote, you should use quotation marks different from the ones you used for the main quote (e.g., double quotation marks instead of single):

> Sidney Katz shows the racial taunts Rocket Richard endured when he says, "Inspector William Minogue, who, as police officer in charge of the Forum, frequently hears opposing players calling Richard 'French pea soup' or 'dirty French bastard' as they skate past." (page 340)

Quotation marks are also used around the titles of short stories and articles, while the titles of the books or newspapers are printed in italics. For example, "The New Heavyweight Champions" was one of Margaret Wente's columns in *The Globe and Mail*; it is reprinted in *Skill Set*. (In some citation styles, underlining is used instead of italics; underlining and italics are considered equivalent.)

Hyphens and dashes

A hyphen is used within a word (such as *co-author* and *self-discipline*), while a dash is used between words in a sentence. Some words have two accepted spellings—with a hyphen and without. Sometimes the word loses the hyphen over time. For instance, the word *e-mail* is now often written *email*. Check your dictionary if you are not sure of the spelling.

If a word cannot fit on a line, a hyphen is used to break the word into two parts. The hyphen must appear between syllables (syllable breaks are shown in dictionaries). You will see this use of the hyphen in publications because the text is written with full justification (both the right and left margins form straight lines). If words were not split, there would be annoying white spaces in the lines. You can avoid this use of the hyphen by simply writing the whole word on the next line. Use only left justification with a ragged right margin in your documents.

A parenthetical dash is used to set words off from the rest of the sentence. These words can be extra information or a comment. The same function can often be met by parentheses (round brackets) or commas, which can set off a clause or phrase that is not part of the main idea—but the dash gives more emphasis. Notice the usage of each in this section.

A parenthetical dash is also called an "em dash" (because of typesetting—it is the same width as the letter *M*). There should be no space before or after the dash.

While a hyphen can be found on a standard keyboard, dashes are not. Word processing programs may replace two typed hyphens with a long dash. Otherwise, it is a symbol that can be inserted, along with the "en dash." The en dash is used with numbers such as dates (e.g., 1947–63) and is the width of the letter *N*, thus not as wide as the em dash.

Capitalization

Capital letters appear at the beginning of sentences and on proper nouns (official names):

> Maria is planning a trip to Saskatoon to visit her grandmother.

> Actually, Mr. Burton earned his M.B.A. at the Haskayne School of Business at the University of Calgary.

The names of school subjects are capitalized if they are official titles but not if they are general subject names:

> I'd like to take another biology course. Here's an interesting one—BIOL 130, Introductory Cell Biology.

The capital letter has been dropping from such common phrases as "French fries," but properly they should have a capital.

The use of capitals in the titles of books or articles mentioned in a text depends on the style used. In MLA style, for example, the title of this book would be written *Skill Set*, and Sidney Katz's article (page 304) would be "The Strange Forces behind the Richard Hockey Riot," with the first and all other words capitalized (except prepositions and articles). In APA style, the titles would be *Skill set* and "The strange forces behind the Richard hockey riot," with only the first word and any proper nouns capitalized.

Exercise 3.27

Capitalize the words that need capital letters in the following sentences:

1. the marine museum of the atlantic in halifax, nova scotia, has exhibits on the 1917 halifax explosion and the response to the sinking of the *titanic* in 1912.

Exercise 3.27 – *continued*

2. sainte-marie among the hurons is a recreated seventeenth-century jesuit mission headquarters in midland, ontario.

3. sir john a. macdonald was canada's first prime minister. his picture is on the 10-dollar bill.

4. john mccrae wrote the poem "in flanders fields," which is on the back of the bill.

5. remembrance day honours canada's war dead. a minute of silence commemorates the end of world war I at 11 a.m. on november 11.

Exercise 3.28

Add capitalization and punctuation where necessary:

1. mr peterson requested the review of the department because of its poor performance the manager thought it was unnecessary

2. shakespeares play romeo and juliet tells the story of two teenagers in love in sixteenth century italy its a tragic tale because the lovers are from two feuding families

3. i dont know what to buy as a gift for joannes baby shower shes having twin boys

4. if youre worried about fitting the english course into your schedule why dont you take it online

5. lets take the train to montreal so we dont have to worry about driving and parking the citys subway system which is called the metro is an efficient way to get around town

6. a man who grew up not having to do housework is less likely to help his wife out around the house

7. to bake a cake you need to assemble the following ingredients butter sugar eggs flour baking powder salt buttermilk baking soda and vanilla

8. i asked him to leave me a copy of the report but he forgot he finally emailed it to me and i had to print out a copy

Exercise 3.28 – *continued*

9. we went over every word of the report however we missed several errors so it didnt look very good when we gave it to the supervisor

10. she asked whether i could take over her shift on saturday night i wanted to go to jacks party so i said no

Paragraph Writing Skills

Essay writing is essentially presenting ideas and supporting them. It is argument in the broader sense of the word. Paragraphs are the building blocks of essays—if you can write a good paragraph, you can write a good essay. A paragraph may even stand as a mini-essay on its own as an independent, developed paragraph.

The first criterion for a paragraph is that it clearly looks like one. Students sometimes get sloppy and do not leave proper spacing in their writing, but readers depend on the space to see where each paragraph begins and ends. Usually, a paragraph begins with an indentation and may end in the middle of a line. In publications, the first paragraph after a title or subtitle is not generally indented. In business writing, block style is common: paragraphs are not indented, but a blank line appears between paragraphs. Indenting the beginning of paragraphs is the most common style for student writing. Whichever style is used, it should allow the reader to distinguish the paragraphs easily.

Length is often an issue in writing for school because students are concerned that their writing meets assignment criteria. Modern writing favours shorter paragraphs. Newspapers and magazines have short, undeveloped paragraphs, often just a sentence or two, because the print is in narrow columns and long blocks of unbroken text are difficult to read. Modern novels have a lot of dialogue, and the convention is to start a new paragraph with each new speaker, so there are many short paragraphs. Academic writing, however, favours longer paragraphs, though not as long as in the past. Books written 100 years ago have paragraphs that can go on for more than a page. Because of the influence of television and the Internet, today's readers lack the attention span to digest that much unbroken text. The paragraph length that you are reading now (about 100 to 150 words) is typical of academic, business, and technical writing today. A single-paragraph writing assignment may extend to more than 200 words.

Essays, reports, and letters are divided into paragraphs. A paragraph is a unit of meaning, as is a sentence. Each paragraph puts forth an idea and supports it. What is in a paragraph depends on the function it serves. It may introduce or conclude an essay; it may be a definition, description, or comparison. The same criteria for a good paragraph apply no matter what its function.

Most academic-style paragraphs start with a topic sentence, which introduces the main idea and is usually the first sentence. The rest of the paragraph is essentially composed of arguments supporting the idea in the topic sentence, with supporting details supplied to prove those arguments. Remember that the main task of academic writing is to put forth an idea and to support it. Writers must connect the dots for the reader, showing the relationship between the ideas in the sentences.

Independent Paragraphs

Sometimes students are required to write single, expository paragraphs for assignments. These independent paragraphs tend to be longer than the paragraphs that would appear in an essay or report. They may have eight to 12 sentences and range from about 150 to 200 words. They begin with a topic sentence, have perhaps three supported points, and end with a concluding sentence. In essence, they are a shorter version of an essay, and they allow students to practise the basics of making arguments and supporting them before moving on to the complexity of a longer piece of writing.

Here is a typical outline for an independent, developed paragraph:

> Topic sentence
>> Elaboration of topic sentence (if necessary)
>
> Point 1
>> Support (explanation, example, illustration)
>
> Point 2
>> Support (explanation, example, illustration)
>
> Point 3
>> Support (explanation, example, illustration)
>
> Concluding sentence

This is not the only way to develop a paragraph, but it is one way that will lead you to success and help you to build your essay writing skills.

Here are examples of developed paragraphs following this pattern. The word count is included to show you typical length. Note that the first one has an elaboration sentence and four points. The second and third paragraphs are different viewpoints on the same subject; note how the opposing arguments are presented.

Students should take notes when they are attending lectures or reading. Note-taking is a skill they can develop in their high school years and is especially vital in college and university. First, by the very act of writing, they are engaging in active, not just passive, learning. Research has shown that students retain less if they only listen or read, but by writing and talking about the material, they retain it better because these actions require more of the brain. Second, note-taking forces students to process the information. Because they cannot write down every word, they have to choose the most important points, paraphrase, and summarize information. Even if the notes are lost, the action of note-taking means that the material is better understood and more firmly fixed in the brain. In addition, college and university classes rely on the lecture to transmit information. The professor might have a different take on the subject than the one offered in the textbook and only explain it in class. Finally, students can use the notes they have taken for review for tests and exams. It is easier to reread notes than to reread the whole textbook. Thus, note-taking is a valuable practice for students. [203 words]

Campus residence is a good choice of accommodation for first-year students. First, it can be economical. Apartments and houses often have to be leased for a full year, while students pay for residence only for the months they are in school. They can also save on the cost of transportation and utilities. In addition, living on campus is convenient. Students do not waste time travelling to and from school. The campus facilities are close at hand and are often open long hours and during the weekend. Finally, residence offers students the chance to socialize and learn to live with other students, who may have very different backgrounds. Often, long-term friendships develop. Students who meet as floor-mates may decide to share off-campus housing in later school years. Students starting at a new school in a new city can make the campus residence their home away from home. [146 words]

Although undeniably convenient, residence may not be the best choice of accommodation for students. First, it can be expensive. Students sharing a house or an apartment can often find a cheaper place to live. If the students know how to cook, homemade food is also less expensive and more nutritious than eating in the cafeteria with a meal plan. Furthermore, living off campus allows students a chance to escape from school. A residential neighbourhood can offer many different amenities and a chance to interact with people who are not students. Students can also escape the noise and partying often found in a residence. They can study in peace and quiet away from the escapades of young people revelling in their freedom away from parents. Although students often choose residence for first year, many prefer living off campus once they are established in the new city. [145 words]

Thanksgiving is known for the "turkey dump," when first-year college and university students break up with high school sweethearts. The six weeks from the start of school until the first holiday weekend is a perfect amount of time for students to have stretched their wings, looked around, and decided that there are many other fish in the sea. They have begun the process of personal growth and no longer need the security of having a special someone at home waiting for them. In addition, Thanksgiving weekend is usually the first face-to-face meeting after the start of school. This allows the student a chance to see whether absence has actually made the heart grow fonder or whether it is time to move on. More importantly, it gives the student the chance to deliver the bad news personally—only a callous person would do otherwise. Moreover, delaying the break-up would force students to wait for Christmas holidays, which is a bad time to break up since gifts may already have been purchased and holiday plans have been made. Therefore, Thanksgiving is the most suitable occasion to slice away ties to past relationships. [190 words]

Writing Topic Sentences

In academic writing, the topic sentence gives the main idea of the paragraph. Generally, it appears at the beginning of the paragraph, although it can be in the middle or at the end of a paragraph and may even be implied and not directly stated. A topic sentence should state a supportable idea that can be explored in the body of the paragraph. It makes a claim that should be proved or explored in the rest of the paragraph. All the other sentences in that paragraph should relate to the topic sentence; these sentences are more specific than the topic sentence, which is quite general.

Topic sentences are particularly important in expository paragraphs that argue or explain an idea. They are found in the body paragraphs of the essay but not in the introduction or conclusion. Narrative paragraphs and process descriptions may open with the first event or step, and so they might not have a topic sentence introducing the paragraph. In an essay, the topic sentences of the body paragraphs take their cue from the thesis statement. A good topic sentence should tell the reader what to expect in the paragraph. For example, for a paragraph that starts, "Editing is an important step in writing an essay," the reader will expect that the paragraph shows why editing is so important. The topic sentence also limits the paragraph—all the sentences should fit under the umbrella of the topic sentence. This is called unity. For example, "Students should brainstorm their topic first" would not fit in the paragraph about editing.

It is important to distinguish a topic from a topic sentence. A topic is what the paragraph is about, such as "living in residence." In a topic sentence, there is a controlling idea that says what idea the writer is going to explore about living in residence, such as "living in residence is the best choice for first-year students."

Activity

Consider these topic sentences, which have a different focus but on are on the same topic. Discuss how they differ and what each paragraph would say. (Note: *Empty nesters* are parents whose children have grown up and left home, and *boomerang children* are adults who come back to live in the family home, usually after college or university graduation.)

1. Boomerang children must make adjustments to their lifestyle in order to live with their parents.
2. Adult children who live with their parents should contribute financially to the household.
3. Adult children who still live at home must take on more responsibility for household chores.
4. Parents with boomerang children should not treat them as children.
5. Many college and university graduates are forced to return to their parents' home.
6. Empty nesters should downsize their homes once their children leave to prevent them from returning.

Note when the focus is on the parents and when it is on their children.

A well-written topic sentence serves as a guideline for the writer, so instructors generally insist that students start with a topic sentence. Practising writing topic sentences will also help students write better thesis statements for their essays. The main difference between a thesis statement and a topic sentence is that a thesis statement gives the main idea of an essay while a topic sentence introduces just a paragraph.

It is good practice to put the topic sentence first because this structure is the most common and easiest for student writers. The topic sentence should be a supportable idea, not a plain fact, and it should state an idea that can be explained in a single paragraph, so it is neither too broad nor too narrow.

It should be a full, grammatical statement. If you are given a question as a writing topic, do not start with "yes" or "no"; the paragraph should stand on its own. Moreover, you should use your own words in your topic sentence and not just copy from the question posed by the instructor.

A topic sentence should state the main idea, not announce it:

> I will talk about the differences between bus and car travel. [announcement]

> Travelling by bus is a different experience from travelling by car. [better]

Because it limits what can be dealt with in one paragraph, a topic sentence should not be too broad:

> Alcohol hurts many people. [too broad]

> Fetal alcohol syndrome affects social development. [better]

A topic sentence should not be too narrow:

> Electronic books are not good to take to the beach. [too narrow]

> Electronic books are less convenient than the paper format. [better]

In most academic writing, a topic sentence should be a supportable idea—a judgment made about an idea, not a straight fact:

> Many high school students have part-time jobs. [fact]

> Part-time jobs have many benefits for high school students. [better]

> Electronic books are read on a computer screen instead of on paper. [fact]

> It would be hard to get avid readers to give up paper books for electronic formats. [better]

A topic sentence should have one main idea, not two:

> The key to success in college is attending class and taking notes. [two ideas]

The key to success in college is attending class. [better]

Avoid using a *because* idea in your topic sentence; it makes your sentence too specific. Moreover, the reasons will be explored in the paragraph itself.

Smoking should be prohibited in restaurants because it creates unhealthy work conditions for servers. [too limited]

Smoking should be prohibited in restaurants. [better]

Do not overload your topic sentence:

With online shopping, you can have the convenience of staying at home, surfing as much as you want among the websites, looking for the item you want, comparing prices, and reading posted reviews. [overloaded]

With online shopping, you can have the convenience of staying at home. [better]

Make sure your topic sentence is a grammatical statement, not a question. It should be understandable on its own, so be careful with pronoun use.

Why should students preview textbook chapters before class? [should be a statement]

Students should preview textbook chapters before class. [better]

They should read children's fairy tale books. [unacceptable— who is "They"?]

Students learning English should read children's fairy tale books.

Exercise 4.1

For each question, discuss which topic sentence is best and why.

1. What criteria should be considered when choosing a ring tone for a cellphone?
   a) Ring tones are set on cellphones to alert the users when there is an incoming call or text message.
   b) People should choose a ring tone for a cellphone by considering several criteria.

Exercise 4.1 – *continued*

c) The cellphone is an important device for our daily life.

d) Instead of just choosing a cellphone ring tone that is catchy, people should make sure it is appropriate.

e) Every person who has a cellphone tends to have a unique ring tone.

f) Ring tones can often be disturbing, depending on the time, place, or situation.

2. How should young adults deal with over-protective parents?

a) There are many ways young adults could try dealing with their over-protective parents.

b) Young adults need to prove that they are responsible.

c) These days young adults and parents seem to have many issues.

d) Many parents are too worried about their children and want to protect them in every situation.

e) No matter the age, parents will always be protective over their children.

3. Should the one-cent coin be eliminated?

a) Canadians no longer need a one-cent coin.

b) There is nothing worse than receiving four pennies, three quarters, a nickel, a toonie, a loonie, and a five-dollar bill from a cashier.

c) Yes, the one-cent coin should be eliminated.

d) Canadians could be a few steps closer to where they need to be, without the hassle from that useless, problematic penny.

e) Should the one-cent coin be eliminated?

Exercise 4.2

From the following groups of sentences, choose the one that would make an appropriate topic sentence for the other sentences in the group:

1. a) The various meanings of words are explained in dictionary entries.

b) Dictionaries are useful tools for students.

c) Students can check their spelling by consulting a dictionary.

d) Useful grammatical and usage information is given in word entries.

2. a) Doing the assigned readings before class is essential for success in university.

Exercise 4.2 – *continued*

    b) If students have not read the assigned reading, the lecture
       will mean little to them.
    c) When students do the reading at home, they can look up
       words or concepts they find difficult.
    d) Students learn the material more easily through repeated
       exposure—from both reading and listening.

3. a) Parents give their children an allowance and let them
       choose how to spend it.
    b) Children are encouraged to try different activities to see
       where their interests and talents lie.
    c) Canadian parents raise their children to be independent as
       adults.
    d) Children are encouraged to make their own decisions,
       starting with choosing what to wear when they are
       preschoolers.

4. a) Novels allow students to exercise their imagination,
       picturing characters and settings in their mind.
    b) High school students need to read more novels in their
       English courses.
    c) Novels expose students to other worlds and times,
       broadening their view of life.
    d) Students develop good reading skills by following a long,
       involved story.

5. a) Just like a fish that cannot comprehend what water is,
       people cannot really understand their culture unless they
       experience another one.
    b) If students see people who live with far less, they will learn
       to appreciate what they have.
    c) Students can improve their communication skills while
       travelling even if they do not speak other languages.
    d) Travelling abroad is a vital part of education.

Exercise 4.3

The following paragraphs lack topic sentences (and concluding
sentences). Choose the best topic sentence from the choices given:

1. _____ *b* _____ First, students must
   really want to study the particular subject. If they are forced to
   take a course they do not like, they will not do as well. On the

Exercise 4.3 – *continued*

other hand, a liking for a subject fosters an interest that will motivate students to do extra reading and learn all they can. In addition, students need motivation to stick to the work when it is difficult. It is human nature to do only what is easy, but course work can be very difficult, and only the most motivated students persevere. Finally, motivation means that students have their eyes on the ultimate goal—a diploma, certificate, or degree. They understand the big picture and can see how everything fits together. They are more likely to put up with the parts of the program that they do not like as much. They are willing to make sacrifices to achieve their goal.

a) Finishing a college program is very difficult.
b) The most important factor in academic success is motivation.
c) If students enjoy a subject, they will read more about it.
d) Sometimes college students have to take compulsory courses that they do not like.

2. _____ d _____ If children have too many organized activities, they have no downtime to relax. They need time to goof off and just be kids. Second, they should not be dependent on others to entertain them. Boredom can spur children on to create their own games. For example, a large cardboard box can become the castle in a game of medieval knights. Furthermore, when children play games that are not controlled by adults, they learn to compromise and negotiate with others. There is no adult intervening to tell them how to play or how to interact.

a) Children are often bored.
b) Our modern technological society is not good for children.
c) Parents hate it when their children complain about being bored.
d) Children need free, unstructured time.

3. _____ b _____ Hoarders are obsessive about collecting things. Some of these items might be quite useless. For example, some people keep every flyer that is delivered to their house or every plastic bag they bring home from shopping. Hoarders cannot bear to throw things out. They are emotionally attached to their collections and feel like a part of them is being ripped away. Finally, hoarding is clearly an illness because sufferers cannot live normal lives. Their homes become huge messes that are unsanitary and unsafe.

One famous hoarder, Langley Collyer, died in 1947 when some of the mountains of junk in his home fell on top of him. It took a month to find him because literally tons of stuff had to be removed from the house to clear the way.

a) Everybody likes to collect things.
b) Excessive hoarding is a psychological disorder.
c) People today don't know how to properly clean their homes.
d) Our society produces too much stuff.

4. _____ C _____ Euchre is played with two teams of two, so it provides a good social grouping. Working with a partner fosters both cooperation and competition. The games are short, so partners can switch and not be stuck with someone for a long time. Because players get only five cards each, the hands are played quickly and require less concentration, unlike Bridge. Therefore, players can chat more during the games. Euchre offers the right balance of challenge and fun.

a) Euchre is a difficult card game to play, but it is a lot of fun.
b) Bridge is too difficult a card game to enjoy.
c) Euchre is one of the best card games for social interaction.
d) Playing cards is a good way to spend time with others.

5. _____ a _____ The music puts them in their own little world, with its own soundtrack. The earbuds or headphones prevent them from hearing what is going on around them and act as a signal to other people—"do not disturb." People are less likely to start a conversation or offer a bit of small talk to people with music players.

a) Portable music players are one more way that people cut themselves off from personal contact.
b) Today, many people walk around with portable music players.
c) Teenagers today are going to suffer hearing loss because of their music players.
d) MP3 players are a great way to carry music around all day.

Exercise 4.4

In groups, generate three topic sentences for possible paragraphs in each of the following subject areas:

1. A problem that needs to be addressed at your school (such as parking or the registration process)
2. Benefits of sport
3. Pets
4. Driver's licences
5. Video games

Making Points

The topic sentence introduces the main idea that is being put forth in the paragraph. That main idea is argued with several points. In the paragraph below, three arguments (marked in boldface) support the idea that teenagers are the main movie-goers:

> Teenagers are the most desirable market for movie producers. They are more likely than any other age group to spend their entertainment dollar on the cinema. **First, teenagers go to the movies as their main social activity.** They are old enough to go out on their own but too young for other social activities such as bar-hopping. They even go to see movies they are not that interested in simply because their friends are going, and they might see a movie more than once. **Moreover, teenagers prefer the theatre as a more enjoyable environment for movies.** They get out from under their parents' watchful eyes and appreciate the full effects of a large screen and superior sound system. Their parents, on the other hand, often prefer to cocoon at home and wait for the DVD. **Finally, teenagers have disposable income to spend at the cinema.** They often have allowances and part-time jobs but do not have to pay for rent or tuition, unlike college and university students. It is not surprising that so many movies today are aimed at teenagers' tastes.

The points made should relate directly to the topic sentence and should have the same focus. The points should be supportable yet more specific than the topic sentence. For example, for the topic sentence "Part-time jobs can be very beneficial to students," your points should say **why** part-time jobs are good and should focus on the students' point of view, not the employers' or the parents'. Consider the following sentences as points for this topic sentence:

Topic sentence: Part-time jobs can be very beneficial to students.

a) Students generally work at low-wage jobs as servers in restaurants. [does not show a benefit]
b) Students can gain many benefits from part-time jobs. [just repeats the main idea of the topic sentence]
c) Employers can pay students less money. [a benefit for employers, not students]
d) Students can learn useful skills on the job.
e) Students have to learn to manage their time efficiently to balance both work and school. [a requirement, not a benefit]
f) Part-time jobs are an important source of income for students.
g) Handling customers is an important part of many entry jobs. [related to a benefit but not the actual benefit]
h) Students eventually have to enter the work world. [does not show the connection to part-time jobs]
i) Students who work gain valuable work experience.
j) It is difficult for students to afford tuition and the cost of living. [shows the reason why students need money but does not focus on benefits of working]

Sentences d, f, and i give the reasons why part-time jobs are useful. Each of these points would be supported with examples and explanations, as shown in the next section on supporting points.

Exercise 4.5

For the topic sentence, choose three sentences that would make the best points for that paragraph:

Cooking a meal from scratch is a worthwhile skill to acquire.   b dg

a) Cooking is a lost skill.
b) Home-cooked meals are more nutritious.
c) People eat too much junk food.
d) Cooking at home is less expensive than eating out.
e) Many prepared foods are available in grocery stores.
f) Few people can cook today.
g) Cooking is useful for entertaining and impressing guests.
h) Cooking is not very difficult to learn.

Supporting Points

When you make a point, you have to support it. Support means giving the reader examples or explanations to make that point clear and to convince the reader of its validity. The supporting sentences are more specific than the point they are supporting. Note that restating a point is not supporting it.

Here are two kinds of support for a statement:

> Documents must be written for the intended audience. [argument]

> The level of vocabulary and the background given should reflect the knowledge the proposed reader has about the subject. [explanation]

> For example, a computer user manual should have simple instructions with no jargon. [example]

Here is an example of a paragraph in which the support is not specific enough:

> Hockey is the best sport to watch in the winter Olympics. First, it is very exciting. The action is fast-paced. Fans can watch what is happening and be very entertained. Second, it is a surprise as to who will win. Fans watch because the game could have any outcome. They do not know who will eventually win the game. Finally, hockey players are athletes playing at the top of their game. They have trained for many years, and they have many skills. It is exciting to watch skilled athletes. For these reasons, hockey is the not-to-be-missed event of the Olympics. [note that the arguments and supporting statements are so general that they could apply to any sport]

Consider again the suggested outline for an independent, developed paragraph:

> Topic sentence
>> Elaboration of topic sentence (if necessary)
>
> Point 1
>> Support (explanation, example, illustration)
>
> Point 2
>> Support (explanation, example, illustration)
>
> Point 3
>> Support (explanation, example, illustration)
>
> Concluding sentence

For the topic sentence "Canadians can do much to reduce environmental harm in their everyday practices," here are three possible points:

1. First, they can reduce the amount of garbage they produce.
2. Canadians can also limit their use of resources.
3. They can safeguard the water supply.

In a developed paragraph, points such as these generally have from one to three sentences in support. For this example on the environment, a reader would expect that each of these three points be followed by statements that explain how Canadians can do this. Discuss how this is accomplished in the following paragraph outline:

Canadians can do much to reduce environmental harm in their everyday practices.

1. First, they can reduce the amount of garbage they produce.

    They can choose products with less packaging, such as bulk food items.
    They can redirect items that they don't need, such as clothing, to recycling depots rather than throwing them into the garbage.

2. Canadians can also limit their use of resources.

    Driving smaller cars instead of J NSS reduces the amount of gasoline burned.
    They can use less electricity by converting to energy-saving appliances and by shutting off unnecessary lights.

3. Finally, they can safeguard the water supply.

    They should use water wisely, not watering their lawn unnecessarily or washing their cars excessively.
    They should not pour toxic waste down the toilet, sink, or sewer.

All Canadians must do their part to protect the environment.

Add a third supporting statement to each of the three arguments.

Exercise 4.6

Choose the sentence or group of sentences (a, b, or c) that makes the best support for the argument:

Topic sentence: Punctuality is important to success in college.

c 1. First, when students arrive on time for class, they create a good impression.
   a) They are less likely to miss important information and tests, and so their marks will be higher.
   b) They impress the teacher. The teacher will be quite satisfied with the impression the students make.
   c) They show that they are interested in the class and are prepared to work hard. Teachers are more likely to give breaks to such hardworking students.

b 2. In addition, students who are late often miss important information.
   a) A lot of important information is given at the beginning of class, and latecomers will lose out. That will result in a lower mark.
   b) For example, they may not get the feedback from the last assignment, which is often handed back first in class. They will also miss the explanation for that day's lesson.
   c) Sometimes there is a pop quiz at the beginning of class. Latecomers who miss it will get a mark of zero.

b 3. Finally, late students miss out on time given for tests and assignments.
   a) They show that they don't care about the test, so the instructor is less likely to take their work seriously.
   b) These students get a lower mark if they do not complete a test. Sometimes they might even miss a test entirely since pop quizzes are often given at the beginning of class.
   c) Tests are very important, and students need to pass these tests to pass the course. Every test mark counts and can make the difference between passing and failing the course.

Exercise 4.7

Academic writing usually moves from general to more specific statements. Pick the most general from the following statements:

b 1. a) College students do not have parents shepherding them through their schedules.

Exercise 4.7 – *continued*

    b) College students have to become self-sufficient when they
       strike out on their own.
    c) College students have to prepare their own meals.
    d) College students have to be responsible for rent, utilities,
       and transportation.

2. a) She won our neighbourhood Monopoly challenge.
   b) She is good at all sorts of games.
   c) She cleaned us all out in poker last night.
   d) She was always the leader of the children in the
      playground.

3. a) Smoking impairs your ability to breathe.
   b) Smoking is bad for your health.
   c) Smoking can lead to lung disease.
   d) Smoking makes your breath stink.

4. a) Contract work can lead to abuse of workers.
   b) Contract workers often receive no benefits.
   c) Contract workers have no job stability.
   d) Contract workers get paid less for the same work.

5. a) Some people put clothes on their pets.
   b) Some people sleep with their pets.
   c) Some people treat their pets like people.
   d) Some people pamper pets with spa treatments or doggie
      daycare.

Exercise 4.8

For the following pairs of sentences, write "For example" or "For
instance" in the blank if the second sentence is indeed an example:

1. Some tattoos show the qualities that people admire.
   _____, they may choose a Chinese character for
   'serenity' or 'joy'.

2. Many parents solve their children's problems, which does not
   help their children's self-confidence. _____, when
   the children grow up, they depend on other people to solve
   their problems.

Exercise 4.8 – *continued*

3. Public transit has several advantages. _____, less polluting exhaust is produced by buses or trains than by individual vehicles.

4. Students need to develop time management skills to prepare for tests. _____, teachers can help by showing how to take notes.

5. One advantage of resort weddings is that the couple and the guests get a vacation. _____, they get time off work and spend it at the resort.

6. One advantage of destination weddings is that the couple and the guests get a vacation. _____, they could spend a week at a luxury resort on a Caribbean island.

7. People sleep better if they wind down before they go to bed. _____, instead of watching television or using the computer, they could read or listen to restful music.

Exercise 4.9

In pairs or small groups, write one or two sentences to support each of these general statements. Compare your answers with your classmates':

1. Students need good study habits to succeed in college. (What habits?)

2. Job candidates need to prepare for an interview. (How?)

3. Hiking in the wilderness can be dangerous. (Why?)

4. Board games can teach children valuable skills. (What skills?)

5. Students can furnish their first apartment very cheaply. (How?)

6. Fashionable clothes are often impractical. (Give examples.)

7. Cellphones are useful in emergencies. (Give examples.)

8. Superstitions can cause people to change their regular routine. (How?)

Writing Concluding Sentences

If you are writing a single-paragraph writing assignment, your paragraph should have a concluding sentence to tie it all up. Generally, the concluding sentence echoes the topic sentence—giving essentially the same main idea but not repeating it in the same words. A body paragraph in an essay or report does not necessarily need to be wrapped up in a concluding sentence. Shorter paragraphs do not need a concluding sentence because the topic sentence is probably still fresh in the reader's mind.

Note the concluding sentence (marked in boldface) in the following paragraph:

> Although working part-time can create a serious time crunch, high school students should consider the many advantages of having a job. The most important consideration is the money. The cost of such desired items as a cellphone or designer clothing can exceed a teenager's allowance. More importantly, however, many students must start saving for their post-secondary education. In addition, part-time jobs give students a taste of the working world. With this taste, they can find out what jobs suit their personality and talents. For instance, they can learn whether they like dealing with the public. They also learn how hard it is to work, especially in minimum-wage jobs. This gives them a greater appreciation for the work itself and for the education required to get a better job. Finally, in the workplace, students gain valuable skills. These skills include practical ones, such as working with cash or answering the telephone and soft skills, such as communication strategies and working as a team. **Therefore, students who can handle the load should work part-time to reap the many benefits of a job.**

Activity

Examine the concluding sentences in the sample paragraphs in this unit. Consider how they differ from the topic sentences.

Go back to Exercise 4.3 and write a concluding sentence for each paragraph.

Exercise 4.10

Here are some topic sentences, some of which are from previous exercises in this chapter. Write a concluding sentence that could complete the paragraph. Use the same basic idea as in the topic sentence, but do not use the same wording.

1. Punctuality is an important part of success in college.

Exercise 4.10 – *continued*

2. Electronic books are less convenient than the paper format.
3. Survival swimming skills should be taught to all children.
4. Travelling abroad is a vital part of education.
5. Cooking a meal from scratch is a worthwhile skill to acquire.
6. The weather is a safe topic of conversation for small talk.

Achieving Unity

A paragraph should have unity—it should have one main idea. The topic sentence sets out this main idea, and all the other sentences should fit under the umbrella of the topic sentence. For example, a paragraph that begins "Part-time jobs can be very beneficial to students" should only have sentences that explain why part-time jobs are good for students. It should not contain sentences that give the disadvantages of working or explain how to find a job.

Exercise 4.11

Identify the two sentences that do not fit in this paragraph:

ESL students can benefit from reading children's fairy tales. First, reading is the best way to improve general language skills because it exposes students to both language and ideas. The simpler vocabulary and sentence structure of children's books make them accessible to ESL students and allow them to build their reading skills gradually. Modern novels are also good reading practice because students have to follow a complex plot with a variety of characters. Second, fairy tales are part of the culture, and ESL students need to be familiar with these stories to understand references in film and other literature. For example, psychology books may refer to a person exhibiting a Cinderella complex. The characters are well-known and can appear in movies, in modern novels, or even in newspaper articles. For instance, a politician's situation might be described as "the emperor's new clothes," a reference to a story by Hans Christian Andersen. Andersen was a Dane who had an unhappy childhood but gained a measure of fame with the stories he wrote. Furthermore, the fantastical worlds of magic, witches, and elves can be entertaining. The popularity of these tales has survived over centuries to modern incarnations such as the Harry Potter books. Rather than dismissing fairy tales as juvenile reading, ESL students should seek them out as supplemental reading.

Exercise 4.12

Choose which sentences would fit under the topic sentence:

The economics of professional sport is detrimental to the fan base.

1. Games often start later in the evening so that they can be broadcast in the more lucrative prime-time spots even though that is often too late for younger viewers.

2. Violence should be better controlled in games so that it does not set a bad example for children.

3. The pace of baseball is too slow for fans accustomed to fast action.

4. Free agents switch teams as they chase bigger salaries, so fans have trouble staying loyal to certain players.

5. Games are paused so that broadcasters can insert commercial breaks.

6. Professional athletes often sign multi-million-dollar endorsement contracts.

7. High salaries of players are often reflected in higher ticket prices.

8. Athletes demand higher salaries not because they need the money but because it is part of a competition—the best-paid athlete is considered the best athlete.

9. Games are less interesting to watch when the team with all the high-priced talent is generally the one that wins.

10. Fans of small-market teams are often in danger of losing their teams to bigger cities.

11. Expansion of leagues requires more players, diluting the talent pool.

12. Only billionaires can afford to buy sports franchises.

13. Owners are not motivated to improve a team as long as it is making money.

14. Amateur athletes are struggling to survive on very little money.

15. Canadians cannot live without hockey.

Using Transition Signals

Writers need to help readers follow the development of their ideas. To this end, they use transition markers or signals—words and expressions that introduce a sentence to show how the sentence relates to other sentences.

For example, a phrase such as *for example* tells readers that the sentence is an example of the point made in the previous sentence. Just as signals on a car tell the drivers behind where the driver is going, the signals in a paragraph tell readers where the ideas are going so they can follow them.

Here are some common transition signals:

Addition: also, finally, first, furthermore, in addition, moreover, next, second

Cause and effect: accordingly, as a result, consequently, therefore, thus

Comparison: likewise, similarly

Contrast: however, in contrast, instead, nevertheless, on the contrary, on the other hand, otherwise

Emphasis or clarity: in fact, indeed, in other words, of course, that is

Special features or examples: for example, for instance, in particular, mainly, specifically

Summary: in brief, in closing, in conclusion, in short, on the whole, to conclude, to summarize

Time relations: afterwards, at that time, earlier, in the meantime, lately, later, meanwhile, now, then

Most of these expressions function as adverbs and are sometimes called conjunctive adverbs or adverbial connectors. It is important to distinguish them from conjunctions such as *although* and *but* so that you join sentences correctly. (This grammar point is discussed in "Writing Adverb Clauses" in Unit 2.)

Here are some examples of transition signals at work. Note that in the following pairs of sentences, the second pair includes a transition signal, making it easier to follow the meaning:

I went through the paper files to scan the older documents into the system. I weeded out the out-of-date papers and checked the accuracy of the information in the system.

I went through the paper files to scan the older documents into the system. At the same time, I weeded out the out-of-date papers and checked the accuracy of the information in the system.

Essay writing helps students develop their thinking skills. They have to understand the relationship between a general idea and a specific example.

Essay writing helps students develop their thinking skills. For instance, they have to understand the relationship between a general idea and a specific example.

Smokers should have the right to decide whether they poison their own bodies or not. They cannot make that choice for the others whom they affect with second-hand smoke.

Smokers should have the right to decide whether they poison their own bodies or not. However, they cannot make that choice for the others whom they affect with second-hand smoke.

Exercise 4.13

Write an appropriate transition signal in each blank:

1. Computer games can give children an opportunity to exercise their problem-solving skills. _____, in a strategy game, children have to work through different scenarios to make the most advantageous move.

2. Many drivers exhibit unnecessary aggressive behaviour on the highway. Some tailgate trying to make other drivers speed up or move out of the way. _____, some drivers weave in and out of lanes looking for any space to advance.

3. Disney movies often have "happily ever after" endings even when the source material is a tragedy. _____, in the Hans Christian Andersen story "The Little Mermaid," the mermaid dies at the end, while in the Disney cartoon she marries the prince.

4. We worked together to paint the room efficiently: Jack used the roller to cover the large surfaces. _____ I used a brush to cut in around the trim and the corners.

5. I missed the class when our instructor taught us how to do a summary. _____, I did not do well on the summary test.

6. The Canadian team was considered a favourite for the championship. _____, the odds changed when a few of the top players were injured.

7. The United States is the most powerful country in the world. _____, it is understandable that many underdog countries feel resentment towards Americans.

Exercise 4.13 – *continued*

8. The story of Laura Secord warning the British troops of an American attack includes many myths. _____, one version says she led a cow through the swamp.

9. A post-secondary education costs students thousands of dollars. _____, graduates can expect greater income.

10. Reading children's books is good reading practice because the stories have simpler ideas, structures, and vocabulary. _____, children's books teach about the culture.

11. First, he went to the bank to withdraw some cash. _____ he went to bargain with the person selling the bike.

12. Modern technology is supposed to improve communication between people. _____, people tend to email strangers across the world rather than actually talk to their next-door neighbour.

Achieving Coherence

The sentences in a paragraph must fit together in a logical, coherent manner. The word *cohere* means "to stick together." Coherence is achieved by the order of the sentences, by the use of transition signals to show the reader how the ideas connect, by the use of pronouns to refer back to nouns in a previous sentence, and by the repetition of words and ideas.

Readers can follow a paragraph better when the ideas are in an order they are familiar with. For instance, a paragraph describing the history of something would most likely be in chronological order. Sub-topics should be dealt with one at a time. For instance, in the paragraph on the benefits of part-time jobs (p. 131), both financial reasons are dealt with together, at the beginning.

Another way to achieve coherence is through the use of transition signals, like *for example* and *in addition*. The use of these signals is shown in the previous section.

Pronouns refer to a specific noun and help to link sentences:

> Andrew had to get his project approved. It [refers to the project] was an orientation film in which he [Andrew] needed to interview first-year students. They [the students] would discuss the problems they had faced.

Demonstrative pronouns (such as *this* and *these*) also help to link sentences:

> Fairy tales, folk tales, and myths are important parts of children's books. **These stories** teach a cultural heritage that is built upon in other kinds of literature.

Remember that in English, an indefinite article is usually used the first time something is mentioned, and then a definite article is used. This grammatical structure also helps readers follow the ideas:

> We wrote **a report** at the end of our project. **The report** summarized our problems and how we overcame them.

Repeating key words, or using synonyms to refer to them, is another way to ensure coherence in a paragraph:

> Luxury **cars** are a waste of money. While these **vehicles** are comfortable and well-made, they are too expensive to purchase, maintain, and insure. Drivers really just need a car to get them safely from point A to point B. The powerful engine of a **luxury car** is useless when a driver is stuck in a traffic jam or restricted by speed limits.

Exercise 4.14

Here is a disassembled paragraph to put back together. Determine which sentence is the topic sentence and which is the concluding sentence. Identify each point and its supporting sentence(s). Once you have put the sentences in an order you find works well, make the paragraph coherent by adding transition markers, combining sentences, using pronouns, and making other changes to smooth out the sentences.

1. The piece of music should appeal to a wide audience, not just the cellphone user.
2. The ring tone should be easy to distinguish.
3. Phone owners should be able to hear it over background noise.
4. An urban cowboy answers a phone playing country music.
5. Instead of just choosing a ring tone in a cellphone that is catchy, people should make sure it is appropriate.
6. The ring tone should not be annoying.

Exercise 4.14 – *continued*

7. No adult wants a phone that sounds like a cutesy cartoon character singing, especially in a business situation.

8. Often phones ring at inappropriate times, and having one that repeats a name or phrase, such as "Harold, pick up the phone," would just make the situation more embarrassing.

9. Phone owners should be able to identify it as their own phone ringing.

10. The ring tone should be pleasing to listen to.

11. The ring tone should project the right image.

12. While cellphones can be individualized to a certain extent, the ring tone is the most public aspect of that personalization.

13. The image should also relate to the user.

Sample Paragraphs

Examine the paragraphs below, reviewing the features of a good paragraph as you read. Compare the topic sentence and concluding sentence of each. Identify the points made to prove the main idea and the specific examples or explanations used to support the points. Identify transition signals and other methods used to achieve coherence.

> Students who enrol in college should choose a career path based on their own interests and talents rather than on a job's earning potential. One reason is that people spend a large part of their lives at work, and it is wrong to waste precious hours of life doing something they do not enjoy. Second, if they choose a career in an area where they are talented, they will probably achieve more. For example, an accountant who wishes she had followed her passion for music will probably not be as successful in her job as someone who actually enjoys working with numbers. Finally, the job market is unpredictable. For example, a diploma in computer programming used to be considered a guaranteed ticket to economic success, but with the high-tech bust, many programmers found themselves unemployed and forced to reinvent themselves in other fields. Thus, high school graduates should follow their passions when they choose a career.

More than a necessary chore, shopping is a good way to spend leisure time. First, instead of sitting at home in front of the TV, shoppers get exercise walking around the stores. Shopping can also be a social activity, a bonding experience. For example, young women enjoy getting together to survey the new merchandise and serve as each other's fashion consultants. Third, living in our material world requires education. Savvy consumers have to learn about products and prices. Spending time in a mall allows shoppers to comparison-shop and to get information from different salespeople. Finally, and most important, shopping is enjoyable. Shoppers can gaze at colourful displays, watch other shoppers, stop for a coffee or a snack, listen to mall music, and imagine how all the high-tech goodies and trendy clothes will make their lives better. It is no wonder that so many people today view shopping as a pleasant pastime.

People who choose to spend their free time shopping are misguided. Shopping is the curse of the modern consumer world, not a leisure activity. First, buying merchandise is stressful. Shoppers have to choose how to spend their hard-earned dollars on a bewildering array of items, including models with practically imperceptible differences. Getting the best price requires hard work, patience, and good luck. While some people argue that shopping is good exercise, the benefits are negligible. Instead of taking a brisk walk in fresh air, shoppers meander about the crowded aisles, spending much of their time standing around looking at items or waiting for service. Worst of all, the fact that so many people spend so much time shopping shows that our society has degraded to the lowest level of materialism. We care more about buying things than spending time with our family and friends in worthwhile pursuits. The evils of shopping cannot be avoided, but the activity should be limited to buying the bare necessities.

Family dinner
Activity
The following paragraphs are all on the same topic—the family meal. Read the paragraphs and examine the structure and language of each paragraph. Look at the main idea in the topic sentence, and identify the points made and the supporting sentences. Determine the approach of each paragraph. For example, is the paragraph discussing causes, effects, or solutions? Is it descriptive? Is it a comparison? Does it describe a process? Can you deter-

mine what topic question might have generated the paragraph? Determine the style of each paragraph—is it personal, conversational, or academic?

Compare the paragraphs. See how the same information can be given differently for a different purpose. You can also compare these paragraphs to an essay on the same topic on page 150–1.

A) The shared family meal is yet another casualty of the hectic modern lifestyle. We do not take the time to sit down to dinner together. One reason is our complicated schedules. Children's after-school and evening hours are filled with sports and music lessons. When they reach the teenage years, these activities are replaced by part-time jobs. Parents not only work long hours, but their return home may also be delayed because of a long commute. As a result, family members often eat separately. Moreover, a sit-down meal requires time to prepare and to consume. People do not want to devote that much time to what they consider a simple act of fuelling their bodies. Finally, many lack the culinary skills to make nutritious and appealing meals. They rely on restaurant take-out and processed foods from the supermarket. It is not surprising that suppliers of ready-to-eat food are doing such good business, and it does not look as though this trend will reverse itself any time soon. Family dining is obviously a thing of the past.

B) As our family sat down to Thanksgiving dinner, I enjoyed the sight of the gathering of the clan for the traditional meal. The whole extended family, all 17 of us, came dressed in Sunday best. My grandfather sported his favourite bowtie, and the younger girl cousins had new dresses to show off. The main table was set with the best linen, china, and crystal, and the centrepiece of gourds and autumn foliage proclaimed the season. The children's table was at the end of the formal dining table, but it looked festive even with the orange polyester tablecloth and everyday dishes. After saying grace, we passed the dishes around the table. Everyone had contributed to the meal: Grandma had cooked the turkey, and Grandpa had carved it. Uncle Garth had brought his special wild cranberry sauce. Aunt Judy's vegetable medley tempted even the most determined of broccoli haters. My mother's pumpkin pie topped with dollops of whipped cream was the traditional dessert. It was a scene played out every year, but I never get tired of it.

C) A shared meal is an important family ritual, worth nurturing and keeping alive even in the fast-paced lives of the twenty-first century. First, families who take the time to dine together are generally eating healthier foods. They are not gobbling down a slice of pizza before running off to a night class or music lesson. Families who value mealtime usually take care with the food itself—making sure it is nutritious and tasty. In addition, the family meal is an opportunity for learning. Children can help prepare and serve the meal, thus acquiring practical cooking skills. They can also learn social skills, such as proper table etiquette, that will serve them well in their future business lunches. Finally, a family meal is above all a time for family members to touch base and talk about what is happening in their daily lives. At the end of the school and work day, the family can sit down together and share what happened that day as they eat their evening meal. Families that eat together have stronger bonds because the shared meal is a uniting element in family life.

D) My mother always insists on a family dinner at least once a week. Us kids all want to rush off somewhere that night, but oh no, I can't schedule that last-minute study and gabfest on Sunday—I have to eat with my family. More than simply showing up and stuffing our faces, however, we have to cooperate in both making and cleaning up the food. As long as I don't have to do dishes! I can't stand getting my fingers all pruney. During the dinner we have to talk: "How was your day?" "You know already, Mom. I spent two hours peeling potatoes." "Anything new with your friends?" "I don't know—I couldn't see them tonight." By the end, however, we always end up talking animatedly about politics or news stories. I get half my Current Events quiz answers from Sunday night. I find I know more about cooking than my friends and feel immensely superior when I exclaim "What? You've *never* peeled a potato?"

E) Over the past three generations, the eating habits of Canadians have changed dramatically. In the past, mealtimes were generally regular, and families often sat down to share a meal together. Today's busy families rarely find the time to eat together; people grab a bite to eat when they can and often eat alone, sometimes taking their food to their bedrooms or eating in front of the TV. Instead of home-cooked meals, Canadians today eat more processed foods and restaurant meals. Supermarkets stock a variety of prepared foods— from frozen dinners to deli meals. The growth of fast-food restaurants shows how important they have become to family life. The types of foods Canadians eat have also changed because of the greater variety of ethnic food available. They used to have very conservative tastes, sticking to the food they knew from home. Now Canadians of all ethnic backgrounds consume Italian pasta, Chinese stir fries, Greek souvlaki, Thai noodles, Tex-Mex tacos, and Middle Eastern hummus. Moreover, fruits and vegetables are shipped in from all over the world, so Canadians are not restricted by what is locally in season. Our food and the way we eat it is in line with the way we prefer to live our lives.

F) Even with today's hectic lifestyle, it is possible to reap the benefits of a shared family meal. First, it is important to acknowledge the importance of the family dinner and to schedule time for it. This may mean cutting down on some activities. At the very least, Sunday dinner should be set aside as family time. Second, if the meal is planned ahead of time, it will go more smoothly. The menu should be decided on and groceries should be bought beforehand. In addition, the work should be shared. If it is up to only one person to do all the preparation, the meal does become more of a chore. Children can start helping with food preparation at a very young age—washing vegetables, for example. Working together not only lessens the workload, it allows family members to talk together and to acquire cooking skills. Furthermore, for the meal to be an important part of family life, it must be acknowledged as a time for discussion. Parents should be careful not to nag but to listen to their children's concerns. Talk about political and social issues can pass on moral values and increase awareness of current events. Proper table etiquette can be taught at the same time. Finally, the family should share cleanup responsibilities. By working, talking, and eating together, families can forge strong bonds and foster communication.

Practice Paragraphs

Here are some suggestions for paragraph writing topics. Some are general topics, which you have to develop into a specific idea to explore in your paragraph, while others are specific questions. Be sure to make your focus clear in your topic sentence.

1. Choose one of the topics you generated with your group in Exercise 4.4 (page 124).
2. Boomerang children (you can use the ideas from the topic sentences on page 117 or use a different focus)

3. What is the best way (or the wrong way) to break up with a boyfriend or girlfriend? (Consider the turkey dump [p. 116] or break-ups by email or Facebook as examples.)
4. Disagree with the idea that the family dinner is important.
5. Explain one problem with using electronic books as textbooks.
6. How should young adults deal with over-protective parents?
7. Should the one-cent coin be eliminated?
8. Choose one common part-time job for students, and explain either the practical skills or the soft skills the job requires.
9. What is the best sport to watch at the Olympics?

Paragraph Recap

For single-paragraph writing assignments:

*   start with a topic sentence that clearly delineates the main idea of your paragraph;
*   give two to four arguments for that main idea;
*   support each argument with explanation or examples;
*   use transition signals to show the relationship between ideas;
*   make sure your paragraph has unity (one main idea);
*   make sure your paragraph has coherence (all the ideas flow logically);
*   check your paragraph for grammar, spelling, punctuation, and style.

Essay Writing Skills

Essays are essentially arguments. The word essay comes from the French word meaning "to try." The writer tries to show or prove something to the reader. The audience for students' essays is their professor or teacher. The purpose is purely academic; instead of giving new information (the purpose of most written communication), student essay writers are charged with the task of showing what they have learned, synthesizing information, and explaining the thesis in a way that shows their understanding of the subject. Students are being tested on both their thinking and their communication skills, so essay writing requires logical organization of ideas.

Understanding Essay Structure

The essay structure often taught in school is the five-paragraph essay. It has an introduction, three body paragraphs, and a conclusion. Even though this type of essay is rarely seen outside the classroom, the form is adaptable to other kinds of writing. Business reports, for example, are longer than five paragraphs, but they too have an introduction, a body divided into different ideas, and a conclusion. Most importantly, the five-paragraph essay model can be expanded by simply adding paragraphs to the three basic sections.

In a five-paragraph essay, the first paragraph is the introduction. It provides background for the reader, gets the reader's attention, and prepares the way for the thesis statement. The thesis gives the main argument of the essay and comes at the end of the introduction.

The thesis statement is supported in the three body paragraphs. The arguments are divided so that each paragraph has a different main idea. The body paragraphs start with a topic sentence giving the main idea of that paragraph. A good body paragraph has support for the points made, has unity (only one main idea), is coherent (the sentences flow and follow logically), and has transition markers (to signal the relationship between ideas). These aspects were explained in Unit 4.

The conclusion generally starts with a restatement of the thesis and goes on to give a "so what?" idea to lead the reader back out of the essay. The conclusion should not give new ideas to support the thesis. In a short essay, the conclusion should not summarize the essay because it would be too repetitive.

Sometimes this type of essay is referred to as a "hamburger essay," with the introduction and conclusion serving as the bun holding the meat of the essay (the body) together. This analogy simply tells students that the body of the essay is the most important part.

Comparing the paragraph and the essay

Unit 4 focuses on the structure of a paragraph. An independent, developed paragraph is like a mini–essay. Moving from paragraph writing to essay writing is not difficult. You need to expand on ideas and write introductory and concluding paragraphs. Compare this independent paragraph and the five-paragraph essay on the same topic that follows:

Even with the wide variety of prepared foods available today, cooking is a worthwhile skill for anyone to have. Most important, home-cooked foods are more nutritious. Processed foods contain high amounts of salt, sugar, and fat. People who cook at home have control over the ingredients. They can tailor the dishes to their family's tastes and avoid any food to which someone may be allergic. Second, being able to cook is a useful social skill. Inviting friends over for dinner is a time-honoured method of entertaining. In Canada, home-cooking has an added dimension when immigrants can share their ethnic foods with people of a different ethnic background. For example, many Canadians would love to try home-cooked Chinese food rather than the typical restaurant fare of sweet 'n sour chicken balls. Finally, knowing how to cook is an important part of self-sufficiency. As much as possible, people should be able to take care of themselves and not rely on others. Cooking is not difficult, and people who cannot even boil water are pitiful. People should start learning to cook when they are children, but it is never too late to start learning. [191 words]

The Value of Home-Cooking

With the modern busy lifestyle, people seek to save time in meal preparation. They often eat out, whether at fast-food places or upscale restaurants. They buy prepared foods from the deli counter of the supermarket or frozen meals that just have to be warmed up in the microwave. As a result, cooking is becoming a lost skill. While it is possible to survive without knowing one end of a chef's knife from the other, the ability to prepare a home-cooked meal is a valuable skill.

The most obvious benefit of home-cooking is the ability to control the quality of the food. Processed foods contain high amounts of sugar, salt, and additives, while fast food is high in fat. Cooks choose their own raw ingredients and control the seasonings, so they can ensure freshness and make the dishes to their taste. This is especially important for people with allergies or restricted diets. An added benefit is the lowered cost. Cooks provide their own labour and can thus spend more on superior ingredients. The same quality of food would not be found outside of expensive restaurants.

Cooking is also a valuable social skill. Hosting a dinner party is a time-honoured method of entertaining guests. Even for casual get-togethers, it is gratifying to be able to serve food that is homemade. In the dating game, moreover, cooking is useful. It is said that the way to a man's heart is through his stomach, but women are also attracted to men who are handy in the kitchen. Parents may also expect their adult children to cook well enough to contribute to holiday dinners and to carry on their family traditions. For immigrant families, preparing ethnic foods is a way to keep their native culture alive.

In addition to the social rewards, cooking has psychological benefits. People can feel personal satisfaction when they produce a delicious meal. Self-sufficiency is a goal in itself because it is humiliating to have to admit to an inability to provide the basic necessities of life. Cooks can also exercise their creativity: They can tweak recipes and even develop new flavour combinations. Working with food takes people back to nature, especially when they avoid modern gadgets in favour of working by hand. For example, kneading bread dough and beating cream can relieve stress as well as give muscles a workout.

These many benefits of cooking show that it is still an important skill despite the proliferation of restaurants. Even people who grew up in homes devoid of the heady aroma of home-cooking are turning to the kitchen. The popularity of cooking shows on television, how-to videos on YouTube, and expensive, illustrated cookbooks shows that cooking is not entirely disappearing from modern life. If foodies can convert more people to the benefits of home cooking, everyone will live better. [470 words]

Planning an Essay

An essay requires more planning than an independent paragraph. Writers must make sure that the essay is well-balanced. For example, the three body paragraphs should be approximately the same length. Each paragraph should have different ideas with no repetition or overlap.

Writing is generally a three-stage process: planning, drafting, and editing. The planning stage includes researching, thinking about the topic, brainstorming ideas, and putting together an outline. The drafting stage is when the actual writing is done. The final stage involves rereading the draft, revising, editing, proofreading, and correcting. However, writing does not always proceed in such a clear-cut way. For instance, writers may revisit the outline once they start writing because they think of a better way to organize it. People who compose on a computer may find their essay evolves from their brainstorming with less of a progression from one step to another.

Students often spend too little time in the first and third stages; they rush to get words on paper without thinking about how they want to develop their ideas, and they are too easily satisfied with what they have written, reluctant to delete sections that do not work or to proofread carefully to catch mistakes. Granted, students are often put into writing situations in which they do not have the luxury of time to plan or edit. If they are required to write a 500-word essay in an hour, they must concentrate on getting words down as quickly as possible. However, if they have practised writing an essay with the three stages, they can work more efficiently when they are under tight time constraints.

Choosing a topic

The first step is choosing a topic. Usually, teachers give their class a choice of topics, perhaps related to assigned readings or current events. Often the topics are discussed in class before students have to write about them. Students should pick the topic they are most comfortable with. They probably have choice within the topic, such as agreeing or disagreeing with a statement, or they may have to narrow the topic down. If students can generate their own topic, they should do this in consultation with their instructor because it is too easy to flounder without direction.

Here are some typical essay topics:

Describe an ideal job.

How can the use of public transit be increased?

What can be done to make post-secondary education more affordable?

Why do people get tattoos?

What are the benefits of married life as opposed to remaining single?

What factors determine how well an immigrant will adapt to life in Canada?

Activity

In groups, make a list of essay topics you would like to write about. Exchange your list for another group's, and rate the other group's list as to which topics you like the best and which the least.

Generating ideas

Before you start writing your essay, make sure you have enough to say. Indeed, if you find you do not have enough to say on one topic after you have brainstormed, then it is a good idea to go back to the topic choices and consider doing a different topic. One of the best ways to brainstorm is just to jot down point-form ideas about your topic. Consider the topic from different viewpoints. For example, if you are going to write about the advantages of wearing school uniforms, jot down points about the disadvantages at the same time. As you think of the disadvantages, you may think of counter-arguments that might fit in your "pro" essay. If you are asked to come up with a solution to a problem, make sure you spend enough time considering the problem itself and the different ramifications.

Here is an example of brainstorming on the topic "Explain the advantages or disadvantages of living in residence":

Advantages	Disadvantages
• less travelling to and from school	• always on campus with students, can't get away
• close to facilities on campus (gym, library)	• may have to live with people you don't know, can't choose roommates
• get to meet other students, not just classmates	• noisy because of student parties
• can be cheaper because you don't pay for 12 months accommodation	• can be more expensive per month
• don't have to cook for yourself	• may have to live on school cafeteria food, if no kitchen facilities

By brainstorming on both sides of the topic, students can then choose to write on the side for which they have more to say.

Brainstorming in this manner is an efficient way to start your essay writing process, but there are other ways of doing it. People who think visually may use bubble diagrams for their points with lines to connect related ideas. Free-writing is a method in which students just write what comes into their heads and then look through the writing for an argument they can develop. Some writers ask themselves questions about a topic ("Why does this happen?" "What can this lead to?" "Who is affected?") to generate ideas.

You may need to experiment to find out what works for you. Whichever method you use, it's important to think about the topic thoroughly to generate enough ideas to choose from and not just grab the first three random arguments that come to mind.

Activity

With your instructor and classmates, discuss the techniques you have found helpful for getting started with an essay or for getting past writer's block. Consider different ways of brainstorming.

Writing a title

A title is not always necessary, but writing one can help you start your essay. It gives you a perspective and helps you limit the scope of your paper. If you need a title for your essay, make sure it is an appropriate phrase. Do not just put the essay topic question on your cover page. Generally, titles are phrases, not full sentences or questions. For example, a story in this book is called "Why My Mother Can't Speak English" rather than "Why Can't My Mother Speak English?"

Newspaper articles have headlines rather than titles. These generally give the main idea. Short forms are common to save space. Often a telegraphic style is used, leaving out grammatical words such as articles and auxiliary verb. This style is not appropriate for essay titles.

Activity

In small groups, look over the titles of the sample essays in Units 5 and 6. In addition, look at the titles of the readings in Part 2 as listed in the table of contents. Discuss the titles. Which ones give you a good idea of the contents of the essay or article, and which do not?

Exercise 5.1

Write an appropriate essay title for the following topics:

1. Why are male children preferred in some Asian cultures? (Specify one country.)

2. Should religious schools be funded by the government?

3. What kind of adjustments do adult children and their parents have to make when the children move back home after college or university?

Exercise 5.1 – *continued*

4. What can people do in their everyday lives to lessen environmental damage?

5. What are the advantages of sending text messages over voice calls?

Writing an outline

An outline is a plan for an essay. Following the plan keeps you on track as you write. An outline can be very detailed or very simple. It can be written in full sentences or have point form. A basic outline for a five-paragraph essay would have the thesis and the three topic sentences; these sentences would be revised as you write the draft. You can also include the supporting points in your outline.

Here is an example of an outline, followed by the full essay:

Thesis: The family meal lets people share food, learn good behaviour, and spend time together.

1. Eating together:
   home-cooked, more nutritious food
   eating slowly
   variety of foods
   traditional foods

2. Good behaviour:
   table etiquette
   sharing chores

3. Time to talk:
   news to share about the day
   current events

The Family Meal

In today's hectic lifestyle, meals have become little more than pit stops. People grab something on the run, often fast food or processed foods, and rarely take the time to sit down and enjoy a meal together with the most important people in their lives—their families. However busy their lives become, they should take the time to gather together for meals. The family meal provides people with an opportunity to share food, learn good behaviour, and spend time together.

A meal is primarily about the food, and a shared family meal offers many health benefits. The food is generally more nutritious, since it is more likely to be home-cooked. It is usually consumed more slowly—which is also good for the digestive system. Children are introduced to foods they might not eat if they are accustomed to having individual meals. Shared dinners often feature food that is traditional to the family and its ethnic culture. Moreover, children may learn how to appreciate and prepare such foods.

The family meal also offers opportunities to learn good behaviour. Children can practise proper table etiquette when they share a relaxed meal at home rather than grabbing a burger at a drive-through. These good manners will serve them well later when they are attending business lunches or wedding receptions. The meal also offers a good opportunity for family members to share the chores of preparing and serving the meal and cleaning up afterward. Children who have learned to work together in this way grow up to be more considerate and less likely to sit around expecting to be waited on.

Finally, dinnertime is an occasion for enjoyable, relaxed conversation. Because the meal is at the end of the day, everyone will have news to share, so it is the best time for conversation. Children can tell what they learned at school, and parents can relate events from their workday. They can discuss current events and exchange opinions. They can even discuss problems and find solutions. Not only will they practise communication skills but also problem-solving techniques. With everyone leading such busy lives, a shared meal is a uniting element, giving family members an opportunity to communicate with one another.

The benefits of a shared family meal are so profound that people should not eliminate it from their lives, no matter how busy they get. Modern families must take a good hard look at their schedules and take some time off from business meetings, extracurricular activities, and clubs to spend time together as a family sharing a meal. Even if they find it impossible to arrange to eat together every evening, they should schedule a family meal once a week at the very least.

You can compare this essay to paragraph C on pages 140–1.

Exercise 5.2

Here are some brainstorming notes on the topic "What factors determine how much second-generation immigrants will maintain their mother tongue?" Arrange the ideas in three paragraphs. Write a topic sentence for each paragraph. Work with a partner or in a small group:

a) whether they attend language school for their mother tongue

b) how well their parents speak English

c) the birth order (oldest child versus youngest)

d) whether they visit their parents' native country

e) whether they live with or frequently visit grandparents who do not speak English

f) whether the children live in a community where many immigrants speak that language

g) the attitude of the second generation toward the ethnic culture

h) whether they can read and write in that language

i) how useful the language is for international business or travel

j) whether the parents encourage the children to speak the language

Writing a Thesis Statement

The thesis statement is the most important sentence in the essay. It comes at the end of the introduction. A thesis statement is a complete, concise, grammatical statement that presents a supportable idea that can be explored in the scope of the essay. The thesis gives the writer's viewpoint. It answers the question posed and narrows the topic. For instance, if the topic question is, "Should religious schools be funded?" a possible thesis would be "Public funding should be extended to all religious schools in Ontario." In addition, the thesis should be in the essay writer's own words and should not repeat the phrasing of the topic question.

A thesis statement should not be a fact:

The size of the average family grew during the baby boom. [poor thesis]

The baby boom had sociological, economic, and political effects in Canada. [better]

It should not present a personal opinion that cannot be argued:

> I like biking. [poor thesis]

> Biking is an enjoyable, healthy, and socially responsible activity. [better]

It should not be too broad for the essay:

> Teenagers face many problems growing up. [poor thesis]

> Children of immigrant parents have to deal with cultural differences. [better]

It should not be too narrow:

> Second-generation immigrants may not like the potential spouse picked out by their parents. [weak]

> Second-generation immigrants may not accept the idea of a traditional arranged marriage. [better]

It should not be an announcement:

> In this essay, I am going to compare big-box stores with independent businesses. [poor thesis]

> Independent stores offer knowledgeable service, good product choice, and shopping convenience. [better]

Note that a thesis statement is a complete, concise, grammatical statement. It cannot be a fragment:

> Working at home. [incorrect]

> Working at home offers several advantages over working in an office. [better]

It cannot be a question:

> What is the best way to stop teenagers from smoking? [incorrect]

> Anti-smoking campaigns need to be tailored to teenagers' concerns. [better]

It cannot be a command:

> Note the differences between King Lear and Macbeth. [incorrect]

> Shakespeare's King Lear and Macbeth are two very different rulers. [better]

It must be one statement, not four:

> Swimming pools in school are a good investment for three reasons. First, swimming is so important that all children should learn how to swim. Second, having pools on-site is very convenient for lessons. Third, the community can use the pool after school hours, making it more economical. [incorrect]

> Swimming pools in school are a good investment because of the need for basic swimming skills, the convenience of the on-site facility, and the potential for community use. [better]

If the thesis lists the arguments of the body paragraphs, it must have parallel structure (see page 84 for an explanation of parallel structure):

> The family meal means that people can share food, spending time together, and they can learn good behaviour at the table. [incorrect]

> The family meal provides people with an opportunity to share food, spend time together, and learn good behaviour at the table.

In a five-paragraph essay, the thesis statement may state the three main ideas to be discussed in the body, but in a longer essay this is not practical and a less specific thesis is presented:

> Teenagers often conflict with their parents on their social life, appearance, and household responsibilities. [good for a five-paragraph essay]

> Teenagers' relationship with their parents is often full of conflict. [good for a longer essay]

If the thesis statement lists the arguments of the body paragraphs, the thesis should be concise, with the three main ideas expressed in short phrases. Care must be taken to ensure that the sentence is grammatical, following parallel structure. In addition, the body paragraphs should explore the arguments in the same order that they are presented in the thesis statement.

Exercise 5.3

Choose which sentences would work best as a thesis statement. Explain why. Look for the statements that actually answer the question. Discuss why the statement is appropriate or not for a thesis.

Topic: In Canada, single adults now outnumber married ones. There is less pressure to get legally married today. Women are not financially dependent on men, and religious and social pressure to marry has diminished. Can marriage survive as a vital social institution?

a) Today people do not get married or stay married long.

b) In this essay, I will show that marriage can survive as a vital social institution.

c) Despite its usefulness, marriage is unlikely to continue to be essential in Canadian life. ✓ *no blueprints*

d) Marriage is a social institution in Canada.

e) People get divorced because they fall out of love, they change their outlook on life, or they get tired of staying with one person. *✗*

f) Today there is no reason to get legally married in North American society.

g) People get married because of financial, social, and religious reasons. *✗. not relate to background*

h) Marriage will remain important in Canadian society because of tradition, legal incentives, and the human desire to mark life events. ✓

i) People do not have to get married any more because our society accepts unmarried couples.

j) It is difficult to stay married through decades of being with one person.

Exercise 5.4

Here are incorrect four-sentence theses. Rewrite them into one concise, grammatical thesis statement. Take out any information that can be explained in the body paragraphs:

1. There's a lot of evidence to show that fast food is unhealthy, but people keep eating it. They like it because it's cheap. It tastes good. Fast food is very convenient.

Exercise 5.4 – *continued*

2. People get tattoos for many reasons. One, they want to decorate their bodies. Two, they want to show that they belong to a specific group. Three, tattoos illustrate what they are attached to.

3. There are three main reasons for leasing a car. First, the monthly payments are lower. Second, you can always drive a new car after the three-year lease is over. Third, I don't have to worry about breakdowns as usually everything is covered under warranty.

4. For students who are at a loss during a teachers' strike, these are things they can do. They can read their textbook and review their notes. They should complete any assignments given before the strike so they will be up-to-date and maybe even ahead when the strike is over. They could do extra reading on the subject material to truly master it.

5. There are several basic types of TV commercial. One is the lifestyle ad where advertisers want consumers to think they will have the kind of life depicted in the commercial if they use the product. Another kind is the humorous commercial that tries to make the consumer laugh and therefore remember the product. Third, there are straight information commercials that tell the consumer what he needs to know.

6. The transportation system can be fixed if everyone cooperates. First, the public transit system needs to be improved to make it more convenient to use. Second, more goods need to be shipped by rail instead of by truck. Finally, use of personal vehicles needs to be controlled with fines or incentive programs.

Exercise 5.5

Rewrite these thesis statements so that they are concise and grammatical, with parallel structure:

1. The government should encourage young people to vote by teaching them about politics in schools, showing political news on television shows geared to them, and how easy voting is.

2. By reducing the workweek, the employment rate would be lower with more people working, productivity would go up, and more time for families and to enjoy life.

3. Parents can help their children go off to college by giving them money for tuition and living expenses, help them choose a

Exercise 5.5 – *continued*

school and program, and to encourage them when they are feeling discouraged.

4. The advantages of shopping online are that buyers can choose from a wide array of items, many of which may not be available in local stores, and they can do this shopping at home which is more convenient than going to the mall, and compare prices and read reviews before they buy.

Exercise 5.6

Write a thesis statement for the following essay topics:

1. What is the key to success in college?
2. Should second-generation immigrants be encouraged to marry within their ethnic group?
3. How do high school students benefit from a part-time job?
4. Why are extracurricular activities important in school?
5. What factors should a student consider when choosing post-secondary education?

You can also write thesis statements for the topics you generated in the activity on page 148.

A thesis statement should
- answer the essay question;
- show the point of view of the writer;
- be one sentence;
- be the last sentence of the introduction;
- be concise;
- have parallel structure.

Writing an Introduction

The function of an introduction is, of course, to introduce the topic to the reader. In a five-paragraph essay, the first paragraph is the introduction, while in a longer essay or report, the introduction may extend to several paragraphs or a whole section or unit. In an essay, the introduction generally ends with the thesis statement. The introduction leads the reader gradually to the thesis, provides any background information the reader may need, and narrows the topic.

What is actually in the introduction depends on the topic. For instance, an essay discussing solutions to a problem should have an introduction that explains the problem for the reader. In an essay discussing one side of a controversial issue, the main opposing arguments can be mentioned briefly in the introduction as a lead-in. If a reading (e.g., a book, a story, an article) is a point of departure for the essay, the point of view of the reading's author may be mentioned before the essay writer goes into his or her own thesis.

Sample introductions

A)   In an essay that discusses the effects of overwork, it would be appropriate to explain the causes first:

> Although it was once predicted that technology would result in too much leisure time for workers, the opposite seems to have happened. Instead of working fewer hours, we are working harder than ever. Downsizing has put pressure on surviving employees. Cellphones and laptops mean that workers are in contact with clients and their work at all times. As a result, stressed-out workers are showing signs of physical, mental, and social problems.

B)   In an essay in favour of euthanasia, the main arguments against it could be mentioned in the introduction:

> Even though euthanasia is already practised in Canadian hospitals, many people do not want the procedure legalized and controlled. They fear that it would lead to the "murder" of the terminally ill, the elderly, and the disabled. They think that life and death should be in the hands of God. However, mercy killing can mean a more humane way of dying, a return to a natural life cycle, and a measure of control to those whose life spans are at an end.

C)   This introduction establishes that starting college is both exciting and challenging before explaining the difficulties:

> Graduating from high school and going off to college is an exciting time. Students look forward to being on their own and pursuing the studies that will lead them to a career. However, many find that this is not as easy as they thought it would be.

First-year students may even drop out when they find they cannot make the transition to college successfully. College students have to adjust to living on their own, being responsible for their studies, and coping with financial limitations.

D) In an essay that responds to a reading, it is useful to recap the author's arguments:

In "The New Heavyweight Champions," Margaret Wente explains that as men are losing their well-paying jobs in the recession, women are becoming the primary breadwinners. Men are not pursuing the education required for employment in the knowledge economy. Wente wonders what will happen to marital relationships in the future. These social changes will require men and women to abandon traditional roles and establish equality in their relationships.

Students often struggle writing the introduction. It is helpful to remember that an introduction does not have to be written first—it appears first in the essay, but it might be easier to write it when the body of the essay is drafted, as long as the writer has a thesis as a beginning point. Because the introduction and conclusion often contain ideas that do not fit the body, writing the introduction later can work. Moreover, writers who are blocked at the introduction might find that drafting the body can cure this block.

One common mistake is starting the introduction with the thesis—this leaves no room to do anything else but proceed to the arguments of the essay. Here is an example for the topic "What are the benefits of studying abroad?"

When it comes to the benefits of studying abroad, it is often said that people who have an opportunity to study abroad will have a new life and a bright future. Because of the development of the global economy and education, an increasing number of students choose to study abroad. This phenomenon has become more common than it was 30 years ago. Studying abroad can help students learn a new culture, have friends from different countries, and acquire an advanced education.

Note that this introduction lacks a linear progression of ideas; it zigzags, giving an advantage of studying abroad, then explaining that the phenomenon is increasing, and then going back to advantages. Note also that the writer keeps repeating the phrase "studying abroad," whereas the improved introduction below uses synonyms:

> Choosing to take a university year in another country is an increasingly popular option. Even though it can be expensive and difficult to arrange, many students take advantage of the opportunity to study overseas. They realize that the benefits are worth the effort. Studying abroad can help students learn a new culture, make friends from different countries, and acquire an advanced education.

While an introduction usually moves from general statements to more specific statements, thus leading to the thesis, it is important not to start too broad, as in this example:

> Technology has advanced greatly through the years. We rely on technology. We cannot live without it. Banning cellphone use in class is unfair.

In a nutshell, the introduction should catch readers' attention and prepare them for the essay. It does not have to be very long (the body paragraphs should be longer), so do not overdo it.

Exercise 5.7

Write an introduction (three to five sentences) for the thesis statements you generated in Exercise 5.6.

Tips for an introductory paragraph
- It should gradually lead the reader to your thesis, which is the last sentence of the introduction.
- It should give background information to the reader or prepare the way for your thesis.
- It should not mention arguments in support of your thesis (i.e., it should not repeat statements that are in your body paragraphs).
- It should not be longer than a body paragraph, in most cases.

Writing Body Paragraphs

Body paragraphs in an essay are essentially the same as the developed paragraphs discussed in Unit 4. Each starts with a topic sentence giving the main idea. The rest of the paragraph has points and support. A body paragraph, however, is generally shorter than an independent paragraph, and it does not require a concluding sentence.

In an essay, the topic sentences of the body paragraphs take their cue from the thesis statement. In other words, they should relate to the thesis by taking the same idea but narrowing it down for the focus of the paragraph. The wording should be different so that the sentences are not repetitive.

Thesis statement:	Public transit is a worthwhile investment because it is good for citizens' health, finances, and quality of life.
Topic sentence #1:	Public transit leads to health benefits for the whole population.
Topic sentence #2:	Investing in a better transit infrastructure ultimately saves money for everyone.
Topic sentence #3:	Citizens' quality of life improves as more people use public transit and the number of cars on the roads decreases.

A topic sentence such as "Cars produce a lot of pollution" does not link directly to the thesis because it does not mention the benefits of transit. The reference is oblique; the readers have to make the connection rather than the writer having made it for them.

Remember that the topic sentence of each body paragraph should be clear on its own. Use nouns, not pronouns, in the first sentence of a paragraph. For example, Topic sentence #1 above cannot read "It leads to health benefits for the whole population" because the "it" cannot refer back to a noun (public transit) in the previous paragraph. Each paragraph is a new beginning, so nouns should be clearly identified.

The topic sentence sometimes links to the previous paragraph. For example, if the first body paragraph of the essay talks about the money earned at a part-time job, the second paragraph might begin "In addition to the much-needed income, part-time jobs offer an opportunity to learn new skills."

Body paragraphs in an essay do not need concluding sentences, especially concluding sentences that just repeat the topic sentence. However, you can use a concluding sentence in the paragraph if it is necessary and works well.

Exercise 5.8

Here is an introduction with a thesis statement. For each body paragraph, choose the best topic sentence of the four choices. Explain your choice.

Personal vehicles have long been recognized as major sources of pollution. While it is relatively easy to give up driving a car in major cities that are well served by public transit and have other initiatives such as car sharing, a personal vehicle is a necessity for most Canadians. Even if they must drive, however, they can reduce the harm caused by their car by changing what, when, and how they drive.

1. a) Bigger vehicles such as SUVs burn more gas and therefore emit more toxic gas.
    b) Canadians should choose a more fuel-efficient vehicle.
    c) All Canadians should buy hybrid cars because they produce less pollution.
    d) People should take public transit instead of driving.

2. a) Most Canadians can reduce the number of trips they take by car.
    b) Car-pooling is a good method to reduce the use of personal vehicles.
    c) The government should improve the public transit system.
    d) When should people use a car?

3. a) Most people drive too fast and too far, and so they burn too much gas.
    b) In addition to using public transit, Canadians should walk and cycle more.
    c) Using a GPS system can prevent getting lost and driving too much.
    d) Good driving habits can also lead to a reduction in the polluting effects of cars.

Exercise 5.9

Write three topic sentences for each of the following thesis statements:

1. Students should pick a post-secondary program based on their interests, their skills, and the job prospects.
2. History courses are important because they teach critical thinking skills, explore life lessons, and inform students about their heritage.

Exercise 5.9 – *continued*

3. How easily immigrants adapt to their new country depends on their educational background, their language skills, and their personality.

Writing a Conclusion

Conclusion paragraphs are similar to introduction paragraphs. Unlike body paragraphs, they are not developed with a topic sentence, arguments, and support. Like an introduction, a conclusion should not contain ideas that support the thesis statement. The conclusion starts with a restatement of the thesis, but that is the only repetition, and it should not be in the same words. In longer essays, you can write a short summary in a conclusion, but this is not advisable in short essays because it is too repetitive. Similar to the introduction, the conclusion should be shorter than the body paragraphs.

A conclusion can give the "so what?" idea showing the significance of what has been argued in the essay. It can offer suggestions for improvement or predict the future. It should not spring on the reader a preference or point of view because this should have been clear in the thesis statement. A conclusion should not apologize for brevity (e.g., "These are only some of the problems teenagers face") or make new points to support the thesis. It is the last thing said to the reader, so the conclusion should have a punch.

Here are sample conclusions for the same topics as the sample introductions on pages 158–160:

A) With all these harmful effects of working long hours, we should make a change in our work habits. Even though cutting hours would result in lower pay, we have to value our health above anything else. We need to make sure we lead a balanced life and not work ourselves to death.

B) Euthanasia must be considered now that life and death is no longer a simple matter. Society must come to grips with the issue, and people must acknowledge that it already happens. Physicians play an important role, as does technology. We cannot turn back the clock, so we must accept dealing with a complex issue in a complex world.

C) If students can make these adjustments to college life, they will be successful in school. Moreover, they will have gained maturity and learned to deal with responsibility. This will be as valuable as their education in their future life.

D) By sharing household responsibilities, pooling financial resources, and avoiding gender stereotyping, couples can adapt to the new economic realities and forge a life together. The future, however, will undoubtedly hold more social change that families will have to adapt to. The key to this adaptation is not to be bound by traditional roles and rules.

Exercise 5.10

Write conclusions to go with the introductions you generated in Exercise 5.7.

Practising Essay Writing

Here are some brainstorming notes you can use for practice. You can work alone, with a partner, or in a group. Working with the same base allows you to compare results in the class. You can focus on different parts of the essay: the outline, the thesis, topic sentences, body paragraphs, introductions, and conclusions. For example, each group can write an introduction for the essay on immigrant assimilation and then compare the introductions to see the range of possibilities. You can add ideas or eliminate any you do not think fit your essay.

You can also start the process from scratch, coming up with essay topics and brainstorming as a class or in small groups. In addition, you can look back over this unit and develop some of the essay ideas in other activities and exercises. You can choose to work on one of the essay assignments from the reading selections or on one of the topics on page 147–8 or page 165–6.

Topic: How can at-risk students be encouraged not to drop out of high school?
  a) arts courses (music, drama, art)
  b) counselling
  c) visits to post-secondary schools, work sites
  d) speakers from the work world, former drop-outs
  e) alternatives to regular courses (co-op, independent study)
  f) tutoring for students who are failing
  g) variety of courses, both academic and hands-on
  h) extracurricular activities to engage the students
  i) mentoring with graduates who have gone on to post-secondary education

Topic: What factors determine how readily immigrants will assimilate into Canadian society?

a) their education level
b) their attitude to their new culture, open-mindedness
c) whether they live in an ethnic neighbourhood or not
d) their age
e) their family structure
f) whether they work with Canadians
g) whether they have immigrated reluctantly
h) how similar their native language and culture are to their new ones
i) how much they have travelled and seen other countries
j) their willingness to learn

Topic: What should parents teach teenagers to prepare them for living on their own?

a) budgeting
b) cooking nutritious meals
c) keeping track of their bank and credit card statements
d) saving money on food purchases
e) cleaning rooms (bathroom, kitchen, living areas)
f) doing their own laundry
g) dealing with utilities (hydro, gas, cable)
h) dealing with emergencies such as toilets flooding and power failures
i) how to use basic tools (hammer, screwdriver, paint brush)

Use the following structure when you divide up the points for your essay:

Outline
Thesis statement:
Topic sentence 1:
    Points for this paragraph:
Topic sentence 2:
    Points for this paragraph:
Topic sentence 3:
    Points for this paragraph:

Additional essay topics

1. Why are some people slaves to fashion?
2. Should textbooks be replaced by e-books?
3. Is money the prime motivator for how hard people work?
4. Why should students read fiction?

5. Why should students study history?
6. What are the advantages of being famous? (Note: focus on fame alone, not fortune.)
7. Why are hairstyles so important to image?
8. People who do not vote do not have the right to criticize their government. Discuss this statement.

Sample Essays

Read the following sample essays, examining the structure. Identify the thesis statement, and see how the topic sentences relate to it. Look at the support given for the points made in the essay. Examine the introductions and conclusions.

The Definition of Success

Many people equate success with wealth. If someone has a mansion and a fleet of luxury cars, that person must be successful. However, even though few people ever attain that degree of affluence, many can look proudly upon their many achievements. Success means making worthwhile contributions in work, finding a place in society, and gaining contentment in life.

Because work is so important in human life, people need to do a worthwhile job to be considered successful. It does not matter whether the job is running a global corporation or cleaning the streets; all work contributes something to society and need doing. Some work may not pay very well, such as artistic endeavours, but it should still be recognized as valuable. Artists contribute memorable performances, written works to educate and entertain, and sculptures and paintings to satisfy the aesthetic needs of their audiences. People need to take pride in their work and do it to the best of their ability to be deemed a success.

A successful life is one that also makes a mark on society. People can do this through their work but also through other achievements, such as participating in political movements or doing volunteer work. Raising children to become valued members of society is a way of making a difference in the world. Having friends and helping those in need are important aspects of human existence. Human beings are social animals above all else, so lives spent in isolation cannot be viewed as valuable as those that involve reaching out to people.

Aside from what they contribute to society, people are not successful if they have not achieved some measure of contentment in their own lives. This may not involve vast sums of money or numerous possessions but enough to have their basic needs met, such as a home and a family. Studies have shown that people in poorer countries actually have more joy in their lives than those in rich Western countries. Moreover, people who gripe and complain about every facet of their existence must be judged as failures.

When people want to evaluate the success of their lives, they must look at what they have accomplished through work, through their contributions to society, and in their individual existence. A life well-lived is one that has made a mark as well as one that satisfies the person living it. People only get one chance at life—they must do what they can with the time they are given.

The Success of Fast-Food Restaurants

Since the first drive-in restaurants of the 1950s, fast food has increased in popularity so much that the industry is a dominant player in the global economy. The golden arches of McDonald's restaurants are one of the most recognized corporate symbols in the world. The industry has so much clout that it can influence government policies such as the minimum wage. Fast-food businesses are successful because they offer food that is cheap, tasty, and convenient.

Price is an important consideration in the food industry, and fast food is less expensive than other restaurant meals. A combo at Harvey's, for example, is less than $10, so a family can get a meal out for less than $25. The industry strives to keep prices low by keeping wages low. The factory approach to meal preparation allows it to hire untrained workers willing to accept this wage. The industry has also sought to control food production costs through vertical integration, getting into the agriculture business and meat processing. The bottom line is that the low price of fast food makes it attractive to most segments of society.

The fast-food industry has mastered the art of offering food that appeals to the taste buds of human beings. High fat content is one of the main characteristics of fast food, and fat makes food taste good, despite the nutritional drawbacks. French fries, for example, are the most consumed restaurant food. Leaner, more nutritious offerings are less appealing and sell poorly. High starch, salt, and sugar content also make the food taste good and satisfy cravings.

Convenience is probably the most important consideration in the popularity of fast food. The restaurants are ubiquitous in both small towns and big cities. The main streets leading into town are often fast-food strips where McDonald's, Wendy's, Taco Bell, and Tim Hortons coexist side by side. Fast service is a hallmark of these restaurants; the name "fast food," after all, suggests speed. Customers can either use the drive-through or walk up to the counter and get a hot meal delivered in a couple of minutes. They do not have to cook or do dishes. With North American families struggling with overloaded schedules, the lure of quick, easy food is irresistible.

Fast-food restaurants offer inexpensive, delicious, and convenient food to a North American market that needs it. Added to these basics is the clever marketing of the industry, such as making fast food particularly appealing to children with toys and play areas. Even though consumers know that fast food is not particularly nutritious, they line up to fill their stomachs and fill the coffers of the franchise owners.

Reasons for Body Art

Many people today sport tattoos and body piercings. Although these adornments have been around for thousands of years, their current popularity is somewhat surprising, since it does not result from long-standing cultural traditions. Now it is not only bikers, soldiers, sailors, and criminals who go for tattoos; middle-aged, middle-class people are also following the current fashion for such epidermal embellishment. The reasons that body art is popular stem from artistic pursuits, personal expression, and image projection.

Tattoos and body piercing can simply be viewed as another form of human decoration. Body art has its place along with make-up, hairstyles, jewellery, and fashion. People want to enhance their physical attributes. A colourful tattoo is just a pretty picture—but one that is permanently inscribed on the skin. A glittering navel stud is considered sexy when a young woman has a well-toned midriff to show it off. Tattoos and piercings draw attention to the body, something people have sought to do since prehistoric times.

In addition to being attractive, body art can express various attachments. Some people have a tattoo of the name or image of a loved one. A biker may have the name of his gang inscribed on his body. People can choose a tattoo that shows their ethnic heritage, such as a Chinese character, which might even express a concept the person admires, such as "joy" or "wisdom." The tattoo shows what the person believes in.

Tattoos and piercings also promote a certain image that young people value. They still have some shock value in society, so they are often chosen by rebellious adolescents. This is no different from earlier generations sporting long hair to annoy their parents. Moreover, because the processes involved are painful, people might enjoy the "tough guy" image associated with these types of body art.

The motivations behind body art vary, but it is currently very much in style. It will be interesting to see how long tattoos and piercings remain on the scene. All fashion and fads have their day. While piercings can be easily removed, leaving only a small hole, tattoos require sophisticated removal treatments. Plastic surgeons may well be busy in the future removing the indiscretions of youth, especially tattoos that have blurred or stretched along with the body.

Personal versus impersonal essays

Some instructors assign personal topics to their students in an effort to engage them more in their writing. Others want students to practise writing objectively and impersonally as training for the work world. You should be able to handle both kinds of essays and know what is called for. Your instructor should make his or her preferences clear. The question asked will also indicate whether the response should be personal. Here are two essays on the same topic, one personal and one impersonal. (See page 8 for more on writing impersonally.) Notice that the personal essay is more specific, while the impersonal one is more general and can apply to a variety of situations.

> Topic: "McJob" is the term coined to refer to low-paying, often menial jobs that frequently involve serving the public, based on the model of working at McDonald's. What can students learn from working in such jobs part-time and during the summers?

The Benefits of McJobs

Students often work at part-time or summer jobs to pay their way through school. These positions are usually "McJobs"—low-paying labour, often involving serving the public. While many people disdain such menial labour, students can actually benefit from such work in more than monetary terms. Students can learn time management, practical skills, and personal skills.

By working part-time, students learn to manage their precious time. First, they have to balance their school and work responsibilities. They know they cannot procrastinate with their academic assignments because they have little time to waste. Moreover, they learn to be punctual because bosses are less accepting of tardiness than teachers are. Finally, they learn to get their work done efficiently and use their time productively.

There is a wide range of practical skills that can be acquired on the job. These skills can be carried over to other jobs or even to everyday household chores. For example, students who work as landscapers will be able to take care of their yard and garden when they become homeowners. Restaurant cooks can serve their future families good meals. Cashiers can handle money for everyday transactions. Clerks in clothing stores become adept at pressing and folding clothing.

Since so many McJobs involve dealing with the public, student workers develop valuable people skills. They learn how to be polite and cheerful and how to listen to a complaint without flying off the handle. Because they deal with such a wide range of people, they have a better understanding of humanity. For example, a cashier in a fast-food restaurant will see people struggling to come up with a few dollars to pay for a meal. Camp counsellors learn how children develop and learn. As a result, students develop the emotional intelligence that will serve them well throughout life.

Part-time and summer jobs allow students to grow and acquire skills. Students have to make sure that they do not take on too many hours, because their school work is still the priority. However, learning does not stop at the classroom door, and students should be open to these experiences that they may not have a chance at again. [358 words]

Topic: What have you learned from working at McJobs?

What McJobs Have Taught Me

As a student, I had my share of McJobs. I worked as a waitress, a cashier, and tour guide. Although some of my friends sneered at my jobs and chose to get into debt with student loans instead, I found that working like this was a good experience. My jobs taught me valuable skills in time management, food and drink preparation, and speaking to the public.

My work experience taught me how to use my time and energy profitably. Not only did I have to balance my studies, work hours, and social life, I learned how to get the most out of my work hours. As a waitress, I never went anywhere empty-handed; I had enough miles to walk without having to do them twice. If I took plates of food or drinks to the tables, I went back to the kitchen with empty plates from other tables. Even today, as I clean house, I find that I work as efficiently as I did in my days as a server, making sure I am carrying something both coming and going.

The skills I learned in the food service industry carry over to everyday life. Sometimes I had to mix drinks, so I picked up some bartending skills that still come in handy at parties. At times I had to help the kitchen staff, so I learned to cook and plate food. I did not even know how to cook eggs before I had to help prepare breakfast at a truck stop restaurant where I worked. When we have large family dinners, my skill at balancing plates is impressive and useful.

Probably the most important skills I acquired were people skills. As a waitress, I had to deal with rude and picky customers. Serving food for a catering company took me to formal functions at embassies and government buildings where I had to contend with a demanding clientele including dignitaries such as Pierre Trudeau and René Lévesque. As a tour guide, I learned to project my voice and keep my audience interested—skills that later helped in my career as a teacher. Because I worked in Ottawa, I had to be bilingual, so my fluency in French increased.

Even though working part-time made it difficult to spend enough time on my school work, I don't regret the hours I worked because of all I learned. I probably would have wasted more time if I didn't have jobs, and my marks would not have been much better. I gained much more than just the income. [424 words]

Essay Checklist
- A five-paragraph essay has an introduction, three body paragraphs, and a conclusion.
- Your thesis statement should be the last sentence of the introduction. You restate this thesis as the first sentence of your conclusion.
- Each body paragraph should start with a topic sentence that relates directly to the thesis.
- The arguments in support of your thesis are in the body paragraphs and not in the introduction or conclusion.
- Support your points with specific examples or explanation.

Rhetorical Skills

Rhetoric is the art of speaking or writing to make an argument or impress someone. Communicating effectively involves knowing the structures of language—the way words, sentences, paragraphs, and essays are put together—and the way language is manipulated to have an effect on the reader.

Writing instructors generally speak of different rhetorical forms: narration, description, definition, comparison, exposition, process description, and persuasion. Each form has its particular use in communicating ideas. For example, if you are asked to tell a story, you will use the narrative form to tell what happened. If you are asked to explain a word or idea, your rhetoric technique is definition to explain what something is. While you may be called upon to write an essay in one specific mode, most writing is a mix. For instance, an author might start with a short narrative and then proceed to argumentation. Of course, there may be an emphasis of one form over another. Most essay writing fits under the general umbrella of exposition—making points and supporting them.

This unit deals with the specific modes of writing. Each is explained and illustrated with sample paragraphs and short essays.

Illustrating

Essay topics assigned to students in college or university often require the writer to show and tell. This is the essence of illustrating as a rhetorical form. Instructors want the students to be able to explain an idea, a concept, a thought. Illustrating then is the ideal mode. (Many of the essays in the previous unit are such expository essays.) Often, merely stating something is not enough; it requires showing.

The following student essay has a little twist in the end, when it becomes personal. This is done for a humorous effect. Skilled writers can get away with bending the rules a bit. If you are comfortable doing this and know that your instructor will accept it, you can try little touches like this.

The Hazards of Treeplanting

Every summer, thousands of Canadian university and college students head north to plant trees. Logging companies reforest a certain percentage of their cut land, so they subcontract to treeplanting companies. The goal of a treeplanter is simple: plant as many trees as possible. Treeplanters are paid per tree, so their fortunes rely on the speed with which they can put seedlings into the ground. It seems, however, that every aspect of the job—the weather, the animal life, and the rough living and working conditions—is designed to slow the planter's pace.

Planters work in the rain, during thunderstorms, and even in snow at the beginning of the treeplanting season. At the end of the day, home is a thin nylon tent, which can be crushed in a spring snowstorm. Later in the season, they have to endure the kind of searing heat that sparks forest fires. A clearcut has no place to hide from the sun, and the pace that kept them warm in May can bring heat exhaustion in June.

The bug situation is like a video game in which increasing levels of difficulty bring new enemies to fight. Level 1 would be early May, easy and relatively bug-free. Level 2 would introduce the blackflies, a few at first and then a psychotic swarm of tiny, persistent flies getting into the planter's eyes, ears, and nose. Level 3 would be blackflies and mosquitoes. After mosquitoes come other bugs, such as friendly flies, deer flies, sandflies and horseflies. Each has their own deadly weapon and method of attack. Unlucky planters have even found wasp nests with the thrust of their shovel. It's not enough to be suffering from the bites themselves; every planter is in constant danger of self-inflicted bug-swatting-related injuries.

In addition to bugs, treeplanters have larger threats from the animal world. For instance, bears are attracted to the food and garbage around camp and become a terrifying nuisance. Hungry bears, undeterred by such defensive systems as noise-makers and flares, sometimes come right into the camp. At the block, planters must make enough noise to warn off any bears that happen upon their assigned planting plot.

Dirt is a constant companion in the bush. It is inhaled, eaten, and ground into a treeplanter's flesh. A planter's hands will not be completely free of dirt until a few weeks after the return to civilization. Locals in "day-off" towns know how to spot a planter: A planter's shovel hand has rough calluses that become havens for dirt and sand. Treeplanters generally go into town once a week to get a decent shower, do laundry, and pour a couple of beers down their throat to chase all that dirt they swallowed.

The job itself entails bending over to put a seedling in the ground 2000 times a day, scrambling over obstacles and unfriendly terrain. Trees cannot be haphazardly shoved into the ground; quality is of the greatest concern to the crew boss. The plug must remain unbent and completely in mineral soil, while the tree itself must be straight, at the proper depth and spacing. A planter has to satisfy several tree-checkers as well as his or her crew boss. In a 10-hour day, allowing for breaks and bag-up times, 2000 trees means a tree planted every 10 seconds. Good planters often plant three or four thousand a day, working quickly because the money earned depends on how many trees get planted. At eight to 10 cents a tree (depending on the terrain), a planter can make $250 a day and earn enough for tuition in the first month.

Because of the repetitive and high-impact nature of the work, planters are prone to injuries. For example, tendonitis strikes ankles, knees, elbows, and wrists. Kicking the ground to expose soil causes a numbness in the toes that can last for months after planting. Bruises and scrapes are inevitable in the rocky, "slash"-covered landscape. A nasty spill is often the consequence of moving at the necessary speed. Rainy or icy conditions are especially hazardous. The weight of three to four hundred seedlings in a planter's tree-bags makes every step an awkward balancing act.

Treeplanting is no summer vacation. It is hard, miserable, competitive work, and those who enjoy it are certifiably insane. Do not go for the experience, to save the environment, or to make money. In fact, do not go at all. As for me, I will be there again next year.

Giving examples

As shown in Unit 3, supporting your general statements is important. Examples are commonly used as specific support because they serve to prove your point. You do not have to give a list of supporting evidence when one judicious example will do. Of course, this example has to be relevant and specific.

The transition signals *for example* and *for instance* are generally used to introduce a sentence example. These expressions usually appear at the beginning of the sentence, but they can be in the middle or at the end.

> People can cut down on unnecessary trips with their vehicles. For example, they can walk or bicycle to the corner store.

> Students can build their readings skills gradually. They can read children's books, for instance, to develop their abilities with simpler vocabulary and sentence structure.

If you are giving a list of examples within a sentence, use the verb *include* or the phrase *such as*:

> My courses this semester include biology, psychology, and chemistry.

> I play many sports, such as baseball, tennis, and hockey.

Both *include* and *such as* tell the reader that these are only some of the examples, so do not end the sentence with *and so on*, *etc.*, or an ellipsis (. . .). Note that the comma appears before *such as*, not after.

Avoid launching into an unnecessary narrative mode for examples in essays. This leads to wordiness and distracts from the point you are trying to make:

> People who live in a messy environment have many problems. One of them is wasting time looking for things that are misplaced. For example, Tom has a job interview. As he is getting ready, he starts looking for a clean white shirt and a copy of his résumé. He digs through all his stuff at home but without any success. As a result, he loses time and arrives at the interview too late. Thus, he lost a good chance to get a good job. [wordy]

> People who live in a messy environment have many problems. One of them is wasting time looking for things that are misplaced. For example, a job candidate who arrives late for his interview because he could not find a clean shirt may lose his chance at the job. [better]

Finally, do not use abbreviations such as *e.g.*, *i.e.*, and *etc.* in your paragraphs and essays. These abbreviations belong in your notes, not in your final drafts.

Assignment
Write an expository essay explaining the duties in a job that you have held.

Narrating

Story-telling is the most ancient of human arts, serving as both entertainment and a teaching tool. Researchers have shown that facts are remembered better if they are delivered in the context of a story. In other words, you may recall the facts of events better if you read them in a historical novel rather than in a history textbook.

Narration is simply telling a story, saying what happened, whether it be a true story or a fictional one. How much detail is in the story, however, depends on the audience and purpose. You may be spinning out a story of something funny that happened to you, perhaps even exaggerating for effect. You may be writing a fantastical children's story to entertain your young nephew. Or you may be relating what happened in a traffic accident for a police report, as in the following account:

> I was driving northbound on Chapel Road, going through an intersection that had no traffic lights or stop sign. A car in the southbound side was in the left turn lane. The car turned left before I cleared the intersection and hit the front of my car, on the driver's side. It pushed my car up onto the snow bank.

Here is another simple narrative:

> My treeplanting crew all know the dangers of bears. I've told them to make a lot of noise when they are out in the bush. Many of them sing as they plant trees. This bear, however, came upon me suddenly. I was unloading the seedlings from the back of the truck. The other crew boss had gone to check on one of her planters. This black bear came around a thicket. I don't know who was more surprised—the bear or me. After a moment's hesitation, it charged at me, knocking me down. It bit on my steel-toed boot but didn't break through to my foot. With my free foot, I kicked it in the snout and yelled at it. It backed off and then charged again. I kicked it again, and it turned back and loped off into the bush. Fortunately, I wasn't really hurt.

Some people are gifted story-tellers, enthralling listeners and keeping their attention. Others have trouble telling a story, confusing their audience by skipping back and forth relating the events that happened or boring their audience with too many unnecessary details.

It is important to keep your audience and purpose in mind. A story for entertainment is generally longer and more detailed. A narrative that simply states the facts of the events would be used in a business report. In addition, how much information you give depends on what your audience already knows. For example, if you are telling what happened to Uncle Joe when he was fishing, you do not need to give as much information to your family members, who already know Uncle Joe, as you need to give to your friends, who may not know the personal quirks of your extended family.

Journalistic essays often start with a narrative—an account of something that happened to the author or someone else. The author uses the narrative to get the reader's attention and to serve as an introduction to the topic. This is the technique used in "White Tops, Grey Bottoms" (page 330). "Over Here I Rarely Lift a Finger" (page 303) is an example of a narrative essay.

Be sure to make the point of your narrative clear. For example, if you are writing a complaint letter to a company and are telling a long, involved story of what happened, you should have an introductory paragraph that succinctly tells what your complaint is and what action you want. The narrative can then support your point.

Sequence is an important consideration in narration. An audience can follow a story better if it is told in chronological order (with the events in the order that they occurred). Use time transition signals such as *then* and *as a result*. The story told in "The Strange Forces behind the Richard Hockey Riot" (page 338) is harder to follow because the author goes back and forth in time, starting with a description of the riot but then going back to explain what caused it. This technique is often used for dramatic purposes. If you choose to use it, as always, remember your audience. The technique can make your narrative more difficult for a reader to follow.

When you relate a story, it is important to keep verb tense in mind. In English, we often use the simple present tense to tell a story since it makes it more immediate. Even though Shakespeare has been dead for 400 years, we say, "Shakespeare tells the story of two lovers in *Romeo and Juliet*." The past tense is also used for narration. It is important, however, not to mix the two tenses unnecessarily. Whether you decide to tell your story in the present tense or in the past, do not switch.

Here are two versions of the same story, a well-known Aesop's fable. The first uses dialogue to spin the story out. The second is a simple reporting of events.

The North Wind and the Sun

The North Wind was a boisterous and blustering fellow. His breath blew cold and strong, and he liked to shake leaves from trees and push the waters of the sea into billowing whitecaps. In particular, he liked to wreak havoc on the people below. He would send their hats flying off their heads, tie their laundry into knots on the clothesline, and scatter important papers across the yard.

"I own the sky, and I rule the Earth," he boasted.

One fall day, as the North Wind was up to his usual mischief, he came upon the Sun, who was covered behind some clouds. The North Wind blew them away so that he could see the Sun clearly.

The Sun smiled. "Thank you, North Wind. I'm sure the people down there appreciate what you have done too."

The North Wind sensed that the Sun was making fun of him with his easy smiles. And he didn't like it. "I'm stronger than you are, you know."

The Sun smiled again. "I'm sure you are, North Wind."

The Wind looked below and saw a traveller walking along the road. The man wore a heavy cloak and a wide-brimmed hat.

"We should have a competition. Do you see that man below? The one who can take his cloak off will be considered the stronger. Do you want to go first?"

"No, you can have the first go at it."

The North Wind came behind the traveller and suddenly burst forth a wintry blast. He caught the traveller unawares—momentarily. Then the man grabbed his cloak and hat tightly against his tiny frame. The North Wind twirled about and sent a powerful gust in front of the man. More determined than ever, the traveller wrapped his clothing about him.

Now, this went on for quite a while, but no matter which way the wind blew, the traveller held onto the hat and cloak for dear life. Finally, the North Wind exhausted all his tricks and withdrew.

When it was the Sun's turn, he merely kept beaming brightly, and soon the traveller felt not only the warmth but the heat of the day. The man began to remove his clothing: first his hat and then his heavy cloak. Pretty soon he was loosening his other garments.

"Sometimes," the Sun said, "gentle persuasion works better than force."

Note that the present tense is used in the next telling of the story:

One day the North Wind and the Sun decide to have a competition to see who is the strongest. They spy a traveller below and agree that the one who is able to get the man's cloak off will be deemed the winner. The Wind blows harder and harder, but the man holds on to his cloak very tightly. Then it is the Sun's turn. As the rays of the Sun beat down on the traveller, he grows very warm and takes off his cloak. The moral is that sometimes gentle persuasion works where force does not.

Narration often has direct quotation and reported speech. See page 250 for more on quoting.

Exercise 6.1

Here is another Aesop's fable, told in past tense. Rewrite it, changing it to the present tense. Or rewrite it adding details to expand the story:

There once was a hare who wanted to race with a tortoise. He believed it would be an easy win since the tortoise crawled on all fours and carried his home on his back. The hare had powerful hind legs, and he could spring forth in great leaps and bounds. The race was unfair, of course. Surprisingly, though, the tortoise said yes to this competition. So on the day of the race, both hare and tortoise agreed that the first to reach the pond across the meadow would be the winner. The hare graciously gave his competitor a head start. In two hops, the hare caught up with the tortoise and in another two leaps he was far ahead, so far ahead that he decided to rest and take a nap. The tortoise, however, steadily plodded on, one leg after another, until he passed the sleeping hare. By the time the hare woke up, the tortoise had reached the pond. The moral of this story is that slow and steady wins the race.

Exercise 6.2

Here is an informal, personal narrative. Write a few sentences to say what happened from the Orc's point of view or the manager's point of view (for an incident report):

Exercise 6.2 – *continued*

So there we were sitting front row centre for one of the preview performances of *Lord of the Rings*. We hadn't wanted to sit that close, but there was a bit of an order mix-up, and there wasn't too much choice. Anyway, even though our seats made it difficult to see everything happening on stage, especially when sections of the stage were elevated, we did get an amazing view of the action. We could have reached out and touched the actors sometimes. I did have the urge to peel the fruit sticker off the bottom of Merry's boot. But sitting in the front row was hazardous. We got lungfuls of the dry ice "smoke" and got covered in tissue paper bits in a "storm." The actors came so close to the edge of the stage sometimes that I started cringing, especially when the Orcs were doing acrobatic tumbles and the stage platforms were rising, creating an ever-changing landscape. Some had walking sticks attached to their arms; thumping the sticks made them even more menacing in their elaborate costumes. And then there was the Orc who I could see losing his balance as he teetered on the edge. Sure enough, he fell over, off the stage—landing right on top of me. It was only a few seconds before he scrambled back up, helped by another actor. Except for feeling sore in my knee and elbow, I could almost believe it didn't happen. At intermission, the actor came out in plain clothes—I would never have picked him out of a line-up—he looked sweet, not terrifying. He introduced himself, "I'm Sean, I'm the one who fell on you" and apologized sheepishly. The manager also came out, apologizing and offering a small (very small) item from the gift shop to "make up for being startled." It's too bad my wits weren't working. I should have asked for Sean's autograph, in case he ever becomes famous. At least I have a good story to tell.

Narratives
- should be in a logical order, with transition signals to help the reader follow the action;
- should give as much detail as required for the audience and purpose.

Assignments and activities

1. Write a one-paragraph account of something interesting that happened to you recently.
2. Write the story of a folk tale or fairy tale that you know. Add dialogue to make the story more detailed.
3. In small groups of two to four students, each group should start a short story, writing the first sentence. The paper should then be handed to another group to continue the story. Afterwards, the whole story can be shared with the group. The stories can be read aloud or projected onto a screen. If an overhead projector is used, stories can be written on a transparency instead of paper.

Describing

Description paints a picture in the reader's mind. Sometimes you need to add description to clarify what you are talking about. Sometimes you want your audience to practically feel and sense it themselves. You may not be called upon to write a descriptive essay, but you may have to include description in other forms of writing. Remember your audience and purpose. For instance, the amount of detail you include will vary, depending on whether you are trying to entertain your audience with a story or just trying to make something clear on the way to explaining something else.

Here are some examples of descriptive paragraphs:

Everybody needs a private place to think, dream, and just escape life. When I was younger, I spent a lot of the summer at our family cottage. It was a chalet-style building, and my bedroom was under the roof. Outside my room was a little balcony, which had a ramp that led to the rocky hill right next to our cottage. The ramp meant that I could leave my room without going through the main door of the cottage and alerting the whole family to my movements. That balcony exit was my personal escape. I didn't really get into mischief, but I liked to go out and climb to the top of the hill. It was mostly rock, but there was an indentation that provided a not-too-uncomfortable seating area. I could look down at the roof of the cottage to one side, deep into the woods on the other, and in front of me was the lake, which I could see between the trees. I often did not see any other people even though I was only a few feet from our neighbour's lot. I loved to sit there and smell the pine, feel the warm sunshine and the cooling breeze, and hear the lapping of the waves. It was my little piece of heaven.

My roommate's brother Ammar is a giant. He's not just tall; he's also broad as a linebacker. He tends to wear clothes two sizes too big for him in a style generally seen in a rap video. His unkempt hair and perennial five o'clock shadow add to his unfriendly giant appearance. If you saw him coming down the street, you'd probably surreptitiously get a better grip on your purse or cross the road outright. However, if instead of doing either of those things, you offered him some ice cream, you'd probably end up being best friends forever and have play dates to watch Disney movies. He once came over specifically to watch *Finding Nemo* with me, while his sister rolled her eyes and stayed in her room. I don't think she appreciates his particular charms.

Sao Paolo, founded in 1554 by Jesuits, remained relatively unimportant until it became the key port for the export of coffee in the late nineteenth century. Today it is the financial and industrial capital of Brazil. Growth has been accompanied by distinct spatial expressions of class. Working-class areas arose close to industrial sites, while elite areas developed on higher ground; in some cases elite areas are enclosed by security fences and patrolled by guards. Squatter settlements, known as *favelas*, are common on the city's outskirts. About one-third of the *favelas* are on riverbanks and subject to flooding; one-third are on steep slopes and may be subject to landslides and erosion; and about one-tenth are located on waste dumps or landfill sites. [From *Human Geography*, 7th edition, by William Norton, Oxford, 2009; p. 546]

Look for descriptive passages in the readings in Part 2. For example, in "The Strange Forces behind the Richard Hockey Riot," Maurice Richard is described as: "Thirty-four years old, five foot nine, he weighs 180 pounds and is handsome in a sullen kind of way. His intense, penetrating eyes seem to perceive everything in microscopic detail" (page 340). Discuss the techniques the authors use for description.

Some pointers to keep in mind for description:
- As with all writing, clarity is vital.
- Organize your details so that your reader can follow you.
- Keep in mind your audience and purpose.
- Use adjectives and adverbs, but don't overload your sentences with them.

Assignments

1. Write a one-paragraph description of your home. It can be your current room in residence, an apartment, or your family home.
2. Write a description of an interesting person you know.
3. Describe an object (such as a can-opener) for someone who has never seen one. You can pretend you are describing it for an alien from another planet.

Defining and Classifying

Sometimes in your writing, you have to explain the meaning of some terms (definition) or show how they are related to similar concepts (classification). This is not as simple as it seems. Defining is more than simply copying a definition from the dictionary. For example, you could be asked to write an essay on the meaning of success—what is it to be successful in life? Some people equate success with wealth, while others focus on achievement and others on quality of life. See the sample essay "The Definition of Success" on page 166. The readings "Internet Addiction" (page 274) and "The Gift of Thanks" (page 316) focus on definition. A definition of the "turkey dump" can be found in the paragraph on page 116.

Classification simply means that you are defining something using different categories. For example, you might write about the kinds of customers you have as a server in a restaurant or different types of marketing approaches that can be used with a product. You might be asked to write a whole paragraph or essay as definition or classification, or you might find you need just a section to make something clear to your reader. "Three Kinds of Drivers" is a sample of a classification essay. Another kind of classification is division, in which the different parts of one thing are described.

Here are two examples of definition paragraphs, followed by a classification essay:

> Narcissism is defined as self-love. The word comes from Narcissus, a character in Greek mythology who was handsome and vain. He fell in love with his own reflection in a pond, staring at it for hours, while the lovesick nymph Echo looked on and tried to call out to him. His name was given to the flower that tends to grow by lakes and ponds. Narcissists can be vain, like Narcissus. Mainly they think they are special and privileged and no one else in the world matters. For instance, students who interrupt the class to demand attention to their needs may be showing this kind of behaviour. Many narcissists are charming and attractive, so they get away with lording it over others. They generally have an exaggerated view of their abilities. For example, some contestants on talent

shows such as "Canadian Idol" often react with disbelief when informed that they have no talent. Unfortunately, narcissism has been fostered in modern society with its emphasis on individual wants and needs.

A concussion is an injury to the brain. It may be caused by a blow to the skull by an object or by falling down and hitting the head on a hard surface. There may not even be a visible fracture to the skull and no signs such as blood loss. The victim may not even be aware of the internal injury. The damage done is usually to the inside of the head. The soft mass of the brain is disrupted as it bounces from one side of the interior to the other. This violent movement brings about bruising to the soft tissues, and then swelling. Pressure is created. The victim may experience a mild headache to loss of consciousness. In severe cases, the victim must seek medical attention; otherwise, he or she may lose the function of limbs or, worse, die from the injury.

Three Kinds of Drivers

Driving to work or school is one of the most dangerous activities people undertake in their daily lives. The possibility of getting hurt or killed in a traffic accident is actually higher than getting killed by a terrorist, but people do not take bad driving seriously enough. The danger on the roads is largely caused by bad drivers. Three of the worst kinds of drivers are those who are over-cautious, distracted, or aggressive.

Some drivers are so afraid of driving that, ironically, they create more hazards trying to be careful. Over-cautious drivers insist on going very slowly. They may go down the highway below the speed limit or the speed of traffic. It would not be so bad if they restricted their movements to the slow lane, but sometimes they take the middle lane to avoid the truck traffic. If they do not know where they are going, they may crawl down a street looking at street signs or even reverse if they miss their turn. Overly careful drivers delay making left turns, waiting for the road to be completely clear, thus causing the drivers behind them to become impatient and perhaps even do something rash, such as pulling around them.

Other bad drivers are those who try to do two things at once. The most common transgression today is using a cellphone while driving. Even using a hands-free set does not prevent a driver from being distracted. Cellphone users often weave in their lane or drive more slowly because they are concentrating on their call. Some drivers try to consult a map while they are actually moving. Some use traffic jams to catch up on their reading, even when the traffic is stop-and-go. Other activities include eating or personal grooming, such as putting on make-up. Any of these actions distract the driver from the most important task—driving. Preoccupied drivers put everyone at risk since it only takes a split second to cause a crash.

Aggressive drivers are probably the worst kind of driver. They drive quickly and take risks because they are always in a hurry. They think the speed limit is for wusses, and they tailgate drivers in the fast lane on the expressway, even if those drivers are driving 120 kilometres per hour in a 100-kilometre zone. They are also annoying because they follow so closely that they have to hit the brake lights often, confusing drivers behind who think there is a traffic slowdown. These drivers have type A personalities— they do not want to be behind anyone. They weave in and out of lanes and take chances. It is only luck and the attentiveness of other drivers that save them from more accidents.

The most dangerous hazards on the road are other drivers. Careful drivers have to watch out for those who are overly cautious, preoccupied, or aggressive. They have to understand the characteristics of the drivers in order to be able to predict their behaviour on the road, and they have to be vigilant for signs of these driving behaviours.

It is also important to understand how definitions are incorporated into other kinds of writing. Definitions for terms that the reader might be unfamiliar with are often given in non-restrictive relative clauses, which are separated from the rest of the sentence by a comma:

> Thanksgiving is known for the "turkey dump," when first-year college and university students break up with high school sweethearts. . . (page 116)

This technique is also used in the story "Why My Mother Can't Speak English" when the author has to define Chinese words and expressions for his audience:

> . . . she cannot understand that you don't give government officials *lai-shi,* the traditional Chinese money-gift given to persons who do things for you. (page 353)

Instead of commas, parenthetical dashes are sometimes used, as in this example from "Appearance: Its Social Meaning":

> Consider the humble uniforms worn by members of the Salvation Army—a religious organization devoted to urban good works, originally involving the moral uplift of fallen people. (page 322)

If the defining information is in the middle of a sentence, a comma or dash must also be placed at the end of the definition, as in this example from "The Strange Forces behind the Richard Hockey Riot":

The day before, Clarence Campbell, president of the National Hockey League, had banished Maurice (The Rocket) Richard, the star of the Canadiens and the idol of the Montreal fans, from hockey for the remainder of the season. (page 338)

Assignments
1. Write a paragraph defining one of these abstract terms: beauty, heroism, intelligence, leadership.
2. New words are coined every day; many come from developments in technology. Write a paragraph defining one of these terms: phishing, cookies, loonie and toonie, rap. Include information on how these words were developed.
3. What is a Canadian? Write a definition paragraph or an essay.
4. Write a classification essay on three kinds of people you encounter in your everyday life. For example, if you work as a salesclerk or restaurant server, you can describe three different kinds of customers or three kinds of supervisor.

Showing Cause and Effect

Academic essays often explain the causes or effects of something. Sometimes an essay can discuss both causes and effects, especially if there is a domino effect or a chain reaction in which one event leads to another, which in turn leads to another. For example, you could explain how trying a drug could lead to addiction and how addiction may lead eventually to crime.

Here is a sample paragraph explaining the effects of using a cellphone while driving:

> Despite the denials of transgressors, the effects of using a cellphone, even a hands-free device, while driving can clearly be seen. Researchers have found that the impact is equivalent to driving under the influence of alcohol, and talking to a passenger or listening to the radio does not have the same effects. Talking on a phone takes the attention away from the road, even when the driver has both eyes on the road and both hands on the wheel. On multi-lane highways, most people have observed cars moving slowly or weaving only to find that the driver is on a phone despite the laws against it. Moreover, researchers have discovered the effects of "inattentional blindness" whereby drivers do not process what they are seeing. This effect has been amply shown in tests like the gorilla test in which observers fail to see something in the picture when they are concentrating on something else. The brain cannot multi-task, and laws prohibiting cellphone use while driving should include hands-free devices.

The following cause/effect essay is nine paragraphs long, showing you how the basic five-paragraph form can be expanded.

Causes of Modern Incivility

Complaining about other people's behaviour is nothing new in any society. Ancient Greek writings show that even in those times, people were concerned that teenagers were disrespectful and impolite. Today, people point to such phenomena as road rage, the lack of formal manners, and vulgarity on television to make their claim that incivility is on the rise. Whether people are in fact ruder today than before is debatable. However, changes in technology, politics, and society in the late twentieth century have influenced human behaviour, making people less considerate of others.

The use of new technologies such as computers is the most obvious influence on behaviour. While technology does open up new ways of communicating with our fellow beings, it also cuts us off from real human interaction. It is much easier to be rude sitting in a car or at a keyboard than it is face-to-face. In road rage incidents, aggression and violence escalate between drivers, from cutting other drivers off to obscene gestures and even physical confrontation between drivers who get out of their cars to fight. Psychologists say people feel dehumanized in their vehicles and therefore freer to act aggressively. Similarly, Internet users can send angry, obscene messages because they feel anonymous and not responsible for their actions.

Another problem is that new gadgets come into widespread use before the social rules for using them can develop. Cellphones offer convenience but also intrude on public space as people talk loudly on their phones in restaurants and let them ring in the middle of a lecture. Sometimes the use of a technology affects behaviour in other situations. People used to chatting with their family while they watch a DVD at home sometimes behave the same way in a movie theatre.

Technology has also sped up our world, making us less considerate of others. With instantaneous communication possible, people do not take the time to reflect on their words. Moreover, this hurry-up world causes stress. People have a lot of information to digest and deal with—and little time to do it. Thus, it is not surprising that the courtesies people generally pay each other have fallen by the wayside.

The late twentieth century also brought a political shift that indicates a change in attitude that fosters selfishness. The right-wing conservative viewpoint preaches lower taxes, fewer social programs, and the rightful dominance of the marketplace. This is, in effect, an every-man-for-himself philosophy. People have to be ruthless to succeed, and they cannot consider others' welfare. Consequently, they behave inconsiderately.

The emphasis on individual needs has many manifestations in behaviour. The 1980s was called the 'me' decade. Education became child-centred, and self-esteem was promoted. Parents and teachers were encouraged to praise children so that they could grow up to be confident and content; even poor results were given good marks for effort. However, this over-emphasis on self-esteem resulted in a false sense of entitlement. People educated in this way may think too highly of themselves and may figure that they deserve special treatment, that what they want is more important than anyone else's needs.

In addition, deference to authority is less than it used to be. In traditional families, ideal children were those who were seen but not heard, because parental authority was absolute. Not only do parents get less respect, but other authority figures, such as doctors, politicians, supervisors, and teachers, are also frequently challenged. Some of this is due to the media revealing the weaknesses of such figures. This lessening of deference to authority can be positive because it leads to such actions as questioning doctors and not just accepting everything they say, but it has also led to increased incivility as protestors smack cream pies into the faces of prime ministers and teachers are harassed.

The media can, of course, be blamed for some of this rudeness and vulgarity. Bad behaviour gets featured on the news—whether it be politicians heckling each other in Question Period, hockey players beating each other to a pulp, or drunken celebrities landing in jail. People get a taste of fame and want to hold onto it. They crave the publicity—even if it is negative. Reality television stars find their 15 minutes of fame is not enough and cook up media stunts, such as pretending a child is aloft in a balloon, to extend the media coverage. While we pretend to be horrified, it is our appetite for celebrity news that feeds the paparazzi and schlock TV.

Although we can find many reasons why people behave with less consideration for others today, we should not be too quick to conclude that society today is uncivil. We have to recognize other truths. First, social rules are cultural. As our world brings people with different values together, some adjustments have to be made, leading to new standards of behaviour. We must also be careful to distinguish between casual and rude. A few decades ago, people dressed up to go an airplane trip and never called an older person by a first name. Does this mean a decline of civility or merely a more relaxed style of behaviour? Finally, our society has made improvements in the way we treat those who have lesser status. Overt racism is less accepted today, and we make fewer class distinctions. Women are no longer considered the possessions of their husbands and relatives. In those respects, we can say modern behaviour is better.

You can see other examples of cause and effect writing in this text. In Unit 4, paragraph A (page 140) discusses the reasons that the family meal has become less common, and paragraph C (page 140–1) explains the effects of having a regular meal together. The essays "The Success of Fast-Food Restaurants" and "The Reasons for Body Art" (pages 167 and 168) both discuss causes. "The Strange Forces behind the Richard Hockey Riot" (page 338) explains the causes of the riot. "White Top, Grey Bottoms" (page 330) mentions both the reasons for choosing school uniforms and the effects of having them, and "The Case against Bottled Water" (page 286) explains results.

Here are some words and expressions used to show cause/effect relationships:

Causes
because, since, as, for, to result from, to be the result of, due to, due to the fact that, because of, the effect of, the consequence of, as a result of, as a consequence of, one reason why, caused by, attributed to, on account of, owing to

Effects
so, as a result, as a consequence, therefore, thus, consequently, hence, to result in, to cause, to have an effect on, to affect, the cause of, the reason for, thereby, cause of

Watch out for the different prepositions used. *Affect* is a transitive verb, so there is no preposition afterwards; however, the preposition *on* often follows the noun *effect*. Both *in* and *from* can follow the verb *result*, but the noun *result* is generally followed by *of*. *Because* is followed by a clause; *because of* is followed by a noun or a noun phrase.

Here are some sample sentences illustrating the use of cause/effect expressions:

1. In Canada, education is under provincial jurisdiction. Consequently, the school system varies from province to province.
2. Because students in humanities courses have to write more essays, they develop their critical thinking skills more than students in the sciences.
3. Due to the changes in the curriculum, students have fewer electives to choose from.
4. Because of the construction of the school addition, noise was a distraction during tests.
5. The inclusion of arts and sports programs affects the drop-out rate as more students stay in school to participate in these activities.
6. Their quick progress had a negative effect on the other teams as they scrambled to catch up.

Assignments

1. In a paragraph, explain how the poor choice of a given name can affect a child.
2. In an essay, explain the reasons that young people start smoking.
3. In an essay, explain how traffic jams affect our society.

Reviewing

When you write a review, you evaluate and give your opinion of a work. You could review a book, a movie, a CD, a concert, or a product. Your review might include comparisons to similar works. You can summarize the story, but remember that your audience might not yet have seen or read it, so do not reveal too much of the plot—especially the ending. Everyone is entitled to his or her own opinion, but this opinion should be clearly and logically supported.

Reviewing is also a base for critical literary analysis. The word *review* means to look over or look at something again. In short, reviewing is a critical evaluation or the close examination of materials. From an academic point of view, reviewing is not just a synopsis of what has been said or written, but rather it gives a perspective, or expresses an opinion, on the content. In a book review, for instance, you state the reasons for liking or for not recommending it and then back those reasons up with relevant details.

In your courses, you may be asked to review readings. Reviews tend to be more personal than some of the other writing you may be called upon to do. Here is a short evaluation of a reading, followed by an informal movie review:

> "The Case against Bottled Water" by Sean Petty and Justin Trudeau was my favourite of the course readings. The authors made a strong, clear argument against bottled water, giving statistics and citing research studies. They gave economic, environmental, and health reasons. The article made me think about the issue, and as a result, I have stopped buying bottled water.

> In the winter of 2009, movie audiences raved about James Cameron's *Avatar*, entranced by the flashy and innovative special effects but sadly blind to the movie's shortcomings. First is tragically mundane dialogue: The "I see you" line is supposed to pass for something both romantic and profound. It's amazing that with such a high budget, none of it could be put toward finding a decent screenwriter. Second, not only is the plot utterly predictable, it is a rip-off of Disney's *Pocahontas, or Dances with Wolves,* or any story in which our hero finds love with an exotic yet sympathetic native

girl and learns to renounce his wicked ways and embrace the environment. With all the hype over the amazing technology used to make the film, it's impossible to avoid the conclusion that Cameron came up with the software first and then decided that blue cat people were a great way to showcase it. *Avatar* is yet another example of technology being deployed for the sake of, "Look how cool this is!" rather than to service a story.

Assignment

1. Collect some reviews from the local newspaper or the Internet. It is easy to find reviews of movies, concerts, plays, books, and restaurants. Look at the techniques used. Choose two different reviews about something you are familiar with, such as a movie you have seen. Write a paragraph on how effective the reviews are. Would they have influenced your decision to see that movie?
2. Write a brief review (about 150 words) of a book, movie, computer game, concert, or CD.
3. Write a review of one of the readings in Part 2 of this textbook.

Describing Process

Process description is often found in technical writing. It is generally "how to" writing common in instruction manuals. There are two main kinds of process writing—instructional and descriptive. Instructions can be written in a list or in prose paragraphs. They are directed at the reader, and so they use *you* and command sentences. The other kind simply describes the process objectively, without giving instructions. For example, if you explain to a gardener how to plant a flower, you are giving instructions. If you give an account of how a plant grows, you are writing a process description without being instructional.

Good process writing is clear and concise. You have to give enough information for your reader to understand the process being described but not too much information. You have to know your audience. If you are describing a technical process, much will depend on how comfortable the reader is with the jargon of the field.

It is important to break the process down into the different steps. Sometimes you will have to subdivide, with some general phases of the process broken down into various steps. For example, the planning stage of essay writing includes researching and thinking about the topic, jotting down ideas, and preparing an outline.

Here is an example of a set of instructions, followed by an instructional process paragraph and then a descriptive process paragraph:

How to take notes:
1. Come to class prepared, having done preliminary reading, and with tools (pen, paper).
2. Pay attention to the lecturer.
3. Write down, in point form, the main points of the lecture.
4. Listen for cues, when the lecturer stresses specific points.
5. Use short forms for common words and the terms of the field.
6. After class, review notes, making sure they will be clear later.

Note-taking is one of the skills you must learn in college, especially since you might not have learned how to do it in high school. First, you have to come to class prepared. It goes without saying that you need to bring your note-taking tools, your pens and notebook, but you should also have read whatever chapters are required for that lecture. Then you will be able to follow it better. Pay attention to everything the lecturer says. Your goal is to write down the main points. To do that, you have to follow the lecturer's cues. For example, if the professor says something like "most importantly," you know that she is stressing something. Similarly, you can ignore any small talk, like the chat with students about the movies they saw on the weekend. To be efficient, use point form and abbreviations. In addition to the standard short forms, you can develop your own system. Make sure you make ones for the technical terms that are often repeated in that subject area. After class, make sure you go over your notes. If the notes are not clear, add information or rewrite illegible bits while the lecture is still fresh in your mind. If you take notes faithfully, you will remember your lectures better and have study notes ready.

Note-taking is one of the skills college students must learn since it is not usually taught in high school. The first step is proper preparation. Students need to bring their tools (pen and paper) and come to class having read the required chapters in the textbook. Careful attention to the lecture is required. Professors usually stress the important points. Students need to develop their own system of point-form notes, including abbreviations for technical terms common in their field. The last step is one that many students neglect. Notes have to be cleaned up and added to after class to make sure they are legible even after the material of the lecture is no longer fresh in the mind. The act of note-taking helps students retain the information better, and good notes serve as useful study guides.

Process description is also found in the description of biological or geological processes:

Tsunamis 101

by Jan Dutkiewicz

Say tsunami and up pops a mental image of a single, giant wave rising out of the ocean to swallow cities whole. In reality, tsunamis (meaning "harbour wave" in Japanese) are a series of waves that start small and grow as they approach land. They are the result of oceans attempting to smooth out their surface after a disturbance.

Tsunamis are triggered by any phenomenon that causes a large part of the water's surface to rise or drop relative to normal sea level. These events are usually the result of earthquakes occurring along undersea fault lines, the cracks in the Earth's crust between tectonic plates. When these plates collide or grind against each other, they can elevate, lower, or tilt major sections of the ocean floor, suddenly offsetting the level of water at the surface. The displaced water then rushes to level out, causing a tsunami. The waves travel outward in all directions from the place where the earthquake occurred, just like the ripples created when a stone is thrown into a lake.

Tsunamis can also be caused by undersea volcanic eruptions, landslides, or explosions on the surface, such as the 1917 Halifax harbour explosion that sent 10-metre-high waves crashing into the city. It has also been suggested that asteroids or other extraterrestrial bodies could cause tsunamis if they plummet into large bodies of water, but there have been no examples of this in recent history.

A popular misconception is that tsunamis are monstrous waves that scour the ocean destroying everything in their path. The displacements caused by earthquakes and other cataclysms move huge masses of water, but they do not dramatically shift the surface level. Tsunami waves travelling in the open ocean can travel hundreds of kilometres per hour, but they are usually less than one metre high, and their crests can be up to 100 kilometres apart. They can be virtually invisible from the air and, for ships, be indistinguishable from the normal movement of the ocean. It is when these waves make landfall that they achieve their destructive potential. There are stories of fishermen who had no idea that a tsunami had struck their villages because they were too far out in the ocean to see or feel any waves at all.

As the ocean becomes shallower near the coast, tsunami waves slow down, compressing and directing their energy and volume upward, some rising to amplitudes of over 50 metres and annihilating whatever they encounter. Depending on the depth and slope of the coastline, it is also possible for the tsunami waves to wash over the shore like a flood or rapid current, as they did in the widely televised video footage taken in Thailand during the recent disaster in Southeast Asia.

Generally, coasts and islands with steep fringes or surrounded by barrier reefs are safer than those with gradually rising fringes or those that are exposed to open ocean. This is because reefs can absorb much of the oncoming waves' impact and deep coastlines do not allow tsunamis to slow down and grow into deadly towers of water.

_____

© 2005, Canadian Geographic Enterprises

http://www.cangeo.ca/tsunami/tsunamis101.asp

Jan Dutkiewicz, MBA, is a freelance writer and photographer.

Describing how to find a job is normally instructional, but this essay shows how it can be written as a process description (in third person, avoiding the use of *you*).

Looking for a Job

The job hunt is a formidable task that everyone has to face many times. Not only is one's livelihood dependent on the outcome, but the hunt can be frustrating and demoralizing. There is no avoiding it, however, and it can be more easily tackled as a step-by-step procedure. Finding a job requires preparing documents, searching for openings, and contacting employers.

The first step is writing the documents required for the job search. The most important one is the résumé, which defines the potential employee. Job seekers must summarize their education, experience, and skills. They have to write a search objective that encapsulates what they are looking for in a position. Second, cover letters need to be drafted. These are important because they can bring the résumé to life and can be tweaked for specific job requirements. A third useful document is a list of references to present at interviews. While the list itself is not difficult to assemble, it does take time to contact the people listed and ask them if they will serve as references. Applicants may also need to make copies of their credentials, such as degrees and certificates.

Once the required documents are assembled, job hunters must start looking for possible openings. The first step is networking. They must let friends, family, and acquaintances know that they are looking for work because more jobs are found through contacts than through actual advertising. Using connections may gain them a foothold they might not otherwise be able to get. Then, employment ads in all media need to be scoured for suitable positions. Job seekers must also identify companies that they would like to work for even if there are no positions currently advertised. A visit to a campus or community employment centre can also prove helpful to identify potential jobs.

All this preparation leads to actually contacting and meeting potential employers. Applicants need to send in their cover letters and résumés to the employers and perhaps follow up with a phone call. When they are called in for an interview, they move on to another step in the job hunting process. Applicants must prepare for the interview by practising answers to possible questions and by researching the company. They must also give attention to their appearance so they make a good impression.

Following these steps will make the job hunt a manageable task. Looking for a job is never easy, but with a positive attitude and good preparation, job seekers should be able to find work that suits their qualifications and provides them with a livelihood.

Assignments

1. Find some process description in a textbook for one of your core courses. Look for an example of point-form instructions, prose instructions, and a prose passage that describes how something happens or is done. Jot down notes comparing the three.
2. Write a process description of a task that you are familiar with. For example, you can write about painting a room, cleaning a kitchen, making a pizza, or taking an inventory.
3. Describe the process of getting a driver's licence.

Making Comparisons

Comparison is an important technique in writing. Sometimes writers must compare two things to show which is preferable. Sometimes they use an analogy, a type of comparison, to explain something. The word *compare* itself is problematic because it actually means to show similarity. Writing teachers refer to "compare/contrast essays" to be precise, but common usage is just to talk about comparison with the understanding that it refers to both similarities and differences, with the stress on differences.

There is a common expression in English that says you cannot compare apples and oranges, which means you cannot compare two very different things. The two things you are writing about in a comparison essay should have some basis for comparison. It would not be logical to write an essay comparing a sock to a tree, for instance. Often, a comparison essay shows a preference for one or the other. For example, in an essay comparing life in a big city to life in a small town, you would probably take a stand that one is better than the other.

It is also important to remember that in an essay, the writer does the work. It is the writer's job to make the comparison clear; the reader should not have to infer it. For example, you cannot write an essay talking about one movie and then another and then say to your reader, "As you can see, these two movies are very different." You need to show how they are different. For instance, you could say something like "The new film shows the director's growth. He uses fewer cheesy special effects and instead relies on character development."

Four-paragraph comparison essays are not recommended because they usually end up as two separate descriptions with little explicit comparison.

Comparison paragraphs are tricky to structure. You have to make sure that your reader can follow the points without getting confused. In block form, you talk about one item, then the other, keeping the elements in the same order. In a point-by-point comparison, you go back and forth like a ping pong ball, but you make sure that you maintain order. In an essay, you can have both kinds of paragraphs. However, instructors may prefer that you use the block style since the point-by-point can be tricky.

Point-by-point example:

When Canadian students graduate from high school, they have the choice of two different kinds of post-secondary institution: university or community college. Colleges are vocational, preparing students for specific careers. Graduates may work as aestheticians, computer technicians, paramedics, or videographers. University studies are more academic, with undergraduates studying in such fields as history, mathematics, and philosophy. They may lead to a profession, such as law, medicine, and engineering. Second, colleges give more practical, hands-on instruction. Future paramedics can be seen practising CPR on fellow students in the hallway, while other students are creating window displays or building models. In contrast, university students are more likely to be found in the library, hunting through books for references for essays. Finally, college and university require different investments, with different results. College students have shorter programs, pay less tuition, and usually study closer to home. In one to three years, they graduate with a diploma or certificate. University students, on the other hand, go to school longer, pay higher tuition fees, and sometimes have the additional costs of living far from home. However, their degree ultimately has more earning potential than a college diploma. While these are the traditional differences between colleges and universities, both institutions are changing, and the distinction is blurring: colleges are forming partnerships with universities, and some even offer degree programs.

```
Point 1  – orientation - college (A)
                       - university (B)
Point 2  – instruction - college (A)
                       - university (B)
Point 3  – value       - college (A)
                       - university (B)
```

Block example:

When Canadian students graduate from high school, they have the choice of two different kinds of post-secondary institution: university or community college. Colleges are vocational, preparing students for specific careers. Graduates may work as aestheticians, computer technicians, paramedics, or videographers. Consequently, colleges give more practical, hands-on instruction. Future paramedics can be seen practising CPR on fellow students in the hallway, while other students are creating window displays or building models. In addition, college students have shorter programs, pay less tuition, and usually study closer to home. In one to three years, they graduate with a diploma or certificate. In contrast, university studies are more academic, with undergraduates studying in such fields as history, mathematics, and philosophy. They may lead to a profession, such as law, medicine, and engineering. On campus, university students are more likely to be found in the library, hunting through books for references for essays. Finally, university students go to school longer, pay higher tuition fees, and sometimes have the additional costs of living far from home. However, their degree ultimately has more earning potential than a college diploma. While these are the traditional differences between colleges and universities, both institutions are changing, and the distinction is blurring: colleges are forming partnerships with universities, and some even offer degree programs.

A) college — orientation (point 1)
— instruction (point 2)
— value (point 3)
B) university — orientation (point 1)
— instruction (point 2)
— value (point 3)

Here are some other comparison paragraphs and a comparison essay. Examine and identify the structure of each paragraph.

Destination weddings offer couples something different from traditional weddings. A destination wedding takes place in an exotic location such as a tropical resort. A couple can have a romantic ceremony on a beach. The style is casual, to fit the environment. The wedding is usually small because only the couple's closest family and friends attend. Costs are also kept down because resorts often offer special package deals for the ceremony and reception. The destination wedding is also a vacation for the guests (who pay their own way) as well as a honeymoon for the couple. In contrast, traditional weddings take place in the couple's hometown, with the ceremony in a church and the reception in a hall. While these weddings can be casual, many are very formal, with the bride in an elaborate gown and the groom in a tuxedo. The size of the reception often gets out of hand as more guests get invited to fulfill social obligations. Therefore, the price can skyrocket to the $50,000 range, and that is before the honeymoon costs figure in. When couples look at these differences, it is not surprising that destination weddings have become a popular trend.

The fundamental differences between Americans and Canadians can be traced to the way their two countries were formed. The United States started with a war, the American Revolution. Canada was born through an Act of the British Parliament. The US Constitution promised its citizens "life, liberty, and the pursuit of happiness" and gave them the right to bear arms. Canada was founded on the principle of "peace, order, and good government," and the country has a police force, the Mounties, as a national symbol. Therefore, while the American hero is the maverick forging his own way, the Canadian character has been moulded by deference to authority. The American system favours individual responsibility, so it is not surprising that so many have fought against national health care. Canadians prefer a strong society and consider their health care system to be a national treasure. While this broad generalization of national differences does not apply to every American and Canadian, it does explain some of the differences in political and social structure.

The Disney Version

In recent years, fairy tales have changed considerably. Children today are more familiar with the sanitized version, the Disney version, than with the raw tellings of the Brothers Grimm or Hans Christian Andersen. The classic tales of Beauty and the Beast, Sleeping Beauty, Snow White, Cinderella, and the Little Mermaid have been transformed into politically correct, cutesy renderings. The hard edge in the originals has been so softened that they have become cotton candy. The three dramatic differences can be found in fairy tale animals, in the level of violence, and in plot resolution.

Animals, big and little, populate the world of the fairy tale and contribute to the plot, but the cartoon versions are softer and more pet-like. For example, in Disney's *Beauty and the Beast*, the 'beast' prince is a cute rendering of an animal. He has a bad temper, but his bark is worse than his bite. In the classic Brothers Grimm version, however, the petulant prince is transformed by a witch into a raging, ugly beast with little compassion for Beauty. Similarly, the little animals such as cute mice and twittering birdies become helpful domestic servants in the cartoons, helping Cinderella sew a dress and Snow White to clean the house. In the classic version, Cinderella has no use for mice, and the birds that separate the lentils from the sand are spiritual manifestations of her dead mother.

The original fairy tales are much more violent than the cartoon versions. Characters are asked to sever limbs, serve up pulsating hearts of virgins, and commit other gory acts. For example, Cinderella's stepsisters each cut off part of their foot to make the glass slipper fit. At the wedding ceremony, their eyes were pecked out by avenging birds befriended by Cinderella. In the Hans Christian Andersen version, the mermaid had to actually cut out her tongue to make herself mute. Moreover, she plotted to murder the prince's bride. The cartoon versions lack this type of violent act. There is no blood spilled in *Cinderella*, and the stepmother is not even very wicked. While the sea witch in *The Little Mermaid* is menacing, she does not actually kill anyone.

Finally, the story lines are softer in the new cartoon versions of the old stories. Sometimes the ending is even changed. Andersen's Little Mermaid kills herself at the end of the story, while Disney's mermaid has a happily-ever-after wedding with the prince. Cinderella's stepsisters are maimed in the original, just jealous and unhappy in the cartoon. Sleeping Beauty was raped by the prince in the Grimm version but awoken with a kiss in later stories. In the story of the three little pigs, the first two pigs are eaten, and the wolf gets his due in a pot of boiling water, while modified versions have no one getting killed.

Fairytales have changed a lot over the years. Sometimes, change is good to keep in tune with the times, but in fairy tales, politically correct retellings have made the stories insipid. The desire to keep young viewers safe from the realities of life has emasculated the power of the classic stories.

Analogy

An analogy is a comparison in which a situation is compared to something well-known in order to make it clear. In the following excerpt, see how the writer uses an analogy to help you understand an abstract concept:

Canada has been described as a patchwork quilt of cultures, religions, etc., and is justly praised for making this work. But to continue the analogy, a patchwork quilt needs a backing to hold it together, and our public schools play part of this role. They provide all of our children the opportunity to interact with people from very different religious and cultural

backgrounds, thus providing an opportunity to develop tolerance and understanding.
[From "The Religious Schools Dilemma," by Wayne Cook, *Toronto Star* 20 January 2005, p. A20]

The basic analogy here is that a quilt is stitched together with separate pieces of fabric, just as Canada is a country of different ethnic groups. In a quilt, you can see the individual pieces. Canada has also been compared to a mosaic in which individual pieces are also visible. In comparison, the United States has been referred to as a "melting pot" because its ethnic groups have been all stirred together and come out as one entity—American. Discuss these comparisons. Are they valid today?

Here is another analogy:

> The English language is like a huge pot of stew. Old English, or Anglo-Saxon as it is known, is the base, a Germanic language. To this base many ingredients have been added. Words from Old Norse were brought to England by the Viking invaders. When William the Conqueror won the Battle of Hastings in 1066, he became the first of many kings of England who did not speak English. Their language, Norman French, gradually blended in with English, changing some of its structures and practically doubling its vocabulary. Another ingredient added to this stew was the huge vocabulary based on Latin and Greek words, used mainly for scientific and technical terms. As these ingredients cook in the stew, they become less distinct, and the flavours blend together.

Assignments

Write a paragraph or an essay comparing:

- two places you have lived in or visited
- two schools or two education systems
- two vehicles, two computers, or two items you have contemplated purchasing
- two people you know
- academic English and conversational English

Persuading

Most essays are a type of argument because you are putting forth ideas and supporting them, but when you are arguing a controversial issue, you need a persuasive argument. Unlike a quarrel, in which you have an emotional dispute with someone, a persuasive essay offers reasoning. You try to make someone understand your point of view or to move someone to an action that you recommend. You must be objective, logical, and forthright to win your case. You must connect and support your ideas.

Logical fallacies

In argument, the term "logical fallacy" is used to explain a mistake in reasoning. Sometimes a fallacy is an unfair or improper method of arguing. Other times, it is a flaw in the process. There are some common logical fallacies:

Against the person: Instead of focusing on the idea, the writer mocks the person:

> You shouldn't listen to such an idiot. Even using all his fingers, he can't count to 10.

Circular argument: The writer goes in circles rather than advancing the reasoning:

> This idea is good because it is fitting. There's nothing bad about a good idea when you know it is right.

Appeal to force: The writer becomes angry and threatens the opponent with harm:

> If you know what's good for you, do as I say. I have a third-degree black belt in karate.

Hasty generalization: The writer uses only one piece of evidence and draws a grand conclusion:

> Don't expand the welfare system. I know a panhandler downtown making $100 a day. These people are making a decent living off the streets.

Appeal to pity: The writer makes the opponent feel sorry for him:

> Sir, I broke my arm in a fall when I helped my sick grandmother to the hospital for emergency surgery today, so can I have an extension on my essay that was due yesterday?

Faulty chronological reasoning: The writer draws a relation between one incident and another illogically:

> His grades started slipping when he moved to the new apartment.

Non sequitur: One idea does not logically follow another:

> Instead of frowning all the time, smiling wins friends. Many people are afraid of the dentist.

Make sure that your arguments are sound when you are writing a persuasive essay. Do not fall into any of the traps of logical fallacy.

Conceding a point

In spoken language, when you are having a discussion over an issue or arguing points of view, you often agree with the other person's arguments but add a counter-argument. It is a "yes, but" strategy. Writers do the same thing when they concede a point but focus on what they perceive to be a stronger argument.

One reason writing is so difficult is that you have to see your work from the reader's point of view and imagine what is going on in your reader's head. What you are saying may be perfectly obvious to you, but it may not be clear to the reader, so it is important that your arguments follow logically. Moreover, if there is a strong argument against your point of view, it is like the elephant in the room—there is no sense ignoring it. Your persuasive essay can become stronger if you anticipate and acknowledge some of the obvious counter-arguments.

One of the easiest ways to make a concession in your argument is to use an *although* statement:

> Although computers have many educational benefits, they stifle children's creativity.

> Although computers may limit children's interaction with their immediate surroundings, they open up the whole world for their exploration.

Note that the first sentence is against computer use, while the second sentence is in favour. The main idea is in the main clause. By using a subordinate clause, you are saying that the statement in the subordinate clause is less important (therefore subordinate) to the idea in the main clause. Make sure that the idea you want to emphasize is in the main clause.

A concession can appear right at the beginning of a paragraph. Note these examples of topic sentences from paragraphs in Unit 4:

> "Although undeniably convenient, residence may not be the best choice of accommodation for students." (page 115)

> "Although working part-time can create a serious time crunch, high school students should consider the many advantages of having a job." (page 131)

You do not have to mention all the counter–arguments in your essay, but if there is one that stands out as an obvious choice, concede it.

Qualifying statements

A good argument has to be reasonable, and so it must acknowledge that the world is not black or white, all or nothing. When you write an essay, you have to choose your words with care so as not to alienate your readers. You do not want to overstate your case.

Readers can accept qualified statements better than absolute statements. In the following statements, the first is absolute while the second is qualified and therefore easier to accept:

> Women do well at language-related tasks while men are good at spatial tasks.
>
> Women generally do better at language-related tasks while men tend to perform better on spatial tasks.

> All smokers develop lung cancer.
> Smokers have a higher risk of developing lung cancer.

Avoid using words like *all*, *always*, and *never*. They are rarely true. Instead, use *often*, *some*, and *many*:

> All teenagers work part-time. [not true]

> Many teenagers work part-time. [better]

Modal verbs (e.g., *may*, *might*, *could*) are another way to qualify statements:

> She is the best film editor in the world.

> She may be the best film editor in the world.

Verbs such as *seem* and *tend* can also make statements less absolute:

> He has no knowledge of physics.

> He seems to lack knowledge of physics.

Remember also that the simple present tense expresses the idea of a general statement, so it does not need additions to express the idea of a common occurrence. Students sometimes try to show the idea of generality by using a future tense or adding *always*:

> First-year students always find it difficult to make the adjustment from high school.

> First-year students will find it difficult to make the adjustment from high school.

> First-year students find it difficult to make the adjustment from high school. [better]

Be careful not to overuse qualifying statements. You still have to take a stand. You do not want to appear wishy-washy and uncommitted.

Assignment

Write a persuasive essay on one of the current issues in the news. For example, take a stand on safe injection sites for drug users, year-round schooling, or stem cell research.

Unit 7

Editing and Proofreading Skills

Word formation, grammatical structures, and mechanics are reviewed in Units 2 and 3. This unit gives you further practice, mostly in error correction. The sentences show common errors, most actually made by students in writing classes. Some of the students were learning English as a second language; some were native speakers of English.

Correcting Vocabulary Errors

Exercise 7.1 Word choice errors

These sentences are based on errors made when students mixed up one word for another, made a poor word choice, or even invented a word. Some of these are tricky, so you may want to work with a partner. Many of the words sound similar to the right words. Change the underlined word for one that fits the meaning of the sentence with any necessary re-phrasing:

1. The young generation today is far too <u>reliable</u> on cellphones.
2. None of the <u>tellers</u> in the clothing store approached me offering help.
3. Harriet Tubman is known for her <u>outrageous</u> contribution to freeing African-American slaves.
4. The blast of the Halifax explosion killed more than 1600 people; some were <u>incarcerated</u>.
5. I chose to study Rocket Richard because he <u>peeked</u> my interest.
6. Louis Riel was <u>trialed</u> for treason.
7. This assignment was <u>uneasy</u> at first.

Exercise 7.1 – *continued*

8. Students need to <u>thrive</u> for improvement.
9. He was caught <u>making</u> a crime and had to do community service.
10. The author <u>narrated</u> a story of his youth, when he fell in love.
11. The problems we faced made the whole trip <u>unjoyable</u>.
12. Through the <u>event</u> of researching Sir Wilfrid Laurier, I came to realize how much he contributed to our country.
13. At McDonald's, I was in charge of <u>sanity</u>. I had to make sure everything was clean and disinfected.
14. They were asked why they took the car, but they did not have a <u>sensitive</u> answer.
15. The author is <u>implementing</u> that the problem is the government's fault.
16. People who choose luxury cars often just want to show off their <u>richness</u>.
17. The plumber could not find the <u>issue</u> with the toilet.
18. I feel very <u>stressful</u> when I have to take an exam.
19. People choose their friends by their <u>outlook</u>.
20. Students need to develop good reading <u>hobbits</u>.

Exercise 7.2 Word differences

Choose the better word to fit the blank. Explain your answer, and discuss the meaning difference in class:

1. Mother Teresa is <u>famous/notorious</u> for helping the poor in India.
2. I didn't want to <u>disrupt/disturb</u> him when he was so busy with his family problems.
3. Jessica felt <u>ashamed/shameful</u> when he pointed out her mistakes.
4. My parents are <u>intolerable/intolerant</u> of the liberal dating practices in North America.
5. My writing still has many <u>shortages/shortcomings</u>.
6. The children were taught to be <u>respectful/respective</u> of their elders.
7. Their assignment was to <u>disapprove/disprove</u> the theory.

Exercise 7.2 – *continued*

8. They are having trouble <u>adapting/adopting</u> to Canadian winters.

9. Cellphones with cameras are now very <u>famous/popular</u>.

10. She chooses to <u>donate/pay</u> money to local charities, especially those that benefit children.

Exercise 7.3 Word choice

Replace the underlined phrase with a word that means the same thing (you might need to make slight changes to the sentence to make the word fit):

1. Teenagers should have a <u>time that they must come in by at night.</u>

2. The <u>man whose wife died</u> found it difficult to participate in the planned social activities.

3. The food was <u>not able to be eaten</u> because it had sat out for too long.

4. She admired his <u>quality of being on time.</u>

5. Parents should never give in to their children's <u>fits of frustration and anger</u> in stores when they don't get what they want.

6. I always plan family parties with <u>the woman who is married to my brother</u> because we have similar tastes.

7. I need a better job to pay for my <u>school fees for college</u>.

8. Part of the employees' salary goes into a <u>plan to give them money when they retire.</u>

9. After the plane crash, many children became <u>children with no parents</u>.

10. The years of <u>time with no rain</u> ruined the economy of the prairie region.

11. The <u>man who had two wives</u> hid his two lives well.

12. Silvia has been working as a social worker for a <u>period of 10 years.</u>

13. He got a job as a <u>person who drives other people around in a limousine.</u>

14. Nada prefers to use a bike <u>that stays in one place</u> rather than exercising outside.

15. When he was a kid, he got in trouble for <u>stealing things from stores.</u>

Exercise 7.4 Collocation

Change the underlined word for a more suitable one:

1. If the passport is lost or <u>robbed</u>, it is important to <u>communicate</u> the embassy.
2. She was so angry that she <u>hit</u> the door shut.
3. People who <u>visit</u> hockey games come to the <u>ice stadium</u> not only to see skating and goals but also fighting.
4. After she heard about the <u>stealing</u> in the neighbourhood, she got new locks <u>established</u>.
5. He is not very <u>true</u>; he will <u>say</u> the secret to someone.
6. I stopped to <u>clean</u> the raindrops from my glasses.
7. His friend is planning to <u>make</u> a bachelor party for him.
8. He went to <u>tell</u> the accident to the police. It took him hours to <u>accomplish</u> all the forms.
9. The committee voted to <u>disagree</u> the plan.
10. While the girls were <u>jumping</u> in the schoolyard, most of the boys were <u>doing</u> soccer.

Exercise 7.5 Parts of speech

Correct the errors in parts of speech:

1. Although Canada is a safety country and the criminal rate is dropping, many people seem worry about dangerous on the streets.
2. Talk on the phone with their parents can decrease their homesick.
3. The Montreal Canadiens loss the game because of Rocket Richard's absent.
4. More trees and flowers can beauty our city. It's importance to develop more parks.
5. Technology ables people to get connected easy and closely.
6. The most commonly use of cellphones is text messaging with people send hundreds of messages a day.
7. Parents' over-protective may cause their children to rebellion and get into trouble.
8. Because they want to success, they have to proceed very careful.

Exercise 7.5 – *continued*

9. Immigrants might have to change their customs and believes to fit in with the cultural.

10. Students can improve their reading comprehend by practice more. They will become more confidence.

Exercise 7.6 Spelling

Correct any errors:

1. I went threw the chapter and hilighted the main points, so studing will be much easyer.

2. It's important for the enviorment that we reduce the amount of polution we create.

3. They're was a problem with the salade, so I thru it into the garbage.

4. The police pulled him over for driving wrecklessly, but after he attack them, he ended up spending the nite in gaol.

5. When we were kids, we idlized Superman and Batman, so we whore caypse and ran around the house.

6. After the accidant, my car was a right-off, so the wreckers took it away.

7. The imigrants' education level will often determine weather or not they adopt to the society easily.

8. If the punishmint were more sever, may be fewer people would run red lites.

9. Cloths that you don't where anymore should be recycled as donations to chairity.

10. Eating a nutrisious, well ballenced diet definately keeps the body healthy.

Exercise 7.7 One word or two?

Choose which of the following choices fits the blank:

1. Jason _____ (maybe/may be) chosen to be _____ (incharge/in charge) of the project _____ (instead/in stead) of Martha.

Exercise 7.7 – *continued*

2. They're on sale now for $5.99 _____ (apiece/a piece),
   but I don't need _____ (anymore/any more).

3. It's _____ (altogether/all together) a new project with
   these specifications. _____ (Furthermore/Further more),
   there is no _____ (downside/down side) at all.

4. We need to get the tools _____ (already/all ready)
   before we begin, _____ (inspite/in spite) of the delay.
   We've _____ (already/all ready) made too many mistakes.

5. Jill and her twin sister look _____ (alot/a lot)
   _____ (alike/a like), but it's not hard to tell them
   _____ (apart/a part).

6. Harry read the instructions _____ (aloud/a loud) and
   then took the pieces _____ (apart/a part) to start again.

7. Melanie had a _____ (faraway/far away) look in her eye
   as she watched the children play _____ (outside/out side)
   the window.

8. I'll be fine with _____ (whatever/what ever) you choose.
   We can check back with _____ (eachother/each other) later.

9. We need _____ (atleast/at least) _____
   (another/an other) boxful, _____ (maybe/ may be) even
   two more.

10. There has to be _____ (away/a way) to fix this. We need
    it _____ (intact/in tact).

Exercise 7.8 Word division correction

Correct the word form errors in the following sentences. Some words
should be separated into two words (e.g., *a lot* instead of *alot*),
while some groups of two or three words should be combined (e.g.,
maybe instead of *may be*).

1. It was quiet on the downtown street. I saw a lone man infront
   of the department store window.

2. He raced a head of the pack and then had to wait for the rest
   to catchup.

Exercise 7.8 – *continued*

3. I don't have alot of time to get the reports all together. I'd like a bit more time.

4. Now a days, people rely on technology far too much. They can't do things themselves.

5. Eventhough she knew he was rude, she was taken aback when he asked her a bout her age.

6. Once in awhile I like to put a side all my work and go for a walk alone to clear my head.

7. Through out the vacation, Fiona could not get along with her parents atall. Never the less, she made some friends and had a good time.

8. Exercise should be apart of everyday life. Even a walk a round the neighbourhood can be beneficial.

9. It was all so strange, but she could not figure out what was amiss. More over, she had to report the malfunction.

10. Inspite of the distance, she wanted to go to her son's university to see what he was upto, whereas her husband was against the idea.

Troublesome words

It is important to learn how words are used in sentences, to recognize word patterns. For instance, a verb might need a direct object or a specific preposition after it. The following words are those that often show up in grammatical errors. They are especially problematic for ESL students. The example sentences show the common patterns for these words. Study the patterns, and discuss them in class. Then correct the errors in the following exercise:

afford

The verb *afford* is a transitive verb, so it takes a direct object. It is generally used with *can*, *could*, and *be able to*. It can also be followed by an infinitive. It is not used in the passive voice.

> I can't afford a Gucci bag, so I have to be satisfied with a knock-off.

> They can't afford to lose another day on that project.

agree

Agree is often followed by *with*, plus a person or a noun referring to some sort of decision or plan. The preposition *to* is used for plans. Infinitives can also follow *agree*.

> I agree with the basic proposal, but I think we should change the timeline.

> She usually agrees with him, but this time she put her foot down.

> They agreed to the proposal, and he agreed to change the fees.

compare

The prepositions *to* and *with* are often used with the verb *compare*. A frequent error is using the active participle *comparing* instead of the passive participle *compared*. *Comparing* has to refer to whoever or whatever is making the comparison, while *compared* refers to what is actually in the comparison.

> Compared to the deluxe model, this one is a better buy. Those features are unnecessary.

> She put together a chart comparing the features of the two cars.

concern

The verb *concern* refers to someone being affected or worried about something. The person is the object of the verb and so is generally described with the passive participle *concerned*.

> This letter concerns his habitual lateness.

> The teachers are concerned about his lack of progress.

easy/difficult

The common ESL error with *easy* and *difficult* (and their synonyms) is using these adjectives to describe the person rather than the task.

> It is easy to follow his argument. His essay is very clear.

> Learning a new language is difficult, but practice makes it easier.

even

Even is an adverb used to strengthen or intensify. It is used just before the surprising part of a statement. *Even though* is stronger than *although* but is used in the same way. A common ESL error is to use *even* as a conjunction, but it cannot stand alone in that position—it must have an accompanying conjunction to make *even though*, *even if*, or *even when*.

Even John was pleased with the results.

I even got my nails done.

I couldn't even see the stitching; it was so fine.

She started working even faster when the bell rang.

Even if the mini-skirt does come back into fashion, I wouldn't be caught dead wearing one.

Even though Monica spent a fortune on her outfit, she didn't look half as good as Rachel.

Alter the following sentences by adding the word *even*. See how many positions *even* will fit in each sentence. You might have to make slight alterations to the sentence:

1. If Fred had notified us a day earlier, I would have been able to fix the problem with less effort.

2. Although Fatima couldn't see the alterations, she approved the new design as a better choice.

3. I had to follow the template, so I couldn't use Jamie's suggestions.

4. If I raised the hemline and took in the seams, the dress wouldn't look better.

hardly, scarcely, barely

Hardly is not the adverb form of the adjective *hard*; instead, it is a synonym of *scarcely* and *barely*.

I could hardly hear him. [I heard him only a bit.]

We have scarcely any money left.

spend

Spend is used with money or time.

> They spent days on the project, but that didn't show in the results.

> I spent $50 on the purse.

> How much did you spend on your vacation?

suppose

Suppose means to think. In the passive voice, it shows expectation. In the past of the passive, it shows something should have happened but didn't. Students who leave off the *d* in the past participle are confused by the pronunciation since the sound of the *d* disappears next to the *t* of *to*.

> I suppose that he could have misplaced the file.

> Remember that you are supposed to change those figures to metric.

> I was supposed to pick him up at four, but I forgot.

used to

Native speakers often do not write the *d* on *used to* because of the pronunciation. ESL learners have trouble keeping the two *used to* expressions separate, in both form and meaning: A past action is expressed with *used* plus the infinitive, while *used to* in the passive voice with a gerund expresses the idea of being accustomed to something.

> I used a credit card to open this door. [the verb *to use* in its basic meaning]
> A credit card can be used to open this door. [passive construction with the verb *to use*]

> I used to work long hours, but now I have a new job. [past action]
> I'm used to working long hours, so I don't mind my new shifts. [I am accustomed to working long hours.]

Exercise 7.9 Troublesome words

Correct any errors in the following sentences:

1. I've been saving my money, but I still cannot afford buying a new car.

Exercise 7.9 – *continued*

2. Comparing to my sister, I lack musical ability.

3. Clothes, toys, or cars are spent too much money on.

4. I suppose to meet him at 4:00, but the bus was late.

5. She use to be his assistant, so she knows a lot about the project.

6. The presentation of the food is another area they should concern about.

7. Even he had contacted us earlier, we would not have been able to fix the problem.

8. Adults are hard to learn a new language.

9. Cellphones are easily to make contact with others.

10. He worked hardly on his manuscript, but he barely got anything accomplished.

11. She used to living in Regina, but she moved to Edmonton for a job.

12. I didn't understand what he was saying even he spoke more slowly.

 Exercise 7.10 Sentence rewriting

Using derivatives for the underlined words, rewrite the following sentences. (Derivatives are other parts of speech—the corresponding noun, verb, adjective, or adverb.)

Example: Thomas did not <u>succeed</u> at increasing the sales in the division. (verb)

Thomas did not have <u>success</u> at increasing the sales in the division. (noun)

Thomas was not <u>successful</u> at increasing the sales in the division. (adj.)

1. I liked that the material was <u>soft</u>. (adj.)

2. Elizabeth enjoys being <u>solitary</u>. (adj.)

3. The whales are in danger of becoming <u>extinct</u>. (adj.)

4. Jason only felt more <u>confusion</u> when the teacher explained it again. (noun)

5. That Brenda was <u>compassionate</u> toward the children surprised me. (adj.)

Exercise 7.10 – *continued*

6. There was no <u>agreement</u> among the members of the committee. (noun)

7. One student from each class was a <u>participant</u> in the project. (noun)

8. What you say in this essay is too <u>repetitive</u>. (adj.)

9. When all the guests arrived, Tracey made the <u>introductions</u>. (noun)

10. I expect <u>responsible</u> behaviour from them while I am away. (adj.)

11. The explosion made Eric <u>deaf</u>. (adj.)

12. Michelle tried to hide that she was <u>disappointed</u> with the results. (adj.)

13. Geoffrey could not see the <u>distinction</u> between the two methodologies. (noun)

14. There was <u>chaos</u> in the city. (noun)

15. The puppy has so much <u>curiosity</u> that it gets into everything. (noun)

16. It is <u>customary</u> to write a thank-you note after receiving a gift or special favour. (adj.)

17. Brian and Susan like to <u>meditate</u> in the morning. (verb)

18. There was no <u>verification</u> for the story. (noun)

Correcting Grammar Errors

Exercise 7.11 Error correction

Correct the errors in the following sentences:

1. The student's completed the assignment quick, so they leave the class.

2. The television is broke. I'll have to downloading that show. I want to know who was the killer.

3. Because he had took the wrong road. He was late for the meeting and miss the important details.

4. In winter, the children go skiing, skating. They don't mind the cold weather as long as their dressed proper for it.

5. I should not of change the date of the meeting the first one was more better.

Exercise 7.11 – *continued*

6. When she reads slow and carefully, she can understand better and making less mistakes.

7. My purse is full of stuffs I don't need even I clean it out regular.

8. Each of projects have a difference advantage choosing one will be difficulty.

9. He is train to be a electrician. When he graduate, he will work for his uncle whom renovates and sell old house's.

10. The student's had to redo there work because they're were to many mistake.

11. He better not wait for her. Its time she learned the consequences of been late.

12. Sylvia rather let Mike runs the workshops. So she can concentrate to the reorganization.

13. For every cases, the detective write's an official report for his client.

14. Even she disagrees about the decision, she try's to support the work the staff is done.

15. The programmers checked the code, ran some test case, and finally they find the problem.

16. The students' asked there teacher whether it was possible to schedule the tutorial for another days. They did not want to missing the career day presentation.

17. I find this grammar point very confused. May be the teacher could explaining it again.

18. Its her boyfriends' fault. Hes so possessive that he never let's her go out with her friend's.

Exercise 7.12 Determiners

Correct any errors:

1. Marilyn Bell was a first person to swim across the Lake Ontario.

2. There are many ways to access information through Internet.

3. Many of students have trouble writing essays. They need to take it one step at the time.

4. Pete is considering going to University of British Columbia or Simon Fraser University.

Exercise 7.12 – *continued*

5. Princess Diana was a most popular and famous woman in the world in the 1980s.

6. Meaning of a gift can be misinterpreted and can cause problems in relationship.

7. He could be success if he took program seriously.

8. The honesty is one of most important traits she is looking for in a man.

9. James wants to be doctor, but he is discouraged because it requires many years of study.

10. The book on the table belongs to the student who usually comes in late.

Exercise 7.13 Countable and uncountable nouns

Correct any errors:

1. I gave him an advice, but he refused to take it. He went ahead and bought the furnitures on delayed payments.

2. They suffered several setbacks in their plans. They didn't have the informations they needed at the start.

3. The teacher gave us many homework to do, but I got a head start on learning my vocabularies.

4. I bought new luggages for the trip—two suitcases and a rolling duffle bag.

5. She did not return the money but instead used them.

6. He restored the car. It's a real beauty now, but it took him a lot of time to do.

7. Many people who live on the street are addicted to alcohols and drugs.

8. The rehabilitation program gave them happiness and hopes.

9. Now that she has finished her assignment, she has another work to do.

10. I don't have the time or money to take on that project.

11. Students were having troubles with their reading and writing tasks.

12. Tattoos are like make-ups, clothes, and jewelleries; they decorate the body.

Exercise 7.13 – *continued*

13. I need to stop at the grocery store. I have to buy a bread, a milk, a cheese, and some fish. [be specific]

14. The graduate students do many researches. The studies are often funded by pharmaceutical companies.

15. I asked him for an information package about the company.

Exercise 7.14 Verb tense and form

Correct any errors:

1. I selected articles that can be helpful for my assignment since I have no previous experience with this kind of research. After I have found several articles, I looked for a website.

2. When I started high school, I have been taking ESL classes to catch up on my English skills. Now in college I still think I need more practice.

3. If children are not teached the difference between right and wrong, they might don't pay attention to their behaviour.

4. Managing money can be very difficult for college students. If they are used to spend their money freely, then when it was time to live on their own, budgeting will be a hard task to accomplish.

5. The change in organization forces people to working more to get the same amount accomplish.

6. If I had finished the project on time, I would not lost so many marks. Now I have to make sure I will do a good job on the final research assignment or I will not have passing the course.

7. People did not take transit because they do not want to wait for buses, hates the overcrowding, and prefer the convenience of a car.

8. Teachers can make reading groups to let the students to have more chance to read.

9. I'm not use to the new system yet, but I think it will helped management to pinpoint problems more quickly.

10. First, I decide to go to the bank because I didn't have any cash. But when I arrive at the bank, I found that I had forgot my bank card.

11. She has had many interesting experiences: She has been bungee jumping in Australia, she has dancing in a Parisian cabaret, and she seen the fall of the Berlin Wall.

Exercise 7.14 – *continued*

12. If I won a million dollars in the lottery, I will still want a job. I would want to use the knowledge I learned in school, and I would still needing to earn money for when I run through the lottery money.

Exercise 7.15 Tense shift

Correct the verb tense errors in the following paragraph:

In "Why My Mother Can't Speak English," the mother wants to get her Canadian citizenship because she was afraid of being deported. She was a Chinese immigrant who has lived in Canada for many years but she spoke limited English. She relies on her son to take care of her domestic affairs after the death of her husband. Her son took her to the preliminary interview at the Citizenship building, and she attempts to bribe a court clerk with *lai shi*. The son tries to teach her English for the citizenship interview, but she just talked about the past. Finally, the mother was able to take the oath of citizenship. Afterwards, she told her son that she will go to the cemetery to tell her husband of her achievement.

Exercise 7.16 Active and passive voice

Correct any errors:

1. An accident was happened on the highway, so I was late for class.
2. I happened to see Jill at the cafeteria, so I didn't have to call her.
3. People often get misleading by salespeople. They buy something they are regret later.
4. People are fear the threat of terrorism even though more people are suffered from cancer and heart disease.
5. I'm afraid I've worried him now. I didn't think he would be taken the news so hard.
6. If I practise enough, my skills will be improved, but I don't think I will make the NHL.
7. Children should assigned some simple housework. Chores need to be share by all family members.
8. Students can also be benefit from playing video games. These games are improve problem-solving skills.

Exercise 7.16 – *continued*

9. The Parliament buildings were build in the early 1860s, before Canada became an official country.

10. Christmas is a time of year to celebrate. Families get together, and gifts are exchange.

Verbs Expressing Emotion

The verbs used to describe emotions can be confusing in English. There are two basic patterns: In one, the person experiencing the feeling is the grammatical subject of the sentence. In the other, the stimulus (the thing causing the feeling) is the subject, and the person feeling the emotion is the direct object of the verb. Sometimes these verbs have a similar meaning but follow a different sentence pattern:

> I fear snakes. [the person is the grammatical subject]
>
> Snakes frighten me. [the person is the grammatical object]

> Hal enjoys jogging.
>
> A walk in the park would please them.

The verbs that take the person as the grammatical object cause problems for ESL students. They create incorrect sentences such as "I am exciting about the field trip" or "I am interesting in the lab work." Because the person experiencing the emotion is the object of the verb, a passive construction is used to describe the person. To really understand the mistake in the participle, you have to go back to the basic verb form. This is shown in the pattern in the following examples:

> Astronomy interests me.
>
> Astronomy is interesting.
>
> I am interested in astronomy.

> This grammar lesson confuses me.
>
> This grammar lesson is confusing.
>
> I am confused by this grammar lesson.

Here are some verbs that follow the same pattern, with the person as the grammatical object:

amuse	appal	bore	charm
annoy	bewilder	bother	confuse

depress	flatter	irritate	scare
disappoint	frighten	mislead	shock
disgust	horrify	offend	surprise
encourage	impress	please	thrill
excite	insult	puzzle	
fascinate	interest	satisfy	

In contrast, here are some verbs for which the person is the grammatical subject:

admire	like	prefer	trust
enjoy	love	regret	
fear	miss	resent	
hate	not mind	respect	

Example sentences:

> I enjoy a walk in the park.

> I don't mind waiting.

> He regrets breaking up with her.

Exercise 7.17 Verbs expressing emotion

Choose the correct form of the verb to complete the sentence:

1. I get _____ [confused, confusing] whenever he talks about the long-term financial prospects.

2. She is _____ [frightened, frightening] because he is stalking her.

3. My mother was _____ [pleasing, pleased] that my sister and I could plan the trip without arguing.

4. The test results were _____ [disappointing, disappointed], but the questions had been _____ [misleading, misled], so it's no wonder we did poorly.

5. Yuri was _____ [offending, offended] by what his supervisor said.

6. The mess in the kitchen was _____ [disgusting, disgusted]. It _____ [bothering, bothered] me that they could live like that.

7. I found the book very _____ [interesting, interested], but I was _____ [shocking, shocked] by the ending.

Exercise 7.17 – *continued*

8. My roommate had many _____ [annoyed, annoying] habits. I was _____ [relieving, relieved] when he decided to move.

9. I was _____ [flattering, flattered] when she chose me for the promotion.

10. The work is _____ [satisfying, satisfied], and my supervisors are _____ [encouraging, encouraged].

Exercise 7.18 Verb form correction

Correct any errors:

1. She admired the skill with which he built the deck and was pleasing with the result.

2. Pooja found the questions confused, so she's relieved to have passed the mid-term.

3. She was surprised that they threw her a birthday party.

4. I don't mind waiting. I'll just read my book. I'm at an excited part—the hero is frightening the bad guys so they will give up their pursuit.

5. I resent his interference. He knows it, and he's trying to charm me into agreeing to the plan.

6. He felt worry about the evaluation, even though his supervisor always seems satisfying with his work.

7. His behaviour was appalling. I can't respect him anymore.

8. I like to talk to her because she's an interested person. She has travelled widely.

9. The party was really boring. There was too much shop talk. I found it annoyed.

10. That dress is not very flattered. I felt insulted that she chose it for me.

Gerunds and Infinitives

The *–ing* forms of the verb when used as nouns are called *gerunds*, as in "<u>Seeing</u> is <u>believing</u>." The base form of the verb preceded by *to* is called an *infinitive*, as in "He didn't know what <u>to do</u>." Both these types of words are called *verbals*. When a verbal follows another form, it could be either the gerund or the infinitive. It depends on the first verb; there is no definitive grammar rule to explain which verbal is used. ESL students, especially, have to memorize each usage. Sometimes verbs can be completed by either a gerund or an infinitive, and sometimes the two expressions have different meanings. Here are some examples:

> I <u>appreciated seeing</u> the plans beforehand because they <u>failed to notify</u> us of the changes.

> After <u>attempting to get</u> a role in the production, he now says he <u>dislikes acting</u> in plays.

> He <u>prefers directing</u>. He <u>prefers to direct</u> plays. [no meaning difference]

> I <u>remembered to take</u> the medicine. I <u>remembered taking</u> the medicine. [different meanings]

Note that the infinitive is also used to express the *in order to* idea, where *in order* can often be left out:

> He quit school [in order] to go to Hollywood.

> I whistled [in order] to attract his attention.

Verbs that take gerunds (+ _____ing):

anticipate	dislike	keep	recommend
appreciate	dread	like	remember
avoid	enjoy	mind	resent
begin	escape	miss	resume
cease	fear	postpone	risk
consider	finish	practise	start
continue	forget	prefer	stop
delay	hate	quit	suggest
deny	involve	recall	try

Verbs that take infinitives (+ to _____):

afford	fail	long	seem
appear	forget	need	start
attempt	happen	neglect	stop
begin	hate	plan	think
choose	hope	prefer	threaten
continue	intend	pretend	try
dare	learn	promise	want
decide	like	remain	wish
expect	live	remember	

Exercise 7.19 Gerunds or infinitives

Choose the correct form of the verb to complete the sentence:

1. I enjoy _____ [taking, to take] a walk after dinner.

2. He intends _____ [waiting, to wait] until she returns even though he'll miss _____ [seeing, to see] the concert.

3. The director threatened _____ [firing, to fire] the whole division.

4. The farmer suggested _____ [taking, to take] the river route to get a better view.

5. Jack happened _____ [seeing, to see] Eliza in the market, so he invited her _____ [joining, to join] us at the sports bar later.

6. The committee decided to postpone _____ [repainting, to repaint] the clubhouse until after some much-needed renovations.

7. Remind me _____ [returning, to return] the books to the library after class.

8. He keeps _____ [telling, to tell] me to invest more money in stocks, but I don't think I can afford _____ [taking, to take] the risk.

9. They neglected _____ [taking, to take] the necessary precautions and so had to postpone _____ [redoing, to redo] the race.

10. I wanted _____ [trying, to try] the bungee jump, but Sam preferred _____ [keeping, to keep] both feet on the ground.

Exercise 7.20 Gerund and infinitive correction

Correct any verb errors in the following sentences:

1. The witness denied ever to see the accused man. She remembered seeing a much taller man.

Exercise 7.20 – *continued*

2. I hope getting a better mark next time, so I will start to study earlier.

3. She promised to be more careful next time, and she seemed to be sincere.

4. Elaine expected seeing him at 4:00, but he had delayed starting the meeting, so he was late.

5. I suggest to try another way. You should pretend agreeing with him and then fix the problem yourself.

6. I resent having to do this over again. He shouldn't have tried doing it without help in the first place.

7. She couldn't decide whether to continue seeing him or not.

8. I recommend to wait until she's older. She'll enjoy riding the roller coaster then.

9. They resumed cutting the budget after the CEO threatened firing more staff.

10. I recall asking him about it before, but he avoided to answer me.

Exercise 7.21 Prepositions

Fill in the blank with the correct preposition where necessary:

1. That new equipment isn't suitable _____ winter conditions. We'll have to replace it _____ something rated for −15.

2. I don't feel sorry _____ you. It was your fault that you weren't ready _____ the test.

3. When she puts her earphones _____ and listens _____ her MP3 player, she becomes oblivious _____ everything around her.

4. You are capable _____ much better work. You should pay attention _____ class.

5. He arrived _____ the airport too late _____ the plane. He had to wait _____ the next flight.

6. I'm not familiar _____ that brand. Is the company known _____ making good products?

7. They were grateful _____ the extra help. They were confused _____ his attempts at explanation.

Exercise 7.21 – *continued*

8. My apartment building is adjacent _____ the park, and I can see the baseball games _____ my window.

9. She's demanding _____ answers. She wants to talk _____ the manager.

10. I depend _____ my brother to calm the situation whenever I argue _____ my parents

Exercise 7.22 Preposition corrections

Correct any preposition errors in the following sentences:

1. She's been living by her own for too long; she has a hard time getting along with people.

2. Here are some solutions about the problem. We need to choose the best one of these.

3. I can store important data at my laptop computer and retrieve it later on my convenience.

4. The family can have a conversation together in front of the dinner table.

5. If someone is acting suspiciously, bystanders should pay more attention on the behaviour.

6. Many people have a desire on a luxury car to show off to their friends.

7. Students should be given reading homework on the textbook at every week.

8. I looked up the company in the Internet, but I couldn't find enough information about it.

9. I can make my meaning clear with choosing good vocabulary.

10. This apartment is a good choice because it's quick to get to downtown from here.

Exercise 7.23 Prepositions and different parts of speech

Sometimes the use of prepositions is confusing because of the differences in parts of speech. Often, the noun may have to be followed by a preposition, but the verb does not. Here are some example sentences:

Exercise 7.23 – *continued*

John <u>influenced</u> his brother. [verb, no preposition]
John is a big <u>influence on</u> his brother. [noun + preposition]

I <u>lack</u> musical talent. [verb, no preposition]
I have a <u>lack of</u> musical talent. [noun + preposition]

Correct any errors:

1. Everybody fears of terrorist attacks, but there's no solution to the problem.

2. He shows a lack of basic arithmetic skills and absolutely no understanding the principles of physics.

3. The course emphasizes on basic first aid treatments and life-saving measures.

4. The techniques used affect on the results and should be taken into account.

5. The author describes about the difficulties he faced enrolling in university. He mentions about the misunderstandings.

6. She expects of Zach to finish on time and to solve the problem.

7. Her desire of privacy has become obsessive. She's becoming a true hermit.

8. With the merger of the two companies, they gained of a new division to take care of the service calls.

9. One way to help homeless people is to increase of charity programs.

10. The new organization structure will have an impact on all day-to-day operations.

Try rewriting the sentences above, switching from the noun to the verb form and vice versa, where possible. For example, "Everyone has a fear of terrorist attacks" is a possible version of the first sentence.

Exercise 7.24 Possessive forms

Correct any errors:

1. I couldn't find out who's keys these are, so I took them down to the Security's Department.

2. Erin lent me her keys to the storage room's because I misplaced mines.

Exercise 7.24 – *continued*

3. A long time ago people had large families, but nowaday's people have fewer children.

4. I didn't have a dictionary, so I borrowed Ron's. I had to go find mine later.

5. The childrens' babysitter needs a ride home if she babysits after midnight.

6. The Johnson's house was broken into last week. They're whole place was trashed.

7. I've been sitting here watching the puppy try to chase its tail. Who's dog is it anyway?

8. Helen and Andy left there backpacks near the bandshell.

9. Sallys car was broken into, and her CDS were stolen.

10. If you don't have you're textbook, you can borrow Elizabeths, but make sure you don't mark it up because she is very fussy about her things.

Exercise 7.25 Singular/plural

Correct any errors:

1. One of the band members are from Australia. He play the trumpet.

2. Working with John and Jane were a pleasure. They are very talented actor.

3. Anton was behaving like a six-years-old. I couldn't take it for another minutes.

4. Every day, the mother goose, along with its five goslings, go across the highway. The drivers all seems to be watching out for the geese.

5. A lot of people leave the city on long weekends. The resulting traffic jams are an ordeal.

6. Each tool has their own place in the case. The compartments is very well organized.

7. Surveillance cameras does not help to make society secure. It only helps to capture criminals after the fact.

8. The number of candidates for the November elections have risen to 20. It should make for an interesting campaigns.

Exercise 7.25 – *continued*

9. If any documents are misplaced, it can be found easily if the information are stored on computers. The search functions allow quick retrieval.

10. You should buy that laptop next week. They will probably go on sale.

Exercise 7.26 Fragments and run-ons

Fix the sentence structure errors to eliminate fragments and run-on sentences:

1. She's pretending to work. But she is just playing solitaire on the computer. And time is running out.

2. Including a list of references in the résumé. It is not necessary. Can be left for the job interview.

3. She lets Jake use the car whenever he asks. Even though he's a terrible driver. Last year he had three accidents.

4. We studied all the readings in class, however many of the students had trouble remembering the material for the test.

5. It's not hard to see what the problem is, the machine won't start because this piece is jamming it.

6. Because he had accumulated so much stuff in residence. He borrowed his parents' van when he was moving out.

7. In most cases, being your own boss and not having to answer to anyone.

8. I had to go to the bank before I could pay him back. Being in debt makes me uncomfortable.

9. He lets his employees have a say in the decision-making process, therefore their job satisfaction is high. Few of them moving on to other jobs.

10. Because of his success with the last project. He was promoted to assistant manager. After a while he was making much more money. So, he asked his girlfriend to marry him.

Exercise 7.27 Sentence structure

Correct the errors, and improve the sentence structure:

1. The law can prevent accidents that were resulted from injuries and death.
2. He wondered why did she not return his calls. He thought that they had hit it off.
3. Success is something that everyone wants it.
4. I come from Saudi Arabia which its national language is Arabic.
5. By going to a fast-food restaurant, it will save time.
6. In a smaller store, you often find the staff more knowledgeable about the products and are more willing to go the extra mile to help you.
7. Pressing hard on the fountain pen, the nib broke.
8. For international students in Canada, they face difficulties in daily life.
9. Because with the fast development happening in China, there are no longer any benefits for studying abroad.
10. The manager cut the staff he reorganized the filing system and got everything to run more smoothly.

Correcting Punctuation and Capitalization

Exercise 7.28 Apostrophes

Correct errors in the sentences below by either adding, moving, or removing an apostrophe where necessary:

1. Jills brother could'n't find a job this summer, so he's visiting her in Winnipeg.
2. This feature let's the user move the icon's over to align with the others.
3. Jack does'nt want to go to the Marshall's cottage next week because its too long a trip.
4. The children's playroom is alway's a mess, so shes given up on keeping it clean.
5. Whose umbrella is that? It cant be hers. She had a blue one.
6. Lets see if Fatima can join us. She know's Montreal very well. Its her hometown.

Exercise 7.28 – *continued*

7. She compared her answers to theirs and realized she had to do them all over again.

8. Were expecting two shipment's of blue jeans—one from each of our regular supplier's.

9. The meetings are held regularly on Tuesday's in the senior's lounge.

10. Thursday's lesson concern's the rampant misuse of apostrophe's in signs.

Exercise 7.29 Mechanics

Add punctuation marks and capital letters where necessary in the following sentences:

1. if i hadnt been paying attention i would have been hit by that ball

2. the japanese garden at ubc is a beautiful restful place i like to visit there on sunday afternoons

3. allison loves horror movies but i hate being scared my favourite movie is gone with the wind

4. tailgating is a traffic violation moreover it is dangerous not only can the tailgater easily hit the car ahead but drivers behind the tailgater get frustrated seeing brake lights because they do not know whether there is an actual traffic slowdown

5. like a drill sergeant steven shouted do not panic walk dont run

6. on my trip to europe i visited paris, monaco, florence, rome, venice, munich, and amsterdam i met a lot of students from different countries who were travelling on the same tour bus

7. the peoples response is predictable they wont support the new party because of its stand on social justice issues

8. i cant say whos coming to the wedding because i havent seen the latest list

9. the womens washroom was closed for maintenance so frances and lee took over the mens room

10. charless mother used to play for a ladies softball team she held a few pitching records

Editing to Improve Style

Exercise 7.30 Conversational style

Rewrite the following passages into a more academic style, and correct errors:

1. I have done both the cellphone and land line thing. Let me tell you, a home phone is the way to go. I can't wait till the end of my agreement to get rid of that cellphone. Well, actually, I can't get rid of it completely. I would still have it for emergencies.

2. Look at residence for example. Residence is a licence to have fun, drink lots, and meet new people; basically a licence to party. Sounds like fun, but there are a few problems.

3. Well, in college it's a big difference. Now students have to budget their money well or they can get really screwed over. Which is the most important part of being on your own.

4. Parents should give help to their children when they asked you to. Otherwise, they will just yell at you for not giving them space. Sometimes they will say you're annoying and stuff like that.

5. No longer can you come home and have Moms home cooking. Welcome to fast TV dinners and a life of Kraft dinner. Now that balanced diet has been thrown out the window to provide more time for homework and studying.

6. The rich people now-a-days have mommy and daddy's moneypit to fall back on if they screw up once in university. But when poor students get in they know if they don't do well they'll be poor for years to come.

7. This guy came to do the landscaping. And he put in a new walkway. And he tore out all the old shrubs. And he made some new planting beds. But we're gonna put in the plants next spring cause we're too late in the season.

Exercise 7.31 Wordiness

Rewrite the following sentences to make them concise by eliminating repetition and unnecessary words:

Example: When large factories are built, they invariably increase road traffic, which makes neighbourhoods far more dangerous places than they were before. (21 words)

Exercise 7.31 – *continued*

Large factories invariably increase road traffic, making neighbourhoods more dangerous. (10 words)

1. Canadian streets and public spaces should have more surveillance cameras. Having more surveillance cameras can help police.

2. The key to success or the most important factor of success in college courses is time management. Managing time in a proper and effective way is the key to success at every part of life. Students all over the world in numerous colleges are facing the same problem of not coping with time.

3. I was shopping along side with a friend of mine.

4. In college, students waste time on socializing and being with friends and waste their time on unnecessary things, such as talking on the phone, sitting in a café for hours, and lots of other things which affects their time.

5. I went to the mall that was close to where I reside. I walked into a store. It was a store only for watches. I was hoping I would definitely find what I was looking for because I spotted a store for watches.

6. Factors such as work, school, and other activities determine how much time and effort one can really put towards a relationship. To begin with, work can determine how much time someone can put into a relationship. For example, a couple where both people work a lot, less time would be put into the relationship but more effort should be put in to make up for the time.

7. Grades should reflect actual student achievement. Giving students a grade that they do not deserve does not help them later in life. When students receive a grade, it should be earned and not given to them as a favour because it is not good for their future. Students need to learn how to earn a grade, rather than receiving a grade that they do not earn. The grade they receive should reflect their actual achievement and skill level. Marks should not be given to students who do not earn them. Later on in life it will not do any good for them due to the fact that they just received a mark instead of actually earning one. Marks should not be given to students just to do a favour for them because they would get credit for something they did not work for. Achievement should be the reason for receiving a good grade, not just being given one as a favour.

Exercise 7.31 – *continued*

8. In our modern day society that we live in, it is understandable that materialism is equated with happiness because people are happy with material goods.

9. What I would do next time would probably be to maybe start my research earlier so I would have extra time to spare if I ran into problems finding the resources needed to complete a complete research assignment.

Exercise 7.32 "For example" narratives

Some students launch into rambling narratives when they give examples in their academic paragraphs and essays. An anecdote can make something interesting, but it can also distract from the main task at hand—proving the points made. Rewrite the examples, preferably in one sentence (see the example on pages 234–5):

1. Some people get a tattoo to remember someone or somebody. For example, a person showed his tattoo to me. He told me this tattoo means his girlfriend's name. When he and his girlfriend fell in love, he got the tattoo. Now they broke up, but he told me he would never erase the tattoo and forget his girlfriend because this is his first love.

2. People can edit their work faster and easier. For example, a student finishes an essay. He finds some mistakes and wants to edit it. If he writes his essay by hand, he needs to write it again. If the essay is in the computer, he can edit it using the cut and paste function.

3. Students should take advantage of their free time and seize the moment while they can. For example, the teacher has just assigned homework. At the end of the class, they know that they have a spare period next. Instead of taking the right step and completing that work, they waste time on something less important.

4. People will chose public transit if it is made more convenient and faster than driving. For example, a business man has to get to work. There are traffic jams on the highway. The driving is all stop and go. But a train bypasses all the traffic. It moves more quickly. Moreover, the man can do work on the train.

Exercise 7.32 *– continued*

5. Sometimes students do not take the time to study for tests and exams. For example, a student is going to have a test next week. Instead of studying for the test, that student decides to go to a party every night and pull an all-nighter the day before the test.

6. People should consider the volume of their ring tone. For example, you are on a bus sitting at the front reading a newspaper. All of a sudden someone's phone from the back of the bus is ringing and you hear everything perfectly clear but are now distracted. If the ring tone was lower, it wouldn't have been heard, and no one would have been distracted.

Reading Skills

The importance of good reading skills cannot be overstated even in the modern world of video on the Internet. It is impossible to become a good writer if you do not read a lot. Written English is different from the spoken variety of the language, so people who do not read much do not know the language—they are not comfortable with the complex sentence structures, the more sophisticated vocabulary, or the conventions, such as using punctuation correctly.

Because students are not sufficiently tested on their reading comprehension skills, some poor readers do not even realize that they have weak reading skills. After all, they know how to "read" the words, but they find it difficult to figure out the writer's main point or to detect tone, such as sarcasm and humour. Their vocabulary is limited, so they misunderstand what the writer is saying. They may read slowly and laboriously.

Reading skills, like all skills, are built gradually. The more you read, the easier it becomes. If you rarely open a book, it will be a chore when you do have to read something. With practice, you can increase your reading speed and level of comprehension. You will learn more words and be exposed to more new ideas. The more familiar you are with a subject, the easier it is to understand stories and articles on that topic.

Your choice of reading material will also determine your success. While most newspapers and magazines are considered to be at a low high school reading level, your familiarity with the topic may make a text easy to understand despite the perceived grade level. It is better to read some easier materials, such as children's books and simplified ESL readers, than to struggle through newspaper articles for which you do not have the background knowledge or the vocabulary. Start with easier texts, and increase the level of difficulty as you get more comfortable. Of course, you do not always have the luxury of time to do this. If you are taking a course with required readings, you must work your way through them as well as you can, even if you find it a struggle. But try to find time for that extra reading that will build your skills.

How you read a text depends on why you are reading it. When you read a chapter of your textbook, you highlight important sections and make notes. When you read a novel for pleasure, you just read through it. You scan a newspaper, reading headlines, looking at pictures, and choosing interesting articles to read. You can skim a chapter in a textbook to get the gist of what is said. If you need to study a story or an article for school, you should do a more careful reading—making notes, highlighting important points, and looking up unfamiliar words in the dictionary.

This unit introduces some of the basics of reading. You can practise and build your skills with the readings in Part 2 of this book.

Distinguishing Fiction and Non-fiction

When you walk into any bookstore or library, you will find that the main division between books is fiction and non-fiction—in other words, between made-up stories and true stories. Even though this distinction becomes blurred when it comes to works such as autobiographical fiction, it is important to differentiate these two kinds of writing. Sometimes students get confused and talk about a character in an essay or about the author doing the actions in a short story.

Even in the "real world" outside school, this distinction becomes important. Theological experts and historians have argued about the theories presented in *The Da Vinci Code*, even though it is a novel, a work of fiction. James Frey was censured in the media because he fabricated part of his memoirs (his life story); readers were expecting a "true" story. Journalists sometimes write about composite characters. We operate on this distinction between fiction and non-fiction even though "truth" is never as clear-cut as we would like. History, for instance, is subject to the interpretation of the writer.

We use the terms *short story* and *novel* to refer to works of fiction. Short stories can be anywhere from 500 to 5000 words. There are three short stories among the reading selections in this textbook. Novels are usually 300 to 1000 pages. Sometimes books are made up of linked short stories. Autobiographical fiction tells the life story of the author, but it is told in a narrative style, events in the story are not exactly as they happened, and the dialogue does not represent the actual words the participants used. Movies are usually works of fiction, unless they are documentaries. Docudramas blur the line between fiction and non-fiction because actual events are dramatized. For instance, the film *United 93* recreates the hijacked flight on 11 September 2001 that ended in a field in Pennsylvania; the recreation is based on transcripts of cellphone calls and other recordings, but much of it is conjecture because no one on the plane survived to tell the true story.

Fiction is more open to interpretation. We can use our imagination to picture characters and settings. And yet fiction can be truer than non-fiction because it can speak to us and stay with us. For instance, the novel *To Kill a*

Mockingbird is a powerful story that can have a greater effect on readers than a textbook reading on racism. Research shows that readers of fiction become more empathetic, that they feel what is happening to the characters.

Moreover, it has been shown that people learn facts better if they are delivered in the form of a story. This is not surprising because it was the way our ancestors learned and passed down knowledge. Readers of historical novels can get a good sense of the history of the period even though they are reading fiction.

Most of the readings in this text are non-fiction. You can call them *essays* or *articles*. Many of them were first published as columns in newspapers or magazines. In newspapers and magazines, news stories are written by reporters and relate the facts as objectively as possible. Columns are usually accompanied by a picture of the columnist in the newspaper or magazine. They give the columnist's opinion and are therefore more like essays. However, these are journalistic essays and therefore not the kind of academic essay you are expected to produce in your English course.

If *I* appears in the piece of writing, the identity of that person depends on what kind of writing it is. An *I* in a work of non-fiction refers to the author himself or herself. Thus, for example, for the article "Immigrants Isolated? Tell That to Their Children," we can say, "Rosie DiManno talks about her childhood in Toronto's Little Italy." However, "Why My Mother Can't Speak English" is a short story based on true events; in other words, it is autobiographical fiction. You cannot say, "Garry Engkent's mother blamed her husband." Because the mother and the son have not been given names in the story, we have to refer to them as *the mother* and *the son*. They are characters, not real people. You can also refer to the son as *the narrator*.

Note that we can refer to characters by their first or last names, depending on what they are called in the short story or novel. When you are discussing a non-fiction reading, you should give the author's full name the first time you mention it but then use just the family name. For example, you can say, "In 'Crushed by Potential,' Doug Howat explains why he is living at home with his parents even though he is a university graduate. Howat compares his position to his experience with his camera."

Identifying the Main Idea

Most essays have one main idea that the author is trying to communicate to his or her audience. Sometimes the idea is stated directly, and sometimes it is not. The reader may have to infer the thesis. If the thesis is not immediately obvious to you, look at the organization of the reading. Remember that you are looking for the most general idea that is supported in the essay. Do not confuse the topic with the main idea. For example, "White Tops, Grey Bottoms" is about school uniforms (that is the topic), but the main idea is that schools are putting too much emphasis on dress codes.

One of the best ways to figure out the main idea of a non-fiction reading is to look at the title. This especially holds true for newspaper stories and columns because their titles are actually headlines, which are sentences with some of the function words (such as determiners) taken out. Take a look at the table of contents of this book, and read the titles of the readings in Part 2. The non-fiction articles are mostly from newspapers; the titles tell you very clearly what the thesis is. For example, "The Case against Bottled Water" clearly shows the position of the authors. Compare these titles to the fiction pieces. It is not as obvious what "Soap and Water" or "The Squatter" is about.

A common organizational pattern for non-fiction writing, especially in newspapers and magazines, is to start with an anecdote—a story of something that happened to the author or to someone he knows. For example, Bev Akerman starts with a specific incident before she gives her arguments about school uniforms. The anecdotal introduction catches readers' attention because it is personal, something they can relate to.

Remember that in an academic essay, the thesis comes at the end of the introduction. This pattern is often used in journalistic essays and articles, except that the introduction may be several paragraphs long instead of the one-paragraph introduction you are used to writing for your essays. (Keep in mind that newspaper and magazine articles have many short paragraphs because they are written in columns.)

In specific sentences, the main idea will be in the main clause. Look at the transitions the author uses. For example, expressions such as *however* and *it is vital to remember* point the way to main points.

Remember that the main idea will be supported by examples and explanations. When you read such specific statements, look for the point that is being made.

Distinguishing Writers' Opinions

When you read essays and columns in newspapers and magazines, you have to make sure you follow different people's arguments. Often, authors mention some popular views before coming to their own. They will start relating these other views and then emphasize their own with a phrase like *the truth is . . .*

Here are some things to watch for:
- expressions like *people think*, which automatically distances that view from the author's view;
- words in quotation marks or expressions such as *so-called*, which show that the author does not agree with the word of expression;
- transition signals such as *however* and *more importantly*, which show a shift in emphasis;
- verbs like *suppose, claim, purport*;
- use of personal pronouns (*I, me*) to emphasize the author's point of view.

Here are some examples:

> "But the truth is that while phones were the best we had for a long time, they have always been profoundly anti-social and alienating inventions." (page 281) Tossell then goes on to prove his point of view about telephones.

> "This is the normal rhythm of the immigrant experience, although apparently a concept poorly understood by the authors of a Statistics Canada report released last week that warned about the isolation of visible minority neighbourhoods in Canada's largest cities where segregation, it claims, has become entrenched." (page 298) DiManno shows that she has problems with what the report is saying.

The reading selections in this text have comprehension and discussion questions that ask you about the author's viewpoint. As you read, look for the cues in the reading, and discuss them in class.

Recognizing Writers' Techniques

Writing is a craft. Writers use a variety of techniques to get their message across to their readers. Each word they put down is chosen from a vast array of possibilities. The way they structure their paragraphs and sentences is part of their craft. They keep in mind their audience and purpose. They want to make sure that everything is clear to the readers. They try to entertain, inform, and convince readers.

The reading selections in Part 2 have notes on the authors' techniques. You can discuss structure and language as you take up the reading in class. Consider the decisions the author made. Look at the connotation of words. Consider how the topic is introduced and concluded. Are you caught up in the story the author tells? Are you convinced by the arguments? Reading attentively will make you a better reader, but do not forget that sometimes you can just sit back and enjoy the ride the author takes you on.

Dealing with Unfamiliar Words

As you read, you will come across unfamiliar words. If you stopped to look each one up in the dictionary, reading would become tedious. Try to get by on guessing the meaning from the context. If you understand the gist of what is being said in the text, you do not have to go to your dictionary when you spot a difficult word. If, however, it is an important reading, such as your English homework, then you should read it the first time through without a dictionary but then go back over it again, highlighting important points, making notes, and looking up unfamiliar words to make sure you understand everything.

Children learn words by hearing them many times and gradually working out the meaning in their own minds. They use their knowledge of their language and of the world to help them. This type of learning continues as they learn to read and encounter a larger body of vocabulary items. The more they read, the more words they learn. This is why people who read little have weak vocabularies. Avid readers generally have a large vocabulary, but they may rarely consult dictionaries. They use them only when they need to be absolutely sure of the meaning of a word or when they are curious about the word. Remember that it is impossible for even the most educated speakers to know all the words of English.

Here are some examples of how context can help you understand words:

> As we passed the rotting garbage, we tried covering our noses to keep out the vile stench.

If you do not know what the words *vile* and *stench* mean, you can figure out from this sentence that they refer to the awful smell of the garbage. And, in fact, *vile* means "terrible, really bad," and *stench* means "bad smell."

> When his father asked, "And where do you think you're going?" the teenager looked back at him sullenly.

Sullenly is an adverb, describing the way the teenager looked at his father. The father is chastising his son, so chances are that the son is not too happy. From what you know about relationship between teenagers and their parents, you can guess that it is not a pleasant expression on his face. The adjective *sullen* means "resentful, unsociable, and sulky."

In addition to looking around the word to the context to figure out its meaning, you can look inside the word. You can look for familiar prefixes, suffixes, and roots. (Many of the common ones were introduced in Unit 2.) For example, the word *indeterminate* has an *in–* prefix, which is probably negative. The root *determine* is recognizable as the verb meaning "to find out the facts about something," so indeterminate means "impossible to know exactly." Another example is the word *naysayer*, which can be easily divided into its three parts: *nay* (meaning "no"), *say*, and *–er* (a suffix showing someone who does something), so a naysayer is someone who says no.

When you come across an unfamiliar word, keep reading and see whether the meaning of the sentence is clear enough. Use context clues and your knowledge of language to help you figure out the word. Go to the dictionary when you need to. You will have an opportunity to practise these vocabulary skills with the reading selections in the text and the accompanying exercises.

Exercise 8.1

Use context clues and word form to help you figure out the meaning of the underlined words:

1. It was <u>serendipity</u> that I came across that article. I wasn't even thinking of my research project when I found it, but it has just what I need.

2. They were <u>at loggerheads</u> over the proposal. In the end, they couldn't work together and had to submit separate proposals.

3. His <u>punctual</u> arrival was a relief since they were so used to waiting for him.

4. The leather sofa was comfortable, but it was <u>cumbersome</u> every time he had to move.

5. They were surprised at his decision to donate the proceeds of the sale because <u>altruism</u> had never been one of his qualities.

6. Simplified novels are <u>abridged</u> versions of the books that also have changes in vocabulary and sentence structure to make them easier to read.

7. I am <u>famished</u>. I only had a cup of yogurt for lunch.

8. The immigrant family was so happy to be here that they <u>assimilated</u> into Canadian society with ease.

9. I love to watch professional soccer because the players have such speed and <u>agility</u>.

10. It's important to eat a good breakfast to <u>fortify</u> yourself for the hard day ahead.

Exercise 8.2

Choose the right meaning of the underlined word, using context clues:

1. She thought that adults would behave better, but this class was as <u>obstreperous</u> as a bunch of preschoolers.
   a) well-motivated and on task
   b) noisy and difficult to control
   c) bored and sleepy

2. Ever since I started taking that medication I feel so <u>listless</u> that I don't get enough of my work done.
   a) without goals or a to-do list

Exercise 8.2 – *continued*

b) wide awake and alert

c) without energy or enthusiasm

3. Because cellphones are <u>ubiquitous</u>, people feel they have the right to use them any time they choose, just as everyone else is doing.

a) everywhere

b) useful

c) expensive

4. Neighbours complained about the local teenagers using the <u>derelict</u> building as a hang-out and were relieved when it was destroyed by a fire.

a) large, impressive

b) abandoned, not cared for

c) historical

5. She presented some <u>cogent</u> arguments and managed to get the opposition to back her plan.

a) angry

b) silly

c) convincing

6. Ever since his girlfriend left him, he's been <u>in the doldrums</u>. His friends are worried and trying to get him to snap out of it.

a) depressed

b) bored

c) happy

7. She found it disgusting when men would <u>expectorate</u> on the street, some barely missing her feet.

a) spit

b) sing

c) smoke

8. Unlike his shy sisters, he is very <u>gregarious</u> and makes friends easily.

a) selfish

b) giving

c) talkative

9. His friends like to tell him crazy, made-up stories because he is so <u>credulous</u>.

a) too ready to believe things

b) dramatic and fond of acting

c) sad and depressed

Exercise 8.2 – *continued*

10. Because the electricity supply can be quite <u>erratic</u>, people have a lot of battery-powered items as backup in case the power goes.
    a) expensive
    b) not regular, not dependable
    c) has mistakes in it

11. Tommy was definitely the <u>instigator</u> of the playground battle, but Amy and Khalid were also punished because they should have known better than to strike back. They should have gone to the teacher.
    a) victim, one who got hurt
    b) witness
    c) person who started something

12. His <u>vociferous</u> complaints angered the salesclerks and embarrassed the other customers all over the store.
    a) drunken
    b) loud
    c) illogical

Researching and Referencing

Some of your reading will be research for your writing. You may be doing just general background reading to help you understand a topic, or you may be doing specific research for a paper.

Like most students today, you probably rely on the Internet for all your research. However, it is often difficult to tell where online information originates from. Respected print newspapers, magazines, and professional journals often post articles online, and this material is reviewed, checked, and edited. Moreover, such publications stand by their work because they value their reputation. However, everything you read on the Internet does not go through that type of formal review. Anyone can start a website on any subject—he or she does not have to be an expert on the subject. Moreover, *Wikipedia*, an online encyclopedia, is open to editing by users and has had misinformation deliberately posted in its entries. Even sites from reputable organizations can be hacked. Misinformation from one site can be copied to another and can go viral, infecting even reliable news sources.

You should try to authenticate any information you get from the Internet. See whether it fits what you already know. Take anything that sounds odd with a grain of salt. Look for independent sources that give the same information. Look at traditional print sources. Check where the websites are based. For instance, an *edu* at the end of the URL, or Internet address, usually denotes a school, and information on the official sites should be reliable—unless they are student project pages.

When you incorporate information from another writer into your essay, you need to reference (cite) it. General knowledge and historical facts do not have to be cited, but interpretation and analysis of the facts should be referenced. Any time you copy phrases and sentences from another writer, you must use quotation marks to show the copied words, and you must include a citation to show your reader where these words came from. Your essay should be essentially your ideas and words, with support from other writers' work.

There are different ways of referencing the material you have used in your research, but essentially in the body of your paper you show when you are quoting or paraphrasing someone's words. The citation you use refers the reader to the full bibliography in the back. The bibliography (also called "references" or "works consulted") gives the reader the information needed to locate that source. You can see examples of referencing in "Internet Addiction" (page 274) and "Appearance: Its Social Meaning" (page 322).

There are three common styles of referencing. The Chicago style is often used in high schools; it uses footnotes for citations. The Modern Language Association (MLA) style is used for humanities subjects, such as English, in universities and colleges. The American Psychological Association (APA) style is used in the sciences and social sciences. Your school library will have information on the format of these styles, often with a style guide on its website. Your instructor will tell you which style you should use and may give you a handout to guide you.

Here is an example of how a reading from this textbook would appear in an MLA Works Cited list:

McQueen, Ann Marie. "Over Here, I Rarely Lift a Finger." *Skill Set:*

Strategies for Reading and Writing in the Canadian Classroom. 2nd ed. By

Lucia Engkent. Don Mills, ON: Oxford, 2011. 303–05. Print.

Avoiding Plagiarizing

Plagiarism is copying someone else's words or ideas and claiming them as your own. It is considered cheating or academic dishonesty. Usually, the punishment gets worse with each offence. For example, a first offence may mean a grade of zero on the paper and a notation on the student record. A second time may mean failing the whole course, while the third may result in expulsion from the school.

Plagiarism is easy to spot. Instructors get to know their students' writing styles and know what they are capable of. Generally, there is a noticeable difference between a student's writing style and a published author's. With modern technology, it is easy to cut and paste from other writers' works, but the same technology also makes the original sources easy to find.

Be careful when you take notes. Make sure you mark quotes accurately and keep references clear. It is also helpful to write your paper without constant consultation of your notes and sources. Make your points and use your research to support those points. Quote only when necessary, and make sure you use quotation marks and include the reference. Follow the techniques for paraphrasing in the next section.

Remember that a writing course is testing your ability to write, not to copy. It is dishonest to claim that the words on the page originated in your brain if they did not. In some cultures, writing does include copying phrases of well-known writers, but in Canadian schools, any such copying must be clearly shown with quotation marks and references. If not referenced otherwise, the words in the essay are assumed to have originated with the student writing the paper.

Paraphrasing

Paraphrasing is the art of reporting what is said in words other than those used in the original. You do this often in the course of a day when you tell someone what somebody else said. Teachers call upon you to paraphrase when they ask you to answer reading comprehension questions "in your own words." They are testing both your reading and your writing skills. A reading comprehension answer that consists of a sentence or two copied from the original article does not show that the student actually understands what he or she has written down. You also use paraphrase when you write a summary or a research paper. A paraphrase is often shorter than the original.

To be able to paraphrase well, you need a strong vocabulary and a good understanding of the original text. Do not just substitute synonyms; you need to reword it entirely. Put the information in the words you would normally use. Use different sentence structure. Be sure to change pronouns. For example, you do not use *I* because it is not you who is speaking.

When told that they have to put something in their own words, students sometimes ask what words from the original they can use in their paraphrase. Avoid phrases particular to the author. You can use the same basic English words if they have no handy synonym. For example, you cannot avoid words like *language* and *immigrant*. You can also use expressions if they are standard English, such as *supply and demand*. One test is that the words you use should be the ones you would normally use to say the same thing.

Study the following examples to see how to paraphrase:

Reading question: In the story "Why My Mother Can't Speak English," what is the main reason the mother does not learn English?

Original text: "For thirty-some years, my mother did not learn the English language, not because she was not smart enough, not because she was too old to learn, and not because my father forbade her, but because she feared that learning English would change her Chinese soul." (page 356)

Poor paraphrase: The mother did not learn English because she was afraid that it would change her Chinese soul. ["Chinese soul" is an expression unique to the author.]

Good paraphrase: The mother did not learn English because she was afraid that she would lose her identity as a Chinese woman. [does not repeat author's words and shows the meaning of "Chinese soul"]

Original text: "What's also problematic, I think, is that Canada has devalued the concept of assimilation, promoting instead a mosaic of ethnic identification that is inherently splintering and isolationist, emphasizing as it does the details that make us different rather than the aspirations that make us so much the same." (page 298)

Poor paraphrase: DiManno is saying that what is a problem, she thinks, is that Canada has made the idea of assimilation less valuable and that it promotes a mosaic of cultural identity that splinters and isolates people, putting emphasis on what makes us different rather than the hopes that make us the same. [words are exchanged for synonyms, and sentence structure remains the same]

Good paraphrase: DiManno is saying that the Canadian government's policy of multiculturalism encourages people to emphasize ethnic differences rather than to look for the values that all Canadians share.

Exercise 8.3

Paraphrase these passages:

1. Appearance is everything. We are constantly being judged by the way we look—to our advantage or disadvantage. Unattractive people may be viewed as inconsequential or ill-favoured, while very attractive people may be thought of as all beauty and no brains.

2. Although some people argue that people today are ruder and less considerate of others, it is easy to find examples of how

Exercise 8.3 – *continued*

we are better behaved than our ancestors. For example, our society has made improvements in the way we treat those who have lesser status. We make fewer class distinctions, and overt racism is not socially accepted today. Women are no longer treated as being nothing more than the property of their husbands or other male relatives.

3. It's hard to say who is more addicted to lotteries—the people who play them or the governments who depend on the revenue they generate. The money goes to support many facilities that should be funded by taxes, such as hospitals and recreation centres. However, taxpayers seem to prefer putting their money toward lottery tickets than toward tax increases.

4. Women's sports have always gotten short shrift. Women golfers and tennis players would play for peanuts compared to the men's prizes. Women's hockey teams have trouble getting ice time. The poor media coverage for women's teams means that even their victories are buried in a few paragraphs in the sports section of the newspaper while losing men's teams get front-page coverage.

5. Halloween has become such a big holiday in North America that spending on it is second to that of Christmas. Houses are elaborately decorated to resemble haunted houses with ghosts and skeletons. Adults wear costumes to scare and delight trick-or-treaters or for parties. An interest in the supernatural is reflected in the current popularity of vampire books and movies.

Quoting and Using Reported Speech

When you report what someone says, you put that person's words between quotation marks, but only if you are quoting the exact words used. More frequently, instead of quoting directly, you use reported speech, also called indirect speech, to paraphrase what is said:

> Quote: Rhett Butler said, "Frankly, my dear, I don't give a damn."

> Reported speech: Rhett Butler said he didn't give a damn.

> Paraphrase: Rhett Butler exclaimed that he didn't care.

Notice the punctuation for a direct quote. The quotation marks curl around the quote and are found at the top of the line. A comma separates the quote from the rest of the sentence. The period of the sentence comes before the quotation mark.

In research papers, you use two kinds of quotations. In one, you incorporate the words of the speaker in your sentences and show the exact words with quotation marks. Longer quotes are set off, separate from your paragraph and indented from the left margin. Both forms require a footnote or a parenthetical citation (the author's name and the page number in round brackets) to show where the reference comes from. The methods used for such referencing differ slightly (see the section "Research and Referencing" earlier in this unit), and you should refer to the style guide you are using to format your quote and citation correctly.

Make sure you choose quotes wisely. Do not quote facts or straightforward, simple sentences. Choose quotes that express something in a unique manner. You should use quotes for impact, not to fill up space.

For reported speech, you must make several changes. Pay attention to pronouns. The speaker's reference to *I* becomes *he* or *she*. Time references may have to change. If the speaker says *today* or *tomorrow*, you may have to change it to *that day* or *the next day*. Verb tense is also tricky. Often, you have to change the present tense verb to past tense. Here are some examples:

> The director said, "Why isn't anyone listening to me?"
> The director asked why no one was listening to him.

> The actor said, "Why am I not getting more auditions?"
> The actor wondered why he was not getting any more auditions.

> Peter said, "You have to do that scene all over again."
> Peter said we would have to do the scene again.
> Peter told us to do the scene again.

> John said, "Why don't you come with me to the game on Saturday?"
> John invited me to the game on Saturday.

> Ivana said, "Let's go to the 8 o'clock show, and then we can go for dessert."
> Ivana suggested going to the 8 o'clock show and going for dessert afterwards.

Exercise 8.4

Change these sentences from direct quotation to reported speech. You do not have to use all the words as long as you get the meaning across:

1. Susan said, "I'm going to work on that assignment tomorrow."

Exercise 8.4 – *continued*

2. Ryan said, "I will help you with the painting this weekend."

3. My sister asked, "What shall we get Mom for her birthday?"

4. Dave said, "Why don't we get tickets for the Great Big Sea concert?"

5. Lulu asked, "Will you help me prepare my oral presentation?"

6. He asked the TA, "Will Unit 6 be on the mid-term?"

7. Hans asked, "Do you know where Michael bought his Vespa?"

8. "I'm sorry. I forgot to call you yesterday," said Amar.

9. Brad said, "I think we should take up curling. It looks like a sport I could handle."

10. Lindy said, "Tomas should buy a new car. His is a piece of junk."

Writing a Summary

Summarizing is a skill used every day. You summarize when you recount the plot of a movie or relate what happened to you in your day; summarizing textbook chapters is an excellent way to study for exams; journal articles are summarized in abstracts; and business reports often include an executive summary.

When you summarize, you give just the main ideas from a reading such as an article, story, or report. You do not include specific details, such as dates, figures, and biographical data, unless they are important. Minor examples should not be included, but if an article depends on the examples to tell the story, then these examples should be summarized.

These main ideas should be in the same order as in the original whenever possible. Sometimes, however, a different order might work better. For example, Sidney Katz does not tell the story of the Richard hockey riot chronologically, but following his order would be too confusing in a short summary.

The summary should be clear enough that someone who has not read the original text can still understand the summary and come away with the same basic information. Avoid vague statements such as "the authors talk about bottled water," which just give the topic and not a main idea. Usually the word *about* signals such a vague statement. One way to check clarity is to ask a friend to read the summary on its own and see whether he or she has any questions.

Conciseness is important because the main purpose is to make something shorter. For school assignments, you may be asked to write a summary that is one-tenth the length of the original so that a 100-word paragraph summarizes a 1000-word article. When you have a strict word limit, it is often easier to write a first draft saying everything that you want to say and then cut it down with careful editing.

Make sure you cover the whole article. When students are faced with a strict word limit, they sometimes stop writing as soon as they reach this limit.

Paraphrase is an important part of summarizing. Use your own words to express the ideas of the author. Copying sentences from the original is not acceptable. One good way to avoid copying phrases from the text is to draft your summary without looking at the original. You can check later to make sure you have covered all the ideas you need. Remember that if the article is in the first person ("I"), your paraphrase will use third person references such as "the author" and "she says."

A summary should maintain good paragraph structure. The first sentence is the topic sentence; it should tell the reader that this is a summary. Usually, the author and title of the article are named, and the source information (the name of the newspaper, the date, and the page number, for example) may be given if necessary.

A summary by itself is objective. You do not give your opinion of what is said in the article or evaluate the author's writing. You just report what the author said.

Steps for writing a summary

1. Read the entire article, story, or report, making sure you understand it all. You may have to read it a few times. Use a dictionary for unfamiliar words.
2. Put the article or story away and think about what it said. Without referring to the original, write a quick draft of your summary, using your own words. Your draft can be in the form of jot notes.
3. Go over the article again, making sure you have covered all the main points in your draft.
4. Rewrite your summary, putting it in proper form.
5. Start a summary paragraph with a topic sentence that identifies the article (title, author's name, and source) and gives the main idea of the original reading.
6. Make sure your summary paraphrases the words of the author. Do not copy his or her specific expressions. Do not quote.
7. Check to see whether your summary says enough to be clear to readers who have not read the original.
8. Edit your summary to meet the required word length.
9. Correct grammar, spelling, and punctuation for your final draft.

Sample summary

Here is a sample summary. You can see the original reading on page 338.

"The Strange Forces behind the Richard Hockey Riot" by Sidney Katz tells of the events that led to the riot on 17 March 1955 in Montreal. In a game against the Boston Bruins, Montreal Canadien Maurice Richard was injured with a high stick and went after the offending player. Richard was penalized for the slashing and fighting. After a hearing on 16 March, National Hockey League president Clarence Campbell suspended Richard for the rest of the season and the playoffs. The citizens of Montreal were upset at the suspension of their beloved hockey hero. The ill-feeling was fuelled by racial tension between French and English Canadians. The riot was touched off when someone exploded a tear gas bomb in the Montreal Forum during a game with the Detroit Red Wings. The people spilled out onto the streets and started on a path of destruction down Sainte-Catherine Street, vandalizing cars and buildings for several blocks. Richard's public statement the next day forestalled any further violence. [166 words]

Note that the summary above has several specific details, such as dates, because these details are necessary for readers to follow the sequence of the story. Moreover, because the article is almost 2000 words (about twice the length of most of the non–fiction essays in this text), the summary is longer than the 100 words asked for in the summary assignments for most of the reading selections in the text.

Here is a sample summary for the reading on page 303:

In "Over Here, I Rarely Lift a Finger," Ann Marie McQueen tries to reconcile her desire for self-sufficiency with her life in the United Arab Emirates where hiring help is the norm. The people in Abu Dhabi rely on cheap labour to clean their homes and look after their children. Businesses employ large staffs to serve customers. These labourers come from poorer countries and depend on the low-paying jobs to support themselves and their families back home. Knowing this, McQueen goes along with the system. [85 words]

Exercise 8.5

Here is a 192-word summary of "Those Mooching, Deadbeat Guests of Summer" (page 310). Eliminate unnecessary phrases and sentences and reduce wordiness to make the summary less than 100 words:

In the article "Those Mooching, Deadbeat Guests of Summer," by Allan Hepburn, the author gives useful advice to house guests based on his own experience as both a host and guest. First, he talks about the timing of the visit. He says guests should arrange a suitable time for their visit. He also thinks they should not stay too long. One of his guests actually wanted him to reschedule his own mother's visit. In addition, guests should bring small gifts each and every day. These can be food items or drink. They should also say nice things about their host's home, such as complimenting the decor and not saying negative things about his or her taste. Another important part of hospitality is mealtime. If the host is cooking, the guests should be prepared to help out. They should not be too picky about the food and eat whatever they are served. Finally, guests should treat their hosts to a meal out. Hosts also deserve some privacy, and so the guests should be prepared to entertain themselves and leave their hosts alone. Essentially, it is very important they not abuse their host's hospitality.

A Good Summary
- is clear to anyone who has not read the original;
- gives only the main ideas of the original;
- is a paraphrase, with no quotes from the original;
- tells the reader it is a summary in the first sentence by identifying the original work;
- is concise, meeting word limits.

Answering Reading Comprehension Questions

Open-ended reading comprehension questions are a good way for instructors to test your reading and writing skills. They are not perfect, because it is difficult to test reading comprehension on its own: instructors cannot get into your head to figure out what you understand. An answer might be poor because you made writing, rather than reading, errors.

Understanding what a question is asking is key for academic success. This applies to essay questions as well as reading questions. Remember that language is communication. If your answer does not address what is being asked, then fundamental communication has failed. One way to get your answer on the right track is to use a few words from the question. For example, if the question asks, "Why does the father encourage the waiters to learn English?" you can start by saying, "He encourages them because . . ."

Look for key words such as *describe*, *compare*, and *explain*. Make sure you understand what those terms are asking. If it is a two-part question, answer both parts. Check to see how many marks each question is worth. A three-mark question requires more than three words.

Instructors generally want you to answer a question in your own words, paraphrasing the original wording. If you copy the author's words directly, your instructor cannot tell how much you understand. Even a person with very little English could be lucky enough to find and copy the right sentence to answer the question.

Each of the reading selections in Part 2 of this text is accompanied by reading comprehension questions that will allow you to practise answering such questions.

Here is an example for the reading on page 266:

> What point is Howat making when he talks about playing catch with the camera?

> Howat wants to see what the camera would look like thrown through the air between two canoes. [poor answer: it does not answer the question, and it is copied word-for-word from the reading]

> Howat is showing exactly how useless the camera has become as a camera. He is no longer worried about its safety because he would risk it landing in the water and being destroyed. [answers the question adequately]

Writing about Readings

You may be called upon to write a literary essay in which you analyze what a writer did in a short story, novel, or play. You might have to discuss plot, symbolism, or theme or compare two literary works. What students find most difficult about this task is doing actual analysis and not just retelling the plot. You can keep on track if you remember what you learned about academic paragraphs—begin each paragraph with your main idea. Then you use examples from the text to support what you said.

This passage simply retells the plot—what you should *not* do:

> In "Why My Mother Can't Speak English," the narrator begins with the old mother wanting to get her citizenship because she is afraid of being deported and of losing her old age pension. After a disappointing interview with a Citizenship clerk, the

narrator recounts the reasons why his mother never learned the English language. While the father in the story encourages the Chinese waiters to learn English, he discourages his own wife from doing so because he is afraid of losing control over her. More interesting is the revelation that the mother does not want to learn because she thinks she may be changed. However, the story ends somewhat happily: The mother does get her citizenship, and she wants to show her achievement to her dead husband at the cemetery.

This is an analysis—what you should do:

In "Why My Mother Can't Speak English," the writer gives some complex reasons for the difficulty immigrant women have in learning a new language. First, learning English opens up the new world to women, and some men have trouble accepting that. For example, the husband does not permit his wife to learn English because he can control her if she cannot speak the language. Moreover, he is afraid that she will learn the ways of white women, something he cannot accept. Second, the wife is reluctant to become more than merely functionally literate in the restaurant because she is afraid that English may change her cultural identity. The writer underscores the point that language is more than a medium of communication.

Building Reading Skills

- Read as often as possible. Carry a paperback novel or magazine with you for the times when you have to wait, such as at the doctor's office or in a line-up for service.
- Read a variety of materials. Read both fiction and non-fiction. Read both short works like newspaper articles and long ones like novels.
- For readings assigned for school, read them more than once. Look up unfamiliar words in the dictionary. Summarize the readings in your notes.
- Read attentively, paying attention to the use of language.
- Keep a reading journal. Writing something down about the reading will help you remember it. You can record your thoughts, a brief summary, or vocabulary notes.
- For non-fiction, read popular treatments of subjects you are interested in. Many science and social science books are written for a lay (non-professional) audience.
- Get in the newspaper habit. Daily newspapers offer articles of interest for everyone, and they are often available online.

- Read books at a level you are comfortable with. They should be challenging enough to enable you to build your skills but not too difficult that they make the reading a chore.
- Try children's literature or books written for teenagers. Some of these books are quite sophisticated. Moreover, the classic books are part of a shared culture and are often referred to. Learning this shared culture is especially important for ESL students.
- Check out simplified novels if you find other novels difficult. They are written at different reading levels and can be found in the public library.
- Try different kinds of literature. Give the book or article a fair chance, but if you decide it is not for you, try something else.
- Ask your instructors and librarians for advice and book recommendations.

Part 2

Reading Selections

From School to Work

The New Heavyweight Champions

by Margaret Wente

1   Something interesting has happened with many of the couples I know. The wives have now become the major breadwinners. They have high-powered jobs in design, consulting, medicine, public affairs, HR, law, and banking. Many of their husbands are underemployed or semi-retired, not always by choice. One works behind the counter in a retail store. Another keeps the books for a small business. One is a freelance writer whose market has nearly dried up, and another husband has gone back to school for a degree. A couple of others work for their wives' businesses. Several of these men also organize the household chores and do the cooking.

2   Thirty years ago, most of these men handily out-earned their wives. But the situation has reversed.

3   Could this be the future? Very likely. At every age and income level, women are more likely than ever before to be the major or sole breadwinner in the family. The reason is not that more women are working but that fewer men are. Three-quarters of the people who lost their jobs in the US recession were men, and the hardest-hit sectors were the male worlds of construction, manufacturing, and finance. Many of those jobs aren't coming back. In the city of Hamilton—once known as Steeltown—just 2 per cent of the population still works in steel. In Sudbury, the town that nickel built, Inco's unionized labour force has shrunk from 12,000 to around 3300 souls, who are currently locked in a futile long-term strike with their foreign owner.

4   Back in 2007, something happened in Canada that got almost no attention. We became the first country in the Western world where women outnumbered men in the work force. At first the gap was small—just one-half of 1 per cent—but by 2009, the gap had grown to 3.5 per cent.

(Note: Statistics Canada's measure doesn't include the self-employed.) This January, the United States followed us across the threshold.

5   All evidence suggests the gender shift is permanent. It would be nice to report that the sons of the striking nickel workers have gone off to university to become metallurgical engineers. But they have not. Just 18 per cent of Canadian males between 18 and 21 are currently attending university. Their sisters, though, are doing fine. They outperform their brothers in school and are far more focused on getting the credentials that will land them jobs as dental hygienists, bank clerks, office managers, and nurses.

6   It's now conventional wisdom that a BA is the new minimum requirement for a good job in the post-industrial economy. Today, 58 per cent of all BAS are earned by women. And nearly all the fields that will yield the most employment growth over the next couple of decades are ones already dominated by women. (An exception: janitors.)

7   A richly reported story in *The Atlantic* magazine ("The End of Men," by Hanna Rosin) argues that these changes in the workplace amount to an unprecedented role reversal, whose cultural consequences will be vast. She notes that even something as fundamental as the sex preferences of parents has changed. Throughout human history, when muscle-power mattered and patriarchy reigned, sons were infinitely more valuable than daughters. But now—from urban America to urban Beijing—people's preferences have tilted toward girls. According to Ms Rosin, one US outfit that offers sperm selection says requests for girls are running at about 75 per cent.

8   At the heart of the *Atlantic* piece is one highly provocative question. What if the modern, post-industrial economy is simply more congenial to women than to men?

9   It's hard not to answer yes. The modern, post-industrial economy rewards people with a high degree of emotional intelligence who can navigate complex social networks. It rewards people who are flexible, adaptable, and cooperative, who have good verbal skills, and who can work diligently, sit still, and focus long enough to get the credentials they need to land a job. Women tend to be better at these things than men. They're also good at all the gender-neutral stuff, such as sales and analytical skills. Meantime, as muscle jobs vanish, men are showing little or no interest in becoming dental hygienists, kindergarten teachers, or anything else that requires a high degree of people skills and nurturing.

10   It seems that just as women have more aptitude for certain jobs than men, they also have more aptitude for schooling—especially the long years of schooling you've got to put in to finish university. As Torben Drewes, an economics professor at Trent University, discovered, it's no mystery why more girls get into university than boys. They're more motivated, and they work harder in high school. "Fewer males had aspirations for university education than females, and this fact might account for the lower levels of effort among them," he wrote. "However, it is also true that males were not

able to produce high school averages (and, therefore, the entry requirement for university) as efficiently as females."

11   Men and women also behave differently once they get there. Here's what guys typically do in first-year university: play video games, work out, watch TV, party. Here's what girls do: study.

12   "If men were operating rationally in an economic sense, they should be flooding into higher education," says Tom Mortenson, a senior scholar at the Pell Institute for the Study of Opportunity in Higher Education in Washington. But people don't always operate rationally. And so we have that most modern of stereotypes—the aimless, slacker man-boy who isn't really qualified for anything and can't quite latch on to the job market.

13   As women bring home more and more of the bacon—and sometimes the whole hog—what will men do? How will relationships between the sexes be renegotiated? How will men figure out new ways to be a man? I have no idea. But for the first time since women relied on men to chase away the lions and bring home a tasty side of mastodon, it's all up for grabs.

[From *The Globe and Mail,* 12 June 2010, p. A25]

Notes

HR: Human Resources, the department of a company concerned with hiring, training, and managing employees

BA: Bachelor of Arts (Note that Wente uses the abbreviation for an arts degree, but she is including all bachelor degrees in her reference.)

Comprehension

1. Explain the title.
2. What is the thesis of the article?
3. Why are fewer men working today? Why haven't they found better jobs?
4. What happened in 2007 and in January 2010?
5. Explain why Wente claims, "All evidence suggests the gender shift is permanent." [5]
6. Why does Wente say, from "urban America to urban Beijing" [7]? What is the significance of the adjective?
7. Why are women succeeding in the workforce?
8. What does "emotional intelligence" [9] refer to?
9. Wente ends her column by saying, "it's all up for grabs" [13]. Explain this statement.

Discussion

1. Did it surprise you to learn that there are more female workers than male workers in Canada? Why or why not?

2. Wente points out that the job statistics do not include self-employment. Do you think this would make much of a difference? Why or why not?
3. Discuss the preference for male or female children in different cultures.
4. Wente suggests that young men are slackers. Is this a fair statement? Is this article anti-male?
5. Do you agree with the reasons given for female university students outnumbering male university students in Canada?
6. Do you think that female domination in the workforce will lead to political and social change? Explain.
7. What are the effects of widespread unemployment among males—both personally and socially?

Assignments

1. Traditionally, women have married men with more education and earning power than they have. How do you think relationships will change now that women are earning more? Write an essay supporting your opinion.
2. Studies show that men who are financially supported by women feel that their masculinity is threatened. Write an essay explaining the causes or the effects of this problem.
3. One of the ways that people are tackling poverty in developing countries is by offering small business loans to women. Find out more about such programs, and write an essay explaining the rationale behind them.
4. Traditional preferences for male children have led to huge population imbalances in countries such as India and China. In an essay, explain either the causes or the effects of a population in which males outnumber females. Or discuss whether this traditional preference is changing and, if it is, why.
5. In many developing countries, women are undervalued. They are not allowed an education or to participate in the workforce without restriction. In an essay, explain how this affects the society.
6. Wente mentions emotional intelligence. Find out more about multiple intelligences. Write an essay on the effects of one kind of intelligence.

Paraphrase and Summary

1. Paraphrase: "The modern, post-industrial economy rewards people with a high degree of emotional intelligence who can navigate complex social networks. It rewards people who are flexible, adaptable, and cooperative, who have good verbal skills, and who can work diligently, sit still, and focus long enough to get the credentials they need to land a job."
2. Paraphrase: "Men and women also behave differently once they get there. Here's what guys typically do in first-year university: play video games, work out, watch TV, party. Here's what girls do: study."
3. Write a one-paragraph summary of the article, of no more than 100 words.

Vocabulary Study

1. *Slacker* is a slang term for someone who is lazy. It is related to the expression *to slack off*. With a partner, come up with other meanings and expressions for the word *slack*. What part of speech can the word be? Use your dictionary to check for other uses of the word.
2. Explain the difference between aptitude, skill, and talent.

Definitions

Use the context to match each word to its definition:

1. breadwinner [1] _____	a) doorway
2. recession [3] _____	b) fixed image of a group of people
3. threshold [4] _____	c) large, extinct mammal resembling a hairy elephant
4. metallurgical [5] _____	
5. credentials [5] _____	d) move towards something
6. conventional [6] _____	e) never seen before
7. yield [6] _____	f) normal, usual
8. unprecedented [7] _____	g) poor economic condition, with less productivity and jobs
9. patriarchy [7] _____	
10. tilt [7] _____	h) produce
11. congenial [8] _____	i) qualities, training, and experience that makes one qualified for a job
12. navigate [9] _____	
13. aspiration [10] _____	j) relating to the science of metals
14. stereotype [12] _____	k) society where males are in control
15. aimless [12] _____	l) steer, find the way
16. mastodon [13] _____	m) strong desire to do something
	n) suitable or pleasant for somebody
	o) the main earner in the family
	p) without a goal or direction

Word parts

Discuss the meaning of these words by looking at their parts:

high-powered	self-employed
underemployed	outperform
semi-retired	muscle-power
out-earned	post-industrial
hardest-hit	gender-neutral
long-term	man-boy
outnumbered	renegotiated

Collocations and expressions

Discuss the following expressions. How clear is the meaning? Which expressions are idiomatic? How useful are the expressions?

to keep the books [1]
to dry up [1]
to land a job [5]
conventional wisdom [6]
at the heart of something [8]
to be good at something [9]
to have an aptitude for something [10]
to be qualified for something [12]
to bring home the bacon [13]
to be up for grabs [13]

Parts of speech

Fill in the following chart:

Noun	Verb	Adjective	Adverb
	organize (tr.)		
			handily
	n/a	futile	
		provocative	
	n/a	complex	
		flexible	
		adaptable	
	n/a		diligently
		analytical	
	discover		n/a
	motivate		
			rationally

Structure and Usage

Note that Margaret Wente begins her column with examples of people she knows. She then goes on to give statistics to support what she is observing. This is a common structure in journalistic essays—the introduction gives a personal anecdote, and then the author makes the point and supports it. If this were an academic essay, what could be said in the introduction instead of the personal report?

Crushed by Potential

by Doug Howat

1   At 26, finished school but lacking a career, I find my thoughts pointed toward the future while my actions are directed toward a screen. A whole life lies in front of me, a clean, bright canvas asking me to paint it. And instead of grabbing a brush I'm updating my Facebook status so my friends can see how clever I am.

2   As far as my life is concerned it feels a bit like somebody has pushed pause. I go nowhere but still keep the world in touch with the minutiae of my day. "Doug is hot for Hillary . . . Doug is a fan of melted cheese . . . Doug is still in his pyjamas." Or, truest of all, "Doug is still living in his parents' house."

3   I would feel weird living here, not doing anything, if not for considerable evidence that lots of other people are doing the same. One of the perks of living at home, beyond the grilled cheeses, family vehicles, and free Internet, is that your parents will read the newspaper for you and point out articles they think you will enjoy—ones about young adults living at home and mooching off their folks.

4   So I've been asking myself, how did I get here? How did I let my chance to be one of the top 25 under 25 so widely pass me by? I had and have dreams, and I'm not exactly a slacker, but I am nonetheless stuck in neutral.

5   In my search for answers, I find myself thinking of a camera I once purchased.

6   When I bought it, the camera was state of the art. It had a big screen, a glut of special functions, and it took great pictures. It was, for a time, my favourite possession. But now it lies dormant on a shelf in my childhood bedroom—my current bedroom—unused for seasons.

7   The camera's problem was not its abilities or performance—both were exceptional. The camera's problem was me. I had spent a lot of money on it at a time when I had very little to spend, and in doing so I fell victim to a scenario I had never considered to be more than a clever play on words: I became possessed of my possession.

8   The camera was far too nice for someone as forgetful and prone to the drink as I am to risk taking it anywhere, and so it stayed at home where it was safe. But it's hard to take nice pictures when your camera is at home.

9   On the few occasions I did brave the wild world with it, I was so preoccupied with its safety that there was little fun to be had. I brought it along to document my crazy nights, and instead documented everyone else's while I stayed sober and my camera stayed safe.

10   Once it became clear to me that the choice to bring or leave the camera was a choice between worry and fun, the camera was afforded few outings. I overvalued and underused it.

11   Now, years later, the camera sits on a shelf for an entirely different reason—it sucks. It eats batteries like I eat my mother's homemade cookies, and all those functions that were so amazing in 2003 really failed the test of time.

12   Now that I have written it off as junk, my camera is more useful to me than ever before. If I decided I really wanted to see what it would look like thrown through the air between two canoes, I could find a partner to play catch with. And if we missed, we missed, and no one would need worry but those concerned with the well-being of fish and other aquatic species.

13   My camera is finally free to be what I want it to be. And here I return to the topic of my life.

14   Like my camera, but in reverse order, my life has been a balance of caution and potential. They told me as a child, "You can do anything you put your mind to." Luckily, as a child I didn't understand what this meant, and did not see the overwhelming profundity inherent in my every decision. As a kid I was free, because kids don't understand consequences.

15   As a teenager, when I understood better but still didn't believe those things they told me, and generally felt a lot of anger and angst toward life and the world, I was perhaps freest of all. I plummeted down hills on my rickety mountain bike, and when I flew over the handlebars it was more funny than scary. As a teenager I was free because teenagers don't care.

16   But now, at 26, I understand and believe those things I was told. I stand on the precipice of a limitless life, and while I stand here my potential is perfect. To step forward is to risk failure, to risk scuffing up that perfectly clean slate.

17   My life, like my camera, has become too well-loved, and I am scared to take it outside and use it.

18   So I figure I can proceed in a variety of ways. I can sabotage myself, destroy my potential, and become free to do all the crazy and dangerous things memorable people do. I can delude myself and pretend people don't fail or become ill or fall off their bikes and that life is entirely safe and easy. Or I can suck it up and unstick the pause button and keep on pushing until I'm brave enough to take my life outside and use it.

[From *The Globe and Mail*, 15 Aug. 2008, p. L6]

Notes

"Doug is a fan of melted cheese" [2] connects to what he says later about a perk of living at home being grilled cheese sandwiches. This also refers to a series of commercials popular at this time, which showed adult children still living at home and their parents being advised to "stop cooking with cheese."

Newspapers and magazines often have features on successful young people such as "the top 25 under 25" [4].

Comprehension

1. What is the thesis (the main idea) of this article?
2. How is the writer spending his time now?
3. Where is he living?
4. What is the tone of Howat's comment about the perks of living at home and the newspaper articles?
5. What was special about the camera he bought?
6. Why did he not use the camera when he bought it?
7. Why does he not use the camera now?
8. Explain what he means by suggesting playing catch with the camera.
9. According to Howat, why are children and teenagers freer than adults?
10. Explain the metaphors: ". . . a clean, bright canvas asking me to paint it. And instead of grabbing a brush . . ." [1]; "stuck in neutral" [4]

Discussion

1. Margaret Wente talks about "that most modern of stereotypes—the aimless, slacker man-boy who isn't really qualified for anything and can't quite latch on to the job market" (page 262). Is Howat just a slacker? Do you feel sympathetic toward him?
2. What are some of the other reasons young adults live with their parents? Consider cultural differences as well.
3. What are the advantages and disadvantages of adult children living at home, for both the children and the parents?
4. Is a strong work ethic lacking among young people today?
5. Give another reason that young people do not succeed.
6. Is the traditional idea of success (such as a good job, financial stability) over-rated?
7. What is the difference between adult children living with their parents and young children living with their parents?
8. What kind of house rules are advisable for adult children moving back in with their parents?
9. Howat says, "I became possessed of my possession." Discuss what this statement means with another example (not Howat and his camera).

Assignments

1. Ask your friends and family for their opinion on adult children living at home. What kind of conditions would they consider acceptable? (For example, some parents would prefer to see adult daughters living at home rather than on their own but would set a different standard for their sons.) Write a report on the information you gathered.

2. Find statistics and demographic reports on young adults living with their parents. Newspapers often report these statistics. Use this information in a research essay explaining why more young adults live with their parents now than a generation ago.

3. Write an essay comparing the place of young adults in your native culture (or another one you know well) and in Canada. In some cultures, the expectation is that young adults will live with their parents until they marry. Often, there are different expectations for males and females.

4. Research the Peter Pan Syndrome. Does this explain young men today? Write an essay on the subject.

5. Write an analysis of the treatment of young men's juvenile behaviour as shown in contemporary American movies. Focus on one or two movies, such as *Knocked Up* (2007), *Step Brothers* (2008), *Failure to Launch* (2006), *About a Boy* (2002), and *Wedding Crashers* (2005).

Paraphrase and Summary

1. Paraphrase: "I plummeted down hills on my rickety mountain bike, and when I flew over the handlebars it was more funny than scary."

2. Paraphrase, using a more academic word choice: "Now, years later, the camera sits on a shelf for an entirely different reason—it sucks. It eats batteries like I eat my mother's homemade cookies, and all those functions that were so amazing in 2003 really failed the test of time."

3. Paraphrase the author's conclusion: "So I figure I can proceed in a variety of ways. I can sabotage myself, destroy my potential, and become free to do all the crazy and dangerous things memorable people do. I can delude myself and pretend people don't fail or become ill or fall off their bikes and that life is entirely safe and easy. Or I can suck it up and unstick the pause button and keep on pushing until I'm brave enough to take my life outside and use it."

4. Write a one-paragraph summary (no more than 100 words) of the article.

Vocabulary Study

1. Look up the pronunciation of *minutiae* [2], and compare it to the pronunciation of *minute* (noun) and *minute* (adjective). Compare the meanings.

2. A *slacker* [4] is a person who "slacks off" and does not fulfill his or her responsibilities. Find out the meaning of the adjective *slack* and the

phrasal verb *slack off*. The adjective "slack" is the opposite of "tight" or "taut" when referring to something like a rope.

3. The word *sabotage* [18] is from the French word *sabot* for a kind of shoe. There are disputed explanations for how the word came to its present meaning. Find some of these explanations on the Internet.

Definitions

Use the context to match each word to its definition:

1. perk [3] _____	a)	anxiety, worry
2. mooch [3] _____	b)	ask for something without paying for it
3. glut [6] _____	c)	benefit, something extra given, usually in a job
4. scenario [7] _____		
5. preoccupied [9] _____	d)	deceive, make somebody believe something that is not true
6. aquatic [12] _____		
7. overwhelming [14] _____	e)	go down quickly
8. profundity [14] _____	f)	mark up a smooth surface, making it rough
9. inherent [14] _____		
10. angst [15] _____	g)	natural quality of something
11. plummeted [15] _____	h)	oversupply of something
12. rickety [15] _____	i)	possibility to succeed
13. potential [16] _____	j)	related to water and swimming
14. scuffing up [16] _____	k)	showing great depth of knowledge
15. delude [18] _____	l)	situation that could possibly happen
	m)	thinking about something so much and neglecting something else
	n)	weak structure, likely to break easily
	o)	with a great effect, overpowering

Parts of speech

Fill in the following chart:

Noun	Verb	Adjective	Adverb
	direct		
		considerable	
		special	
function			
possession			
	n/a	exceptional	

Noun	Verb	Adjective	Adverb
	risk		n/a
variety			
	destroy		
		dangerous	
		memorable	
		safe	
		brave	

Collocations and expressions

Discuss each of the following expressions. How clear is the meaning? Is it idiomatic? Which expressions are slang? How useful is each expression?

stuck in neutral [4]
state of the art [6]
to lie dormant [6]
to fall victim to something [7]
a play on words [7]
to be prone to something [8]
to fail the test of time [11] (opposite: to stand the test of time)
to write something off [12]
to stand on the precipice [16]
a clean slate [16]
to suck it up [18]

Structure and Technique

1. This essay is written in conversational, personal style to meet the needs of the newspaper. Moreover, the author is a young adult, so he would be comfortable with a casual style.

   Here's an example of a conversational style sentence: "So I've been asking myself, how did I get here?" Note that it starts with a co-ordinate conjunction (*so*), uses a contraction, and has a direct question after a comma. To be more formal, Howat could have written, "I have been asking myself how I got here."

   Find examples of words, expressions, and sentence structures that make this piece of writing conversational. Convert them to academic style.

2. An analogy is a comparison used to make something better understood. In this essay, Doug Howat compares his life to a camera he owns. Discuss this analogy. Does it work well? For instance, does it help the reader understand how he feels about his life? Can you think of another analogy to describe this period of life?

Some common expressions describing the relationship between adult children and their parents are based on analogy:

> Parents whose children have grown up and left are referred to as "empty nesters."
> Adult children who return home after they have left for a period of university or work are called "boomerang children."
> Parents who do too much to take care of their adult children are called "helicopter parents." They "hover."

Explain these expressions. Use your dictionary when necessary.

Same-Sex Schooling

One of the perennial issues in education is whether classes should be mixed or whether students should be separated. The ideal of public education is that all children should be taught together—boys and girls, the academically gifted and the learning disabled, and students of different religions and ethnic backgrounds. In the early days of public education in Canada, many students were taught in one-room schoolhouses. The school had a mixture of students from Grade 1 to Grade 8, both boys and girls, all taught by a single teacher.

In the latter part of the twentieth century, the education movement focused on girls not achieving to their potential. Much of this was deemed to be based on social reasons. For instance, higher education for girls was considered a waste, since they would grow up to be housewives and not use this schooling. With the large-scale entry of women into the workforce, this view changed and so did education figures. Women even challenged for typically male occupations such as police officers and engineers. Now the pendulum has swung to the other side, and the worry is that males are underperforming in academics and therefore have fewer career prospects.

It has been observed that boys and girls behave and learn differently. While girls are more verbal and obedient, boys are more physical and hands-on learners. Consequently, some educators argue that boys and girls should be taught separately, at least for some subjects, such as math and reading. This remains a contentious issue.

Essay Topics

1. Argue for or against same-sex schooling. You can take a position in the middle—arguing that some classes should be separate.

2. Would same-sex schooling solve the problem Margaret Wente talks about in "The New Heavyweight Champions"?

3. Argue for or against another type of specialized education, such as religion-based schools or those for academically or artistically gifted students.

4. Explain the issue of segregation in another country. For example, in Saudi Arabia male and female students are separated completely—even at the university level. Discuss causes or effects.

5. Compare one aspect of the Canadian education system with that in other country. For instance, you can compare teaching styles, the way schools are organized, or the tasks students are asked to perform.

Unit 10

Communication Technology

Internet Addiction: New-Age Diagnosis or Symptom of Age-old Problem?

by Roger Collier

1   Doctors don't tell patients with broken limbs or open wounds that their health problems aren't real, but ambiguity creeps in when a trauma is mental rather than physical. One topic stirring debate in the mental health community is Internet addiction. Some say it's becoming a major problem and can be as destructive to a person's life as an addiction to alcohol or gambling. But some say the very idea of being addicted to a communications medium is ludicrous. Others are loitering on the fringe of the debate, waiting for mental health researchers to agree on a definition of Internet addiction.

2   Kimberly Young, director of the online resource The Center for Internet Addiction (www.keithadkins.com/netaddiction), says that Internet addiction may not yet be clearly defined but you know it when you see it. People who use computers excessively suffer many of the same problems as other addicts: failed marriages, lost jobs, neglected children, sleep deprivation. Some addicts—whether their problem is gaming, pornography, gambling, social networking, day trading, or shopping—spend up to 18 hours a day online, which can also lead to physical problems, such as back strain, eye strain, and carpal tunnel syndrome.

3   "Some describe the Internet as just being a tool, but if it is causing a detriment to your life, then you have a problem," says Young, author of *Caught in the Net*.

4   Few in the mental health community dispute that pathological use of technology is a problem, but there is disagreement about whether Internet addiction is worthy of the ultimate stamp of approval: inclusion in the

fifth edition of the *Diagnostic and Statistical Manual of Mental Disorders,* tentatively scheduled for publication in 2012.

5   Some mental health experts say this is unlikely, because although the Internet has become a ubiquitous presence in modern society, the research community has been slow to examine how it is affecting mental health. In 2008, researchers from South Korea and the United States performed a meta-analysis of empirical studies on Internet addiction published in academic journals from 1996–2006 (*Cyberpsychological Behavior* 12: 203–7). They concluded that "researchers should work to develop a standardized definition of Internet addiction with supporting justification."

6   Another problem, says Young, is that the story of the Internet has, for the most part, been a love story. Luddites excepted, most people praise technology as a means to eradicate drudgery and improve productivity. The Internet has made many things, from banking to communication to accessing music and movies, more convenient. Therefore a sort of "halo effect" surrounds the Internet, and the problems it causes are viewed as paltry when compared to its many benefits. And the last thing computer companies, Internet providers, and makers of video games want is for psychologists to claim that their products can be destructive to some people's lives, says Young. "The Internet has inherent value and utility . . . but there is this dark side."

7   Or is there? Not according to Vaughan Bell, a visiting research fellow with the Department of Clinical Neuroscience, Institute of Psychiatry, King's College London in the United Kingdom. Bell has argued that the Internet is not an activity, and therefore Internet addiction is a flawed idea (*Journal of Mental Health* 16: 445–57).

8   "Fundamentally, the Internet is a medium of communication," says Bell, who claims that one can no more be addicted to the Internet than to radio waves. "The concept itself doesn't make sense."

9   Bell acknowledges that some people use the Internet and other technologies to excess but believes they do so to avoid dealing with underlying problems, such as depression or social anxiety disorder, which have well-established treatments. Mental health problems often result in obsessions, which could range from watching too many hockey games to reading too much science fiction. In Japan, for instance, many youth are obsessed with comic books, though this is framed as a social withdrawal problem, not a comic book addiction.

10   Creating new "addictions" is misleading and confusing, says Bell, and will only prevent people from getting the help they need, while undermining their self-efficacy.

11   "The overmedicalization of life's problems is damaging," he adds. "Your actual difficulty may be that you are in a bad relationship or you are depressed, not addicted to the Internet. It's a neat placebo explanation that doesn't fully address the complexity of people's problems."

12   As for adding Internet addiction to the *Diagnostic and Statistical Manual of Mental Disorders*, it's often a challenge as it must be demonstrated that symptoms are of such severity as to cause impairment or distress, that the disorder is unique from others already in the manual, and that it won't generate false positives.

13   Bell believes Internet addiction won't meet the test, if for no other reason than the inconsistency of the research in the field. His opinion is shared by Dr. Elias Aboujaoude, director of the Impulse Control Disorders Clinic at the Stanford University School of Medicine in California, who laments the lack of biological data about the effects on the brain of human–technology interaction. "The science is just not there yet, unfortunately, for something that has so radically and irreversibly changed our lives," says Aboujaoude.

14   Some mental health experts are, however, trying to rectify that. For example, researchers from the National Health Insurance Corporation in Seoul, South Korea, have been using functional Magnetic Resonance Imaging to study neurophysiologic differences between hardcore and casual online gamers while observing video of the game World of Warcraft. Their initial findings, presented in May at the American Psychiatric Association's 162nd annual meeting, suggest that activity in the frontal lobes of the brains of the study group (whose members played online games an average of eight hours a day) was significantly different than for the control group (whose members played online games an average of three hours a day), though the researchers admit they aren't yet sure how to interpret these results.

15   Although the scientific evidence is spotty and inconclusive, Aboujaoude, unlike Bell, believes Internet addiction is a real problem and that the Internet is not a typical communications medium. Unlike television or movies or print, the Internet is not inanimate. It communicates back, in a sense, allowing users to feel a sense of connectedness with others. But the ease and appeal of substituting virtual relationships for real-world friendships can be dangerous for some.

16   "By and large, these relationships tend to be superficial," says Aboujaoude. "They do not provide the kind of nurturing connectedness that will help you navigate your way through life. If social networking has replaced long-term, grounded friendships, that's a problem."

[From *Canadian Medical Association Journal* 181 (2009) (9): 575+. http://www.cmaj.ca/cgi/content/full/181/9/575]

Notes

Luddites [6] are people against technological advancements. The word means "followers of Ned Ludd," an eighteenth-century Englishman who supposedly destroyed some knitting frames, textile-making equipment that was taking away people's jobs.

A halo effect [6] occurs when a positive impression in one area makes for a positive one in another. This can also work for a negative impression. A halo is the circle of light around a holy person, so the expression can be seen as this glow extending beyond the holy person to something else.

Academic articles contain jargon related to the field of study. Jargon can include words that have a general meaning to most people but a highly specific meaning in that field. It is easy enough to follow this article without knowing what a "meta-analysis of empirical studies" [5] exactly entails. Essentially, the researchers studied various research studies.

Comprehension

1. What is the main issue discussed in this reading? On which side does the author stand?
2. Explain what the author means in the first sentence.
3. How is an addiction identified?
4. Why is the 2012 event significant for this issue?
5. What do researchers need to do?
6. Why are people reluctant to criticize the Internet?
7. Explain Bell's argument.
8. What have Korean researchers found?
9. What is Aboujaoude's position?

Discussion

1. Consider the different views in this piece. Which statements do you agree with?
2. What are the most addictive elements of Internet use?
3. What are the signs that someone is spending too much time on the Internet?
4. What are your experiences with Internet addiction? Have you felt the pull of the Internet taking you away from other responsibilities? Have you witnessed friends or family members affected by Internet addiction?
5. Because the Internet is so important in everyday life, is it harder to deal with an addiction?
6. What are the social stigmas attached to mental illness? Why does our society have a harder time accepting mental illness than physical illness?

Assignments

1. Write an essay on the causes or the effects of Internet addiction.
2. Korea and China have been in the news for widespread Internet addiction and treatment programs. Research these programs, and analyze one in an essay.
3. Find out about the halo effect in business. Write a definition paragraph.

4. Write a process essay describing how a person could cure an Internet addiction.
5. Write an essay comparing Internet addiction to another kind of addiction.

Paraphrase and Summary

1. Paraphrase: "Therefore a sort of 'halo effect' surrounds the Internet, and the problems it causes are viewed as paltry when compared to its many benefits." [6]
2. Paraphrase (and put in indirect speech): "'By and large, these relationships tend to be superficial,' says Aboujaoude. 'They do not provide the kind of nurturing connectedness that will help you navigate your way through life. If social networking has replaced long-term, grounded friendships, that's a problem.'" [16] Start by saying, "Aboujaoude says that . . ."
3. Write a one-paragraph summary of about 100 words.

Vocabulary Study
Definitions

Use the context to match each word to its definition:

1. ambiguity [1] _____
2. ludicrous [1] _____
3. loitering [1] _____
4. fringe [1] _____
5. deprivation [2] _____
6. dispute [4] _____
7. pathological [4] _____
8. tentatively [4] _____
9. ubiquitous [5] _____
10. eradicate [6] _____
11. drudgery [6] _____
12. paltry [6] _____
13. undermining [10] _____
14. self-efficacy [10] _____
15. placebo [11] _____
16. lament [13] _____
17. rectify [14] _____

a) ability to produce the right result
b) argue against
c) caused by a physical or mental disorder
d) completely unreasonable, stupid
e) dull, hard work
f) eliminate, get rid of
g) existing everywhere
h) false medicine
i) feel sad or sorry about something
j) hanging around a public place without a clear reason
k) insignificant, small
l) lacking something important
m) make right
n) not definitely, may be changed later
o) outside edge
p) state of being unclear, having two interpretations
q) weakening, destroying

Word parts

Discuss the meaning of these words by looking at their parts:

underlying [9]
overmedicalization [11]
inconsistency [13]
irreversibility [13]
inconclusive [15]
connectedness [15]

Parts of speech

Fill in the following chart:

Noun	Verb	Adjective	Adverb
trauma			
		destructive	
			excessively
inclusion			
productivity production			
utility			n/a
anxiety	n/a		
complexity			n/a
		initial	
	interpret		

Collocations and expressions

Discuss each of the following expressions. How clear is the meaning? Is it idiomatic? How useful is the expression?

the very idea of something [1]
stamp of approval [4]
false positive [12]
meet the test [13]
if for no reason than [13]

Structure and Technique

Note that this is an article in an academic journal, so it has citations. Referencing styles vary from discipline to discipline, and even for different publishers or publications.

Using Your Cellphone for Talking? That's So 2007

by Ivor Tossell

1   So, the brain trust at Research In Motion has popped out a new BlackBerry. This is all over the news, since we're told that the new BlackBerry is a very important smart phone indeed.

2   "It's a really special product because so much new goodness has been added to it," Mike Lazaridis, RIM's president and co-chief executive officer, told reporters at its launch in what, apparently, is a real quote.

3   What sets this particular phone apart, it seems, is the fact that it has both a touch screen and a keyboard. This means that it can be both stroked and prodded, which are two very popular things to do with a phone these days. Talking, not so much.

4   Meanwhile, across the way, Apple's new iPhone 4 has caused a media sensation because it was said to drop calls. Curiously, though, customer surveys are showing that buyers are actually very happy with the phone. Why? It could be that the whole dropped-call affair was overhyped. Or maybe, just maybe, it didn't matter that the iPhone drops calls. People want to do many things with phones these days, but actually calling each other isn't one of them.

5   Welcome to the age of the phoneless phone. The *New York Times* reported that in the last year, US cell networks carried, for the first time, more data than voice traffic. Surveys from firms such as Nielsen are showing that, after peaking in 2007, the length of cellphone conversations has been shrinking. After a century in the sun, a consensus is emerging that the telegraphy part is better than the talking.

6   We'll text our thumbs off, we'll email novellas, we'll send pictures of ourselves, we'll tweet, we'll light up our phones and use them as flashlights in what may be a form of semaphore. We just don't like to talk to one another through little black boxes.

7   There are two reads on this. One is that smart phones are rendering people more insulated and less social. (That criticism may not be entirely as crotchety as it sounds.) But instead of bemoaning the decline of talk, we may be better off asking why exactly we thought talking on the phone was a hot idea in the first place.

8   Much has to do with romance. As the sole supplier of telecommunications for half a century, phones accrued an awful lot of cultural baggage. For so long, they were the implements of "phoning home," and as such they were weapons against modernity: tools that could reconnect families despite the vast distances of the modern diaspora and the separations that come with a hurried, jet-setting world. They were the most humane thing about technology. (And, lord knows, the telephone companies were smart enough to market them that way.)

9   But the truth is that while phones were the best we had for a long time, they have always been profoundly anti-social and alienating inventions. There is nothing natural about listening to a disembodied voice coming from a speaker. Phones cut off every non-vocal cue we rely upon in conversation, from facial expression to posture to context. They're torture for people who are more expressive than verbose. You can comfortably sit in silence with someone in person, but on the phone, it's completely excruciating.

10   I polled around online for text-happy young adults and came back with a list of grievances against phones: Phone calls are an invasion of personal space, hijacking your immediate attention and holding you hostage until the end of the conversation. They're inconvenient. They're fleeting and don't leave written transcripts.

11   And let us not even start on voice mail, that anachronism that costs you three minutes to check, only to pick up a message informing you that Reginald called and would you please call back, which you already knew because you can see that he called and presumably not for the purposes of not speaking with you.

12   Imagine if some inventor in Silicon Valley came up with a new online service that made a loud noise come from your kitchen wall, or your office desk or possibly inside your pants. When this gadget went off, you'd be expected to drop everything and pick it up, to hell with whatever else you were doing.

13   If you failed to answer a certain number of times, the person on the other end would be entitled to start leaving aggrieved messages about why you're not picking up. ("Jerome! It's your mother! Answer your pants!") It would be, I predict, the kind of service people would complain bitterly about. Kids these days! With their things that ring!

14   Sure enough, like people who emerge, blinking, from bad relationships, smart phone users today are realizing that perhaps talking on the phone is not worth all the emotional weight we had formerly ascribed to it.

15   The fact that the phone has so many intensely personal uses has overshadowed the fact that it has even more uses that are intensely impersonal, from verifying movie times to sharing short, inane snippets of gossip.

16   In the end, the slow decline of phone talk is nothing to bemoan. There are times when you want to hear the sound of someone else's voice and times when you really, truly don't. Here's to having the choice.

[From *The Globe and Mail*, 9 Aug. 2010, p. L1, L4]

Notes

Writers use different techniques to make sure their readers understand the names of people, places, and companies. For instance, the company Research in Motion is first mentioned with the full name and then with its abbreviation, RIM. The president of the company is identified by name first, and then his position is given in an appositive phrase set off by commas. The product, the BlackBerry, is called "a very important smart phone."

As new technology develops, the words to describe it are also introduced and then gradually change and stabilize. The term "cellular phone" got shortened to "cell phone" and now is used as one word, "cellphone." In Europe, however, "mobile phone" was the starting point and is now shortened to "mobile." New verbs are formed—"sending text messages" becomes "texting," and "searching" becomes "googling." Sometimes it takes a while for one term to dominate. For example, portable computer memory is referred to as "flash drives," "USB drives," "memory sticks," and other expressions.

Comprehension

1. What is the main idea of this article?
2. What prompted the writing of this article?
3. How has cellphone use changed?
4. What does Tossell mean about the cultural baggage of the telephone?
5. Why does he call telephones anti-social?
6. Why do people not like talking on the phone?
7. Explain Tossell's dislike of voice mail.
8. Explain the illustration about Jerome and his pants. What point is Tossell making?
9. What is Tossell's conclusion?

Discussion

1. Do you agree with Tossell's analysis of smart phone usage and movement away from voice communication? What effect will this have?
2. Why do you prefer texting?
3. Would adding video to a phone conversation make much difference to the problems of voice communication? Do you prefer video with phone calls?
4. What are the advantages and disadvantages of cellphone cameras?
5. Can you ignore a ringing phone? Why or why not?

Assignments

1. Are smart phones "rendering people more insulated and less social" [7]? Discuss this statement in an essay.
2. Write an essay comparing voice and text communication on cellphones.
3. Write an essay explaining what the most important features of cellphones are. You can extend this to possible future features. Be sure to categorize and explain, not just list.
4. Write an essay comparing two new telecommunications products. Focus on the features relevant to students as a specific user group.

Paraphrase and Summary

1. Paraphrase: "they have always been profoundly anti–social and alienating inventions. There is nothing natural about listening to a disembodied voice coming from a speaker. Phones cut off every non-vocal cue we rely upon in conversation, from facial expression to posture to context. They're torture for people who are more expressive than verbose. You can comfortably sit in silence with someone in person, but on the phone, it's completely excruciating." [9]

2. Paraphrase, eliminating the *you* and the specific example of "Reginald": "And let us not even start on voice mail, that anachronism that costs you three minutes to check, only to pick up a message informing you that Reginald called and would you please call back, which you already knew because you can see that he called and presumably not for the purposes of not speaking with you." [11]

3. Write a one-paragraph summary of no more than 100 words.

Vocabulary Study

1. The telegraph was one of the first communication devices. Tossell, however, is not referring to this device when he uses the word *telegraphy* [5]. Use the chart of Greek and Latin roots and affixes (page 49) to determine what the two parts of the word mean. How does this word compare to *telephone* (consider the other root word)? Do you think the word *telegraphy* will be accepted and will replace the older meaning of the word? Is it a useful coinage?

2. Check your dictionary for the noun meanings of *read* [7] to determine which one is used here.

3. Explain the difference between the adjectives *human* and *humane* [8].

Definitions

Use the context to match each word to its definition:

1. consensus [5] _____	a) bad-tempered, angry
2. novellas [6] _____	b) belief that one has been treated unfairly
3. semaphore [6] _____	c) claim that something is caused by something
4. rendering [7] _____	d) complaining about
5. crotchety [7] _____	e) extremely painful
6. bemoaning [7, 16] _____	f) general agreement of opinion
7. accrued [8] _____	g) increased, grew
8. diaspora [8] _____	h) making
9. verbose [9] _____	i) short novel
10. excruciating [9] _____	j) something that belongs to the past, not the present
11. grievances [10] _____	k) spread of people to other countries
12. anachronism [11] _____	l) stupid, meaningless
13. ascribed [14] _____	m) system of sending messages with flags
14. inane [15] _____	n) using a lot of words

Word parts

Discuss the meaning of these words by looking at their parts:

brain trust [1]
overhyped [4]
disembodied [9]
snippets [15]

Parts of speech

Fill in the following chart:

Noun	Verb	Adjective	Adverb
modernity			n/a
		humane	
	alienate		n/a
invention			
		natural	
		expressive	
			comfortably
invasion			
		personal	

Structure and Technique

1. Tossell uses a sarcastic tone in this article. Identify the phrases that are sarcastic.
2. Tossell uses the first four paragraphs as his introduction. How effectively does he lead into his main point? Does he capture audience attention? If this were an academic essay, would the same ideas work in an introduction? How would they have to be rephrased?

Technology and the Generational Divide

Young people today have grown up not only surrounded by communication technology but also tethered to it. This generation, the millennials, cannot imagine their lives without their cellphones, personal music players, and laptops. They send hundreds of text messages a day, constantly access their social networking sites to update their status, and worry about being unreachable if they are denied access.

Their parents and many of their instructors have trouble understanding this attachment to electronic gadgets. They cannot understand why millennials prefer to socialize through the medium of screens rather than face-to-face. Even dining together at a restaurant, young people spend more time looking at their phone than at their companions. Although baby boomers have also become dependent on the technology, they can more easily live without it and do not put their trust in the machinery as much. For example, they may print hard copies of documents and arrange social get-togethers in advance. Their children, on the other hand, rely on cellphones to inform their friends about impromptu get-togethers.

Millennials often do not understand school policies limiting cellphone use in school. Phones provide yet another distraction from the lesson at hand, and, of course, they can be used for cheating on tests. Students argue that there might be an "emergency call," while teachers scoff at this worry, knowing that not only is it unlikely that a "real emergency" would occur but that if one did, students could be contacted through the school.

Another point of contention is multi-tasking. Tech-savvy millennials use their gadgets with incredible ease and speed—text-messaging practically without looking, for instance. Therefore, they think warnings against multi-tasking, such as not using a phone while driving, do not apply to them.

Communication technology is no doubt changing lifestyle and even social structure. Already people spend more hours using media such as computers and cellphones than they spend working or sleeping. It is impossible to imagine what will happen with the next generation.

Essay Topics

1. Is the prohibition against cellphones in school unfair?
2. Research "inattentional blindness" and some experiments studying cellphone use. Discuss the implications of these studies in your essay. For example, evaluate the current laws against driving while using a cellphone.
3. Explain young people's reliance on their communication devices. Use strong arguments that would convince the sceptical older audience.
4. Are people today too dependent on communication technology?
5. Are online relationships as satisfying as face-to-face ones?
6. How are millennials going to change society because of their dependence on communication technology?
7. How does access to cellphones change lives in developing countries?

The Environment

The Case against Bottled Water

by Sean Petty and Justin Trudeau

1   Canadians have long been proud of the mighty rivers and beautiful lakes that make this country one of the greatest repositories of fresh water on the planet. So, it's a sad statement about our society that we are increasingly choosing to drink bottled water, often from foreign companies.

2   A recent Statistics Canada study found that three in 10 Canadian households used bottled water as their main source of drinking water in 2006. The study results are surprising, as there are so many good reasons to avoid drinking bottled water.

3   Many Canadians buy bottled water because they think it's safer and healthier than tap water. Certainly, advertising by bottled water companies—dominated by images of pristine glaciers and mountain streams—leaves consumers with that impression. The reality is that Canada's water supply—with rare exceptions—is extremely safe. Furthermore, according to Health Canada, there is no evidence to support the belief that bottled water is any safer than tap water. Indeed, if anything, our tap water may well be safer and healthier than bottled varieties.

4   The municipal water supply is more stringently tested than bottled water supplies. In Canada, the CBC reports that local water supplies are inspected every day while bottled-water plants are inspected just once every three years. In addition, according to MSN News, water-bottling plants are required to test for coliform bacteria just once a week whereas most municipal water systems test for the bacteria several times a day.

5   Consumers should also consider the safety and health risks posed by the bottles themselves. Many plastic water bottles are made using the chemical polyethylene terephthalate or PET. A recent study by Dr. William

Shotyk, the Canadian director of the Institute of Environmental Geochemistry at the University of Heidelberg, found PET bottles leach a dangerous toxin called antimony into the water they contain. The study found that the levels of antimony rise the longer water stays in the bottle.

6   Before reaching for bottled water, Canadians need to think about the serious environmental consequences of their water choice. These include: release of millions of tons of carbon dioxide into the atmosphere from manufacturing, transport, and marketing, which contributes to global warming; depletion of scarce energy and water resources; release of toxic chemicals into our air, land, and water; and absorption of poisons into the food chain.

7   According to the Pacific Institute, the energy required to produce plastic water bottles for the American market alone in 2006 was equivalent to more than 17 million barrels of oil and created 2.5 million tons of carbon dioxide.

8   Producing bottles consumes a huge amount of water too, with the Pacific Institute estimating it takes three litres of water to produce one litre of bottled water.

9   It also takes energy to fill the bottles; ship them by truck, train, boat, or plane to the consumer; refrigerate them; and recover, recycle, or dispose of the empty bottles. The Pacific Institute estimates the total amount of energy used to provide a bottle of water to the consumer could be equal to filling 25 per cent of that bottle with oil.

10   Unfortunately, most empty bottles—more than 85 per cent according to the David Suzuki Foundation—are thrown into the trash. These bottles don't just disappear—they either get buried in the landfill or they're incinerated. The buried bottles take up to 1000 years to biodegrade and may leak toxic additives into the groundwater. The incinerated bottles release toxic chemicals into our air. Moreover, some of the bottles make their way into our oceans, where they break down into increasingly tiny pieces and can enter the food chain when they're eaten by marine animals and birds.

11   The economics of bottled water are as startling as the health and environmental considerations. While we don't tend to think of it in this way, buying bottled water is an incredibly expensive habit: a bottle of water costs more than a litre of gasoline. If we buy a bottle a day for a toonie from the vending machine, we're spending more than $700 a year on water.

12   What's more, bottled water is an example of price gouging at its most outrageous. More than one-quarter of the bottled water consumed by Canadians is nothing more than filtered tap water. Two of the top-selling brands in Canada are Dasani, which is owned by Coca-Cola, and Aquafina, which is owned by its beverage rival PepsiCo.

13   As Pepsi was forced to admit last year, both brands take the water they bottle directly from municipal water systems; Dasani uses water from Calgary and Brampton taps while Aquafina uses tap water from Vancouver and Mississauga.

14   Shocking, isn't it? These companies are taking our tap water, which on average in Canada costs us less than one-tenth of a cent per litre, filtering it, although it is already perfectly clean, and selling it back to us at a markup that can be several thousand times its original price.

15   What's perhaps even more galling is that not only is the consumer paying exorbitant prices for filtered tap water but the taxpayer is also heavily subsidizing these companies on the back end by allowing them to draw water from municipal systems that were built with their tax monies.

16   From a marketing perspective, bottled water is unquestionably one of the great success stories of modern times. However, from a social, environmental, and economic perspective, the success of bottled water has created a myriad of problems.

17   Responding to these problems, governments, universities, schools, companies, and restaurants around the country have stopped buying and selling bottled water. They are thinking before they drink. You can too.

[From the *Toronto Star*, 11 Aug. 2008, p. AA8]

Comprehension
1. What is the thesis of this article? What are the three main arguments used to support this thesis?
2. Why do so many Canadians drink bottled water?
3. Why is tap water safer than bottled water?
4. Why is plastic an environmental hazard?
5. Where do many bottled water companies get their water from?
6. Why do the authors say that bottled water producers are gouging consumers?
7. Why do the authors say that bottled water is a marketing success?

Discussion
1. Do you drink bottled water? How often? Why? Will this article change your practice?
2. Are the authors' arguments sound? Give counter-arguments.
3. What can people do in their everyday lives to lessen environmental damage?
4. Sometimes people choose bottled water over a soft drink or juice that also comes in a bottle. Should they feel guilty?

Assignments
1. Although ideally products are designed and made to meet human needs, often the need is as manufactured as the product. Trudeau and Petty show that bottled water is unnecessary. Consider another product for which the perceived need is exaggerated. Write an essay explaining why.

2. While consumers should reduce their use of bottled water, an outright ban on the product could be counter-productive. In an essay, explain when bottled water is necessary.

3. Rewrite this journalistic essay to make a five-paragraph academic essay. Paraphrase; do not copy the authors' words.

Paraphrase and Summary

1. Paraphrase: "What's perhaps even more galling is that not only is the consumer paying exorbitant prices for filtered tap water but the tax-payer is also heavily subsidizing these companies on the back end by allowing them to draw water from municipal systems that were built with their tax monies." [15]

2. Write a one-paragraph summary (no more than 100 words) of this article.

Vocabulary Study

1. *Dominated* [3] is the past particle (used as an adjective) of the verb *domi-nate*. What are some related nouns and adjectives with the same root?

    This verb is transitive, which means it is usually completed by a direct object and is often found in the passive voice. Working with a partner, make a list of five nouns that could complete the following sentence. Compare your list with those of your classmates to see which nouns collocate most often with the verb *dominate*.

    John dominated _____.

2. The adjective *municipal* [4] refers to a level of government. What is the noun form? What are four other adjectives ending in *–al* used to describe levels of government in Canada? Give the noun form of each.

3. What are two corresponding noun forms for the adjective *toxic* [6]? What is the opposite of toxic?

4. *Subsidize* [15] is a verb. The participles *subsidizing* and *subsidized* are used as adjectives. What are the two noun forms? Fill in the correct forms of the verb or the noun in the blanks in the sentences. What adverb collocates with the adjective *subsidizing* in the reading?

    There are too few _____ daycare spaces.

    After the rule infractions, they decided to withdraw the _____.

    The provincial government _____ the education costs.

    Family farms would not survive without _____.

Definitions

Match the words to their definitions:

1.	repositories [1] _____	a)	an extremely large number of something
2.	pristine [3] _____	b)	burned up
3.	stringently [4] _____	c)	decompose through biological processes
4.	leach [5] _____	d)	increase in the price of something
5.	depletion [6] _____	e)	making somebody angry because it is unfair
6.	incinerated [10] _____		
7.	biodegrade [10] _____	f)	much too high (usually used with price)
8.	startling [11] _____	g)	place where things are stored or may be found
9.	gouging [12] _____		
10.	markup [14] _____	h)	remove a chemical from something as the result of water passing through it
11.	galling [15] _____		
12.	exorbitant [15] _____	i)	strictly, precisely
13.	myriad [16] _____	j)	surprising, shocking
		k)	taking an amount of money from somebody with no justification
		l)	the act of emptying or reducing something
		m)	very clean, pure

Collocations and Expressions

Discuss each of the following expressions. How clear is the meaning? Is it idiomatic? How useful is the expression?

to leave somebody with an impression (How is this different from "to impress somebody"?)

to support a belief that (How is this different from "to believe"?)

to pose a risk (What other words collocate with *pose* and *risk*?)

Structure and Technique

This essay is similar to the classic five-paragraph essay taught in school because there is an introduction, three main arguments, and a conclusion. Each argument has specific support. Of course, it has more than five paragraphs because it was written for a newspaper and not a school assignment. Identify the thesis and the three main arguments. Look at the facts used to support the arguments. Which argument do you think is the strongest?

Grammar analysis

Compare the use of *as* in these two sentences from paragraph 2:

1. A recent Statistics Canada study found that three in 10 Canadian households used bottled water <u>as</u> their main source of drinking water in 2006.

2. The study results are surprising, <u>as</u> there are so many good reasons to avoid drinking bottled water.

What is the difference between the two uses of *as*? Which of the two could be replaced by another word? Which words would work as a replacement?

Analyze the two sentences. Find the core of the sentence (the main subject and verb). Identify clauses and phrases.

Battle of the Bag

by Peter Shawn Taylor

1   It could be worse. Cathy Cirko could be the official spokesperson for the Somali Brotherhood of Pirates, or the Mosquito Breeders Association. As it is, Cirko is vice-president of the Canadian Plastics Industry Association and the country's chief advocate of plastic shopping bags.

2   The once-ubiquitous plastic bag has quickly become an environmental bogeyman in Canada. Earlier this month, citing concerns over litter and landfill, Toronto launched the country's first municipal bylaw requiring all stores to charge a five cents per bag fee to discourage their use. Several retail chains—including Home Depot and Canada's largest grocer, Loblaw Co. Ltd—have taken the fee nationwide. Emboldened by the speed with which this policy has moved, environmental groups are now talking of the day when plastic bags will seem as repellant as in-flight smoking sections. "It's taking off everywhere as people realize this is the next right thing to do," says Steven Price, the senior conservation director of the World Wildlife Fund.

3   Tasked with the unenviable job of defending plastic bags in the face of this momentum, Cirko has fought back with a host of independent scientific studies and government data that appear to undercut the substantive arguments made against the bags. "Even if we assume every plastic bag went straight to the dump, it would only represent 0.2 per cent of the 25 million tonnes we send to landfills annually," she says, citing federal and provincial documentation. And she points to a 2007 Decima poll that found more than eight out of 10 Canadians reused their shopping bags for household garbage or pet waste.

4   She also notes a 2006 City of Toronto street litter audit that examined 4300 individual pieces of garbage at 300 sites citywide. Of this total urban detritus, just six were plastic retail shopping bags. That's 0.15 per cent of total litter.

5   "Bags are not a litter issue, and they are not a landfill issue," she says. "And we have the numbers to show that. Unfortunately, this has become an emotional issue rather than a debate based on facts. It is very frustrating." She argues municipal efforts would be better directed towards recycling plastic rather than discouraging its use.

6   Glenn de Baeremaeker, a Toronto councillor, is the architect of his city's bag bylaw. The ardent environmentalist disputes the notion that bags are a minor issue. "Nothing is insignificant," he says. "We are drowning in a sea of garbage. So we are coming after plastic bags, and we are coming after everything else that's bigger as well." From disposable coffee cup

lids to consumer electronics, it is all in his sights. De Baeremaeker argues that beyond the practical benefits of reducing landfill usage, if only by a tiny amount, his campaign is emblematic of a broader issue. "The plastic bag is a symbol of our wasteful and gluttonous lifestyle. It all has to change."

7   Still, it's hard to escape the sense that the plastic bag crusade is largely a political statement. The bags, for instance, are frequently held up as the biggest blight on the world's oceans. But this month, the United Nations Environmental Programme (UNEP) released a major report on marine waste which cited garbage cleanups along the Mediterranean Sea showing plastic bags accounted for just 8.5 per cent of total marine litter. Cigarettes and cigars were 37 per cent, plastic bottles, 10 per cent. With respect to entanglement of marine life, a 2007 study identified fishing nets, lines, and ropes as being responsible for over 70 per cent of such incidents. Plastic bags, including garbage and shopping bags, caused less than 10 per cent. The report recommended that bag use be "discouraged" in coastal areas. Instead, the executive director of the UNEP, Achim Steiner, issued a press release calling for a sweeping worldwide ban on "pointless" plastic bags. Based on the evidence, a ban on fishing line, plastic bottles, or cigarettes would make more sense.

8   Then there's the possibility that, regardless of the symbolism, throwaway plastic bags might simply be better than the alternatives. Cirko also commissioned two independent labs to examine the health implications of replacing plastic shopping bags with reusable woven "green" bags. Bags randomly obtained from shoppers were tested for bacteria, yeast, mould, and E. coli. The results were then interpreted by Dr. Richard Summerbell, the former chief of medical mycology for Ontario.

9   The tests found surprisingly high levels of bacteria in two-thirds of the reusable bags. One-third had levels above those set for safe drinking water. The fact that some people used the bags to carry items other than food— gym clothes or beer empties—greatly increased the risk.

10   "This study provides strong evidence that reusable bags could pose a significant risk to the safety of the food supply if used to transport food from store to home," Dr. Summerbell concluded. He recommended that all meat be double-wrapped before being placed in reusable bags and that the bags themselves be washed and discarded regularly. None of the throwaway bags were found to be contaminated in any way.

[From *Maclean's*, 2 July 2009, p. 46]

Notes

Not mentioned in the article, but important to understand, are other problems that surface in the battle against the plastic bag. Biodegradable bags do not work well unless they are placed in composting; they contaminate the recycling stream. People who do not have grocery bags to recycle as garbage bags may turn to buying bags especially for these purposes; these bags, however, are made with more plastic and are only used once.

Comprehension

1. Explain the first sentence.
2. Who is Cathy Cirko?
3. What is being done to reduce the use of plastic bags?
4. What are the main arguments that Cirko gives? Why does she say that it has become an emotional issue?
5. What is de Baeremaeker's position? How does he justify it?
6. What point is being made with all the figures given in the article?
7. What is the problem with reusable grocery bags?

Discussion

1. Where do you stand on the plastic bag issue? Do you use reusable bags? Why?
2. What kind of controls should be placed on plastic bags? Should they be taxed or banned? Could an education program be enough to curtail use? Should there be no controls?
3. Do you think it was right to target plastic bags in this way? Is there any pollution that you think is worse?
4. Although Taylor presents both sides of the argument, he reveals a bias. What is his opinion about plastic bags? How do you know?

Assignments

1. Write an essay giving your opinion on the controls on plastic bags.
2. Write an essay on either the benefits or the problems of one specific kind of recycling.
3. Choose one garbage problem (such as excessive packaging, discarded electronic equipment, or paper diapers), and suggest solutions in an essay.

Paraphrase and Summary

1. Paraphrase: "The once-ubiquitous plastic bag has quickly become an environmental bogeyman in Canada." [2]
2. Paraphrase: "Tasked with the unenviable job of defending plastic bags in the face of this momentum, Cirko has fought back with a host of independent scientific studies and government data that appear to undercut the substantive arguments made against the bags." [3]
3. Paraphrase: "Glenn de Baeremaeker, a Toronto councillor, is the architect of his city's bag bylaw. The ardent environmentalist disputes the notion that bags are a minor issue. 'Nothing is insignificant,' he says. 'We are drowning in a sea of garbage. So we are coming after plastic bags, and we are coming after everything else that's bigger as well.' From disposable coffee cup lids to consumer electronics, it is all in his sights." [6]
4. Write a one-paragraph summary of this article, of no more than 100 words.

Vocabulary Study

What are two homophones (words that sound the same) for *cite* [2, 7]? What is the meaning and part of speech for each word? What is the noun form for *cite*?

Definitions

Use the context to match each word to its definition:

1. advocate [1] _____	a) campaign to get something done, long war
2. ubiquitous [2] _____	b) consuming too much
3. bogeyman [2] _____	c) development that is getting stronger
4. momentum [3] _____	d) disagree with something
5. substantive [3] _____	e) existing everywhere
6. audit [4] _____	f) having strong positive feelings for something
7. detritus [4] _____	g) important, serious, actual
8. ardent [6] _____	h) leftover bits, waste material
9. dispute [6] _____	i) publicly support a way of doing something
10. emblematic [6] _____	j) somebody or something that people think is evil
11. gluttonous [6] _____	k) sign of something, symbolic
12. crusade [7] _____	l) something that spoils or damages something
13. blight [7] _____	m) systematic review or assessment

Word parts

Discuss the meaning of these words by looking at their parts:

emboldened [2]
unenviable [3]
undercut [3]
reused [3]
insignificant [6]
disposable [6]
entanglement [7]
reusable [9]

Parts of speech

Fill in the following chart:

Noun	Verb	Adjective	Adverb
		repellant repellent★	n/a
argument			
		emotional	
		political	

Noun	Verb	Adjective	Adverb
	identify		
symbolism			
			randomly
		significant	
safety			

*Note that both spellings are acceptable.

Structure and Technique

Taylor reports on other people's words, finding, and opinions. Note how he uses both quotes and indirect speech. (You can refer to Unit 8, p. 250, for an explanation of these forms.) Note both the format and usage. Are the quotes effective? Are there any that should be indirect speech instead? Is it clear where each idea is coming from?

Living Green

Most people want to follow environmentally friendly living habits, but it is often difficult to know what to do. One problem is that expert advice often conflicts and may not take into account individual situations. For instance, while local foods travel shorter distances to the table, areas father away may have more hospitable growing conditions, requiring less use of pesticides and fertilizers, thus offsetting the gains from shorter transportation. Moreover, "green" alternatives may be impractical. For example, the weather, the design of cities, and long commuting distances often make cycling to work impractical in Canada. In addition, the system often works against environmental choices. Citizens may dutifully separate recyclables from their garbage only to find that the city has no market for the items and they end up in landfill anyway. Finally, the "green" alternative is not always as good as advertised. For instance, compact fluorescent bulbs use less electricity but contain toxic mercury. Lighter fuel-efficient cars may break down earlier and have to be replaced sooner than heavier cars. It is clear that consumers must educate themselves about the choices they make.

Essay Topics
1. What food choices can people make to reduce environmental damage?
2. How can Canadians limit environmental damage from their personal vehicles?
3. Explain the advantages or disadvantages of hybrid cars.
4. How can people reduce their use of water?
5. How can people reduce their use of toxic chemicals?
6. Should incandescent light bulbs be banned?

7. Explain a specific recycling process, such as glass or electronics.
8. When is educating the public better than banning a product outright?
9. How can the need for oil be reduced?
10. Explain the environmental damage of oil spills.
11. Explain the causes and/or effects of light pollution or noise pollution.
12. Research a huge garbage problem, such as the Great Pacific Garbage Patch or space junk, and discuss the problem or suggest solutions.
13. Explain the environmental effects of clearing rainforests.

Migration

Immigrants Isolated? Tell That to Their Children

by Rosie DiManno

1   I liken the immigrant neighbourhood where I grew up to a jawbreaker, the orbicular candy that used to cost a penny from a bubblegum dispenser, changing hues and flavours the longer you sucked on it.

2   A more gifted writer would probably come up with a better metaphor, a more elegant way to describe the generational metamorphosis of a community that was sequentially transformed by every ethnic wave that settled within its ragged boundaries. The urban neighbourhood as a recycled oil canvas, perhaps; a painting that, when scratched, reveals an earlier piece of work beneath the surface patina.

3   At the centre of the jawbreaker was English Canada, which in my west-end enclave of Toronto meant blue-collar Irish and Scots, although not so dominant as they were elsewhere in the city. Then, in succeeding layers, came the Jews and the Italians, the Germans, the Greeks, the more ambiguous—to me—Eastern Europeans, the blacks, and then later the Chinese, the East Indians, the Koreans. And so on: A rubric of what would become multicultural Canada, although none of us thought of it then in those terms, this being the era before Multiculturalism became capitalized and politicized and hyphenated in its ethnic subdivisions.

4   We may have lived within our ethnic pockets—Little Italy or Little Greece and the like—because that is the natural tendency for immigrants venturing into a new world, seeking the sheltering embrace of the known in an unknown environment, a niche where people speak your language and eat your food, share your beliefs and understand your cultural otherness.

This companionship of like to like took the edge off our strangeness, allowed us to feel less alien.

5   It was, and remains, the normal coalescing of newcomers who huddle in cultural clans—for at least one generation, before the native-born offspring of immigrants begin to assert their own imperatives on the dichotomy of the family, on their transplanted parents. This is the normal rhythm of the immigrant experience, although apparently a concept poorly understood by the authors of a Statistics Canada report released last week that warned about the isolation of visible minority neighbourhoods in Canada's largest cities where segregation, it claims, has become entrenched.

6   I suspect the problem, if one exists (and I'm not broadly convinced of this), is largely about time—not giving these uprooted and transplanted constituencies enough of it before expecting that they become something else entirely, particularly if they come from non-European, non-white countries with their own millennia of traditions, where attitudes have been shaped by vastly different experiences, where the liberal virtues we cherish in Canada do not have the same traction, indeed where they are viewed with suspicion and alarm.

7   What's also problematic, I think, is that Canada has devalued the concept of assimilation, promoting instead a mosaic of ethnic identification that is inherently splintering and isolationist, emphasizing as it does the details that make us different rather than the aspirations that make us so much the same.

8   The ethnic neighbourhood—the cultural ghetto, as clearly disapproved by the StatsCan report—was like the warmth of a womb for postwar immigrants only a decade removed from a global conflagration and surely no less so for more recent arrivals fleeing other tyrannies, other unpromising futures. Those of us born here as first-generation offspring, as gestated Canadians, sprang from this same amniotic sac of cultural nourishment but grew up rapidly absorbing the dominant ethos, pining to assimilate, glad to shed old country peculiarities. I see little evidence that a new generation of made-in-Canada Canadians feels greatly different.

9   It was harder for our parents, and no wonder, but they tried, they did try. We were a polyglot of peoples, fusing gradually, by osmosis, by a generosity of spirit that found its expression in church, at christenings and weddings where neighbours of different backgrounds were welcome—in the exchange of ethnic food—have some homemade wine, try this strudel—in the early and quite scandalous phenomenon of intermarriage and, most critically, in the public schools attended by that first generation of immigrant children. We were Canadian tadpoles, swimming into the mainstream, even within the ethnic patchwork of our neighbourhoods.

10   The street where I lived was primarily Italian in the '60s, a postwar influx that steadily displaced the Jewish families that had converged there previously. I remember my mother using a knife to remove the mezuzahs that former owners had affixed on the doorframes in our house on Grace St.

But when my parents arrived in the neighbourhood, the Jewish presence was still strong, and our existences overlapped. Remarkably, there was very little clash of culture. My father worked for a Jewish-owned industrial laundry on Shaw St. For two decades, that Jewish family spent Christmas with our extended Italian family. I don't recall any resentment, on my parents' part, toward this earlier wave of immigrants who had preceded them up the economic ladder. We wanted more to emulate their success than to grumble about it.

11   Our separate cultures, confident within their own essence, were not averse to engaging with each other. It was the overlapping, I think, that encouraged this engagement and made us less alien to each other, certainly less threatening.

12   Maybe that, in its clumsy and unsophisticated fashion, is what the StatsCan report was trying to get at. But the isolation indexes applied in this overview put too much emphasis on where people live and too little on *how* they live, where their lives intersect, socially and economically. It is entirely normal for a Jamaican family, say, to patronize a Jamaican grocer or for an Indian family to buy from an Indian retailer. It's natural to hire one another, to support one another's business ventures, even to gather in social clubs and puzzle over this weird thing called Canadian society.

13   Perhaps it was indeed easier, in another time, to mingle with different cultures when most families lived in tidy houses and couples strolled along the street at night, neighbours stopping to chat in variously accented English on one another's front stoop. Those high-rise suburban clusters are not conducive to neighbourliness. But the children of newer immigrants still, overwhelmingly, go to school with one another, watch the same TV shows, listen to the same pop music, have the same rebellious conflicts with their parents. It is the segregation of religious-based schools and the imposition of ethnocentric exclusivity on young social groups that should be discouraged.

14   But, you know what? The children of immigrants, straddling two cultures, inevitably turn away from their parents' experience and assert their own commingled identity. The ethnicity becomes diluted. They will keep the bits that they value and discard the rest.

15   It has always been thus, one generation to the next.

16   Just give it time.

[From the *Toronto Star*, 15 March 2004, p. A2]

Notes

A mezuzah [10] is a parchment inscribed with religious texts, usually in a decorative case, attached to a doorway of Jewish homes.

First-generation immigrants are the ones who come to a new country; the second generation is their children who are born and raised in the new country. Immigrant children who are very young when they arrive can be considered second generation because they are more at home with the new country.

Comprehension

1. What is the thesis (the main argument) of this article?
2. What do you think was in the StatsCan report of March 2004?
3. What does she mean when she says "Multiculturalism became capitalized" [3]?
4. Why do new immigrants move to ethnic neighbourhoods?
5. Why do "non-European, non-white" [6] immigrants have to make more of an adjustment?
6. When DiManno says "postwar" [8, 10], which war is she referring to?
7. Why was it easier to get to know neighbours when DiManno was young than it is today?
8. Why does DiManno dislike "religious-based schools" [13]? (See an explanation of the different kinds of Canadian schools in the note for the second reading, Unit 14, page 332.)
9. Who do you think DiManno is addressing at the end of the essay when she says, "Just give it time"?

Discussion

1. Do you agree with DiManno's arguments? Discuss your own experiences with, and observations of, immigrant assimilation.
2. What culture clash problems do second-generation immigrants face?
3. Do you think Canada should promote assimilation rather than multiculturalism? Explain why or why not.

Assignments

1. DiManno says that second-generation immigrants "will keep the bits that they value and discard the rest" [14] of their ethnic culture. Write an essay explaining what is usually kept from an ethnic culture in Canada. Do not just list items—categorize them, and then give specific examples. You can focus on one specific ethnic group if you wish.
2. Read the short story "Why My Mother Can't Speak English" (page 352). Is the son in the story a typical second-generation immigrant according to what DiManno says? Write an essay explaining your viewpoint.

3. In addition to articles about politics, social issues, and sports, Rosie DiManno has written about her childhood growing up in Toronto as the child of Italian immigrants in such essays as "Growing up on Grace" (28 June 1997). These works, published in the *Toronto Star*, may be found in your school library's periodical databases. Read and summarize one of these articles, or write an essay comparing her childhood with today's immigrants' experience.

Paraphrase and Summary

1. Paraphrase: "What's also problematic, I think, is that Canada has devalued the concept of assimilation, promoting instead a mosaic of ethnic identification that is inherently splintering and isolationist, emphasizing as it does the details that make us different rather than the aspirations that make us so much the same." [7]
2. Paraphrase: "I don't recall any resentment, on my parents' part, toward this earlier wave of immigrants who had preceded them up the economic ladder. We wanted more to emulate their success than to grumble about it." [10]
3. Write a one-paragraph summary of no more than 150 words of this article.

Vocabulary Study

1. *Like* is a very versatile word in English. DiManno uses the verb *liken* [1] and the expressions *and the like* [4] and *like to like* [4]. Explain what each term means.
2. While *rubric* [3] can refer to a designation or category, as in this reading, it has other meanings. The word comes from the Latin word for red earth because titles were often written in red. Ask your instructors how the word is used in academia—whether they use a rubric to grade papers.
3. Explain the difference between *venturing* [4] and *ventures* [12].
4. What is the difference between *segregation* [5, 13] and *separation*?
5. Explain the difference in connotation between "ethnic neighbourhood" and "cultural ghetto" [8].

Definitions

Use the context to match each word to its definition:

1. orbicular [1] _____
2. hues [1] _____
3. metamorphosis [2] _____
4. patina [2] _____
5. enclave [3] _____
6. ambiguous [3] _____
7. niche [4] _____
8. coalescing [5] _____
9. dichotomy [5] _____
10. mosaic [7] _____
11. aspiration [7] _____
12. conflagration [8] _____
13. tyrannies [8] _____
14. ethos [8] _____
15. polyglot [9] _____
16. osmosis [9] _____
17. emulate [10] _____
18. averse [11] _____

a) a small area within a larger area, where a different group of people live
b) change of character and condition
c) characteristic attitudes of a group of people
d) colours
e) comfortable or suitable place to live or work
f) coming together to form a whole
g) cruel and oppressive governments
h) division into two
i) gradual absorption of ideas
j) hope, goal, strong desire to have something
k) huge fire or violent situation like a war
l) opposed to something
m) pattern or picture composed of small pieces
n) smooth, shiny surface
o) spherical, shaped like a globe
p) try to equal or copy
q) unclear, difficult to understand, with two different interpretations
r) with many languages

Word parts

Discuss the meaning of these words by looking at their parts:

entrenched [5]
uprooted [6]
transplanted [6]
devalued [7]
neighbourliness [13]
commingled [14]

Parts of speech

Fill in the following chart:

Noun	Verb	Adjective	Adverb
	n/a		sequentially
	politicize		
		hyphenated	n/a
		alien	n/a

Noun	Verb	Adjective	Adverb
	assert		
suspicion			
	promote		
	n/a	problematic	
		isolationist	n/a
	emphasize		
	absorb		
peculiarity peculiarities	n/a		
		scandalous	
	patronize		
exclusivity			
		diluted	n/a

Collocations and expressions

Discuss each of the following expressions. How clear is the meaning? Is it idiomatic? How useful is the expression?

> to come up with something [2]
> to try to get at something [12]
> to put emphasis on [12]

Structure and Technique

DiManno uses analogies, metaphors, and similes. Review the sections on analogy as a literary device in Unit 6 (pages 198–9).

1. She starts her essay with an analogy, comparing her neighbourhood to a jawbreaker. She then suggests another possible analogy. What is her second one? Which one is better? Can you suggest another analogy?
2. A common metaphor compares immigrants to trees. What words in paragraph 6 relate to this metaphor?
3. What is the simile in paragraph 8? What words in the paragraph relate to that simile?
4. Explain the metaphor in paragraph 9.

Over Here, I Rarely Lift a Finger

by Ann Marie McQueen

1   I resisted the affordable help for a little while after moving to the United Arab Emirates. More than a year later, I rarely do anything for myself.

2   Back in Ottawa, where I lived before coming here, I felt guilty if I stopped to pick up dinner at Farm Boy's deli counter, or drove from the ByWard Market up to Elgin Street on the weekend because I felt lazy. I once struggled to haul a giant plant pot out of Home Depot; I don't recall anyone offering to help.

3   In the capital of the Emirates, Abu Dhabi, there is valet parking at hospitals, hotels—where the restaurants and bars are—and malls. Most everyone has a nanny, one who has invariably left her own children to care for someone else's. A friend of mine pays more than triple the going wage; she can hear her nanny crying after hanging up from a long-distance phone call with one of her children back in the Philippines.

4   My apartment was the last thing to go when, two months ago, I broke down and hired a cleaner. A neighbour mentioned that Zara, a slight Sri Lankan woman who has been here for 24 years, could use the work. Now, even the area under my sink is spotless.

5   For months I've had my clothes laundered and meticulously pressed at a tiny shop steps from my apartment, picked up from my door and delivered back. I don't even have to ask for it—the owners spot me when I walk past, and a few minutes later, my doorbell rings.

6   If I wake up in the morning and don't have milk, water, or anything else I might need, I ring the corner store. They deliver, fast.

7   As with many locations in the world, the cheaper the labour, the bigger the staff. All these people clamour for a chance to work for any wage, no matter how low, regardless of the conditions or distance from their families, because it's way more than they could get back in India, Pakistan, Nepal, or any number of other poor countries.

8   When I went to buy a new camera, I counted 11 men behind the counter. Three asked if I wanted any help, and the majority seemed to pitch in to complete the transaction.

9   If I happen to go to the local market and clutch a few items to my chest, one of the staff will approach me with a basket and wait nearby after I wave him away, just in case I really do need it. At the larger grocery store, a staffer bags my items, wheels out the cart, and waits in front of the long taxi queue until it's my turn.

10   That's another thing: I haven't bothered to buy a car. Traffic, parking, and other drivers are a nightmare, and taxis are plentiful, each trip just a few dollars. It's not uncommon to take a half-dozen taxis on a day off.

11   When I sit down at work each morning, I am greeted by Ismeal, one of the office "tea boys." He wears a bow tie and an orange vest, and he won't let me fill my own water bottle, get my own tea or coffee, or wash any dishes from my lunch. I try to sneak around, but he catches me. He is one of the hardest workers I have ever met, sending his earnings back to a wife and baby, scraping together any extra to build a home with his brothers in Bangladesh. He came here on his own when he was just 14 and like most of the diaspora, gets home just once every couple of years.

12   Everyone gets takeout because it's almost cheaper than shopping. Then there are the manicures and pedicures, each one given by a giggling Filipino woman. They laugh at me, incredulous because I have not married yet, and then tell me about their far-off husbands and children while massaging my toes.

13   This situation isn't right, and while I try and fail to square my own role in it, I tip heavily. I do know this: Although widely criticized for its treatment of labourers, the United Arab Emirates, and the wider Middle East, is just one piece of the problem. Relentless poverty in their home countries will continue to drive people like Zara and Ismeal to leave for a paltry salary that is much more than they could ever hope to earn back home.

14   I see them each weekend, all the people who would not be here if they had a choice, laughing and joking while they line up at the wire-transfer offices. While many white-collar expats dig themselves deeper in debt, and everyone else counts how much they lost in the economic downturn, these people earn a fraction of a proper salary. And yet they manage to save and send whatever they can back home. I could learn a lot from them and how they just get on with it. We all could.

15   Loads of people have judged me for coming to a place that so relies on immigrant labour. I suppose it could be argued that by taking a paycheque I am somehow sanctioning the situation. By funding it unofficially, perhaps I go that much further.

16   Would my conscience be cleaner if my apartment was sometimes messy and cuticles occasionally ragged? I'm not so sure. After all, Zara and Ismeal would just earn their dirhams somewhere else.

_____

[From *The Globe and Mail*, 6 July 2009, p. L6]

Notes

The dirham is the principal monetary unit in the United Arab Emirates and Morocco. Find out what the current exchange rate is for a Canadian dollar.

Comprehension

1. What is the author's main point?
2. Where was the author living when she wrote this article?
3. What point is she making when she gives examples from her life in Ottawa?
4. Why does her friend pay so much for a nanny?
5. Why did McQueen end up hiring a cleaner?
6. How are McQueen's shopping excursions different from typical shopping in Canada?
7. Where are the labourers from? Why are they in Abu Dhabi?
8. What does McQueen admire about the labourers?
9. Explain what the author is worrying about when she talks about "sanctioning the situation." What does she conclude?

Discussion

1. Which adaptation is easier: to move from a culture where self-sufficiency is the norm or from a culture where servants are the norm? Explain why.
2. Discuss the adaptations we have to make to a different culture when we live and work somewhere else. Discuss your own experiences.
3. McQueen says, "I could learn a lot from them and how they just get on with it. We all could." She is implying that Canadians lack a strong work ethic. Is this a valid criticism? Do you think most students have a strong work ethic?
4. What kind of jobs would you want to hire someone to do for you? For example, would you want someone doing your laundry and cleaning your home, or would you prefer to do it yourself?
5. Why do many Canadians value self-sufficiency? Is self-sufficiency over-rated? Is it important to you?

Assignments

1. Is the work ethic important in Canadian society? Is it "old-fashioned," as many people claim? Write an essay arguing your position.
2. The saying "When in Rome, do as the Romans do" proclaims that we all must make adjustments when living in a different culture. In an essay, explain adjustments that immigrants to Canada must make.
3. In an essay, define good service in a store. How much help do people want and need?
4. In a paragraph, discuss one factor that determines whether a wage is fair or not. For example, you could discuss the value of the work in society or the effort, training, talent, or danger involved.
5. In an essay, discuss the value of self-sufficiency.

Paraphrase and Summary

1. Paraphrase: "For months I've had my clothes laundered and meticulously pressed at a tiny shop steps from my apartment, picked up from my door and delivered back. I don't even have to ask for it—the owners spot me when I walk past, and a few minutes later, my doorbell rings." [5]
2. Paraphrase: "While many white-collar expats dig themselves deeper in debt, and everyone else counts how much they lost in the economic downturn, these people earn a fraction of a proper salary. And yet they manage to save and send whatever they can back home." [14]

Vocabulary Study

1. What is the four-letter verb at the root of the word *invariably*? Explain the meaning of the prefixes and suffixes and ultimately of the word itself.
2. What is the opposite of *spotless*?
3. Since *staff* is a mass noun, the term *staff person* is often used to specify one member of the staff. McQueen uses another word. What is it?

4. The words *conscience* (n.) and *conscious* (adj.) are sometimes confused because they sound almost the same and both concern mental states. Your conscience is the voice inside your head that tells you whether something is right or wrong. If you listen to your conscience and do the right thing, you can be considered *conscientious* (adj.). If you are conscious, it means you are awake and aware. Related words include *unconscious* (adj.), *subconscious* (n.), and *consciousness* (n.). Use your dictionary to find definitions, example sentences, and other uses of the words.

Definitions

Use the context to match each word to its definition:

1. haul [2] _____
2. launder [5] _____
3. meticulously [5] _____
4. clamour [7] _____
5. transaction [8] _____
6. clutch [9] _____
7. queue [9] _____
8. diaspora [11] _____
9. incredulous [12] _____
10. relentless [13] _____
11. paltry [13] _____
12. expats [14] _____
13. sanction [15] _____
14. cuticle [16] _____

a) a piece of business done between people
b) an amount too small to be considered useful
c) demand something loudly
d) ethnic group of people who have moved away from their own country
e) give permission for something to take place
f) hard skin at the base of fingernails and toenails
g) hold tightly
h) individuals who have moved to another country, from expatriate
i) line-up
j) not believing something
k) pull something with a lot of effort
l) wash clothes
m) with careful attention to detail
n) without stopping, refusing to give up

Parts of Speech

Fill in the following chart:

Noun	Verb	Adjective	Adverb
	resist		n/a
		affordable	
	n/a	guilty	
	judge		
	rely (on)		
	manage		
		messy	

Collocations and expressions

Discuss each of the following expressions. How clear is the meaning? Is it idiomatic? How useful is the expression?

to lift a finger (usually used in a negative way, as in "she never even lifted a finger", "he barely lifts a finger around the house") [in title]

to do something for yourself [1]

to break down [4] (Discuss the different meanings of this expression.)

to wave somebody away, to wave somebody off [9]

to pitch in [8]

to wheel out something [9]

to scrape together something [11] (usually used with money)

to dig oneself deeper in debt [14]

to get on with it [14]

to have a clear conscience (note that McQueen uses the word *clean*, but *clear* is more common) [16]

Structure and Usage

McQueen uses semi-colons, colons, and parenthetical dashes. Discuss the way these punctuation marks have been used. What other ways could she have fulfilled the same functions?

Article use with country names: Note that the definite article *the* is used before the United Arab Emirates (and the Middle East) but not before the city name Abu Dhabi. In English, article usage can be confusing for place names. The definite article is used with a country name if there is a word that means country or state included in the name. For instance, *Emirates* refers to the domain controlled by an emir.

Here are some examples of country names:

Canada, but originally the Dominion of Canada
the United States of America, but America
China, but the Republic of China
Russia, but the former Soviet Union
Saudi Arabia, but the Kingdom of Saudi Arabia
England, Scotland, Ireland, but the United Kingdom
Holland, but the Netherlands

Immigration Issues

Canada is a country built by immigrants, but immigration has always been a controversial issue—from the seventeenth-century boatloads of *filles du roi* (French women sent to marry settlers in Quebec) to recent boatloads of Tamil refugees from Sri Lanka. Strangely, people who have come as immigrants or are the children of immigrants themselves are often against opening Canada's doors to let more people in—especially if those people are of different ethnic stock.

With Canada's birthrate below replacement level, the country counts on immigration for demographic, and therefore economic, growth. Moreover, immigrants are motivated to work hard and to work at jobs that Canadians are reluctant to do. One of the ironies of the immigration system is that it favours educated professionals, who often find it difficult to find employment in their field. However, many cities need labourers, who can find work but may be unable to come to the country legally.

Immigrants sacrifice so much to come here. They leave family and friends to come to a strange land. They must change their lifestyle to adapt to Canadian language, laws, and culture. They often do this for the sake of their children. This puts pressure on the children to succeed. It is not surprising, therefore, that second-generation immigrants have such high academic achievement. They work hard to justify the sacrifices their parents made.

The second generation is often caught between Canadian lifestyle and values and those of their parents. Many walk the tightrope between two different cultures. They may wish to please their parents by following their cultural traditions, but they also want to be part of Canadian society. Sometimes this can result in terrible conflict. For example, some Canadians have been forced into arranged marriages or have even fallen victim to "honour killing" when their behaviour has been seen by their parents as shameful. Most issues are resolved as compromises are made, but the clash of wills and desires can create resentment, anxiety, and frustration for both first- and second-generation immigrants.

Essay topics

1. What kind of immigrants should Canada seek?
2. Should there be amnesty for illegal immigrants?
3. What should the government do to help immigrants settle in Canada?
4. What kind of adjustments should immigrants make? What should they maintain of their own culture?
5. What factors determine how well immigrants assimilate?
6. What factors determine whether second-generation immigrants will keep their mother tongue?
7. Research a specific group of immigrants (such as Chinese railway workers, Ukrainian farmers, or Vietnamese boat people), and write an essay on their settlement in Canada.

Etiquette and Culture

Those Mooching, Deadbeat Guests of Summer

by Allan Hepburn

1   Being a perfect house-guest requires talent and tact. In July this year, I had visitors three weeks out of four. I welcomed friends for stays lasting between one night and one week. As the perfect host, I brewed coffee in the morning and grilled tuna for dinner. I kept towels laundered and the bathroom clean.

2   As a guest myself in the past, I have benefited from the largesse of others. I once spent an entire summer in Amagansett, NY, at the invitation of friends. I was on my best behaviour. All summer, I improvised clafouti recipes and pasta sauces to please my hosts. I shopped every day and cooked every night. I went to the beach with a book so my friends could have time alone. In a word, I was grateful.

3   I love my friends. They are excellent company—independent and easy-going. Some of them, however, need remedial advice on guesting.

4   *Schedule*: I have fewer beds than the Ritz-Carlton. People are already booked with me until November, mostly for weekends, although one New Zealander is coming for a fortnight. The perfect guest calls ahead, commits to dates of arrival and departure, and does not whimsically change plans. A guest once announced she wanted to stay longer—I was living in Paris at the time—and demanded that I reschedule my mother's impending visit. The unwanted guest had already stayed for 24 days, which, in retrospect, was 23 days too long. If you want to remain friends, you've got to know when to leave.

5   *Gifts*: I operate on the "one gift a day" principle. The perfect guest arrives with a present and offers some token every day thereafter. The gift doesn't have to be extravagant, just a sign of appreciation. Flowers, candles, a movie ticket, or a half-kilo of coffee will do. Appropriate gifts fall

into four categories: things to eat, things to drink, things that amuse, things your host expressly likes. Do not redecorate your host's abode. If your host is a minimalist, don't clutter his space with tchotchkes. When in doubt, bring booze; somebody will drink it.

6   (Note to Manhattan friends: Deutz champagne, a splendid beverage, is not regularly available in Canada. Sherry-Lehmann on Madison Avenue sells it.)

7   *Flattery:* Do not tell your host that his taste sucks. One of my guests recently commented, "Wow, that carpet has seen better days! I can't believe you still have that thing!" If I hated it, I wouldn't have it on my floor, would I? It is far better to flatter your host than to critique his interior decorating. "I love that Jens Risom chair!" you should gush. "Your home is beautiful and functional at the same time!"

8   *Meals:* Your host is not a restaurant. Recently a guest who stayed six days watched as I roasted chicken, tossed salad, and whisked sabayon. I served her three meals a day. On her last night in town, I suggested we go out to eat, I was too weary to cook. Within minutes, queasiness overcame her, and she took to her bed. I foraged in the kitchen. Fifteen minutes later, she weakly suggested I go to the restaurant alone. "Oh, I've nibbled on leftovers," I said. Within minutes, my guest had recovered her health and good spirits. It is uncharitable to say so, but I think her queasiness was brought on by the spectre of a bistro tab for two.

9   Be grateful for what you get. One guest blurted out as I placed a dish of penne in front of her. "Not this again! You made this last time I was here!" The perfect guest eats anything, provided that the perfect host has inquired into kosher prohibitions, vegan preferences, and gastro-intestinal ailments.

10   Although guests need not assist with every meal, they can pitch in as required. Cook dinner in lieu of your present-of-the-day if you feel indigent. Display unstinting generosity when it comes to food. If your host leads you to a pricey restaurant, indulge him the way he's indulging you. Do not blanch at the cost of a meal. Remember how much money you are saving by not staying in a hotel.

11   (Note to Canadians: Americans will buy expensive dinners if you convert prices to US dollars. Steak at $18 US tastes better than steak at $25 Canadian.)

12   *Privacy:* You are on holiday, but your host is not. He has work to do, so leave him alone. When your host gives you a house key and a map, take them. Venture out on your own. Hook up with him for dinner. Converse charmingly. Do not ask how he spent his afternoon. Some things should remain private.

13   *Appreciation:* After you leave, send a bread-and-butter note saying you appreciated the hospitality. Email messages and phone calls are acceptable. If you say thanks, you'll be invited back.

14   (Note to slackers: there's no room at the inn.)

[from The *Globe and Mail*, 9 Aug. 2000, p. A16]

Notes

The term *house guest* refers specifically to people who come to stay for a few days—not a dinner guest. Note that Hepburn hyphenates it. It is more commonly written as two words. Moreover, he uses the word *guest* as a verb [3]; this usage is unusual.

Some of the terms Hepburn uses are proper names of products and names of specific dishes that may not be in your dictionary. You can use the Internet to find out more about: Amangasett, NY (where it is located); the Ritz-Carlton chain of hotels; recipes for clafouti and sabayon; Deutz champagne; the Sherry-Lehmann wine store; the kind of furniture Jens Risom designs; and anything else you are curious about.

Note that the exchange rate for American dollars changes. At the time this article was written, the American dollar was worth considerably more than the Canadian.

The expression "there's no room at the inn" [14] is an allusion to the Nativity story when Mary and Joseph could not find a room at the inn and Jesus was born in the stable.

Comprehension

1. What is the main idea of this article? Who is Hepburn addressing his remarks to?
2. Why does Hepburn think he is qualified to give this advice?
3. What is most important about the scheduling of a visit?
4. What makes an appropriate gift for a host?
5. What is important at mealtime?
6. What are "kosher prohibitions, vegan preferences, and gastro-intestinal ailments"? What other factors may determine what people can and cannot eat?
7. How should guests ensure their host's privacy?
8. What should guests do after the visit?

Discussion

1. Do you agree with Hepburn, or do you think he is too demanding of what a house guest should do? Support your answer.
2. Do you think Hepburn's guests are too "high maintenance" (i.e., are too demanding)? Which of his guests do you think was the worst behaved?
3. Do you think Hepburn is too hospitable? Would you like to visit him?
4. How do host/guest expectations vary from culture to culture?
5. Talk about some of your experiences as a host or a guest.
6. In addition to staying with friends, what are other ways to save accommodation costs when travelling? Would you consider couch surfing and home exchange as viable options? (If you are unfamiliar with these practices, look them up.)

Assignments

1. House guest etiquette varies from culture to culture and even from family to family. In South Asian tradition, for example, the host is responsible for everything. House guests are given royal treatment and are not expected to do anything until it is their turn to host. South Asian immigrants often find it difficult to keep up these traditions in a Canadian lifestyle. In an essay, describe a different style of hospitality and why it fits the society. Or compare two different styles of hospitality and explain the differences.

2. Note that one of Hepburn's guests was there for each meal. This means she could not have spent much time out exploring the city (which in this case would have been Montreal). Imagine that someone like this is going to visit you. Write an email to the person suggesting a few places to visit in your local area. Be persuasive; imagine that your visitor will be a reluctant tourist and you want the person to be out and about as much as possible.

3. Write an essay explaining what factors should be considered when choosing a gift for someone. Discuss gifts in general, not just gifts for hosts. (Hint: Imagine a friend has asked you to help shop for a gift. What questions would you ask before you suggested a possible present?)

4. Write an essay explaining what makes a good traveller. You should focus on a particular aspect, such as being environmentally conscious, getting the most out of the experience personally, or adapting to the culture.

5. Hepburn lived in Paris and now lives in Montreal—two wonderful cities to visit. Choose a city anywhere in the world that you would like to visit. Write a paragraph explaining what makes it attractive as a destination.

Paraphrase and Summary

1. Paraphrase: "I love my friends. They are excellent company—independent and easy-going. Some of them, however, need remedial advice on guesting." [3]

2. Paraphrase, eliminating specific details: "On her last night in town, I suggested we go out to eat, I was too weary to cook. Within minutes, queasiness overcame her, and she took to her bed. I foraged in the kitchen. Fifteen minutes later, she weakly suggested I go to the restaurant alone. 'Oh, I've nibbled on leftovers,' I said. Within minutes, my guest had recovered her health and good spirits. It is uncharitable to say so, but I think her queasiness was brought on by the spectre of a bistro tab for two." [8]

3. Note that this article is written as instructions for readers. The author therefore uses *you* and command sentences. Rewrite one of the following paragraphs in more academic English, eliminating the *you* forms: 7, 12, 13, or other sections that address the reader.

4. Do Exercise 8.5 (p. 254–5), which is a summary of this article that needs to be edited to the required length.

Vocabulary Study

1. What is the opposite of the adjective *appropriate*? (Hint: add a prefix.)
2. What is the difference between the two verbs *critique* and *criticize*? What are the corresponding noun and adjective forms?
3. The word *gush* here is used to describe emotional speech, which is a more figurative meaning. In the literal meaning, what kinds of things gush?
4. A common noun related to the verb *venture* is formed with a prefix. What is this noun form?
5. The prefix *re* means "again." Find two words in the reading that use this prefix. Be careful not to choose words that just start with *re*; make sure the prefix changes the meaning of the original word to show that something is done again.

Definitions

Match the words to the correct definition:

1. tact [1] _____
2. launder [1] _____
3. largesse [2] _____
4. remedial [3] _____
5. whimsically [4] _____
6. minimalist [5] _____
7. tchotchkes [5] _____
8. queasiness [8] _____
9. forage [8] _____
10. indulge [10] _____
11. blanch [10] _____

a) ability to deal with difficult situations carefully and graciously
b) aimed at solving a problem
c) be generous by allowing somebody to have whatever he or she wants
d) become pale from fear or shock
e) by whim (a sudden decision to do something that is based on a feeling)
f) feeling of sickness, nausea
g) generosity, giving to others
h) knick-knacks, small decorative objects in a house
i) look for food, usually picking berries and nuts outdoors
j) someone who prefers to have few possessions and likes a simple, clean decor
k) wash clothes

Parts of speech

Fill in the following chart:

Noun	Verb	Adjective	Adverb
	benefit		
invitation			n/a
	improvise		
	n/a	extravagant	
appreciation			
category, categories			
flattery			
		functional	
	n/a	weary	
	inquire		
generosity	n/a		
	convert		n/a
	converse		

Collocations and expressions

Discuss each of the following expressions. How clear is the meaning? Is it idiomatic? How useful is the expression?

    to commit to something [4]
    in retrospect [4]
    to fall into a category [5]
    to have seen better days [7]
    to be brought on by something [8]
    provided that [9]
    to pitch in [10]
    in lieu of [10] (*lieu* is a French word meaning *place*)
    bread-and-butter [13] (something basic and fundamental)

Slang

to mooch off somebody. [title]
deadbeat [title]
booze [5]
Wow! [7]
it sucks [7]
pricey [10]
hook up [12] (note that this term has different meanings, depending on the context)
slacker [14]

Structure and Technique

This article is written in an informal, humorous style. Discuss what makes it funny. The author teaches English at McGill University. Does this surprise you? What kind of teaching style would you imagine he has?

Note that Hepburn uses subtitles (in italics) and asides directed to different groups of readers (in brackets). How effective are they? Are they necessary?

As a journalistic article, this reading is not organized in the same way an academic essay would be. Which sentence would you consider his thesis statement? Where would this statement come in an academic essay? Is it a good thesis statement? Does its location work well in this article?

The Gift of Thanks: "What Do You Say?"

by Margaret Visser

1   People whose native language is English traditionally feel that gratitude is a good thing, that "the least they can do" for people who help them, give them presents, or do them favours is to thank them. To begin with, they usually have the habit of saying "thank you" drummed into them at an early age. And linguistic custom requires them to produce "thank you" and "thanks" not only when they feel gratitude but also when it is thought they *should* feel grateful even though they do not. Indeed, they often feel obliged to say "thanks" in situations where gratitude is irrelevant . . .

2   Thanking, in English, is like greeting, apologizing, and politely requesting in that it is achieved by means of what linguists call "conversational routines." These include conventional phrases, iron-clad in their invariability, commonly said in a preordained order, and often hard to account for through traditional grammar. "Thank you" means "I—or we—thank you": "thank" is a verb spoken without its subject. The further abbreviation, "Thanks," stands for something like "I offer you my thanks." "No, thanks" is an expression that appears to have arrived during the late nineteenth century. Mrs. Humphry announces in 1897 that "'No, I thank you,' is a form of words no longer heard in good society, having some time since been replaced by: 'No, thanks.'"[1] The word had become a noun—in the plural.

3   These words and other routines like them are learned as phrases, or references to phrases, even when the original expressions are unknown to their speakers. As spoken phrases, they often become unbreakable chunks of words, so much so that they have each become more like one word than a phrase. "How do you do?" seems to be a question, but the speaker really does not require—or even want—an account of how the other is doing. The equally fixed response is to repeat "How do you do?": the two parties have simply and formally assured each other that they belong to the group of those who can be expected to be polite. They are doing what is customary, not "insolent," and correct. Other conventional greeting and parting rituals involve saying "Good morning," "Good evening," "Good night," and "Good-bye," or "Bye-bye," the original and literal meaning of which is "God be with ye." "Please," tied as it is to request, is less common than "thank you" but may be even more rigorously required. It means "If you please," which sounds archaic nowadays. The whole phrase may therefore, when found, and especially with a strong stress on the first word, be sarcastic: "*If* you please." For "please" we would now say (but we do not), "If it would please you, or at least not inconvenience or trouble you," and the idea includes "It would certainly please *me*."

4   The routine phrase "thank you" is far more difficult to account for than "please." Its meaning is so involved and complicated, indeed, that this book-length treatment of the idea will not exhaust its complexity. For example, nobody is supposed to do a kindness or give a present in order to receive thanks. We are likely to be enraged, however, if thanks are not forthcoming. Gratitude—we feel—ought to be felt and must be expressed. Yet a person owed thanks often feels constrained to protest that the debtor owes nothing. "Not at all," he or she will protest. "It was nothing." What meets the eye, when we talk of thanks, is merely the tip of an iceberg.

---

1 Mrs. Humphry. 1897. *Manners for Men.* p. 136. Exeter: Webb and Bower.

Notes

These four paragraphs come from the first chapter of Margaret Visser's 2008 book *The Gift of Thanks* (Harper Collins). Note that Visser refers to her whole book when she says "this book-length treatment." In this excerpt, the second and third paragraphs of the original have not been reproduced here, so some references may not be clear. For example, Visser explains the meaning of the word *insolence* as "what is unaccustomed," which is why she talks about what is customary as "not 'insolent'" [3]. The modern meaning of *insolent* is "extremely rude."

In her book, Visser explains that saying "thank you" is not common in all cultures, but that it is a heavily used expression among English-speaking people. The chapter title, "What do you say?", refers to what parents say to their children when they are teaching them to say "thank you." Visser points out that children have to be trained to say it and that it is not as natural or easily learned as greetings and other expressions.

Comprehension

1. Why does Visser say, "People whose native language is English" and not just "people"? What do you expect her to explain later on?
2. In what kind of situations would gratitude be irrelevant?
3. Explain why Visser says that conversational routines are "often hard to account for through traditional grammar."
4. Why is "How do you do?" not a real question?
5. How do people feel when someone does not say "thank you"?

Discussion

1. Discuss how Canadians use "please," "thank you," and "sorry." Do they use these expressions too much? What do you think of the custom of drivers waving their gratitude when another driver lets them in the lane? Compare the customs in Canada with those you know in other cultures.
2. Was there an occasion when you did not receive the thanks you thought you deserved (for a favour or a gift)? How did you feel? Why do you think you did not get thanked?
3. Answering "no problem" has become a common response to "thank you." However, some people argue that it is not as polite as "you're welcome." Do you think the two responses are interchangeable—that they mean the same thing?
4. Would you be offended or would you understand when someone does not respond to your expression of thanks with any gesture or words? Why?
5. If these expressions are ritualized and meaningless, why do we still use them?

Assignments

1. Write a definition paragraph about an expression used in a conversational routine in either English or another language you speak. Research the etymology (the history) of the expression. You can explain both meaning and usage. Here are some possible expressions to write about: Hello, How are you?, Good-bye, So long, Farewell, You're welcome, Adieu, Ciao.
2. Write an essay explaining the guidelines for when and how people should be thanked.
3. Write a process paragraph explaining how parents teach their children to say "thank you."
4. Write a thank-you note for a gift or a favour.

Paraphrase and Summary

1. Paraphrase: "These words and other routines like them are learned as phrases, or references to phrases, even when the original expressions are unknown to their speakers. As spoken phrases, they often become unbreakable chunks of words, so much so that they have each become more like one word than a phrase." [3]
2. Write a 60-word summary of this reading.

Vocabulary Study

Definitions

Use the context to match each word to its definition:

1. linguistic [1] _____	a) decided beforehand
2. irrelevant [1] _____	b) normal, usual, predictable
3. conventional [2] _____	c) not useful or related to a particular situation
4. iron-clad [2] _____	
5. preordained [2] _____	d) old and no longer used, outdated
6. archaic [3] _____	e) related to language and words
7. sarcastic [3] _____	f) restricted, not allowed to do something else
8. constrained [4] _____	g) saying the opposite of what is really meant
	h) strong and sure, cannot be argued against

Word parts

Discuss the meaning of these words by looking at their parts:

invariability [2]
unbreakable [3]
forthcoming [4]
debtor [4]

Parts of speech

Fill in the following chart:

Noun	Verb	Adjective	Adverb
gratitude			
custom			
		obliged	obligingly
	apologize		
	expect		
	n/a		rigorously
complexity			
		enraged	n/a

Collocations and expressions

Discuss each of the following expressions. How clear is the meaning? Is it idiomatic? How useful is the expression?

the least someone can do [1]

to be drummed into somebody [1]

to account for something [2, 4]

to stand for something [2]

the tip of the iceberg [4]

Structure and Technique

Note that this passage is much more academic in style than "Those mooching, deadbeat guests of summer" (even though author Allan Hepburn is an English professor). The paragraphs are longer and more developed. There is no slang or conversational language.

Examine the structure of the paragraphs. Are the topic sentences effective? Do the paragraphs have unity and coherence?

Grammar Analysis

Academic writing has more complex sentence structure, which can be difficult to read. Analyze the following sentences by identifying the core (the subject and predicate) and the phrases and clauses:

1. "These include conventional phrases, iron-clad in their invariability, commonly said in a preordained order, and often hard to account for through traditional grammar."
2. "The whole phrase may therefore, when found, and especially with a strong stress on the first word, be sarcastic: '*If* you please.'"

Etiquette

Etiquette is a French word that refers to the formal rules for polite behaviour in society. It includes the way you greet someone, set the table, issue an invitation, thank someone, and apologize, as well as other social niceties. North American society has become more casual in the past few decades, and many of the old rules have fallen by the wayside. Moreover, social events have been complicated by such social changes as mixed, blended, and even gay marriages, which change family structure. For more on modern life and behaviour, read the essay "Causes of Modern Incivility" on page 186.

Assignments

1. Write a one-paragraph comparison of the two readings in the unit. Focus on one area of difference, such as writing style or content.

2. Write a comparison essay about the social rituals in two different cultures. Choose one specific kind of custom. For example, you could compare the way Canadians greet each other or apologize with the way it is done in your native culture.

3. Choose one kind of rude behaviour, and write an essay explaining the causes and effects. You can talk about driving, the use of cellphones, or anything you observe in daily life.

4. Look up some advice columns on etiquette. You can use local newspapers, etiquette books, or online sources. Choose one letter and response, and analyze it in an essay, or write a different response. As a group activity, students can write their own etiquette questions, and other students can write responses.

Clothing and Fashion

Appearance: Its Social Meaning

by Lorne Tepperman

1   In his classic sociological work *Asylums*, Erving Goffman (1961) notes that the first step taken by a total institution, such as a prison or mental hospital, is to re-socialize an inmate, by separating the inmate from old identities and identifiers. Interestingly, this process begins by changing the inmate's appearance—for example, by forcing the inmate to wear an institutional uniform, while removing all individual identifiers such as jewellery or personal assets. Often the inmate is forced to wear a generic hairstyle, which is another way of regimenting the body and eliminating individuality. The loss of one's own clothing signifies the loss of an old identity and social status. The adoption of an institutional uniform represents entry into a low-status community of identical inmates or subjects. In this real sense, the old maxim is true that "clothes make the man" (or woman). Humble clothes make humble people.

2   Consider the humble uniforms worn by members of the Salvation Army—a religious organization devoted to urban good works, originally involving the moral uplift of fallen people. Winston (2003) notes that the popular image of Salvation Army women changed during the period 1880–1918, due in part to their adoption of plain, unfashionable clothing, which enabled them to enter public places such as saloons to do their work without criticism. So dressed, Salvation Army women practised spiritual warfare on establishments that promoted sin and vice. Their uniform, dramatically severe, came to represent traditional service and old-fashioned virtue.

3   The connection between appearance, clothing, and self has been known and commented on for a long time. The nineteenth-century Scottish

novelist and essayist Thomas Carlyle wrote about clothing metaphorically in his comic work *Sartor Resartus*. There he used clothing to stand in for all symbols of self. People use clothing and other items related to their appearance to construct, confirm, and modify their personal identities within the context of their daily lives. However, personal identities are linked to social identities. Clothes define our place, role, and position in the social order. Carlyle believed that "clothes present us to ourselves and to the world" as we negotiate our freedom of dressed self-expression.

4   In turn, society affects both what we reveal and conceal of our bodies (Keenan 2001). Social pressures constantly undermine our realm of choice and reduce the basic right of self-expression. As a result, clothes never reveal the whole self, since they may be imposed on us or we may use clothes to conceal ourselves. However, given some modicum of choice in how we dress, the choices we make tell the world who we think we are and who we want to be.

5   Not surprisingly, appearance norms are gendered—like many other social norms. Not only are men and women judged by different appearance standards; they also wear different kinds of clothing, connoting their different social roles and statuses. Take pockets: historically, pockets on women's clothing have been smaller and fewer than pockets on men's clothing. For women, pockets have been decorative, for men practical. Even today, men and women use their pockets differently (that's why women carry purses), and pockets play a part in the construction of gender.

6   Underwear is also gendered, though usually unseen except by their wearers and intimate acquaintances. Men's underwear tends to be sturdy and plain. Women's underwear tends to be flimsy and decorative, as though it was on display as part of the mating game. When middle-class women began to wear underpants in the early 1800s, their "drawers" were feminized by fabric, ornamentation, and an open crotch (Fields 2002). Such open drawers on respectable, supposedly passionless women presented female sexuality as both erotic and modest. In the twentieth century, however, women demanded crotches in their drawers to establish their sexual propriety. Women increasingly chose to wear closed drawers during a period of women's greater public presence and feminist activism. This change symbolically closed the gap between men and women.

7   Even today, the type of underwear known as "lingerie" is particularly invested with meanings of femininity, sexuality, and pleasure (Storr 2002). Mass-market lingerie, sex toys, and other "personal" products are sold to women through the use of particular strategies and images. The processes of choosing and buying lingerie involve identifications of gender, sexuality, and sensuality, even though the garments themselves are rarely if ever worn in public. Moreover, they hold implications of class (and classiness). The class connotations of mass-market lingerie are used by working- and lower-middle-class women to distinguish themselves from higher-class women who are thereby defined as pretentious, boring, or tasteless.

8   Fashions, then, declare a person's gender and class, and they also declare ethnic origins. In multicultural urban areas, women's fashion choices are closely tied to issues of self-definition. For example, young Asian and white women living in urban, "multicultural" areas in the United Kingdom express their differently sexualized and racialized female identities through styles of appearance and tastes in clothing, hairstyles, and cosmetics (Malson, Marshall, and Woollett 2002). In doing so, they are making statements about who they are and how they differ from conventional United Kingdom style and culture.

9   As we saw with degradation ceremonies in total institutions, when people in authority want to control people, they try to control their modes of dress. This has been evident in the history of fashion in fascist countries, and it is true of dress codes for schoolchildren in our own society. Paulicelli (2002) notes that Italy under the fascist dictator Mussolini used fashion to discipline the social body—especially women's bodies—and to create an identifiable national style. The issue of school uniforms in our society—a practice of imposing dress codes to regiment people's self-expression—brings up a variety of issues that include safety, egalitarianism, social inclusion, and marketing that encourages students to dress competitively (Bodine 2003).

10   Left on their own, and unless required to wear uniforms, young people develop clothing aspirations very early in life. Even before adolescence, at ages 8 to 12, children begin making product decisions and building knowledge about different products and brands (Meyer and Anderson 2000). A desire to conform to appearance norms influences their shopping behaviour, especially with regard to clothing purchase criteria and shopping independence. As preadolescents age, they acquire more of the norms and information needed to make informed clothing decisions. Conformity concerns influence how children shop, whom they shop with, and what they purchase.

11   Clothing is an expression of both individual and collective identity even among 10 to 11 year olds (Swain 2002). Relaxing the enforcement of school appearance norms (i.e., a dress code) allows pupils to use clothing to gain recognition, forge common bonds, and share interests within peer group cultures. It also, however, serves to distinguish and separate those who fit in with social expectations of dressing in popular fashions and those who do not. Certain items and brand names—for example, Doc Martens—acquire a specific, symbolic value for purposes of conformity or rebellion. Pupils who conform to the school dress rules may satisfy the formal requirements of their institution but run a high risk of being stigmatized and excluded by their peers.

12   Our tendency to conform to appearance norms, learned from childhood onward, largely continues throughout life. This results in a widespread interest in "fashion."

References

Bodine, Ann. 2003. "School Uniforms and Discourses on Childhood". *Childhood* 10 (1): 43–63.

Fields, Jill. 2002. "Erotic Modesty: (Ad)dressing Female Sexuality and Propriety in Open and Closed Drawers, USA, 1800–1930." *Gender and History* 14 (3): 492–515.

Goffman, Irving. 1961. *Asylums: Essays on the Social Situation of Mental Patients and Other Inmates*. Garden City, NJ: Doubleday Anchor.

Keenan, William J.R., ed. 2001. *Dressed to Impress: Looking the Part*. Oxford: Berg.

Malson, Helen, Hariette Marshall, and Anne Woollett. 2002. "Talking of Taste: A Discourse Analytic Exploration of Young Women's Gendered and Racialized Subjectivities in British Urban, Multicultural Contexts." *Feminism and Psychology* 12 (4): 469–90.

Meyer, Deborah J.C., and Heather C. Anderson. 2000. "Preadolescents and Apparel Purchasing: Conformity to Parents and Peers in the Consumer Socialization Process." *Journal of Social Behaviour and Personality* 15 (2): 243–57.

Paulicelli, Eugenia. 2002. "Fashion, the Politics of Style and National Identity in Pre-fascist and Fascist Italy." *Gender and History* 14 (3): 537–59.

Storr, Merl. 2002. "Classy Lingerie." *Feminist Review* 71: 18–36.

Swain, Jon. 2002. "The Right Stuff: Fashioning and Identity through Clothing in a Junior School." *Gender and Education* 14 (1): 53–69.

Winston, Diane. 2002. "Living in the Material World: The Changing Role of Salvation Army Women, 1880–1918." *Journal of Urban History* 28 (4): 466–87.

Notes

This is an excerpt from a sociology textbook. Note the academic style of language and the use of references. After each quote or reference to another author's work, Tepperman cites the work by giving the name of the author and the year of the work in round brackets. These references point the reader to the full information in the references section at the end of the book. This information allows readers to find the original article or book and read it for themselves.

The term "total institution" is used by Goffman to denote a place where people live in a group cut off from the regular society.

Comprehension

Choose the best answer according to what is directly said in the reading:

1. Which method of re-socializing inmates is not mentioned?
   a) wearing uniforms
   b) having common haircuts
   c) tattooing ID numbers on forearms
   d) removing jewellery

2. The Salvation Army had its female members change clothing in order to:
   a) have them look like poor people.
   b) show that they were different from authoritarian figures like the police.
   c) protect them from being beaten by those they wished to help.
   d) enable them to enter bars and brothels and do their good works.

3. According to Thomas Carlyle, appearance and clothing are important because:
   a) they reveal personal identity and social status.
   b) they keep people happy.
   c) they played an important role in the novel he wrote.
   d) people want to attract the opposite sex.

4. What does social pressure do?
   a) It makes us reveal our whole self.
   b) It limits our choice of clothing.
   c) It makes us choose unflattering clothes.
   d) It restricts our modicum.

5. Pockets on women's clothes:
   a) don't show social norms.
   b) are mainly ornamental.
   c) are a substitute for a purse.
   d) serve a practical purpose.

6. How did closed drawers reduce the gap between men and women?
   a) It let them both show their underwear.
   b) It made lingerie more erotic.
   c) The underwear made women seem less like sex objects.
   d) The underwear wasn't worn in the 1800s.

7. According to the reading passage, which statement is correct?
   a) Mussolini started Italian high fashion.
   b) Dress codes in schools tend to liberate rather than to restrict.
   c) Controlling dress is one way of controlling people.
   d) Regimenting people's self-expression is not a good way to run a society.

8. When young people choose their clothing:
   a) they have no fashion sense at all.
   b) they would prefer to wear school uniforms.
   c) they are not concerned with conformity.
   d) they try to follow the fashion for their group.

9. Students who follow the school dress code:
   a) may be unpopular.
   b) are rebelling against the norms of their society.
   c) become mature faster.
   d) cannot afford designer clothes and expensive brand names.

10. The main idea of this reading selection is:
    a) clothing can be racially motivated.
    b) underwear is sexy.
    c) conformity in appearance is important.
    d) fashion is based on illogical conclusions.

Discussion

1. What does Tepperman mean when he says, "clothes never reveal the whole self, since they may be imposed on us or we may use clothes to conceal ourselves"? Give examples.
2. What was the dress code in your high school? Do you think it was fair? Should there be dress codes?
3. How important are designer labels in your clothing?
4. Consider different forms of self-expression through appearance: hairstyles, makeup, jewellery, tattoos, and piercings. Discuss these elements and specific styles such as goth, punk, jock, and prep. What and how is the image portrayed?
5. Clothing for babies and toddlers has become more gendered. It used to be possible to dress a small child in plain T-shirts and sweatshirts that would suit either gender. Today, however, baby clothing is either feminine (pink and frilly) or masculine (decorated with pictures of trucks and racing cars). Why has the clothing industry moved in this direction? What does this say about our society?

Assignments

1. Write a paragraph or an essay arguing that men should use purses (or that women should use pockets).
2. Research the use of uniforms by the Salvation Army, and write a brief report.
3. Although traditionally underwear is supposed to remain hidden, recent fashions have exposed underwear. For instance, young men have the top of their boxer shorts showing at the top of their low-slung pants. Young women wear lacy camisoles that can be seen under jackets and

show bra straps along with the thin straps of tank tops. Write an essay explaining what this trend says about society and fashion. Or write an essay arguing for or against bans on such revealing clothing.

4. Tepperman says, "when people in authority want to control people, they try to control their modes of dress." In an essay, discuss one example of clothing used in this way. For example, you can discuss the burka in Afghanistan or the Mao suit in China.

Paraphrase and Summarize

1. Paraphrase: "A desire to conform to appearance norms influences their shopping behaviour, especially with regard to clothing purchase criteria and shopping independence. As preadolescents age, they acquire more of the norms and information needed to make informed clothing decisions. Conformity concerns influence how children shop, whom they shop with, and what they purchase." [10]

2. Paraphrase: "Certain items and brand names—for example, Doc Martens—acquire a specific, symbolic value for purposes of conformity or rebellion. Pupils who conform to the school dress rules may satisfy the formal requirements of their institution but run a high risk of being stigmatized and excluded by their peers." [11]

3. Read paragraph 3 carefully, and reword the ending: "as we negotiate our freedom of dressed self-expression."

4. Summarize this article in no more than 120 words.

Vocabulary Study

1. What kind of places can you call an institution? What does the verb *institute* mean? What is the verb that means "to put someone in an institution"?

2. The nouns *identity*, *identifier*, and *identification* and the adjectives *identical* and *identifiable* are all related to the verb *identify*. What are the differences in meaning?

3. The word *generic* [1] is often used to talk about product names. What is the opposite of a generic name?

4. From the reading passage, find 10 adjectives ending in *−al* (a common adjective ending). Give the related adverbs, nouns, and verbs. For example, related to the adjective *individual* are the adverb *individually*, the noun *individuality*, and the verb *individualize*. Explain any meaning differences. Look for common patterns in your completed list, such as the *−ity* ending in nouns.

5. Note that in the second paragraph, the author says "devoted to urban good works." The word *work* is almost always uncountable. Can you think of another use in which *work* is countable?

6. In the second paragraph, find two words that mean the opposite of each other and start with the same letter.

7. Use a dictionary to find the different meanings of *drawer* and *drawers*.

8. Use a dictionary to find the pronunciation and origin of *lingerie*.

9. What word does *pretentious* look like? What do you think it means? Look at the context (the last sentence of paragraph 7). What clues does the sentence give you? Check the dictionary definition to see if your guess is correct.

10. The suffix *−ism* denotes a belief in something (*racism, feminism, capitalism*), and the *−ist* ending is the person who believes in that "ism" (*racist, feminist, capitalist*). Paragraph 9 contains the word *egalitarianism*. Use the context to help you figure out the meaning. A knowledge of French can also help you. Check the meaning in the dictionary.

11. The words *cloth, clothes,* and *clothing* can be difficult for ESL students to use correctly. *Clothes* and *clothing* are synonyms, but *clothes* is often more specific to the owner, and *clothing* is more general. Both words are nouns, but *clothes* is a plural form with no corresponding singular, and *clothing* is uncountable. *Cloth* refers to the material used to make clothes.

    Fill in the correct word (more than one word may be possible):

    a) After his growth spurt, all his _____ were too small.
    b) Her wedding dress is made of some shiny _____, perhaps satin.
    c) She was still wearing her work _____ when we met.
    d) I need a damp _____ to clean this mess up.
    e) The immigrant family needed to buy winter _____.
    f) The _____ store has re-opened after the fire.

    Here are some other nouns that refer to clothing: *apparel, attire, dress, garment, wear,* and *wardrobe*. Find out the difference in meaning and usage, and write a sentence for each word.

Parts of speech

Fill in the following chart:

Noun	Verb	Adjective	Adverb
individuality			
	signify		
	enable		
criticism			
	practise		
			dramatically
	n/a	severe	
	construct		

Noun	Verb	Adjective	Adverb
	confirm		n/a
	modify		n/a
	impose		
		decorative	
strategy			
implication			
inclusion			
		collective	
		symbolic	

Collocations and expressions

Discuss each of the following expressions. How clear is the meaning? Is it idiomatic? How useful is the expression?

    rarely if ever [7]
    gain recognition [11]
    forge common bonds, forge a bond between [11]
    share interests [11]
    to fit in with something [11]
    to run a risk of (+ gerund) [11]

Structure and Technique

1. In the first paragraph, the author uses a singular form—"the inmate"—but avoids the sticky he/she pronoun problem. What techniques does he use to do this?

2. Unlike the short paragraphs used in journalistic style, this reading has longer, developed paragraphs. Using the topic sentences, identify the main idea of each paragraph.

3. Which words are italicized in the text? Why?

White Tops, Grey Bottoms

by Bev Akerman

1   Not long ago, my 15-year-old son received a detention. He had to stay after school not for inappropriate language or behaviour but because his shirttail was untucked. Although I usually allow room for some embellishment—and even, at times, truth-twisting—in his version of events, I believe him on this one. And that's because I've become acquainted with the Uniformists. In Quebec, they're among the parents, teachers, and school administrators on the governing boards that run the schools.

2   My three children, all in the public system, go to elementary and high schools with strict dress codes. I've never been completely in favour of all this uniformity. When I was in kindergarten in 1965–66, I had to wear a navy, box-pleated tunic to school. Not long after that, the school abandoned this requirement because, according to the then-latest thinking, wearing a uniform stifled self-expression and creativity. Now, the received wisdom is quite different: uniforms are supposed to "create an environment conducive to learning" and a sense of "community among students." Fair enough, I suppose, given the intense, competitive consumerism and cliquishness that plague many schools today.

3   Still, I have a number of questions, starting with: How much uniform is uniform enough? All my kids and all their schoolmates wear some variation of white shirts and grey flannel skirts or slacks. The school my 15-year-old attends also insists on a particular brand of shoe. I can understand requiring a certain style, but no one has yet explained to me why one make should be sanctioned. Meanwhile, both schools keep changing which style of shirt they deem acceptable. Oxford, T-shirt, polo—who can keep track? And the latest dictates: monograms on collars or pockets.

4   So why all the white and grey? Do we want our schools to be sensory deprivation zones? I see nothing wrong with letting a child wear a blue, pink, or yellow shirt as long as it's in the prescribed style. Besides, there's the environmental degradation that keeping white shirts white is causing—I'd never used bleach before my kids entered these schools!

5   I have other concerns. Our high school has a devoted cadre of volunteers who run the uniform store, generating tens of thousands of dollars a year. This money is put toward many things that really are the school board's responsibility: new musical instruments, a fresh coat of paint more than once every seven years, equipment for classrooms, computers, libraries, etc. It also gets spent on extras: lavish graduation exercises, an unbelievable number of academic prizes for graduates, European exchange trips. So requiring students to wear uniforms, in effect, functions as an invisible school fee, over and above the taxes we all pay. Maybe if we were more up-front about this we'd demand more money from our governments, or at least that our school boards make better use of the existing funds.

6   The surprising truth is most parents I speak with feel the uniforms are a blessing: they are relieved to not have daily arguments about appropriate dress. As for the school officials, it seems one reason they've chosen a particular monogrammed shirt is that it's only available in adult sizes. The previously acceptable shirt was also available in children's sizes, which on some high school girls were extremely tight and skimpy.

7   But I question whether we are really doing our kids any favours by abdicating our authority to the school bureaucracy. Parents need to face head-on the challenges these uniforms try to cover over with grey flannel. If we have a problem with the downright sluttish dress of some of our daughters, tattoos, body piercing, or outlandish hair colour, we should deal with these

things ourselves. Buck up, people! Learn to say, "No, that is not appropriate dress for school. When you are a responsible adult, you can choose whether or not to conform to society's expectations." No further explanation necessary.

8   Finally, I suspect the Uniformists have a secret motivation behind their fashion agenda: it makes public schools resemble, in the most superficial way, the exclusive private schools that pepper my Montreal neighbourhood. I simply do not share that aspiration. We should be proud that our kids go to public schools, where all races, religions, and socio-economic groups form a community—just like the real world they will eventually enter.

9   My kids love their schools. And I'm grateful for all the hard work the decimated custodial staff, devoted teachers, concerned administrators, and dynamic parent volunteers put in. I know—and so does my son—that by his age, he shouldn't be wandering about with his shirttail hanging out. But I wish the administration was more concerned with the originality of my kids' minds and less concerned about the conventionality of their dress. In the final analysis, shouldn't their education be more about content and less about form?

[from *Maclean's*, 7 March 2005, p. 57]

Notes

The terminology for different kinds of schools differs from country to country and even from province to province in Canada. History explains the split between public schools and separate schools. When Canada became a country in 1867, there were two main ethnic groups—English Protestants and French Catholics—so two public school systems were set up, according to both language and religion. As Canada became multicultural, some provinces were left with the legacy of the split system. In Ontario, for example, the schools serving English Protestants became the public system, for students of all religions, with a further division into French and English systems depending on linguistic area. The separate school system is essentially for those of the Catholic faith. This has led to discrimination because other religious groups do not have public school funding. However, private schools may be established for specific religious groups. Private schools in Ontario do not receive tax funding, so parents must pay high school fees to send their children there. While private schools can be religion-oriented, many are elitist institutions, the kind referred to by Akerman as "exclusive" [8].

School uniforms are more commonly worn in private and separate schools than in the public system.

Comprehension

1. What is the thesis (the main argument) in this article?
2. Why did Akerman's son receive a detention? What is her complaint about this?

3. What is the author's personal experience with uniforms?
4. What argument for wearing uniforms does she accept as valid?
5. What objections does she have to the colours of uniforms?
6. What objections does she raise regarding the financial issue?
7. What objections does she have to parents letting the schools dictate what is acceptable clothing?
8. What does she see as an advantage of the public school system?

Discussion

1. Do you think more Canadian schools should adopt uniforms? Why or why not? Discuss your experience with school uniforms.
2. Do Canadians dress too casually? Consider work as well as school.
3. What is your opinion about "tattoos, body piercing, or outlandish hair colour"?
4. Should religious schools be funded by the government? Why or why not?
5. Are private schools better than public schools?
6. Akerman refers to the "intense, competitive consumerism and cliquishness that plague many schools today." Discuss this statement. Is it true? How does consumerism and cliquishness manifest itself? What are the problems caused?
7. Consider the educational necessities and luxuries Akerman lists in paragraph 5. What do you think the government should pay for?

Assignments

1. Write an essay for or against uniforms in high school.
2. How important is appearance in our society? Write an essay focusing on one particular group. For example, you can write about store clerks, job candidates, or people in court.
3. Write a classification essay explaining different cliques that existed in your high school.
4. Are teenagers today too materialistic? Write an essay explaining your view.
5. What rules and guidelines should parents set down for their teenagers' appearance? Explain your choices.

Paraphrase and Summary

1. Paraphrase: "the Uniformists have a secret motivation behind their fashion agenda: it makes public schools resemble, in the most superficial way, the exclusive private schools that pepper my Montreal neighbourhood." [8]
2. Paraphrase: "But I wish the administration was more concerned with the originality of my kids' minds and less concerned about the conventionality of their dress. In the final analysis, shouldn't their education be more about content and less about form?" [9]
3. Write a one-paragraph summary of this article. Keep your summary under 100 words.

Vocabulary Study

1. *Uniformist* is a term the author has made up. It has a double meaning—referring to both the championing of school uniforms and the desire to have everyone look the same. In the latter meaning, it would be similar to the word *conformist*.

2. *Cliquishness* [2] is a noun formed from an adjective (*cliquish*) formed from a noun (*clique*). Another adjective form is *cliquey*. *Clique* is pronounced "cleek," although some people pronounce it as "click." The word refers to a small, exclusive group of people and generally is used for the groups formed at high school. It has a negative connotation. The word is originally French (as you can tell by the *–que* ending.) Paragraph 5 has another French word for a group of people. Find the word, check its meaning, and determine how it is different from the word *clique*.

3. In paragraph 3, a word that is more commonly a verb is used as a noun. What is it? What does it mean?

4. In paragraph 8, a word that is more commonly a noun is used as a verb. What is it? What does it mean?

5. What distinguishes the different types of shirts mentioned in paragraph 3?

6. *Decimate* [9] comes from the Latin word for the number 10. How does this meaning relate to the verb's current meaning?

7. *Aspiration* and *inspiration* both come from the Latin word meaning breathe. For each word, find out the meaning, how they relate to breath, and the corresponding verb forms.

Definitions

Use the context to match each word to its definition:

1. embellishment [1] _____
2. stifled [2] _____
3. conducive [2] _____
4. plague [2] _____
5. sanctioned [3] _____
6. deem [3] _____
7. dictates [3] _____
8. degradation [4] _____
9. lavish [5] _____
10. up-front [5] _____
11. abdicate [7] _____
12. superficial [8] _____
13. dynamic [9] _____
14. conventionality [9] _____

a) added details to a story that are not true but make it more interesting
b) bother or annoy somebody or something
c) conditions that make something happen easily, contributing
d) consider, think
e) full of energy and ideas
f) give up one's responsibility for something
g) honest, not hiding anything
h) large, impressive, expensive
i) officially accepted or approved
j) on the surface only, not deep
k) reduction in condition, worse
l) rules, regulations
m) state of following the usual way of doing things
n) stopped from happening or developing

Parts of speech

Fill in the following chart:

Noun	Verb	Adjective	Adverb
creativity			
		competitive	
variation			
	insist (on something)		
		acceptable	
deprivation			n/a
	prescribe		
	generate		n/a
responsibility			
		unbelievable believable	
		relieved	n/a
argument			
		skimpy	
		exclusive	

Collocations and expressions

Discuss each of the following expressions. How clear is the meaning? Is it idiomatic? How useful is the expression?

    to receive/get/have a detention [1]
    to run a school (or other institutions) [1]
    to be in favour of something [2]
    to keep track of something [3]
    to see nothing wrong with something [4]
    money put toward something [5]
    to do somebody a favour [7]
    to face something head on [7]
    buck up [7] (informal, idiom)

Structure and Technique

1. This essay is less formal than an academic essay would be. It contains personal references, sentence fragments, sentences that begin with conjunctions, exclamation marks, over-use of questions, and conversational expressions. Identify examples of this type of usage, and explain what could be used instead in an academic essay.
2. Note the use of parenthetical dashes and colons in the text. Examine each use, and determine whether it is correct and effective. Could alternatives be used?
3. The use of a quote in paragraph 7 is also not academic style. Reword the sentence using indirect speech.

Clothing Controversies

While Canadians generally have fairly liberal standards toward clothing, some controversial issues have surfaced, especially when religious dictates clash with other rules and regulations. Accommodations and compromises have generally been made. For example, the Sikh turban was allowed as alternate headgear in the RCMP and other police forces, but it remains a problem when helmets are mandated for safety. The ceremonial knife-like kirpan worn by Sikh males has not received acceptance, especially in schools and courts.

Currently, much controversy swirls around Muslim women and their donning of the hijab (head scarf), niqab (face veil), or burka (the complete covering demanded by the Taliban in Afghanistan). Some women choose to wear such garments in religious observance, although most theologians say that while modesty is important in Islam, such covering is not required by the Koran. While the hijab has not been banned in Canada as it has in some European countries, teenage girls wearing such head scarves have been stopped from participation in some sports, such as soccer. The issue with the niqab is often one of security, as officials need to see the face to verify identification. Objections were raised when a witness wearing a face veil testified in court in Ontario and when a student restricted her participation in a Quebec French class for immigrants. In addition, there have been reports of bank robbers wearing burkas as a disguise. However, that item of clothing has not made much of an appearance on Canadian streets. While many Canadians agree that such clothing represents a misogyny they find abhorrent, they support freedom of religion and do not want to go to the length of banning it.

Essay Topics

1. Choose an item of clothing that has significance in a religion, such as a nun's habit, the yarmulke, or the items mentioned in the passage. Explain the significance of the item and any controversy surrounding it.
2. Should the niqab be banned in Canada?

3. What accommodations should be made for Muslim women who insist on wearing a niqab?
4. Why is seeing the face so important in society?
5. Just as wearing a burka can be seen as treating women as sexual objects (protecting them from the lustful gaze of men who have no right to them), Western clothing such as tight jeans, low-cut tops, and high heels also objectifies women. Agree or disagree with this statement.

Sport

The Strange Forces behind the Richard Hockey Riot

by Sidney Katz

1   On March 17, 1955, at 9:11 p.m. a tear-gas bomb exploded in the Montreal Forum where 16,000 people had gathered to watch a hockey match between the Montreal Canadiens and the Detroit Red Wings. The acrid yellowish fumes that filled the stadium sent the crowd rushing to the exits, crying, shrieking, coughing, and retching. But it did more. It touched off the most destructive and frenzied riot in the history of Canadian sport.

2   The explosion of the bomb was the last straw in a long series of provocative incidents that swept away the last remnant of the crowd's restraint and decency. Many of the hockey fans had come to the game in an ugly mood. The day before, Clarence Campbell, president of the National Hockey League, had banished Maurice (The Rocket) Richard, the star of the Canadiens and the idol of the Montreal fans, from hockey for the remainder of the season. The suspension couldn't have come at a worse time for the Canadiens. They were leading Detroit by just two points. Richard's award for individual high scoring was at stake, too—he was only two points ahead of his teammate Bernie (Boom-Boom) Geoffrion.

3   At one time there were as many as 10,000 people packed around the outside of the Forum. For a time it looked as if a lynching might even be attempted: groups of rioters were savagely chanting in unison, "Kill Campbell! Kill Campbell!" The windows of passing streetcars were smashed and, for no apparent reason, cab drivers were hauled from their vehicles and pummelled. The mob smashed hundreds of windows in the Forum by throwing bricks and bottles of beer. They pulled down signs and tore doors

off their hinges. They toppled corner newsstands and telephone booths, doused them in oil, and left them burning.

4   When the mob grew weary of the Forum, they moved eastward down Ste-Catherine Street, Montreal's main shopping district. For 15 blocks, they left in their path a swath of destruction. It looked like the aftermath of a wartime blitz in London. Hardly a store was spared. Display windows were smashed, and looters carried away everything portable.

5   The cost of the riot was added up later: an estimated $30,000 worth of damage; 12 policemen and 25 civilians injured; eight police cars and several streetcars, taxis, and private automobiles damaged.

6   But the greatest damage done was not physical. Montrealers awoke ashamed and stunned after their emotional binge. Canadian hockey was given a black name on the front pages of newspapers as far apart as Los Angeles and London, England. "Ice hockey is rough," observed the London *News Chronicle*, "but it is now a matter of grim record that Canadian players are spring lambs compared to those who support them."

7   The newspapers and radio were blamed for whipping up public opinion against Campbell before the riot. Frank Hanley, of the Montreal city council, said that Mayor Jean Drapeau must accept at least some of the responsibility. Drapeau, in turn, blamed the riot on Campbell, who "provoked it" by his presence at the game. Frank D. Corbett, a citizen of Westmount, expressed an opinion about the riot which many people thought about but few discussed publicly. In a letter to the editor of a local paper, he said bluntly that the outbreak was symptomatic of racial ill-feeling. "French and English relationships have deteriorated badly over the past 10 years and they have never been worse," he wrote. "The basic unrest is nationalism, which is ever-present in Quebec. Let's face it . . . the French-Canadians want the English expelled from the province."

8   All of these observations contained some germ of truth, but no single one of them explains satisfactorily what happened in Montreal on St. Patrick's Night.

9   In the case history of the Richard riot, the night of March 13, four nights before the Montreal outburst, is important. The Montreal Canadiens were playing against the Boston Bruins in Boston. Six minutes before the end of the game, Boston was leading 4–2, playing one man short because of a penalty. In a desperate effort to score, the Canadiens had removed their goalie and sent six men up the ice. Richard was skating across the Boston blue line past Boston defenceman Hal Laycoe when the latter put his stick up and caught Richard on the side of his head. It made a nasty gash which later required five stitches. Frank Udvari, the referee, signalled a penalty to Laycoe.

10   Richard skated behind the Boston net and had returned to the blue line when the whistle blew. He rubbed his head, then suddenly skated over to Laycoe. Lifting his stick high over his head with both hands Richard pounded

Laycoe over the face and shoulders with all his strength. Laycoe dropped his gloves and stick and motioned to Richard to come and fight with his fists.

11   A linesman, Cliff Thompson, grabbed Richard and took his stick away from him. Richard broke away, picked up a loose stick on the ice and again slashed away at Laycoe, this time breaking the stick on him. Again Thompson got hold of Richard, but again Richard escaped and with another stick slashed at the man who had injured him. Thompson subdued Richard for the third time, forcing him down to the ice. With the help of a teammate, Richard regained his feet and sprang at Thompson, bruising his face and blackening his eye. Thompson finally got Richard under control and sent him to the first-aid room for medical attention.

12   Richard was penalized for the remainder of the game and fined $100. Laycoe, who suffered body bruises and face wounds, was penalized five minutes for high-sticking and was given a further 10-minute penalty for tossing a blood-stained towel at the referee as he entered the penalty box.

13   Many observers feel that the Richard riot was merely another example of how lawlessness can spread from players to spectators. Team owners, coaches, and trainers have promoted disrespect for law and authority in hockey by their attitude. They complain bitterly when referees apply the rules strictly. In this new brand of hockey which permits rough play and often ignores the rules, the most harassed player in the NHL is Richard. Thirty-four years old, five foot nine, he weighs 180 pounds and is handsome in a sullen kind of way. His intense, penetrating eyes seem to perceive everything in microscopic detail. It's possible that Richard is the greatest hockey player who ever lived. Canadiens were once offered $135,000 for him—the highest value ever placed on a player. Frank Selke, Canadiens managing director, refused, saying, "I'd sooner sell half the Forum."

14   Opposing teams recognize Richard's talents and use rugged methods to stop him. Sometimes two players are specifically detailed to nettle him. They regularly hang on to him, put hockey sticks between his legs, bodycheck him, and board him harder than necessary. Once he skated 20 feet with two men on his shoulders to score a goal. His opponents also employ psychological warfare to unnerve him. Inspector William Minogue, who, as police officer in charge of the Forum, is regularly at the rink side during games, frequently hears opposing players calling Richard "French pea soup" or "dirty French bastard" as they skate past.

15   Because of these tactics, Richard frequently explodes. But he is a rarity among men as well as among hockey players. He is an artist. He is completely dedicated to playing good hockey and scoring goals. "It's the most important thing in my life," he told me.

16   On the night of the Boston fracas, Clarence Campbell was travelling from Montreal to New York by train to attend a meeting of the NHL board of governors where plans for the Stanley Cup playoffs were to be made. In Grand Central station next morning he read about the rumpus in the *New York Times*. Hurrying to his hotel, he phoned referee Frank Udvari and

linesmen Sam Babcock and Cliff Thompson to get a verbal report. Disturbed by what he heard, he set a hearing in Montreal to ascertain all the facts and decide on what punishment should be given to the players involved. The time set was two days later—March 16 at 10:30 a.m.

17 The hearing lasted for three hours. The attacks on Laycoe and Thompson were deliberate and persistent, Campbell found. The room was completely silent as Campbell then pronounced the punishment. "Richard is suspended from playing in the remaining league and playoff games."

18 No sports decision ever hit the Montreal public with such impact. It seemed to strike at the very heart and soul of the city. A bus driver became so upset by the news that he ignored a flashing railway-level-crossing signal and almost killed his passengers.

19 There were portents of what was to happen on the night of March 17 in the phone calls received by Campbell. Many of them were taken by Campbell's secretary, Phyllis King. "They were nearly all abusive, and they seemed to grow worse as the day wore on," says Miss King. One of the first callers said, "Tell Campbell I'm an undertaker and he'll be needing me in a few days."

20 The strong racial feelings engendered by the decision should have sounded an ominous warning. One of the letters that Campbell received said, "If Richard's name was Richardson, you would have given a different verdict."

21 Many prominent people added fuel to the fire. One French weekly published a cartoon of Campbell's head on a platter, dripping blood, with the caption: "This is how we would like to see him."

22 A few minutes after the Canadien–Detroit game started, Richard slipped into the Forum unnoticed and took a seat near the south end of the rink. He gazed intently at the ice, a look of distress on his face: the Canadiens were playing sloppy hockey. At the 11th minute of the first period, Detroit scored a second goal and the Canadiens saw their hopes of a league championship go up in smoke. It was at this minute that Clarence Campbell entered the arena. He couldn't have chosen a worse time.

23 As soon as Campbell sat down the crowd recognized him and pandemonium broke loose.

24 Richard was still asleep when reporters knocked on the door of his home at 8 o'clock. It was answered by his six-year-old son who said, "I hope you didn't come to talk to him about hockey." When the reporters returned later, Richard was attired in a white T-shirt and a pair of slacks. His face was lined with fatigue. "This certainly isn't the time for me to say anything," he said. "It might start something again." By 3 o'clock he changed his mind. He showed up in Frank Selke's office and said that he wanted to make a public statement. At 7 o'clock, seated in front of a battery of microphones, he made the following short speech in French:

25 "Because I always try so hard to win and had my troubles in Boston, I was suspended. At playoff time it hurts not to be in the game with the boys.

However, I want to do what is good for the people of Montreal and the team. So that no further harm will be done, I would like to ask everyone to get behind the team and to help the boys win from the Rangers and Detroit. I will take my punishment and come back next year to help the club and younger players to win the cup."

26   As he repeated the speech in English, Richard appeared restless and upset. He rubbed his eyes, tugged at his tie and scratched his left ear. His words seemed to have a settling effect on the city. The question of his suspension was laid aside, at least for the time being. Mayor Drapeau and other leaders followed Richard with strong pleas for law and order. There was to be no further violence for the remainder of the season, despite the fact that the Canadiens lost the championship.

[From *Maclean's* 17 September 1955; reprinted 10 October 2005]

Notes

Note that "Maurice Richard" is a French name, so his surname is not pronounced the same as the English first name "Richard." Also, note that the spelling of his team's name is with an *e*, the French spelling—Canadiens, not Canadians.

This article was written more than 50 years ago. Some of the language sounds quaintly old-fashioned today. For example, a sportswriter today would be unlikely to use words such as *rugged* and *nettle* [14] and *rumpus* [16]. The writing style is more formal than is used in modern journalism.

Comprehension

1. What was significant about this riot?
2. Who were the rioters angry at? Why?
3. Why was Maurice Richard suspended?
4. Why was Richard such a great player?
5. How did Richard help defuse the situation?

Timeline

You may find this article difficult to follow because of the shifts in time. Look for transition signals to figure out the sequence. Most paragraphs deal mainly with one time period, but a few span two dates. Fill in this chart with corresponding paragraph numbers. One paragraph can fit more than one category. Some have been done to help you:

	Paragraphs:
13 March 1955	9
16 March 1955	2
17 March 1955	2
18 March 1955	
Unidentified later time	5
Background information/explanation	13

Discussion

1. Why would people be reluctant to talk about racism in regard to the riot? Why are people reluctant to talk about racism in general?
2. Is the author overly sympathetic to Richard? Does he imply that Richard's violent attack was somehow justified, that he was provoked, that it was the straw that broke the camel's back?
3. How is trash talk used in sports today?
4. Why is hockey such a popular sport in Canada? Do Canadians take hockey too seriously?
5. Is hockey too violent? How does it compare to other sports?
6. Do sports fans still get worked up so much that they could run riot in the streets? Why?

Assignments

1. There is an expression in French *plus ça change, plus c'est la même chose*, which means the more things change, the more they remain the same. One reason to read older pieces is to find out the truth of this statement. Obviously, we still have hockey violence, hooliganism, and rioting in the streets. Write an essay comparing something from the Richard story with a recent event, such as soccer hooliganism. Or write a paragraph comparing Richard's attack on Laycoe with similar famous incidents, such as Todd Bertuzzi's sucker punch to Steve Moore in 2004.
2. Write a review of one of the films about Maurice Richard, such as *The Rocket* (2005) or the documentary *Fire and Ice: The Rocket Richard Riot* (2000).
3. Research athletes' salaries. Find out what $135,000 in 1955 would be worth today. Find out more about free agency and the increase in salaries. Do athletes deserve this much money? Write an essay explaining, criticizing, or defending athlete salaries.
4. Katz says, "Many observers feel that the Richard riot was merely another example of how lawlessness can spread from players to spectators" [13]. Write an essay explaining crowd behaviour using the Richard hockey riot and other similar events as examples.
5. Choose a current famous NHLer, and compare him to Richard in a paragraph.
6. Find another famous public apology, and compare it to Richard's.

Paraphrase and Summarize

1. Summarize what Richard did to get suspended.
2. Summarize the actions that led to the riot.
3. Paraphrase: "Opposing teams recognize Richard's talent and use rugged methods to stop him. Sometimes two players are specifically detailed to nettle him." [14]
4. Paraphrase: "The strong racial feelings engendered by the decision should have sounded an ominous warning." [20]

Vocabulary Study

The word *pandemonium* [23] means "all demons." The Greek prefix *pan–* can be seen in words like *Pan-American* and *panorama*.

Definitions

Use the context to match each word to its definition:

1. acrid [1] _____		a)	beaten with the fists
2. provocative [2] _____		b)	cause a particular feeling or situation
3. remnant [2] _____		c)	dressed
4. pummelled [3] _____		d)	harsh, stinging
5. binge [6] _____		e)	important or well-known
6. bluntly [7] _____		f)	intentionally causing anger or other strong feeling
7. symptomatic [7] _____		g)	make not as loud or bright as usual
8. subdue [11] _____		h)	make someone lose confidence
9. unnerve [14] _____		i)	period of uncontrolled eating or drinking
10. engender [20] _____		j)	remaining piece
11. prominent [21] _____		k)	showing signs of an illness or problem
12. attired [24] _____		l)	without softening, directly, honestly

Parts of speech

Fill in the following chart:

Noun	Verb	Adjective	Adverb
	explode		
restraint			
	promote		
			bitterly
	apply		
			specifically
		psychological	

Noun	Verb	Adjective	Adverb
	ascertain		
		deliberate	
		persistent	
		abusive	
	n/a	ominous	
effect			

Hint: Remember that verbs can be formed with a prefix when you deal with *bitterly* and *ascertain*.

Note the pronunciation of *ascertain* and the two pronunciations of *deliberate*.

Collocations and expressions

Discuss each of the following expressions. How clear is the meaning? Is it idiomatic? How useful is the expression?

> touch off [1]
> the last straw [2]
> could not have come (or happened) at a worse time [2]
> at stake [2]
> in unison [3]
> for no apparent reason [3]
> a swath of destruction [4]
> to be given a black name [6]
> a matter of record [6]
> contain a germ of truth [8]
> to play a man short [9]
> strike at the very heart and soul of something [18]
> go up in smoke [22]
> to have a settling effect on something [26]

Structure and Technique

1. Katz starts the article with the thick of the riot to give a dramatic opening to his article. He then has to go back to explain what led up to the riot. You can also see this done in movies and TV shows. Look at the cues Katz gives to help readers follow the time sequence. Are there paragraphs that could be better marked for time? Discuss.
2. Notice the journalistic style of giving the person's full name the first time he or she is mentioned and then just using a surname to refer to the person. What different techniques and grammatical structures are used to give additional information about the person?
3. Look at the use of quotation in this article, including the punctuation. What does the ellipsis (. . .) mean in paragraph 7?

Fighting Hockey Violence Will Give You a Concussion

by Jeffrey Simpson

1   Specialists in diagnosing and treating concussions should know about the perils of bashing heads against a brick wall. But, nonetheless, bravo to those who know about concussions for having recently recommended an end to fighting in hockey.

2   Medical experts, minor hockey executives, and former National Hockey League players who suffered from concussions recently gathered in London, Ont., to try to improve safety in the game. They made many suggestions about better head protection, but they also said: Stop the fighting.

3   Concussions can be caused by many aspects of hockey and by numerous rules that leave heads inadequately protected. Shots to the head are endemic in hockey, and the NHL has always been fitfully attentive, at best, in trying to protect against them. But some damage to the head, even the occasional death, occurs from fighting as a player's head is struck, either by a fist or when he falls against the ice.

4   The medical experts were right: An end to fighting would reduce head injuries. But just as threatened legal cases against on-ice thuggery have come to naught, so medical advice won't change the cultivated culture of violence in professional hockey.

5   Fighting, however, is to professional hockey as hearts are to Valentine's Day. People just love it. Those noble souls who wish to ban it will give themselves concussions trying to end it, although the case against fighting, rationally speaking, is overwhelming.

6   Those who gathered at the concussion conference were bashing their heads against not just one wall but many. There's the wall of tradition; fighting has always been there. There's the wall of the NHL Players' Association, some of whose members are fighters, lacking any other skill that would give them a job in professional hockey. There's the wall of the owners, who know—and rightly so—that fighting means excitement, and excitement means money. There's the wall of commissioner Gary Bettman, who knows that fighting puts bums in seats. And, sad to say, there's the wall of the fans.

7   Attend an NHL game in any arena. When a fight starts, fans throughout the building rise, shout, and gesticulate as vigorously as when a goal is scored. A few Canadians like to insist that fighting really only appeals to Americans. Fighting exists in hockey to sell the game in US markets where people carry guns, watch football players smash each other and where television is overrun with violence.

8   Alas, such an argument merely reflects Canadian conceit about Americans in general and American hockey fans in particular. Watch a fight in any Canadian city with a professional team, or attend a junior hockey

game where fights break out even more frequently than in the NHL. Canadian fans eat up fighting.

9   It's in Canada, don't forget, where the highest media priests who defend fighting reside. And not only in Canada but on the CBC. As if Don Cherry were not already the country's leading cheerleader for fisticuffs, the CBC went out and hired the worst general manager of the past 20 years, Mike Milbury, as an "analyst." He quickly joined Mr. Cherry in trotting out the old clichés about the indispensability of fighting as an outlet for aggression. He then added his own denunciation of "pansification" in hockey, for which he had his knuckles rapped.

10   Fortunately for literate hockey fans, there is TSN, where the quality of hockey commentary vastly outstrips anything on the CBC. On that hockey-savvy network, there are some defenders of fighting in hockey, but the brilliant Pierre McGuire opposes it and, of course, he is right. Even on TSN, however, the highlight package each night usually features a brawl or two, rather than some extraordinary defensive play or slick passing move.

11   Fighting is not endemic to hockey, except for the evident fact that the sport allows it. Fighting could be eliminated with the snap of a finger if owners and players didn't believe that the fans want fighting. It is, after all, the only professional sport that allows fighting. Hockey is no rougher than football or Australian-rules football or rugby, where to fight is to be expelled from play. The argument that fighting is a necessary outlet for aggression is wholly bogus.

12   Go to the Hockey Hall of Fame, or watch films of classic encounters of yesteryear. You won't remember the fighters, but rather the skilled players. Today, the NHL markets the Sydney Crosbies and Alexander Ovechkins for national and international purposes. But the owners also watch us, the fans, and our reaction to fighting. We, or at least most fans, like it.

13   It used to be that North American players fought and Europeans did not. True, most of the fighters remain North American, but we have passed on bad habits to a handful of Europeans, too. The Cherryfication of hockey that glorifies fighting has spread and will not be stopped, notwithstanding the excellent advice of the concussion experts.

[From *The Globe and Mail*, 14 February 2009, p. A19]

Notes

See the definition paragraph on concussions on page 183.

The expression about bashing, hitting, or banging one's head against a brick wall refers to frustration and being unable to make progress. It has a double meaning here because concussions are often caused by hitting one's head against a hard surface like a wall. In paragraph 6, Simpson takes the expression further by suggesting different figurative walls that those against fighting are up against. The walls here are like barriers to the rule changes.

Don Cherry is a former hockey coach who is a commentator on CBC's "Hockey Night in Canada." He is so well-known for glorifying hockey violence that Simpson even makes up a word to describe his influence—"Cherryfication" [13].

Sidney Crosby and Alexander Ovechkin are hockey players known for their skill rather than their fighting ability. Players who are known as fighters are often referred to as "enforcers."

Comprehension

1. What is the thesis (the main idea) of this article?
2. Who are "those who know about concussions" [1]?
3. What is the other cause of concussions besides fighting that Simpson mentions?
4. What does Simpson mean by the "cultivated culture of violence in professional hockey" [4]?
5. Explain: "Fighting, however, is to professional hockey as hearts are to Valentine's Day." [5]
6. What are the many walls that those against fighting are up against? Explain each one.
7. What does Simpson think of the argument "that fighting really only appeals to Americans" [7]? Explain.
8. Explain Simpson's comments about the coverage of hockey on CBC and TSN.
9. What point does he make when he mentions other sports?
10. What point does he make when he mentions Crosby and Ovechkin?

Discussion

1. What is your opinion about this issue? Should fighting in hockey be banned? Why or why not?
2. Are enforcers necessary in hockey? Why or why not?
3. Why do people like to watch fighting?
4. Are sports a substitute for war?
5. Athletes always face a risk of injury. Where should they draw the line and no longer take the risk?
6. When Simpson talks about the "Canadian conceit about Americans in general" [8], he is saying that Canadians like to think they are better than Americans. Do you agree with this statement? Discuss other beliefs Canadians hold about Americans.

Assignments

1. Write an essay explaining the effects of concussions. Use examples from hockey or another sport, and discuss how careers can be cut short because of concussions.

2. Simpson says "the case against fighting, rationally speaking, is over-whelming." Write an essay arguing for or against fighting in hockey.
3. Should hockey players who attack other players on the ice be charged with criminal assault?
4. Write an essay explaining how the media feeds viewers' appetite for violence.

Paraphrase and Summary

1. Paraphrase: "Those noble souls who wish to ban it will give themselves concussions trying to end it, although the case against fighting, ration-ally speaking, is overwhelming." [5]
2. Paraphrase: "It used to be that North American players fought and Europeans did not. True, most of the fighters remain North American, but we have passed on bad habits to a handful of Europeans, too. The Cherryfication of hockey that glorifies fighting has spread and will not be stopped, notwithstanding the excellent advice of the concussion experts." [13]
3. Write a one-paragraph summary of this article. Do not exceed 100 words.

Vocabulary Study

1. What is the verb that is the root word of *indispensability*? Explain the meaning of the root word and the suffix and prefix. What does *indis-pensability* mean? What is the adjective form? Find synonyms for the positive form of this adjective.
2. A *pansy* is a flower. Find out what the term means when a man is called a pansy. The word *pansification* [9] is a noun formed from a derived verb form "to pansify" (to make into a pansy). The same word forma-tion can be seen in the word *Cherryfication*. This kind of word creation is common. It needs to have a clear root word and common affixes in order for the word to be understood. In small groups, make up your own words following the same pattern. Have a class vote to choose the most useful new word.
3. Look up the meaning of the adjective *savvy* to figure out the meaning of *hockey-savvy*. Find out the origin of this adjective. What are syno-nyms of *savvy*?

Definitions

Use the context to match each word to its definition:

1. diagnosing [1] _____
2. endemic [3, 11] _____
3. fitfully [3] _____
4. thuggery [4] _____
5. gesticulate [7] _____
6. conceit [8] _____
7. fisticuffs [9] _____
8. denunciation [9] _____
9. brawl [10] _____
10. bogus [11] _____

a) a wild, noisy fight, especially in a public place
b) always present
c) an imaginative idea
d) fake, not real
e) fighting with the bare hands
f) figuring out what illness someone has
g) make movements with the hands while talking
h) not regular, starting and stopping
i) public statement criticizing somebody or something
j) violent behaviour related to gangsters

Parts of speech

Fill in the following chart:

Noun	Verb	Adjective	Adverb
specialist			
peril			
		attentive	
			vigorously
	reside		
	n/a		vastly
	glorify		
		excellent	
advice			

Hint: The verb forms for *peril* and *vigorously* are formed with prefixes.

Collocations and expressions

Discuss each of the following expressions. How clear is the meaning? Is it idiomatic? How useful is the expression?

> to come to naught [4]
> to eat up something [8]
> to trot out something [9]
> to have one's knuckles rapped [9]
> a snap of the finger [11]

Structure and Technique

As this is a newspaper article, the paragraphs are short. However, Simpson does follow many of the principles of essay writing. He has an introduction, which ends in a thesis statement. Which sentence would you consider to be his thesis? Identify the main arguments in support of his thesis and the specific details that are given to support each of these arguments.

Fair Play and Sportsmanship

At issue in every contest is the question of fair play and sportsmanship. We want sport to be pure—to reflect actual skill and achievement. However, this ideal is rarely realized. Sports can be a huge money-making proposition. It is no wonder that athletes are motivated to win at any cost—even if that requires cheating at the game.

High-level athletes train for thousands of hours, and they look for any boost they can get. Some go beyond vitamins and protein powder to performance-enhancing drugs such as steroids. These drugs have been banned, not only because of the edge they give athletes but because of the harm they do to the body. In addition, every technological innovation in equipment, from clap skates to skintight swimsuits that increase buoyancy, is scrutinized to determine whether it is just a step in the evolution of the sport or whether it constitutes an unfair advantage.

On the field of play, other actions call into question fairness and sportsmanship. Players indulge in trash talk and physical intimidation to improve their chance at victory. Other times, results can be fixed, either by the judges and referees or by the athletes themselves. Especially when high-stakes gambling is involved or when the honour of a nation stirs patriotic fervour, the temptation to break the rules to win overpowers athletic participants.

Sometimes what is perceived as cheating differs. For instance, the soccer "dive," when players pretend that they have been fouled, is considered part of the game by some players despite the rule against it. They are unapologetic whether they get away with it or are caught. However, such antics are generally criticized. We have high expectations of sport, expecting both winners and losers to be gracious and accept the outcome of the match.

Essay Topics
1. Explain the risks of cheating in sports.
2. Compare the risks versus the rewards of cheating in sports.
3. Explain causes and/or effects of one specific kind of cheating in sports.
4. What makes for a gracious winner or a sore loser?
5. Analyze a famous cheating incident—such as Ben Johnson in the 1988 Olympics, the judging scandal in pairs figure skating at the 2002 Olympics, the Tour de France, and the 1919 Chicago White Sox baseball scandal. Be sure to explain the incident and the results—do not just tell the story.
6. Life is unfair, so why should we expect sports to be any different? Discuss this statement.
7. What is considered cheating can vary from culture to culture—whether it be sports, politics, academia, or even marriage. Choose one kind of cheating, and compare and explain two different views of it.

Unit 16

Fiction Readings

Why My Mother Can't Speak English

by Garry Engkent

1   My mother is 70 years old. Widowed for five years now, she lives alone in her own house except for the occasions when I come home to tidy her household affairs. She has been in *gum san* for the past 30 years. She clings to the old-country ways so much that today she astonishes me with this announcement:

2   "I want to get my citizenship," she says as she slaps down the *Dai Pao*, "before they come and take away my house."

3   "Nobody's going to do that. This is Canada."

4   "So everyone says," she retorts, "but did you read what the *Dai Pao* said? Ah, you can't read Chinese. The government is cutting back on old age pensions. Anybody who hasn't got citizenship will lose everything. Or worse."

5   "The *Dai Pao* can't even typeset accurately," I tell her. Sometimes I worry about the information Mother receives from that bi-weekly community newspaper. "Don't worry—the Ministry of Immigration won't send you back to China."

6   "Little you know," she snaps back. "I am old, helpless, and without citizenship. Reasons enough. Now get me citizenship. Hurry!"

7   "Mother, getting citizenship papers is not like going to the bank to cash in your pension cheque. First, you have to—"

8   "Excuses, my son, excuses. When your father was alive—"

9   "Oh, Mother, not again! You throw that at me every—"

10   "—made excuses, too." Her jaw tightens. "If you can't do this little thing for your own mother, well, I will just have to go and beg your cousin to . . ."

11   Every time I try to explain about the ways of the *fan gwei* she thinks I do not want to help her.

12   "I'll do it, okay? Just give me some time."

13   "That's easy for you," Mother snorts. "You're not 70 years old. You're not going to lose your pension. You're not going to lose your house. Now, how much *lai-shi* will this take?"

14   After all these years in *gum san* she cannot understand that you don't give government officials *lai-shi*, the traditional Chinese money-gift given to persons who do things for you.

15   "That won't be necessary," I tell her. "And you needn't go to my cousin."

16   Mother picks up the *Dai Pao* again and says: "Why should I beg at the door of a village cousin when I have a son who is a university graduate?"

17   I wish my father were alive. Then he would be doing this. But he is not here, and as a dutiful son, I am responsible for the welfare of my widowed mother. So I take her to the Citizenship Court.

18   There are several people from the Chinese community waiting there. Mother knows a few of the Chinese women, and she chats with them. My cousin is there, too.

19   "I thought your mother already got her citizenship," he says to me. "Didn't your father—"

20   "No, he didn't."

21   He shakes his head sadly. "Still, better now than never. That's why I'm getting these people through."

22   "So they've been reading the *Dai Pao*."

23   He gives me a quizzical look, so I explain to him, and he laughs.

24   "You are the new generation," he says. "You didn't live long enough in *hon san*, the sweet land, to understand the fears of the old. You can't expect the elderly to renounce all attachments to China for the ways of the *fan gwei*, white devils. How old is she, 70 now? Much harder."

25   "She woke me up this morning at six and Citizenship Court doesn't open until 10."

26   The doors of the court finally open, and Mother motions me to hurry. We wait in line for a while.

27   The clerk distributes applications and tells me the requirements. Mother wants to know what the clerk is saying so half the time I translate for her.

28   The clerk suggests that we see one of the liaison officers.

29   "Your mother has been living in Canada for the past 30 years, and she still can't speak English?"

30   "It happens," I tell the liaison officer.

31   "I find it hard to believe that—not one word?"

32   "Well, she understands some restaurant English," I tell her. "You know, French fries, pork chops, soup, and so on. And she can say a few words."

33   "But will she be able to understand the judge's questions? The interview with the judge, as you know, is a very important part of the citizenship procedure. Can she read the booklet? What does she know about Canada?"

34   "So you don't think my mother has a chance?"

35   "The requirements are that the candidate must be able to speak either French or English, the two official languages of Canada. The candidate must be able to pass an oral interview with the citizenship judge, and then he or she must be able to recite the oath of allegiance—"

36   "My mother needs to speak English," I conclude for her.

37   "Look, I don't mean to be rude, but why didn't your mother learn English when she first came over?"

38   I have not been translating this conversation, and Mother, annoyed and agitated, asks me what is going on. I tell her there is a slight problem.

39   "What problem?" Mother opens her purse, and I see her taking a small red envelope—*lai-shi*—I quickly cover her hand.

40   "What is going on?" the liaison officer demands.

41   "Nothing," I say hurriedly. "Just a cultural misunderstanding, I assure you."

42   My mother rattles off some indignant words, and I snap back in Chinese: "Put that away! The woman won't understand, and we'll be in a lot of trouble."

43   The officer looks confused, and I realize an explanation is needed.

44   "My mother was about to give you a money-gift as a token of appreciation for what you are doing for us. I was afraid you might misconstrue it as a bribe. We have no intention of doing that."

45   "I'm relieved to hear that."

46   We conclude the interview, and I take Mother home. Still clutching the application, Mother scowls at me.

47   "I didn't get my citizenship papers. Now I will lose my old age pension. The government will ship me back to China. My old bones will lie there while your father's will be here. What will happen to me?"

48   How can I teach her to speak the language when she is too old to learn, too old to want to learn? She resists anything that is *fan gwei*. She does everything the Chinese way. Mother spends much time staring blankly at the four walls of her house. She does not cry. She sighs and shakes her head. Sometimes she goes about the house touching her favourite things.

49   "This is all your dead father's fault," she says quietly. She turns to the photograph of my father on the mantle. Daily, she burns incense, pours fresh cups of fragrant tea, and spreads dishes of his favourite fruits in front of the framed picture as is the custom. In memory of his passing, she treks two miles to the cemetery to place flowers by his headstone, to burn ceremonial paper money, and to talk to him. Regularly, rain or shine, or even snow, she does these things. Such love, such devotion, now such vehemence. Mother curses my father, her husband, in his grave.

50   When my mother and I emigrated from China, she was 40 years old, and I, five. My father was already a well-established restaurant owner. He put me in school and Mother in the restaurant kitchen, washing dishes and cooking strange foods like hot dogs, hamburgers, and French fries. She worked seven days a week from six in the morning until 11 at night. This lasted for 25 years, almost to the day of my father's death.

51   The years were hard on her. The black-and-white photographs show a robust woman; now I see a withered, frail, white-haired old woman, angry, frustrated with the years, and scared of losing what little material wealth she has to show for the toil in *gum san*, the golden mountain.

52   "I begged him," Mother says. "But he would either ignore my pleas or say: 'What do you need to know English for? You're better off here in the kitchen. Here you can talk to the others in our own tongue. English is far too complicated for you. How old are you now? Too old to learn a new language. Let the young speak *fan gwei*. All you need is to understand the orders from the waitresses. Anyway, if you need to know something, the men will translate for you. I am here; I can do your talking for you.'"

53   As a conscientious boss of the young male immigrants, my father would force them out of the kitchen and into the dining room. "The kitchen is no place for you to learn English. All you do is speak Chinese in here. To survive in *gum san*, you have to speak English, and the only way you can do that is to wait on tables and force yourselves to speak English with the customers. How can you get your families over here if you can't talk to the Immigration officers in English?"

54   A few of the husbands who had the good fortune to bring their wives over to Canada hired a retired school teacher to teach a bit of English to their wives. Father discouraged Mother from going to those once-a-week sessions.

55   "That old woman will get rich, doing nothing. What have these women learned? *Fan gwei* ways—make-up, lipstick, smelly perfumes, fancy clothes —like whores. Once she gets through with them, they won't be Chinese women any more—and they certainly won't be white, either."

56   Some of the husbands heeded the words of the boss, for he was older than they and had been in the white devils' land longer. These wives stayed at home and tended the children, or they worked in the restaurant kitchen, washing dishes and cooking *fan gwei* foods, and talking in Chinese about the land and the life they were forced to leave behind.

57   "He was afraid that I would leave him. I depended on him for everything. I could not go anywhere by myself. He drove me to work, and he drove me home. He only taught me to print my name so that I could sign anything he wanted me to, bank cheques, legal documents . . ."

58   Perhaps I am not Chinese enough any more to understand why my mother would want to take in the sorrow, the pain, and the anguish and then to recount them every so often.

59   Once I was presumptuous enough to ask her why she would want to remember in such detail. She said the memories didn't hurt any more. I did not tell her that her reminiscences cut me to the quick. Her only solace now is to be listened to.

60   My father wanted more sons, but she was too old to give him more. One son was not enough security he needed for old age. "You smell of stale perfume," she would say to him after he had driven the waitresses home.

Or, to me, she would say: "A second mother will not treat you so well, you know," and, "Would you like another mother at home?" Even at that tender age, I knew that in China a husband could take a second wife. I told her that I didn't need another mother, and she would nod her head.

61   When my father died five years ago, she cried and cried. "Don't leave me in this world. Let me die with you."

62   Grief-stricken, she would not eat for days. She was so weak from hunger that I feared she wouldn't be able to attend the funeral. At his graveside, she chanted over and over a dirge, commending his spirit to the next world and begging the goddess of mercy to be kind to him. By custom, she set his picture on the mantel and burned incense in front of it daily. And we would go to the cemetery often. There she would arrange fresh flowers and talk to him in the gentlest way.

63   Often she would warn me: "The world of the golden mountain is so strange, *fan gwei* improprieties, and customs. The white devils will have you abandon your own aged mother to some old age home to rot away and die unmourned. If you are here long enough, they will turn your head until you don't know who you are, what you are—Chinese."

64   My mother would convert the months and the days into the Chinese lunar calendar. She would tell me about the seasons and the harvests and festivals in China. We did not celebrate any *fan gwei* holidays.

65   My mother sits here at the table, fingering the booklet from the Citizenship Court. For thirty-some years, my mother did not learn the English language, not because she was not smart enough, not because she was too old to learn, and not because my father forbade her, but because she feared that learning English would change her Chinese soul. She only learned enough English to survive in the restaurant kitchen.

66   Now, Mother wants *gum san* citizenship.

67   "Is there no hope that I will be given it?" she asks.

68   "There is always a chance," I tell her. "I'll hand in the application."

69   "I should have given that person the *lai-shi*," Mother says obstinately.

70   "Maybe I should teach you some English," I retort. "You have about six months before the oral interview."

71   "I am 70 years old," she says. "*Lai-shi* is definitely much easier."

72   My brief glimpse into mother's heart is over, and it has taken so long to come about. I do not know whether I understand my aged mother any better now. Despite my mother's constant instruction, there is too much *fan gwei* in me.

73   The booklet from the Citizenship Court lies, unmoved, on the table, gathering dust for weeks. She has not mentioned citizenship again with the urgency of that particular time. Once in a while, she would say: "They have forgotten me. I told you they don't want old Chinese women as citizens."

74   Finally, her interview date is set. I try to teach her some ready-made phrases, but she forgets them.

75   "You should not sigh so much. It is bad for your health," Mother observes.

76   On the day of her examination, I accompany her into the judge's chamber. I am more nervous than my mother.

77   Staring at the judge, my mother remarks: "*Noi yren.*" The judge shows interest in what my mother says, and I translate it: "She says you're a woman."

78   The judge smiles "Yes. Is that strange?"

79   "If she is going to examine me," Mother tells me, "I might as well start packing for China. Sell my house. Dig up your father's bones, I'll take them back with me."

80   Without knowing what my mother said, the judge reassures her. "This is just a formality. Really. We know that you obviously want to be part of our Canadian society. Why else would you have gone through all this trouble? We want to welcome you as a new citizen, no matter what race, nationality, religion, or age. And we want you to be proud—as a new Canadian."

81   Six weeks have passed since the interview with the judge. Mother receives a registered letter telling her to come in three weeks time to take part in the oath of allegiance ceremony.

82   With patient help from the same judge, my mother recites the oath and becomes a Canadian citizen after 30 years in *gum san*.

83   "How does it feel to be Canadian?" I ask.

84   "In China, this is the eighth month, the season of harvest." Then she adds: "The *Dai Pao* says that old age pension cheques will be increased by nine dollars next month."

85   As we walk home on this bright autumn morning, my mother clutches her piece of paper. Citizenship. She says she will go up to the cemetery and talk to my father this afternoon. She has something to tell him.

1985

Notes

This story is autobiographical fiction. It is based on true events, but these events have been dramatized in the story-telling.

Second-generation immigrants are those born or raised in Canada, like the son in the story. Many have a first language that is different from their mother tongue. (*Mother tongue* refers to the language first learned and still understood, usually their parents' native language. *First language* means the language the person is most comfortable speaking.) Most second-generation immigrants become very comfortable in English or French, especially as they progress through their schooling in that language. They do not develop their ability to speak their mother tongue in the same way. For example, they might be able to talk about history and do math in English but only talk about household concerns in their native language. A common situation is that the immigrant parents speak the mother tongue to their children, but the children answer back in English or French. In this story, the son cannot read Chinese but does speak to his mother in Chinese.

Unlike other ethnic groups, the Chinese were not encouraged to establish families in Canada. While the men were welcome as workers, Canadian immigration policies such as the Head Tax (1885–1923) and the Chinese Exclusion Act (1923–47) prevented them from bringing over family members. This is why the father in the story was in Canada before his wife and son.

Comprehension

1. Why does the mother want to get her citizenship?
2. Describe the process by which the mother gained her citizenship.
3. Why did the mother want to use *lai-shi*? Why did the son not want her to do that?
4. What was the father's attitude toward immigrants learning English? What double standard did he have?
5. What reasons contribute to the mother's not learning English? What is the most important reason she does not learn?
6. Explain the author's reference to the mother's "Chinese soul."
7. What is ironic about the last bit of dialogue in the story—the last exchange between the mother and son?
8. How does the writer make the story humorous?

Discussion

1. How realistic is the portrayal of the mother? Do you know any immigrants like her?
2. Are the mother's fears justified? Why or why not?
3. What is the most important factor in learning a second language? Could the mother have overcome her age and her husband's disapproval had she really wanted to?
4. What are some of the problems faced by immigrant women learning English?
5. What kinds of conflicts are common between first- and second-generation immigrants?
6. Discuss the immigration and citizenship procedures in Canada. Use examples of the experience of friends, family, or yourself.

Assignments

1. What factors determine how well an immigrant assimilates? Explain these factors in an essay.
2. What factors determine how much a second-generation immigrant will keep his or her mother tongue? Explain these factors in an essay.
3. Research the history of the Chinese in Canada or that of another immigrant group. Write a report on the factors that played a part in their settlement. Or write an essay comparing two immigrant groups.
4. Write an essay explaining the process of becoming a Canadian citizen.
5. What are the rights and responsibilities of Canadian citizenship? Is Canadian citizenship too easy to obtain? Should dual citizenship be

allowed? Write an essay on one of these issues or another issue related to Canadian citizenship.

6. Review the information given in *Discover Canada: The Rights and Responsibilities of Citizenship*, the booklet given to people studying to become citizens (available on the website of Citizenship and Immigration Canada). Is it a good introduction to Canada? What do you think of the coverage? Is there any other information you think should be included in the booklet?

Paraphrase and Summary

1. Paraphrase: "Perhaps I am not Chinese enough any more to understand why my mother would want to take in the sorrow, the pain, and the anguish and then to recount them every so often." [58]

2. Paraphrase: "Once I was presumptuous enough to ask her why she would want to remember in such detail. She said the memories didn't hurt any more. I did not tell her that her reminiscences cut me to the quick. Her only solace now is to be listened to." [59]

3. Paraphrase: "She turns to the photograph of my father on the mantle. Daily, she burns incense, pours fresh cups of fragrant tea, and spreads dishes of his favourite fruits in front of the framed picture as is the custom. In memory of his passing, she treks two miles to the cemetery to place flowers by his headstone, to burn ceremonial paper money, and to talk to him. Regularly, rain or shine, or even snow, she does these things." [49]

4. Write a 200-word summary of the story.

Vocabulary Study

1. The noun *welfare* [17] has the same parts as the word *farewell*. The verb *to fare* means to progress and get on, so *welfare* means the well-being of someone. Note that in Canada we also use the word *welfare* as a short form for "welfare benefits," the government payments people receive if they cannot earn their own living. We can say someone is "on welfare." Check the dictionary for other meanings of the word *fare* and its homophone *fair*.

2. The verb *agitate* [38] means to shake up and disturb, so a person who is agitated is disturbed or nervous. What are the two noun forms? Which one can refer to a part of a top-load washing machine?

3. For *conscientious* [53], see the note on *conscious*, p. 306.

4. The word *presumptuous* [59] is hard to get a handle on. The verb form is *presume*; what is the noun? Use your dictionary, and discuss the meanings and usage in class.

5. The compound adjective *grief-stricken* [62] shows the old past participle of the verb *strike*, which is also used in *poverty-stricken* and *panic-stricken*. The more commonly used past participle is seen in such compounds as *awe-struck* and *thunderstruck*. See if you can find other compounds.

6. Paragraphs 49, 62, and 63 have some of the words related to grief and funerals. Check the meaning for any of these words that you do not know: *cemetery*, *headstone*, *grave*, *graveside*, *funeral*, *dirge*, and *mourn* (the negative adjective *unmourned* is used in the reading). Notice that the author says "the memory of his passing"; people who have died are said to have "passed away." Discuss different mourning customs.

Collocations and expressions

Discuss each of the following expressions. How clear is the meaning? Is it idiomatic? How useful is the expression?

to cut back on [4]
little you know [6]
to have a chance (at something) [34]
to stare blankly at something [48]
to be better off [52]
to cut somebody to the quick [59]
to gather dust [73]

Definitions

Use the context to match each word to its definition:

1. astonish [1] _____
2. misconstrue [44] _____
3. clutch [46] _____
4. trek [49] _____
5. vehemence [49] _____
6. robust [51] _____
7. heed [56] _____
8. anguish [58] _____
9. reminiscences [59] _____
10. solace [59] _____
11. improprieties [63] _____
12. obstinately [69] _____
13. retort [70] _____
14. glimpse [72] _____

a) answer back angrily
b) pay attention to, follow advice
c) behaviour that is morally wrong
d) emotional comfort
e) hold tightly
f) memories
g) misunderstand
h) severe misery or mental suffering
i) showing strong feelings, usually anger
j) small look
k) strong and healthy
l) stubbornly
m) surprise
n) take a long, hard walk; hike

Parts of speech

Fill in the following chart:

Noun	Verb	Adjective	Adverb
		quizzical	
	distribute		
application			n/a

Noun	Verb	Adjective	Adverb
requirement			n/a
	suggest		
appreciation			
	depend		
	survive		n/a
formality			
	n/a	patient	

Structure and Technique
First person, unnamed narrator
This story is told in first person narration: *I*. The narrator's name is not given. Note that this story is fiction, so the *I* is a character, and you cannot refer to him as "Garry Engkent." Instead, you can call him "the son" or "the narrator."

In first person narration, the *I* tells the story from the *I* perspective, not from a general one. The reader gets only the narrator's way of seeing or interpreting an action and must trust that what the narrator says is valid and true. Often, the reader identifies with the narrator.

Present tense narration
Although most stories are told in the simple past tense, the use of the present tense brings a sense of immediacy. The reader follows the story-telling at the same time that the narrator says anything. The present tense creates the illusion that everything is happening right at that moment.

Dialogue
Notice that much of this story is told in dialogue. Look at the punctuation used and the wording that sets up the speech. When a new speaker begins, there is a new paragraph.

Use of foreign words
Words from a foreign language that are not a standard part of English are generally printed in italics. Engkent uses words in Chinese to add flavour to the story. The author knows that his audience will not know what these words mean; even Chinese-speaking readers would be unlikely to know this particular dialect. Therefore, he gives the readers many clues to help them figure out the meaning.

The most common technique is to put the translation in apposition. This means it is set off by commas. For example, in "for the toil in *gum san*, the golden mountain," Engkent shows that the translation of *gum san* is "golden mountain," which is the way the Chinese referred to Canada and the United States. (The term reflects the fact that the first Chinese came to North America as part of the gold rush.)

Context is also important for understanding the meaning of the words. Note how the meaning of *Dai Pao* gradually becomes clearer, as something the mother slaps down and reads. Look at all the Chinese words in the text, and find the clues the author gives you. Figure out what each word means. Sometimes the translation or definition does not come with the first use of the word in the story.

Soap and Water

by Urs Frei

1   The other day a man walked into the store, carrying a cat. I don't know which I noticed first, the cat or how the man was crying. The cat was his, I guess. Its legs were mangled, and blood was dripping through his fingers. He was crying so hard he didn't notice that this wasn't a vet hospital anymore.

2   "I need you to put my cat to sleep," he said.

3   There he stood, dripping onto the carpet. We had three customers in the store. Of course they were staring.

4   "The vet moved out last month, sir," I said. I came around the counter to show my concern. But also to move him out of there. You have to understand, we'd only been open a month. "We sell computers."

5   The man was silent. The cat was crying low, strange cries.

6   "Where's the vet?" he said.

7   "Where'd that vet go?" I said. Robert, one of my sales reps, was staring back at me. It was a pointless question, actually, because I knew the vet hadn't moved anywhere near. I was pretty sure there was no vet within a mile. "Have a look in the phone book," I told him.

8   The man was sobbing again. I couldn't decide if the best thing to do would be to ask him to step outside or if this would antagonize the customers. I had a closer look at him. He had earrings in both ears. His hair was shaved on the sides of his head. He was wearing a leather jacket, and it was hard to say for sure, but he seemed handsome, the kind of man who would talk about his successes with women. What was he doing crying about a cat?

9   The stock boy had heard the cat and come in from the stock room. He wasn't supposed to be in the store.

10   Robert said, "There's a vet over on K- road."

11   K- road was the other side of town.

12   "Should I call them?" he said. "They have a pet ambulance, it says here."

13   "Call the pet ambulance," I said. "Get that pet ambulance over here."

14   The stock boy wasn't a boy at all. He was a Mexican man, about 40 years old, named Ricardo, who spoke almost no English. He was wearing

dirty blue jeans and a blue work shirt. Also, he wasn't legal. He was taking off his shirt. I thought, Lord in heaven—Lord in heaven. There was that cat, dripping on my new carpet, and there was the stock boy, taking off his shirt.

15   He walked up to the man, spreading the shirt on his palms, and took the cat, and wrapped it in the shirt. The man said nothing. Ricardo turned his back so that no one could see, but everyone heard the snap as he broke the cat's neck. The cat went silent. One of the customers, a lady, made a horrified sound. Then Ricardo, with his head bowed, handed the cat back, along with his shirt.

16   I was glad I'd got that in about the pet ambulance. You have to understand that this was before I learned that blood comes out easily with just soap and water. It was that lady customer who told me.

_____

1997
Reprinted by permission of the author.

Notes

The stock boy "wasn't legal," which means he didn't have proper status from the Immigration Department.

Comprehension

1. Describe the narrator: male or female? age? occupation?
2. Is the narrator portrayed as an admirable character? Support your answer.
3. What is the setting for the story? Why is this significant? Could this story happen somewhere else with the same impact?
4. Why did the man with the cat come into the store?
5. What do you think had happened to the cat? Support your answer.
6. How did the various characters react to this?
7. What is the narrator concerned about?
8. What is the narrator apologizing for in the last paragraph?
9. Compare the narrator and the stock boy. How do their different backgrounds explain their reactions?
10. What is the significance of the title?

Discussion

1. What would you do in this situation?
2. How far would you go to save the life of a pet? Would you pay thousands of dollars for surgery, for example?
3. Do Canadians care too much about their pets? Consider, for example, people who have severe allergies and yet refuse to get rid of their pets.
4. Could you kill an animal if necessary? Could you, for example, kill a chicken, clean it, and prepare it for dinner? Could your parents do it? Could your grandparents? What has changed? Does this matter?
5. What is the stereotype of someone who works with computers?

6.   What is this story saying about modern society? Is this a valid criticism?

7.   Canadians use the terms *illegal immigrant* and *landed immigrant*, while Americans say *illegal alien* and *resident alien*. Discuss the difference in terminology.

Assignments

1.   Write an essay explaining the criteria that should be considered for euthanasia for both animals and humans.

2.   Have Canadians become too urbanized? Have we lost touch with nature? Write an essay explaining the problems this causes. Or write an essay arguing that it does not matter.

3.   Take one of the controversial issues surrounding animal rights, and discuss it in an essay. For example, how should farming practices be changed to be more humane? Or are vegans going too far?

4.   Consider the problems of illegal immigrants. Canadians rely on them for cheap labour, but Canadian immigration favours educated immigrants, many of whom have trouble getting jobs that suit their education level. Some people argue that illegal immigrants should be given amnesty since they have established themselves here, often having children born in Canada and therefore Canadian citizens. Yet they live in an underground economy and cannot avail themselves of simple services such as health care and education. Suggest a possible solution, and discuss it in an essay.

Paraphrase and Summary

1.   In one short paragraph, summarize what happens in the story.

2.   Write a one-sentence description of each character, paraphrasing what the narrator says.

Vocabulary Study

Both *rep* and *vet* are short forms of longer words. What does each word stand for? What other words use the same short forms?

Connotation

Explain the meaning of these terms and the differences:

1.   put an animal to sleep
2.   put an animal down
3.   euthanasia
4.   mercy killing
5.   kill
6.   murder
7.   die
8.   pass away
9.   to be six feet under
10.   a visit from the grim reaper

Make a list of other idioms and expressions that describe death. You can also discuss cultural differences. For example, why are euphemisms used? We prefer to say "my grandmother passed away" instead of "my grandmother died," and we would never say "my grandmother kicked the bucket."

Structure and Technique

1. The author has used first person narration, with an unnamed narrator. What is the effect of this type of narration in this story?
2. The author gives us the narrator's internal dialogue. How does this reveal the narrator's personality?
3. The story hinges on an implied contrast between the narrator and the stock boy. Should this contrast have been made more explicit?

Tempest in the School Teapot

Excerpt from Chapter XV, *Anne of Green Gables*, by L. M. Montgomery

1   Mr. Phillips was back in the corner explaining a problem in algebra to Prissy Andrews, and the rest of the scholars were doing pretty much as they pleased, eating green apples, whispering, drawing pictures on their slates, and driving crickets, harnessed to strings, up and down the aisle. Gilbert Blythe was trying to make Anne Shirley look at him and failing utterly, because Anne was at that moment totally oblivious, not only of the very existence of Gilbert Blythe but of every other scholar in Avonlea school and of Avonlea school itself. With her chin propped on her hands and her eyes fixed on the blue glimpse of the Lake of Shining Waters that the west window afforded, she was far away in a gorgeous dreamland, hearing and seeing nothing save her own wonderful visions.

2   Gilbert Blythe wasn't used to putting himself out to make a girl look at him and meeting with failure. She should look at him, that red-haired Shirley girl with the little pointed chin and the big eyes that weren't like the eyes of any other girl in Avonlea school.

3   Gilbert reached across the aisle, picked up the end of Anne's long red braid, held it out at arm's length, and said in a piercing whisper:

4   "Carrots! Carrots!"

5   Then Anne looked at him with a vengeance!

6   She did more than look. She sprang to her feet, her bright fancies fallen into cureless ruin. She flashed one indignant glance at Gilbert from eyes whose angry sparkle was swiftly quenched in equally angry tears.

7   "You mean, hateful boy!" she exclaimed passionately. "How dare you!"

8   And then—Thwack! Anne had brought her slate down on Gilbert's head and cracked it—slate not head—clear across.

9   Avonlea school always enjoyed a scene. This was an especially enjoyable one. Everybody said, "Oh" in horrified delight. Diana gasped. Ruby Gillis, who was inclined to be hysterical, began to cry. Tommy Sloane let his

team of crickets escape him altogether while he stared open-mouthed at the tableau.

10   Mr. Phillips stalked down the aisle and laid his hand heavily on Anne's shoulder.

11   "Anne Shirley, what does this mean?" he said angrily.

12   Anne returned no answer. It was asking too much of flesh and blood to expect her to tell before the whole school that she had been called "carrots." Gilbert it was who spoke up stoutly.

13   "It was my fault, Mr. Phillips. I teased her."

14   Mr. Phillips paid no heed to Gilbert.

15   "I am sorry to see a pupil of mine displaying such a temper and such a vindictive spirit," he said in a solemn tone, as if the mere fact of being a pupil of his ought to root out all evil passions from the hearts of small imperfect mortals. "Anne, go and stand on the platform in front of the blackboard for the rest of the afternoon."

16   Anne would have infinitely preferred a whipping to this punishment, under which her sensitive spirit quivered as from a whiplash. With a white, set face, she obeyed. Mr. Phillips took a chalk crayon and wrote on the blackboard above her head.

17   "Ann Shirley has a very bad temper. Ann Shirley must learn to control her temper," and then read it out loud so that even the primer class, who couldn't read writing, should understand it.

18   Anne stood there the rest of the afternoon with that legend above her. She did not cry or hang her head. Anger was still too hot in her heart for that, and it sustained her amid all her agony of humiliation. With resentful eyes and passion-red cheeks she confronted alike Diana's sympathetic gaze and Charlie Sloane's indignant nods and Josie Pye's malicious smiles. As for Gilbert Blythe, she would not even look at him. She would never look at him again! She would never speak to him!

1908

Notes

Unlike most of the other reading selections in this textbook, this is an excerpt from a longer work. Excerpts are often harder to understand because the context is missing. Some of the context is usually explained in notes.

The most famous Canadian book in the world is undoubtedly *Anne of Green Gables* by Lucy Maud Montgomery. It was first published in 1908 and is the first in a series of books about Anne Shirley. When the book begins, Anne, who is then 11 years old, comes from an orphanage in Nova Scotia to live with Matthew and Marilla Cuthbert, an elderly brother and sister who need help on their family farm in Prince Edward Island. Anne has red hair (which she is very sensitive about), a lively imagination, a keen intelligence, a tendency to daydream, and a talent for getting into trouble. Her best friend is Diana.

Avonlea school was a one-room rural school, typical of that day. Children from six to 16 studied in the same classroom. Students wrote on slates (small, individual blackboards). Girls often wore their hair in long braids, which were irresistible to boys; a typical prank was to dip the braid in an ink bottle. This scene takes place early in the school year, on the first day Gilbert is at school.

Note that Mr. Phillips misspells Anne's name on the blackboard—another thing that Anne is sensitive about.

Comprehension
1. Why was the teacher oblivious to what the students were doing?
2. What was Anne doing during the class?
3. What did Gilbert do to provoke Anne? Why did he do it?
4. What was Anne's reaction to Gilbert's provocation?
5. How was Anne punished? How did she react to the punishment?
6. Who were Anne's friends in the classroom? How were their reactions to Anne's punishment different?

Discussion
1. Who was most at fault in this incident?
2. Is Anne's anger at Gilbert justified? Did she over-react?
3. Do you think she deserves her punishment?
4. How is this school scene different from what one would expect today? Do you find this kind of school life appealing?
5. What would modern students do if their teacher was preoccupied or out of the classroom?
6. What kind of teasing went on in school when you were a child?
7. What were common methods of discipline in your school? How effective were they?
8. What do you imagine happened to Anne and Gilbert afterwards? Do you think she ever spoke to him again?

Assignments
1. Write a narrative retelling the basic story but updating it to modern times. For instance, the students could be using laptops instead of slates.
2. Write a paragraph comparing a modern classroom to the one in the story.
3. Read more of the book. It can easily be found in the library or online. Write a book report.
4. Watch the TV miniseries from 1985, starring Megan Follows. Write a review of the series.
5. Research the book's fame and position in Canadian literature. Find out about the role of the story in the tourist industry of Prince Edward

Island. Do you find this interest surprising, or is the book's fame justified? Write an essay.

6. In small groups, act out the scene in class. Do not read or memorize the text; feel free to interpret it. Compare your version to the one in the 1985 miniseries.

Paraphrase and Summary

1. In less than 75 words, summarize the main action of the story.
2. Paraphrase: ". . . Anne was at that moment totally oblivious, not only of the very existence of Gilbert Blythe but of every other scholar in Avonlea school and of Avonlea school itself. With her chin propped on her hands and her eyes fixed on the blue glimpse of the Lake of Shining Waters that the west window afforded, she was far away in a gorgeous dreamland, hearing and seeing nothing save her own wonderful visions." [1]
3. Paraphrase: "Anne returned no answer. It was asking too much of flesh and blood to expect her to tell before the whole school that she had been called 'carrots.'" [12]
4. Paraphrase: "Anger was still too hot in her heart for that, and it sustained her amid all her agony of humiliation. With resentful eyes and passion-red cheeks she confronted alike Diana's sympathetic gaze and Charlie Sloane's indignant nods and Josie Pye's malicious smiles." [18]

Vocabulary Study

1. *Scholar* is an old-fashioned word for *student*. You can easily see that it is related to the word *school*. The connotation for the word today is that it is used for a serious student. Another word for student is *pupil*, which is used for younger students, but it is not as commonly used today.
2. The verb *afford* in the reading is the less common meaning of "provide something." See page 212 for examples of how the word is generally used.
3. The use of *save* [1] as a preposition is old-fashioned. Which word would be used instead in this sentence?
4. Explain the relationship and differences between these words: *vengeance, avenge, revenge, vindictive.*
5. The verb *quench* is often used in the expression "to quench one's thirst." How is this use different from the one in the reading?
6. "Thwack!" is an example of onomatopeia—a word that imitates the sound made. Give other examples.

Definitions

Use the context to match each word to its definition:

1. slate [1] _____
2. harnessed [1] _____
3. utterly [1] _____
4. oblivious [1] _____
5. propped [1] _____
6. glimpse [1] _____
7. gorgeous [1] _____
8. piercing [3] _____
9. fancies [6] _____
10. indignant [6, 18] _____
11. hysterical [9] _____
12. quiver [16] _____
13. primer [17] _____
14. legend [18] _____
15. malicious [18] _____

a) brief look, a partial view
b) completely
c) easily upset and excited
d) evil, showing hatred
e) feeling anger and surprise because of unfair treatment
f) high, loud, unpleasant sound
g) imaginings, daydreams
h) not noticing anything
i) piece of writing on a sign
j) primary grades (1–3)
k) shake, be affected
l) small chalkboard in a wooden frame that schoolchildren use to write on
m) strapped together
n) supported
o) very beautiful

Parts of speech

Fill in the following chart:

Noun	Verb	Adjective	Adverb
failure			n/a
			equally
			passionately
		enjoyable	
		horrified	n/a
	n/a		heavily
			angrily
humiliation			
		resentful	
	confront		
		sympathetic	

Hint: Note that the verb form for *passionately* is made with a prefix.

Collocations and expressions

Discuss each of the following expressions. How clear is the meaning? Is it idiomatic? How useful are the expressions?

> to do as one pleases [1]
>
> to put oneself out to do something [2]
>
> to be inclined to be something [9]
>
> at arm's length [3] (Note that in this reading, the expression is used literally. More commonly today, the expression is used to talk about a figurative distance.)
>
> with a vengeance [5] (with great force)
>
> to ask too much of somebody [11]
>
> flesh and blood [11]
>
> to speak up [12]
>
> to pay no heed to somebody/something [14] (pay no attention to something)
>
> to have a bad temper, to control one's temper [17]
>
> to hang one's head [18]

Structure and Technique

1. Note that the paragraphs are longer for the descriptions and shorter for the dialogue sections.

2. Change the sentence structure of "Gilbert it was who spoke up stoutly" to one that would be commonly used today. What effect does the original sentence have? In other words, why does Montgomery start her sentence with "Gilbert"?

3. Explain Montgomery's technique in this sentence: "And then— Thwack! Anne had brought her slate down on Gilbert's head and cracked it—slate not head—clear across." Does the word "thwack" give a good idea of the sound? Why is the verb ("had brought") in the past perfect tense? Is the use of parenthetical dashes effective? Is it humorous? Would it be as effective if Montgomery had instead written "cracked her slate and not his head"?

The Squatter

by Sara McDonald

1   I woke up, and there was a naked man sleeping beside me. I turned on the light to have a look at him. Not bad, but he wasn't anybody I knew. And certainly not someone I knew well enough to give an apartment key. If he'd broken in, surely I would've heard him. Mind you, he did manage to sneak into bed without waking me, and this isn't a very big bed.

2   Hello, I said. Nothing. His eyelids didn't even flicker. I prodded him in the ribs. He murmured and turned, throwing his leg over mine. Hey you, I

shouted in his ear. Hello darling, he said. Then he kissed me and rolled back over, snuggling deeper into the pillows.

3   I got out of bed and looked for something to put on. I couldn't see his clothes anywhere and began to wonder if he had arrived naked. I pulled on jeans and a T-shirt and went to see how he'd gotten in. The windows were all closed, and the deadbolt was on the door. There were no signs that anything was wrong.

4   A drink, I said aloud. What I need is a drink. There wasn't anything in the cupboard but a bottle of Peppermint Schnapps. It had been there so long I couldn't remember where it came from. So I poured myself a tall glass.

5   It tasted like mouthwash, but it seemed to help me think more clearly.

6   I could have phoned the police, but the problem there was my neighbours. I live in this townhouse complex where everybody can see what everybody else is up to. And if the police were to pull in here on a Saturday night, everybody would be out on their balconies in no time. They'd all be real casual about it, mind you. That's the sort of neighbourhood this is. They'd make like they were having a midnight barbeque or just wanted to look at the moon. Anyway, if the police escorted a naked man out of my place, that would be it. I'd simply have to move. And I like this place, I really do. It took me so long to get the furniture where it should be, and I went all over town to find drapes to match the carpets. And I've only just memorized the bus schedule. Moving is out of the question.

7   Darling, he called from the bedroom. Come back to bed.

1988

Notes

This is a complete short story from a collection called *Open Window: Canadian Short Short Stories*, edited by Kent Thompson. A short short story can be as few as 50 words. This one is 402 words.

Comprehension

1. What is happening to the narrator?
2. What is her reaction? Why is this strange?
3. Describe the narrator. What kind of person do you think she is?
4. What is Peppermint Schnapps? What do you think it says about a person who would have it in his or her cupboard?

Discussion

1. What do you think is going on? Can you explain this story?
2. Did you enjoy this story? Why or why not?

Assignments

1. Write a brief continuation of the story. Keep it in the same style.
2. Write your own short short story. Do not go over 400 words.

Paraphrase and Summary

1. Summarize the story in less than 50 words.
2. Paraphrase: "And if the police were to pull in here on a Saturday night, everybody would be out on their balconies in no time. They'd all be real casual about it, mind you. That's the sort of neighbourhood this is. They'd make like they were having a midnight barbeque, or just wanted to look at the moon" [6]

Vocabulary Study

Mind you is an expression like *you know*. It does not really mean much.

Check out the verbs in the story, and determine what kind of verb each one is. Find five transitive verbs, five intransitive verbs, and five phrasal verbs. Be careful not to confuse phrasal verbs with verbs followed by a prepositional phrase. Compare:

> I like to <u>sleep in</u> whenever I can. [phrasal verb]

> I <u>sleep</u> in a double bed. [verb + prepositional phrase]

Structure and Technique

1. This story is told in a very conversational style—as if the author were talking to a friend. How is this effective?
2. Notice how the first sentence gets the reader's attention right away. Explain why it is effective.
3. The author does not use quotation marks around the words said by the characters. What effect does this have?

Appendix A

Following Format Guidelines

Presenting your work properly is important whether you are in elementary school, college, or the workforce. The two most important criteria for school assignments are that the work is easy to read and that it leaves the marker plenty of room for comments and corrections. Instructors with specific format guidelines generally make them clear with assignment instructions. Here are some common format guidelines:

- Type your assignments on a computer. The printout should be black ink (not faded) on medium-weight 8½-by-11-inch white paper.
- Use a plain type face in a size that is easy to read, such as Times New Roman 12 point. Do not use typefaces that look like printing or handwriting.
- Double-space your essay. (Set paragraph line spacing at 2.)
- Leave a one-inch margin on all sides of the page.
- Number your pages, often in the bottom centre or bottom right. MLA and APA formats require page numbers in the top right corner. Start your numbering with the first page of the essay, not the cover page.
- Use only one side of the paper.
- Indent your paragraphs with five spaces, the default tab setting.
- Use left justification and a ragged right margin. (Full justification often makes large gaps between words.)
- Make sure your sentences are clearly shown with a capital letter at the beginning and a period at the end.
- Use one space after a period. Do not put spaces before periods or commas.
- Include a cover page that gives the title of the assignment, your name and student identification number, the course code including section number, the date, and the professor's name. Note that even though MLA style asks for identifying information on the first page of the assignment instead, many professors prefer a cover page.
- Avoid unnecessary artwork. Include illustrations only when necessary.
- Staple the pages together in the top left corner. Do not use a cover or folder unless your instructor has specifically asked for one.

Sample cover page:

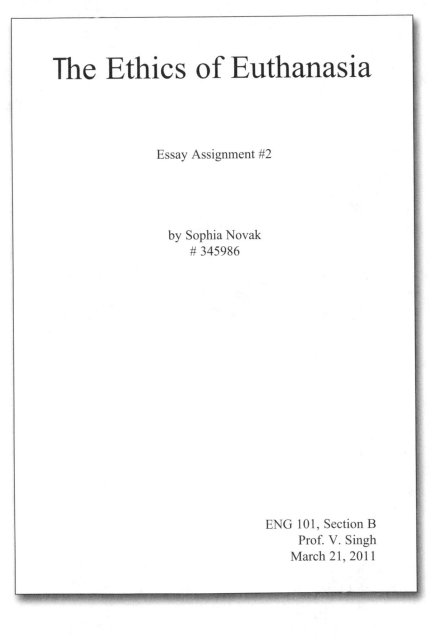

The Ethics of Euthanasia

Essay Assignment #2

by Sophia Novak
345986

ENG 101, Section B
Prof. V. Singh
March 21, 2011

Appendix B

Writing Email

Most students use email to communicate with their professors, and it is important to write messages that communicate effectively. Here are some guidelines.

Using a Subject Heading

You should always give your email a brief, descriptive subject heading. "Hi, this is Jung" is not an appropriate subject heading. Be as specific as possible. Here are some examples: "question about midterm," "absence on Friday," and "appointment request."

Identifying Yourself

Make sure that any email from you includes your full name. The recipient should be able to tell immediately whom the message is from. This should be evident from your email address. If it is not in the address, you may have to include it in your subject heading.

Do not start your message with "Hi, my name is May Novak. I'm one of your students." Instead, give your full name at the bottom of the email as a signature. You can also use an automatic signature with information about yourself, such as your title, address, and phone number.

You will generally be given a school email address; use it for correspondence with your instructor. It is not professional to send out email with an address like "sexyguy@hotmail.com," and the messages may end up in the trash as suspected spam. For a web-based email service, you can set up separate accounts for social contacts and more professional uses.

Including a Salutation

Letters generally start with a salutation, such as "Dear Professor Brown," but memos do not have salutations since the information at the top of the page gives the addressee's name. An email message is more like a memo since it includes "to," "from," and subject information. Therefore, salutations are considered optional in email. They are a good idea when you initiate an email conversation but unnecessary once you get into a back-and-forth exchange of information.

Email etiquette is still evolving. It seems that "Hi" with the person's name is becoming the common salutation in email messages. As North American business style has become more casual, first names are commonly used even in business communication. However, if you do not know the person, it is wise to be formal and use title and last name, especially if you are contacting your professor. In other words, say "Professor Chu" instead of using the professor's first name.

Using Correct, Standard English

You can use abbreviations such as "U R" in chat messages or in email to your friends, but your mail to your instructor should be written in correct, standard English—especially for an English course and especially if you are asking for something such as an assignment extension. Use a spell checker, and proofread carefully before you send your message.

Making Your Message Clear and Concise

Like all writing, email messages should be clear and concise. No one wants to read a long, rambling message only to come to the end with no clear idea of what the sender wants.

Write an email message like a business letter. State right away what the purpose of your message is. You can give necessary details in subsequent paragraphs.

Being Prudent

Before you hit the "send" button, re-read and rethink your message. Remember that email is recorded forever. Keep in mind that business email is legally the property of the institution, so your supervisor is entitled to read any message you send from a company address. If you are sending an emotional message, such as a response to an insult, save your message and read it again the next day before you send it.

Reducing Email Traffic

Do not hit "reply all" unless your information must actually go to every recipient on the list. For example, if someone is setting up a meeting, you probably do not have to tell everybody on that mailing list whether you will attend or not.

Do not request a "received receipt" unless it is absolutely necessary.

Do not let messages get longer and longer as the back-and-forth correspondence goes on. Delete any of the copied information from previous messages unless it is important reference information.

Print messages only if the hard copy is important as a reference. Cutting and pasting the message into a word processing document allows you to control the way it is printed, so you can save paper, eliminate unnecessary parts, and increase the print size.

Attachments

Your instructor will probably have definite preferences on whether or not work can be submitted electronically, so ask if your instructor does not tell you this in the course information. Some instructors prefer to get essays by email, while others are wary of opening attachments. Many instructors prefer assignments in hard copy so that they do not have to print out your work (especially if they do not have access to school facilities for this purpose). If you have questions about your draft, you can cut and paste the text into the body of the message.

School Policies

Your institution may have official policies for appropriate use of email. Check these policies for further information.

Answer Key

Exercise 1.1

1. Driving on the highway presents fewer distractions. The traffic is all travelling in the same direction, so it is only necessary to watch out for lane changers and the occasional traffic jam.
2. Tattoos are often a mistake. People regret them when they get older. They may no longer have the same interests, and the tattoo may not look as good later when the ink fades and skin changes with age.
3. Large batches of food can be cooked on the weekend and then frozen in order to cut down on food preparation time. Chili, stews, spaghetti sauce, and some soups freeze well.
4. Children should not have TVs and computers in their bedrooms because they are too distracting. Children would not do their homework if they could play electronic games instead. They would just stay in their room and never talk to parents and siblings.

Exercise 1.3

1. The smallest problem with a luxury car costs more money because the parts are harder to find and labour is so expensive.
2. All the rules and road signs in the driver's handbook must be memorized for the test.
3. College students can be successful if they attend class, pay attention to the instructor, and do their homework.
4. People can spend hours watching TV and YouTube videos and waste their whole day.
5. Teenagers can be seen hanging around the mall with nothing to do.

Exercise 1.4

(Note that the dividing line between slang and conversational language is not distinct, so expressions could be considered one or the other.)

1. Features of conversational English: the use of *you*, verb contractions, questions that address the reader, sentences that start with co-ordinate conjunctions (*and, but, so*)
2. Conversational expressions: let's face it, well, right?, plain wrong, now there, why not . . .
3. Idioms: going straight into the toilet, gone up in smoke, getting your shorts in a knot
4. Slang: suckers, guys, bunch of . . . , suck, really neat
5. Legalese: be it resolved that, it is acknowledged, without prejudice , we must accept, within the realm of possibility, as responsible nations, it is hereby affirmed, aforementioned
6. descendants
7. geek, nerd

Exercise 2.2
1. competence; 2. enrichment; 3. speech; 4. wealth; 5. clarity; 6. reality; 7. invitation; 8. stability; 9. denial; 10. contribution

Exercise 2.3
1. describe; 2. evade; 3. inspire; 4. facilitate; 5. whiten; 6. threaten; 7. authorize; 8. defy; 9. pursue; 10. expand

Exercise 2.4
1. misty; 2. comic, comical, comedic; 3. operational, operative; 4. forceful; 5. experimental; 6. acceptable; 7. stressful; 8. disastrous; 9. scientific; 10. public

Exercise 2.5
1. secret ballot; 2. brute force; 3. frantic haste; 4. jagged hole; 5. masked intruder; 6. tempting offer; 7. tough opponent; 8. heartfelt sympathy; 9. limited visibility; 10. extensive vocabulary

Exercise 2.7
1. simply; 2. really; 3. truly; 4. significantly; 5. uneasily; 6. brutally; 7. hazily; 8. absurdly; 9. frequently; 10. evidently

Exercise 2.10
agreement, agree, agreeable, agreeably; anger, anger, angry, angrily; beauty, beautify, beautiful, beautifully; development, develop, developmental, developmentally; excess, exceed, excessive, excessively; height, heighten, high, highly; legality/legalization, legalize, legal, legally; management, manage, managerial/manageable, manageably; politics, politicize, political, politically; softness, soften, soft, softly

Exercise 2.11
1. smiling; 2. tiled; 3. requirement; 4. fades; 5. wading; 6. completed; 7. comprising; 8. shades; 9. settled; 10. eroding

Exercise 2.12
1. wedding; 2. waited; 3. dreamless; 4. dipped; 5. controlled; 6. chugging; 7. occurrence; 8. keeping; 9. grunted; 10. dripping

Exercise 2.14
1. woman, whose, too; 2. cite, your, lose; 3. affects, whether; 4. to, two; 5. passed, there; 6. their, hear, Then; 7. than, advice

Exercise 2.16

unable/disabled, inability/disability, inactive, non-addictive, moral, counterargument, unappetizing, inaudible, unbelievable, misbehave, unclassified/ non-classified, incompetent, discontinue, colour, indivisible, inexcusable, unfavourable, infinite, inflexible, unforgettable, informal, malfunction, ungrateful, anti-hero, plausible, uninformed/ill-informed, uninteresting, unjustified, illiterate, nutrition, mismanage, impatient, malpractice, misquote, unreadable, irregular, non-renewable, misrepresent, unsuccessful, non-toxic, worthy, unusable, invisible, unwise

Exercise 2.17

1. a; 2. k; 3. g; 4. h; 5. n; 6. d; 7. e; 8. f; 9. b; 10. l; 11. o; 12. c; 13. j; 14. m; 15. i

Exercise 2.18

1. j; 2. a; 3. o; 4. e; 5. d; 6. h; 7. m; 8. n; 9. k; 10. b; 11. f; 12. c; 13. g; 14. i; 15. l

Exercise 2.20

1. take a test, run a test; 2. make a request, grant a request; 3. conduct research, carry out research; 4. drop a hint, take a hint, give a hint; 5. lack experience, acquire experience; 6. run up a debt, settle a debt; 7. adopt a method, follow a method; 8. give a reason; 9. run a risk, take a risk; 10. gain support, provide support

Exercise 2.21

1. border patrol; 2. calculated risk; 3. daring attack; 4. hazardous material; 5. momentary hesitation; 6. reasonable request; 7. subtle reminder; 8. torrential rain; 9. urgent matter; 10. weak tea

Exercise 2.25

1. medicine; 2. law; 3. computer science; 4. real estate; 5. police work

Exercise 2.26

1. became angry; 2. rejected; 3. unable to cope; 4. doing nothing; 5. stealing; 6. pessimistic; 7. vomited; 8. did nothing

Exercise 3.1

1. Peter/whistled/tune; 2. team/won/game; 3. we/went; 4. she/can afford/vacation; 5. one/has decided; 6. friend/is throwing/party; 7. neighbour/signed, forgot; 8. flight/leaves, he/has packed

Exercise 3.2

1. brought, behaved; 2. saw, avoided, had warned; 3. ate; 4. leaves, have; 5. play; 6. will meet; 7. did not sleep; 8. decided; 9. did you buy, bought; 10. has already seen, will go, will meet

Exercise 3.3

1. been, have; 2. waiting; 3. written; 4. be, contact; 5. solved; 6. have, been; 7. take; 8. be; 9. follow, been; 10. read

Exercise 3.6

1. cars; 2. apple, is; 3. is, has; 4. members, are; 5. lamp, was; 6. posters, market; 7. takes, dance, lessons, Tuesday; 8. errors; 9. pieces, is; 10. mistakes, ones

Exercise 3.7

1. Charles'/Charles's, Peter's; 2. Her, Tim's; 3. children's, their; 4. Megan's; 5. Murphy's; 6. boys', their; 7. students'; 8. our; 9. Ian's, our

Exercise 3.8

Here are the places where articles or other determiners are required:

1. on my/the trip, A student, the University of Ottawa, her French, a tutor, an asset
2. a picnic for the park's anniversary, The neighbourhood high school band, the band shell, the afternoon
3. a wonderful trip, the museum, at the pier, to their final destinations, the name of the ship that my family, a trip on the *Bluenose*, a tall ship was a real thrill, the display about the *Titanic* at the Maritime Museum of the Atlantic, the *Titanic* victims, The story of the 1917 Halifax explosion, A munitions ship, in the harbour, the entire downtown area
4. an apartment, near the university, the bus when the weather, a two-bedroom apartment, my cousin, a high-rise building, on the seventh floor, The living room, a picture window with a view of the river, a few pieces, the thrift shop, my own place

Exercise 3.10

1. in the summer, for his regular games on ice in the winter; 2. on Friday night, in the highest part of the stadium in the nosebleed section; 3. near my sister's house, to/for work, with my nephews, to the park, on the monkey bars; 4. on the couch on Sunday afternoons, on television; 5. out of the park for his second home run of the game; 6. in the early morning at the cottage, off the end of the dock, across the bay to the small beach; 7. on the bookshelf by the door, on the top shelf near/next to/by/with the other dictionaries; 8. in/at the park after class on Wednesday afternoons, By the time; 9. at a resort on the island; 10. on the hook, in my purse, on the desk, in the junk drawer, under the desk

Exercise 3.12

1. Peter had to get the transmission and the brakes fixed.
2. Zach thought he passed his driver's test, but he had to book another one.
3. Kate plays the piano and guitar.
4. My uncle was killed in a motorcycle accident, so my mother won't allow me to get a motorcycle.
5. Erin's brother and her brother-in-law are engineers.
6. Melissa could go to the University of Calgary or the University of Alberta.
7. Ben thought he had a job on the oil ri g, but the job fell through.
8. We thought of holding my parents' anniversary party on a dinner cruise boat or in the revolving restaurant.
9. Christine was supposed to pick Jim up at the train station, but she forgot.
10. Suji couldn't understand the formula, so she read the chapter again.

Exercise 3.15

1. to rake the leaves, plant some bulbs, and spread the mulch; 2. canoeing, sailing, and waterskiing; 3. reasonable financial compensation, a good work environment, and friendly co-workers; 4. coloured, cut, and straightened; 5. excessive violence, swearing, and nudity.

Exercise 3.18

1. Nunavut, which was created from the Northwest Territories in 1999, has an Aboriginal government and Inuktitut as an official language.
3. Janice, whom I taught last year, is planning to be a teacher herself.
5. The president of the college, who uses a wheelchair, has done much to improve the accessibility of campus facilities.

Exercise 3.20

1. While Tim Horton had a hand in starting the business that bears his name, Laura Secord had nothing to do with the candy-making business.
2. The candy store was named after Laura Secord because the founder wanted a Canadian heroine as a trademark.
3. Although the Canadian flag is such a recognized symbol today, it did not have an easy road to design and official acceptance in 1965.
4. While the first explorers came to Canada seeking a route to the Orient, they came back for the valuable fish and furs.
5. British Columbia agreed to join Canada if a railroad would be built to connect it with the eastern provinces.
6. The Canadian Pacific Railway took many years to complete because it was so difficult to build through the rock of the Canadian Shield in central Canada and the mountain ranges in British Columbia.
7. The United Empire Loyalists came north to Canada after the American Revolution because they wanted to remain British subjects.

8. Even though lacrosse is one of Canada's national sports, it is not very popular, especially when compared to hockey.
9. When Tommy Douglas became a member of Parliament, he wanted to introduce the same reforms to Canada that he brought to Saskatchewan.
10. After the Acadians were expelled from Nova Scotia, they settled in Louisiana.

Exercise 3.22

1.Touring the house; 2. located in a prime downtown area; 3. tucked under the stairway; 4. Having worked for his father's construction company; 6. Marc's wife Elena, not wanting to live in a construction zone for years; 7. Although handy with power tools and a paint brush; 9. Doing the work themselves; 10. After weighing all the pros and cons

Exercise 3.25

Cleaning out my grandmother's cluttered, musty old house after she died was a monumental task. Like many old people who had lived through unspeakable war and famine, she was an incurable hoarder. She kept old newspapers, plastic bags, and cardboard boxes. She didn't trash out-of-date calendars; she just tacked up a new one in a different spot on the wall. We found new clothes that had been saved for a special occasion and never used. Her husband's clothes still hung in the closet even though he had passed away a dozen years earlier. In the cold cellar were jars of pickled food that must have been 20 years old. Two full-size freezers were crammed with food. Some of the packages were many years old. She felt safe with all her possessions and never wanted to let anything go.

Exercise 3.26

1. Susan's brother, grandfather's house, He's missed, he's planning, university's; 2. Let's go, Johnsons' cottage, We've, I'll just give, it's okay, It'll, don't go, we'll be; 3. his teachers' instructions; 4. he's willing, father's business; 5. students'/student's work, I don't

Exercise 3.27

1. The Marine Museum of the Atlantic in Halifax, Nova Scotia, has exhibits on the 1917 Halifax explosion and the response to the sinking of the *Titanic* in 1912.
2. Sainte-Marie among the Hurons is a recreated seventeenth-century Jesuit mission headquarters in Midland, Ontario.
3. Sir John A. Macdonald was Canada's first prime minister. His picture is on the 10-dollar bill.
4. John McCrae wrote the poem "In Flanders fields," which is on the back of the bill.
5. Remembrance Day honours Canada's war dead. A minute of silence commemorates the end of World War I at 11 a.m. on November 11.

Exercise 3.28

1. Mr. Peterson requested the review of the department because of its poor performance. The manager thought it was unnecessary.
2. Shakespeare's play *Romeo and Juliet* tells the story of two teenagers in love in sixteenth-century Italy. It's a tragic tale because the lovers are from two feuding families.
3. I don't know what to buy as a gift for Joanne's baby shower. She's having twin boys.
4. If you're worried about fitting the English course into your schedule, why don't you take it online?
5. Let's take the train to Montreal so we don't have to worry about driving and parking. The city's subway system, which is called the metro, is an efficient way to get around town.
6. A man who grew up not having to do housework is less likely to help his wife out around the house.
7. To bake a cake, you need to assemble the following ingredients: butter, sugar, eggs, flour, baking powder, salt, buttermilk, baking soda, and vanilla.
8. I asked him to leave me a copy of the report, but he forgot. He finally emailed it to me, and I had to print out a copy.
9. We went over every word of the report; however, we missed several errors, so it didn't look very good when we gave it to the supervisor.
10. She asked whether I could take over her shift on Saturday night. I wanted to go to Jack's party, so I said no.

Exercise 4.1

1. d; 2. b; 3.a.

Exercise 4.2

1. b; 2. a; 3. c; 4.b; 5.d

Exercise 4.3

1. b; 2. d; 3. b; 4. c; 5. a

Exercise 4.5

b, d, g

Exercise 4.6

1. c; 2. b; 3. b

Exercise 4.7

1. b; 2. b; 3. b; 4. a; 5. c

Exercise 4.8

Pairs of sentences where the second is an example of the first: 1, 3, 6, 7.

Exercise 4.11

Modern novels are also good reading practice because students have to follow a complex plot with a variety of characters. Andersen was a Dane who had an unhappy childhood but gained a measure of fame with the stories he wrote.

Exercise 4.12

Sentences 1, 4, 5, 7, 9, 10, 11, 13

Exercise 4.13

Only one transition signal for each blank is given here, but you can use a different one if it has the same meaning.

1. for example; 2. in addition; 3. for example; 4. at the same time; 5. consequently; 6. however; 7. therefore; 8. for instance; 9. however; 10. in addition; 11. then; 12. nevertheless

Exercise 4.14

Instead of just choosing a ring tone in a cellphone that is catchy, people should make sure it is appropriate. First, it should be easy to distinguish. Phone owners should be able to hear it over background noise and identify it as their phone ringing. Second, the ring tone should be pleasing to listen to. The piece of music should appeal to a wide audience, not just the cellphone user. The ring tone should not be annoying. Often phones ring at inappropriate times, and having one that repeats a name or phrase, such as "Harold, pick up the phone," would just make the situation more embarrassing. Another criterion is that the tone project the right image. No adult wants a phone that sounds like a cutesy cartoon character singing. The image should also relate to the user, so that an urban cowboy answers a phone playing country music, for example. While cellphones can be individualized to a certain extent, the ring tone is the most public aspect of that personalization.

Exercise 5.1

1. Preference for male children in India
2. Funding of religious schools
3. New rules for boomerang children
4. A greener lifestyle
5. Advantages of text messaging

Exercise 5.3

c, h

Exercise 5.4

1. Despite the evidence that shows fast food is unhealthy, people keep eating it because it's cheap, tasty, and convenient.
2. People get tattoos to decorate their bodies, to show group membership, and to illustrate their attachments.
3. Leasing a car means lower monthly payments, access to new cars, and warranty coverage.
4. Students at a loss during a teachers' strike can read their textbook and notes, complete their assignments, and do extra reading.
5. The basic types of TV commercial include lifestyle ads, humorous commercials, and straight information.
6. The transportation system can be fixed by improving the public transit system, shipping more goods by rail, and controlling the use of personal vehicles.

Exercise 5.5

1. The government should encourage young people to vote by teaching them about politics in schools, showing political news on television shows geared to them, and demonstrating how easy voting is.
2. With a reduced workweek, the employment rate would be lower, productivity would go up, and employees would have more time for their families.
3. Parents can help their children go off to college by giving them money, helping them choose a program, and encouraging them.
4. When shopping online, buyers can choose from a wide array of items, shop in the convenience of their own home, and compare goods before they buy.

Exercise 5.8

1. b; 2. a; 3. d

Exercise 7.1 Word choice errors

1. reliant; 2. salesclerks; 3. outstanding; 4. incinerated; 5. piqued; 6. tried; 7. difficult or not easy; 8. strive; 9. committing; 10. told; 11. unenjoyable; 12. process; 13. sanitation; 14. sensible; 15. implying; 16. wealth; 17. problem; 18. stressed out; 19. appearance; 20. habits

Exercise 7.2 Word differences

1. famous; 2. disturb; 3. ashamed; 4. intolerant; 5. shortcomings; 6. respectful; 7. disprove; 8. adapting; 9. popular; 10. donate

Exercise 7.3 Word choice

1. curfew; 2. widower; 3. edible; 4. punctuality; 5. tantrums; 6. my sister-in-law; 7. tuition; 8. pension plan; 9. orphans; 10. drought; 11. bigamist; 12. decade; 13. chauffeur; 14. stationary; 15. shoplifting

Exercise 7.4 Collocation

1. stolen, contact; 2. slammed; 3. attend, arena/rink; 4. break–ins/
burglaries; installed; 5. trustworthy, tell; 6. wipe; 7. throw; 8. report, fill
out/complete; 9. oppose; 10. skipping, playing

Exercise 7.5 Parts of speech

1. safe, crime, worried, dangers; 2. Talking, homesickness; 3. lost,
absence; 4. beautify, important; 5. enables, easily; 6. common, sending;
7. over-protectiveness, rebel; 8. succeed, carefully; 9. beliefs, culture; 10.
comprehension, practising, confident

Exercise 7.6 Spelling

1. through, highlighted, studying; 2. environment, pollution; 3.There,
salad, threw; 4. recklessly, attacked, night, jail; 5. idolized, wore, capes;
6. accident, write-off; 7. whether, adapt; 8. punishment, severe, maybe,
lights; 9. Clothes, wear, charity; 10. nutritious, well-balanced, definitely

Exercise 7.7 One word or two?

1. may be, in charge, instead; 2. apiece, any more; 3. altogether,
Furthermore; downside; 4. all ready, in spite, already; 5. a lot, alike, apart;
6. aloud, apart; 7. faraway, outside; 8. whatever, each other; 9. at least,
another, maybe; 10. a way, intact

Exercise. 7.8 Word division correction

1. in front; 2. ahead, catch up; 3. a lot; 4. nowadays; 5. Even though,
about; 6. a while, aside; 7. Throughout, at all, nevertheless; 8. a part,
around; 9. Moreover; 10. In spite, up to

Exercise 7.9 Troublesome words

1. afford to buy; 2. Compared; 3. People spend too much money on
clothes, toys, or cars. 4. was supposed to; 5. used to be; 6. be concerned;
7. Even if; 8. It is hard for adults to learn a new language; 9. make it easy;
10. worked hard; 11. She used to live; 12. even when

Exercise 7.10 Sentence rewriting

1. I liked the softness of the material.
2. Elizabeth enjoys solitude.
3. The whales are in danger of extinction.
4. Jason only felt more confused. The teacher's explanation confused
   Jason. The teacher's explanation was confusing.
5. Brenda's compassion toward the children surprised me.
6. The members of the committee did not agree.
7. One student from each class participated in the project.
8. This essay has too much repetition. You repeat too much in this
   essay.

9. When all the guests arrived, Tracey introduced them to one another.
10. I expect them to behave responsibly.
11. The explosion deafened Eric. Eric's deafness was caused by the explosion.
12. Michelle tried to hide her disappointment with the results. Michelle found the results disappointing, but she tried to hide that.
13. Geoffrey couldn't distinguish between the two methodologies.
14. The city was chaotic.
15. The puppy is so curious that it gets into everything.
16. The custom is to write a thank-you note after receiving a gift or special favour.
17. Brian and Susan like meditation in the morning.
18. The story was not verified.

Exercise 7.11 Error correction

1. The <u>students</u> completed the assignment <u>quickly</u>, so they <u>left</u> the class.
2. The television is <u>broken</u>. I'll have to <u>download</u> that show. I want to know who the killer <u>was</u>.
3. Because he had <u>taken</u> the wrong road, <u>he</u> was late for the meeting and <u>missed</u> the important details.
4. In winter, the children go skiing <u>and</u> skating. They don't mind the cold weather as long as <u>they are/they're</u> dressed <u>properly</u> for it.
5. I should not <u>have</u> changed the date of the meeting <u>because</u> the first one was <u>better</u>.
6. When she reads <u>slowly</u> and carefully, she can understand better and makes <u>fewer</u> mistakes.
7. My purse is full of <u>stuff</u> I don't need <u>even though</u> I clean it out <u>regularly</u>.
8. Each of <u>the</u> projects <u>has</u> a <u>different</u> advantage. <u>Choosing</u> one will be <u>difficult</u>.
9. He is <u>training</u> to be <u>an</u> electrician. When he <u>graduates</u>, he will work for his uncle <u>who</u> renovates and <u>sells</u> old <u>houses</u>.
10. The <u>students</u> had to redo <u>their</u> work because <u>there</u> were <u>too</u> many <u>mistakes</u>.
11. He <u>had</u> better not wait for her. <u>It is/it's</u> time she learned the consequences of <u>being</u> late.
12. Sylvia <u>would</u> rather let Mike <u>run</u> the workshops <u>so</u> she can concentrate <u>on</u> the reorganization.
13. For every <u>case</u>, the detective <u>writes</u> an official report for his client.
14. Even <u>when</u> she disagrees <u>with</u> the decision, she <u>tries</u> to support the work the staff <u>is doing/has done</u>.
15. The programmers checked the code, ran some test <u>cases</u>, <u>and finally found</u> the problem.

16. The <u>students</u> asked <u>their</u> teacher whether it was possible to schedule the tutorial for another <u>day</u>. They did not want to <u>miss</u> the career day presentation.
17. I find this grammar point very <u>confusing</u>. <u>Maybe</u> the teacher could <u>explain</u> it again.
18. <u>It's</u> her <u>boyfriend's</u> fault. <u>He's</u> so possessive that he never <u>lets</u> her go out with her <u>friends</u>.

Exercise 7.12 Determiners

1. the first person, across Lake Ontario; 2. the Internet; 3. Many of the students, at a time; 4. the University of British Columbia; 5. the most popular; 6.The meaning, a relationship; 7. a success, the program; 8. Honesty, one of the most important; 9. a doctor

Exercise 7.13 Countable and uncountable nouns

1. gave him advice, the furniture on delayed payment; 2. the information; 3. much homework, my vocabulary; 4. new luggage; 5. used it; 7. to alcohol; 8. and hope; 9. another project (or more work); 11. having trouble; 12. and jewellery; 13. a loaf of bread, a jug of milk, some cheese; 14. much research

Exercise 7.14 Verb tense and form

1. could be, I had, After I found several articles; 2. I took; 3. are not taught, they might not pay attention; 4. are used to spending, it is time; 5. is forcing people to work, amount accomplished; 6. would not have lost, to make sure I do, I will not pass; 7. do not take, hate; 8. let students have; 9. used to, will help management pinpoint problems; 10. I decided, I arrived, I had forgotten; 11. has danced, she saw; 12. I would still want, I would still need

Exercise 7.15 Tense shift

she is afraid, She is a Chinese immigrant, but she speaks limited English, her son takes her, but she just talks, is able to, tells her son

Exercise 7.16 Active and passive voice

1. happened; 3. get misled, they regret; 4. People fear, people suffer; 5. he would take; 6. will improve; 7. be assigned, to be shared; 8. can also benefit, games improve; 9. were built; 10. are exchanged

Exercise 7.17 Verbs expressing emotion

1. confused; 2. frightened; 3. pleased; 4. disappointing, misleading; 5. offended; 6. disgusting, bothered; 7. interesting, shocked; 8. annoying, relieved; 9. flattered; 10. satisfying, encouraging

Exercise 7.18 Verb form correction

1. was pleased; 2. confusing; 4. exciting part; 6. felt worried, seems satisfied; 8. an interesting person; 9. annoying; 10. flattering

Exercise 7.19 Gerunds or infinitives

1. taking; 2. to wait, seeing; 3. to fire; 4. taking; 5. to see, to join; 6. repainting; 7. to return; 8. telling, to take; 9. to take, redoing; 10. to try, to keep

Exercise 7.20 Gerund and infinitive correction

1. seeing; 2. hope to get, start studying; 4. expected to see; 5. suggest trying, pretend to agree; 8. waiting; 9. to fire more staff; 10. answering

Exercise 7.21 Prepositions

1. for winter conditions, with something; 2. for you, for the test; 3. earphones on, listens to, oblivious to; 4. capable of, in class; 5. at the airport, for the plane, wait for; 6. with that brand, known for; 7. grateful for, confused by; 8. adjacent to, from my window; 9. talk to; 10. depend on, argue with

Exercise 7.22 Preposition correction

1. on her own; 2. to/for the problem; 3. on my laptop computer, at my convenience; 4. at the dinner table; 5. to the behaviour; 6. for a luxury car; 7. from/in the textbook every week; 8. on the Internet; 9. by choosing; 10. get downtown

Exercise 7.23 Prepositions and different parts of speech

1. fears terrorist attacks; 2. understanding of; 3. emphasizes basic first aid treatments; 4. affect the results; 5. describes the difficulties, mentions the misunderstandings; 6. expects Zach; 7. desire for privacy; 8. gained a new division; 9. increase charity programs

Exercise 7.24 Possessive forms

1. whose keys, Security Department; 2. storage rooms, misplaced mine; 3. nowadays; 5. children's babysitter; 6. Johnsons' house; Their whole place; 7. Whose dog; 8. their backpacks; 9. Sally's car; 10. your textbook, Elizabeth's

Exercise 7.25 Singular/plural

1. is from Australia, plays the trumpet; 2. was a pleasure, actors; 3. six-year-old, minute; 4. goes, seem; 6. its own place, compartments are; 7. cameras do; They only help; 8. has risen, campaign; 9. they can be found, is stored; 10. It will

Exercise 7.26 Fragments and run-ons

1. She's pretending to work, but she's just playing solitaire on the computer, and the time is running out.
2. Including a list of references in the résumé is not necessary. It can be left for the job interview.
3. She lets Jake use the car whenever he asks even though he's a terrible driver.
4. We studied all the readings in class; however, many of the students had trouble remembering the material for the test.
5. It's not hard to see what the problem is. The machine won't start because this piece is jamming it.
6. Because he had accumulated so much stuff in residence, he borrowed his parents' van when he was moving out.
7. In most cases, the advantages of self-employment are being your own boss and not having to answer to anyone.
9. He lets his employees have a say in the decision-making process; therefore, their job satisfaction is high. Few of them move on to other jobs.
10. Because of his success with the last project, he was promoted to assistant manager. After a while, he was making much more money, so he asked his girlfriend to marry him.

Exercise 7.27 Sentence Structure

1. prevent accidents resulting in injuries and death; 2. why she did not; 3. that everyone wants; 4. where the national language; 5. Going to a fast food restaurant will save time; 6. and more willing; 7. he broke the nib; 8. International students in Canada face difficulties in daily life; 9. Because of the fast development; 10. The manager cut the staff, reorganized the filing system, and got everything to run more smoothly.

Exercise 7.28 Apostrophes

1. Jill's brother couldn't; 2. lets, icons; 3. doesn't, Marshalls', it's; 4. always, she's; 5. can't; 6. Let's, knows, It's; 8. We're, shipments, suppliers; 9. Tuesdays, seniors/seniors'; 10. concerns, apostrophes

Exercise 7.29 Mechanics

1. If I hadn't been paying attention, I would have been hit by that ball.
2. The Japanese garden at UBC is a beautiful, restful place. I like to visit there on Sunday afternoons.
3. Allison loves horror movies, but I hate being scared. My favourite movie is *Gone with the Wind*.
4. Tailgating is a traffic violation. Moreover, it is dangerous. Not only can the tailgater easily hit the car ahead, but drivers behind the tailgater get frustrated seeing brake lights because they do not know whether there is an actual traffic slowdown.

5. Like a drill sergeant, Steven shouted, "Do not panic! Walk! Don't run!"

6. On my trip to Europe, I visited Paris, Monaco, Florence, Rome, Venice, Munich, and Amsterdam. I met a lot of students from different countries who were travelling on the same tour bus.

7. The people's response is predictable. They won't support the new party because of its stand on social justice issues.

8. I can't say who's coming to the wedding because I haven't seen the latest list.

9. The women's washroom was closed for maintenance, so Frances and Lee took over the men's room.

10. Charles's mother used to play for a ladies softball team. She held a few pitching records.

Index